Volume 3
by Lee Vin

HAMBURG // LONDON // LOS ANGELES // TOKYO

CONTENTS

•ONE VOLUME 3•

Behind the Music...

It's American Idol, Korea-style! Eumpa is a talented star-in-the-making...but if he won't play the corporate game, will he still have a shot at the bigtime?

Teen queen Jenny Yu is reinventing herself (a la Madonna), but will it be enough to revive her career? And when Issue Productions holds auditions to create a new boy band, will they find a diamond in the rough? Find out this and more in this exciting volume of One, where the hits just keep on a'comin'...

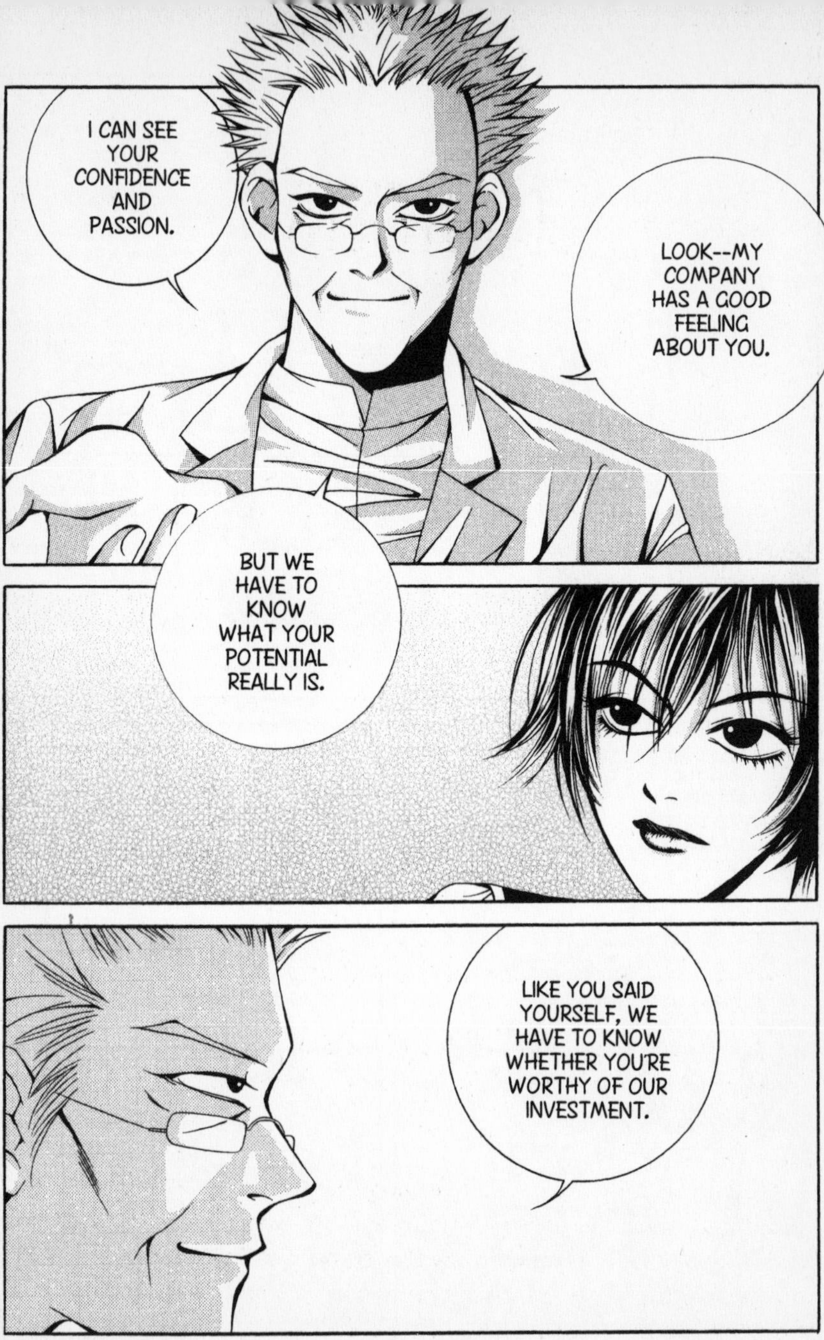
I CAN SEE YOUR CONFIDENCE AND PASSION.
LOOK--MY COMPANY HAS A GOOD FEELING ABOUT YOU.
BUT WE HAVE TO KNOW WHAT YOUR POTENTIAL REALLY IS.
LIKE YOU SAID YOURSELF, WE HAVE TO KNOW WHETHER YOU'RE WORTHY OF OUR INVESTMENT.

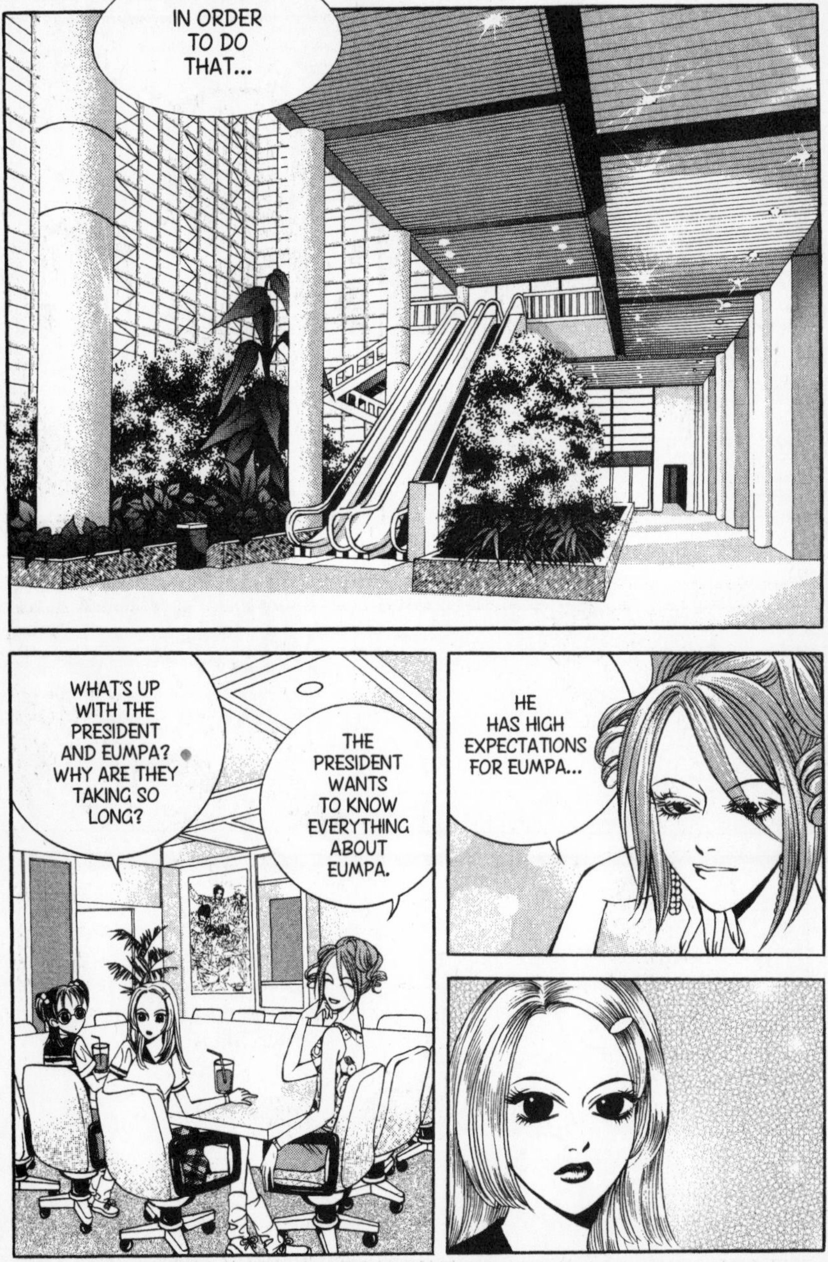
IN ORDER TO DO THAT...
WHAT'S UP WITH THE PRESIDENT AND EUMPA? WHY ARE THEY TAKING SO LONG?
THE PRESIDENT WANTS TO KNOW EVERYTHING ABOUT EUMPA.
HE HAS HIGH EXPECTATIONS FOR EUMPA...

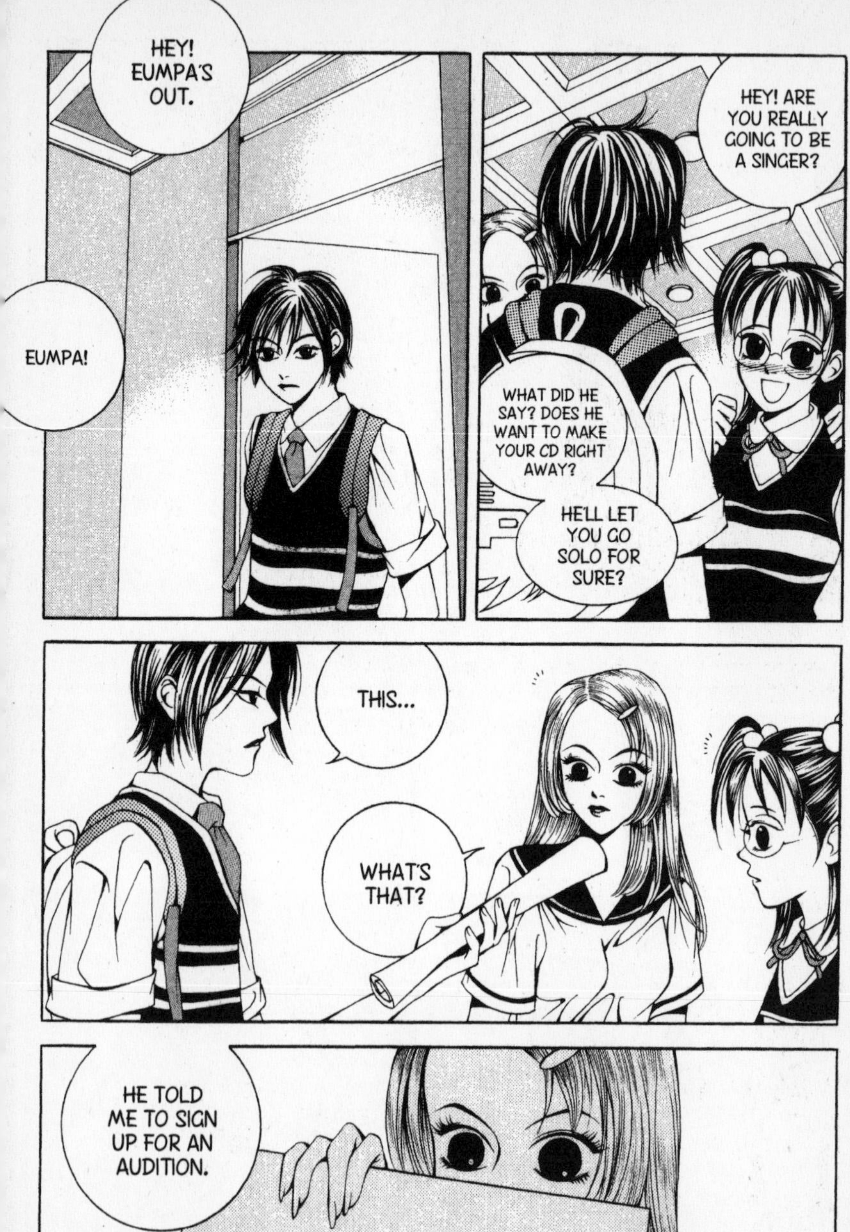
HEY! EUMPA'S OUT.
EUMPA!
HEY! ARE YOU REALLY GOING TO BE A SINGER?
WHAT DID HE SAY? DOES HE WANT TO MAKE YOUR CD RIGHT AWAY?
HE'LL LET YOU GO SOLO FOR SURE?
THIS...
WHAT'S THAT?
HE TOLD ME TO SIGN UP FOR AN AUDITION.

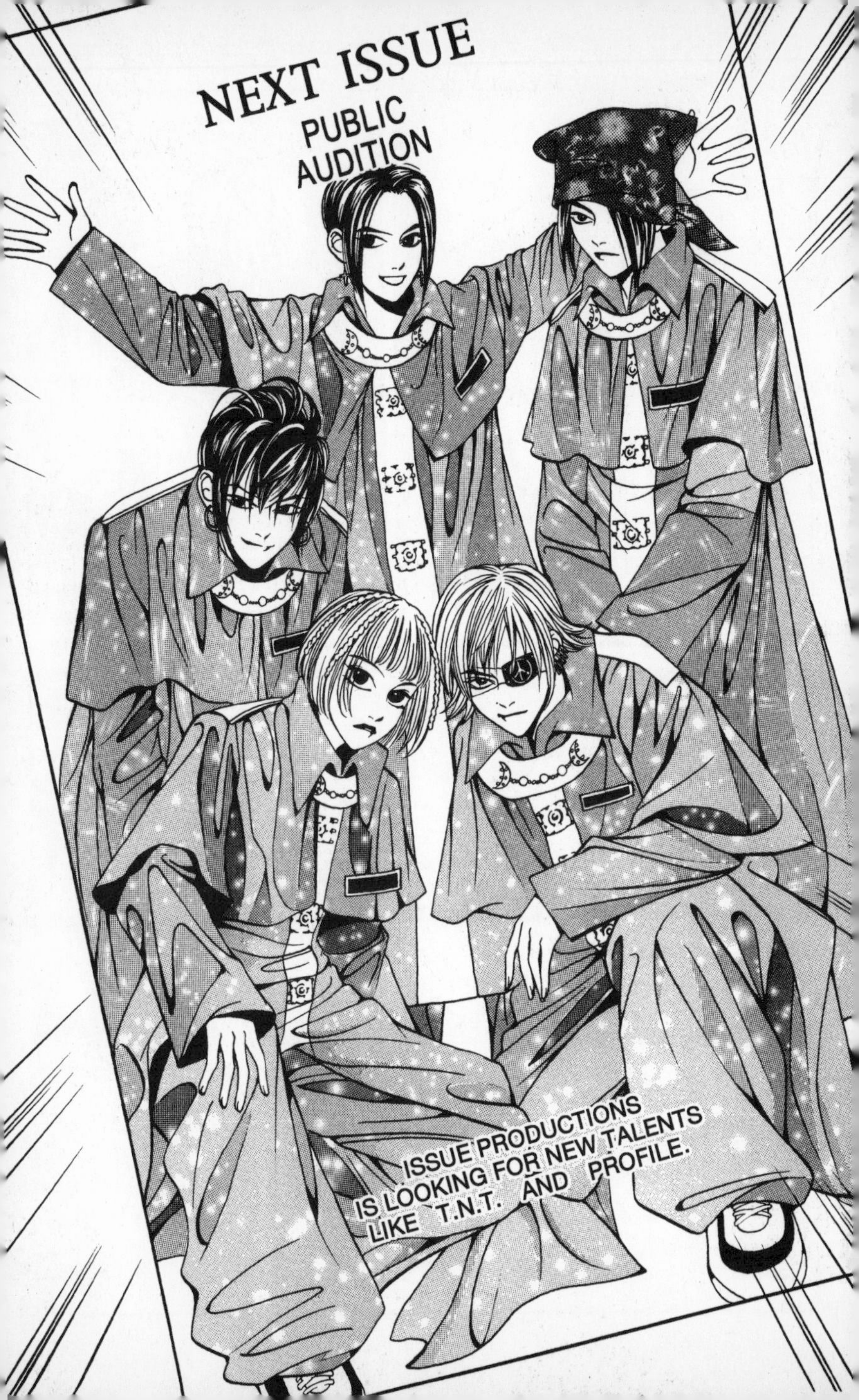
NEXT ISSUE
PUBLIC AUDITION
ISSUE PRODUCTIONS IS LOOKING FOR NEW TALENTS LIKE T.N.T. AND PROFILE.

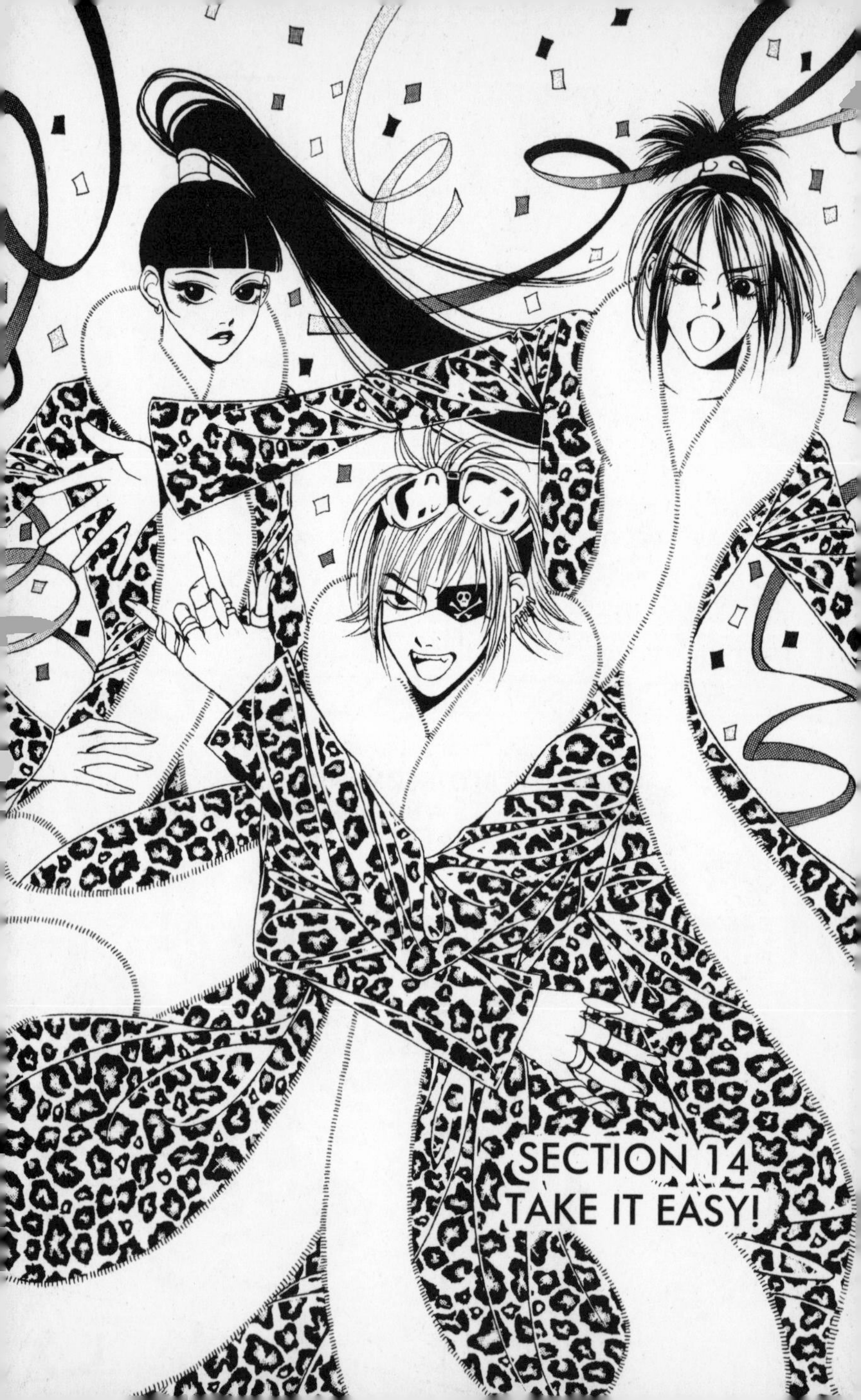
SECTION 14
TAKE IT EASY!

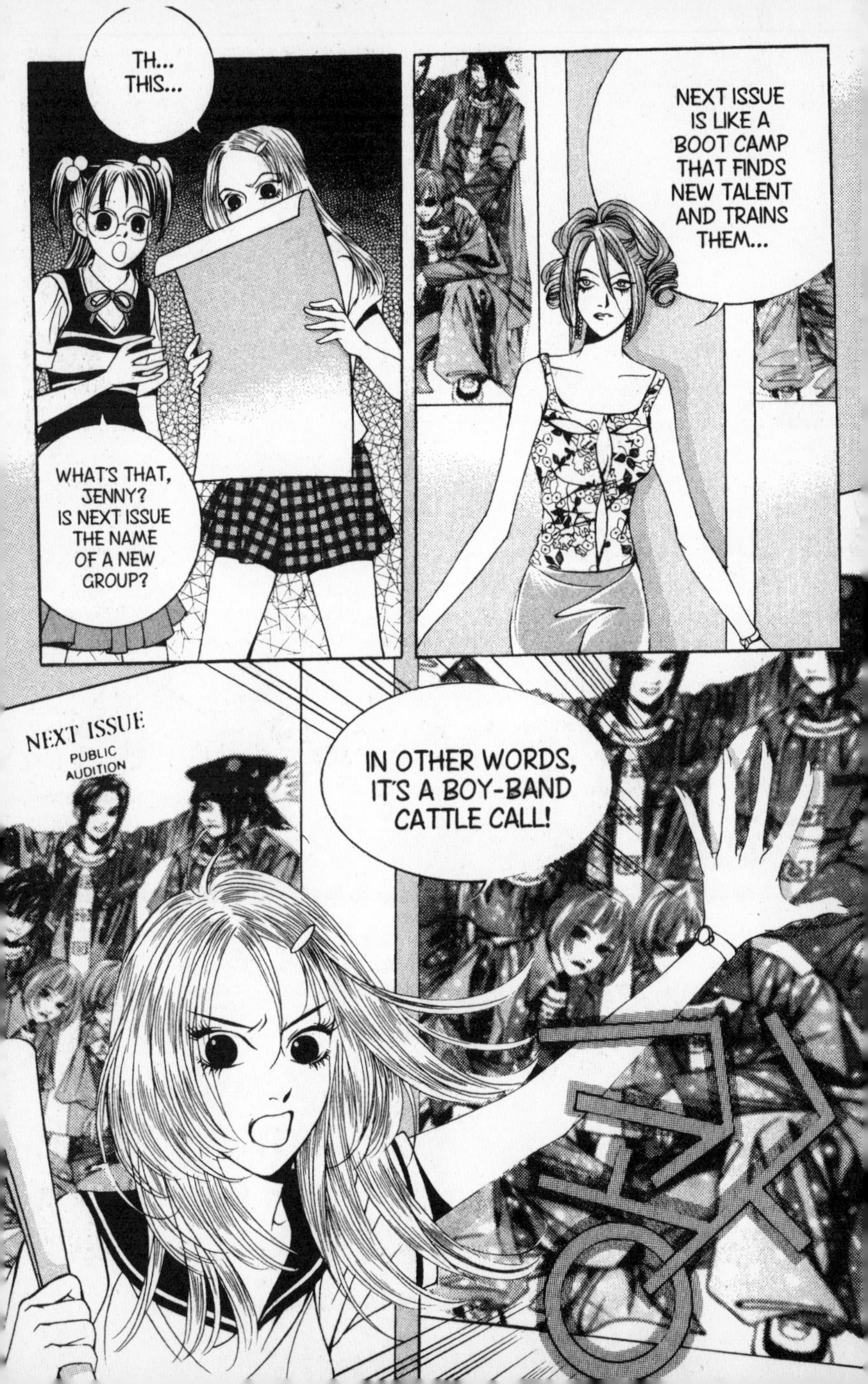
TH... THIS...
WHAT'S THAT, JENNY? IS NEXT ISSUE THE NAME OF A NEW GROUP?
NEXT ISSUE IS LIKE A BOOT CAMP THAT FINDS NEW TALENT AND TRAINS THEM...
NEXT ISSUE
PUBLIC AUDITION
IN OTHER WORDS, IT'S A BOY-BAND CATTLE CALL!

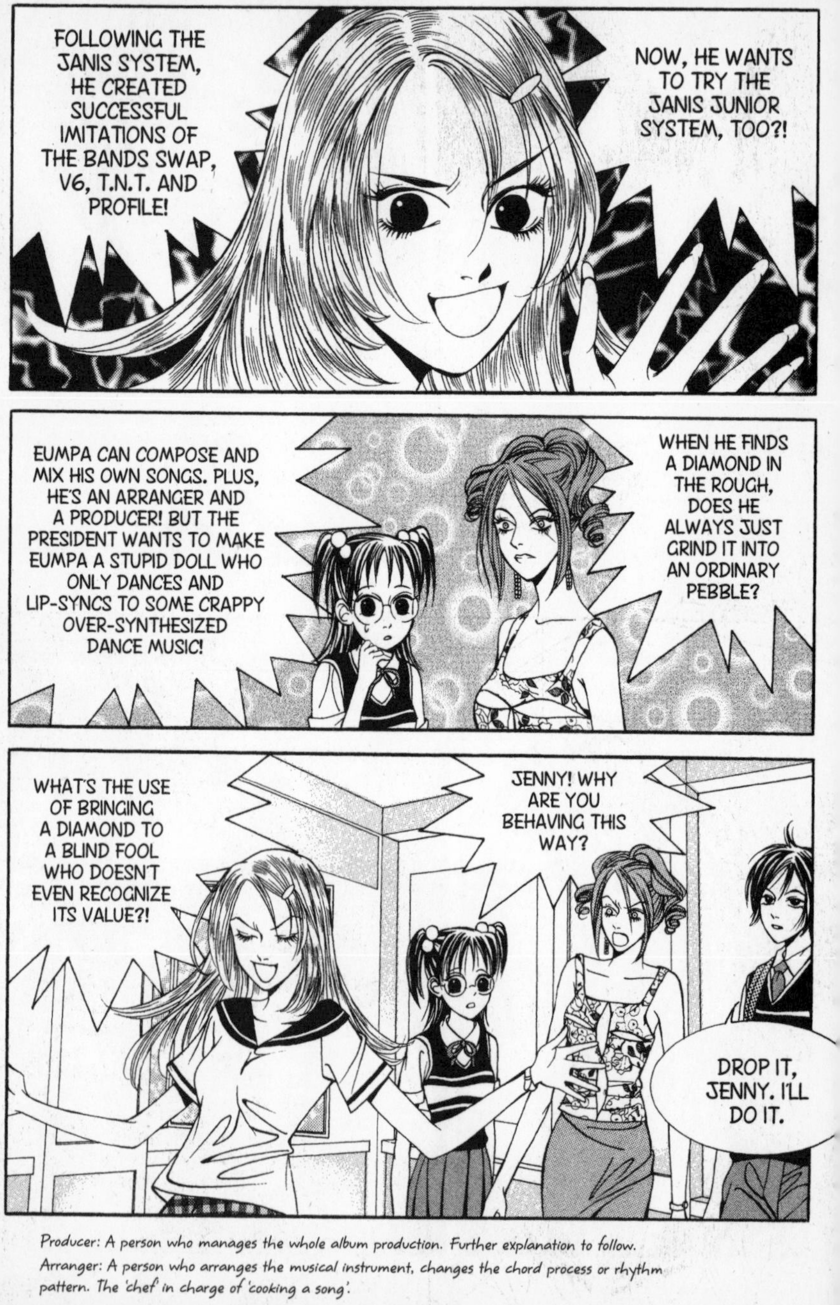
FOLLOWING THE JANIS SYSTEM, HE CREATED SUCCESSFUL IMITATIONS OF THE BANDS SWAP, V6, T.N.T. AND PROFILE!
NOW, HE WANTS TO TRY THE JANIS JUNIOR SYSTEM, TOO?!
EUMPA CAN COMPOSE AND MIX HIS OWN SONGS. PLUS, HE'S AN ARRANGER AND A PRODUCER! BUT THE PRESIDENT WANTS TO MAKE EUMPA A STUPID DOLL WHO ONLY DANCES AND LIP-SYNCS TO SOME CRAPPY OVER-SYNTHESIZED DANCE MUSIC!
WHEN HE FINDS A DIAMOND IN THE ROUGH, DOES HE ALWAYS JUST GRIND IT INTO AN ORDINARY PEBBLE?
WHAT'S THE USE OF BRINGING A DIAMOND TO A BLIND FOOL WHO DOESN'T EVEN RECOGNIZE ITS VALUE?!
JENNY! WHY ARE YOU BEHAVING THIS WAY?
DROP IT, JENNY. I'LL DO IT.

Producer: A person who manages the whole album production. Further explanation to follow.

Arranger: A person who arranges the musical instrument, changes the chord process or rhythm pattern. The 'chef' in charge of 'cooking a song'.

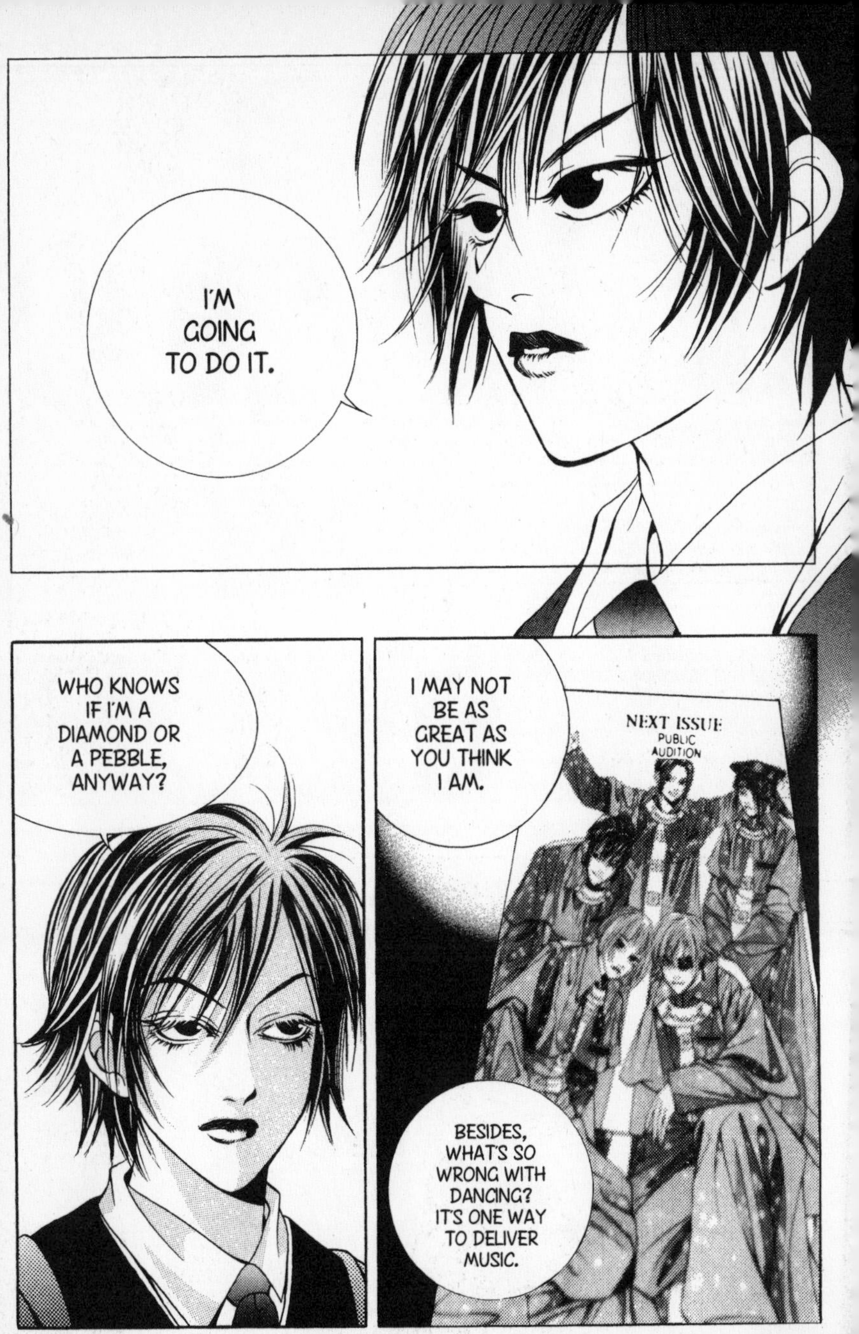
I'M GOING TO DO IT.
I MAY NOT BE AS GREAT AS YOU THINK I AM.
NEXT ISSUE
PUBLIC AUDITION
BESIDES, WHAT'S SO WRONG WITH DANCING? IT'S ONE WAY TO DELIVER MUSIC.
WHO KNOWS IF I'M A DIAMOND OR A PEBBLE, ANYWAY?

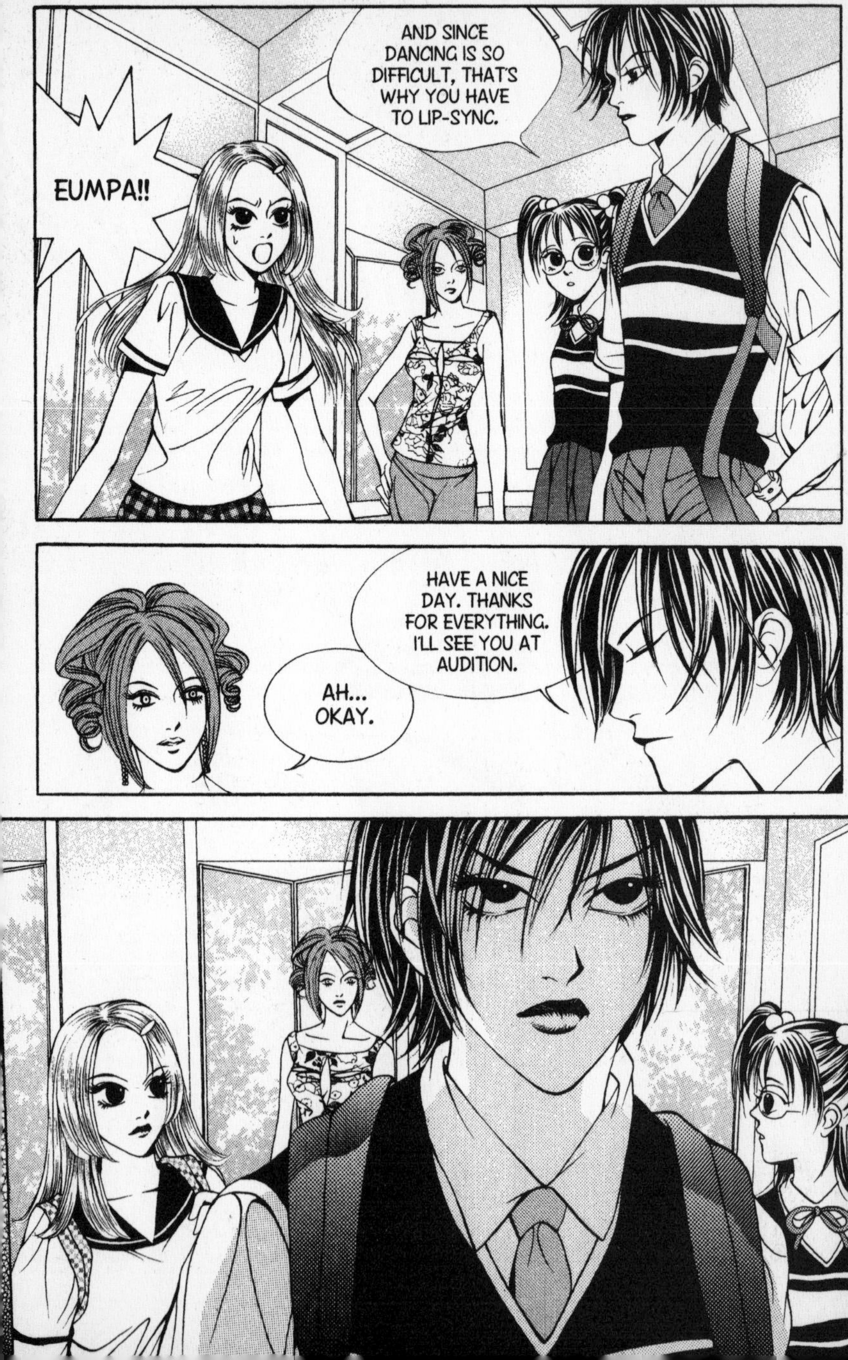
AND SINCE DANCING IS SO DIFFICULT, THAT'S WHY YOU HAVE TO LIP-SYNC.
EUMPA!!
HAVE A NICE DAY. THANKS FOR EVERYTHING. I'LL SEE YOU AT AUDITION.
AH... OKAY.

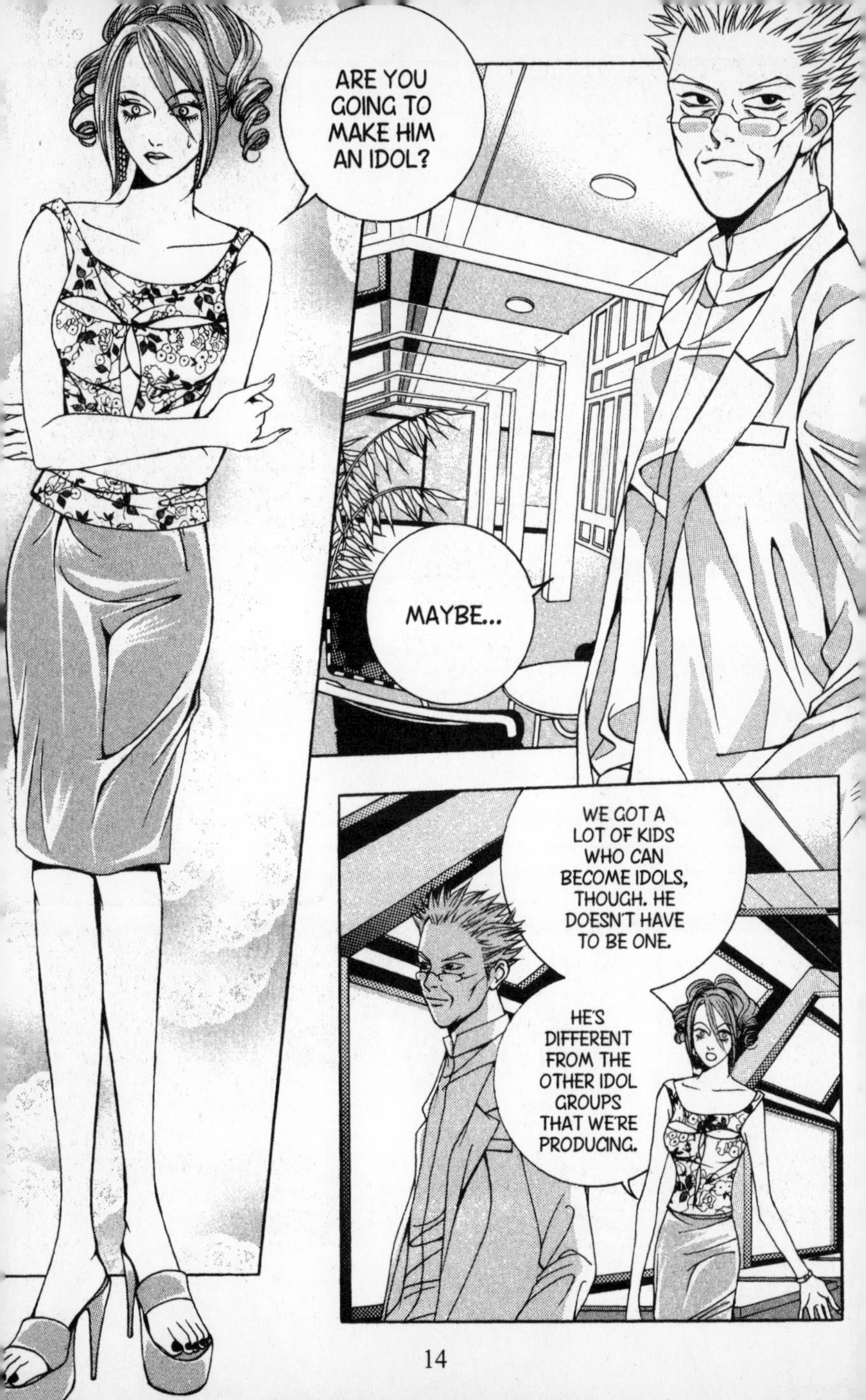
ARE YOU GOING TO MAKE HIM AN IDOL?
MAYBE...
WE GOT A LOT OF KIDS WHO CAN BECOME IDOLS, THOUGH. HE DOESN'T HAVE TO BE ONE.
HE'S DIFFERENT FROM THE OTHER IDOL GROUPS THAT WE'RE PRODUCING.

HE RADIATES LIGHT ALL ON HIS OWN.

HE'S LIKE A TIGER THAT GOES OUT TO HUNT BY HIMSELF.

A TIGER DROPS ITS BABY FROM A CLIFF.

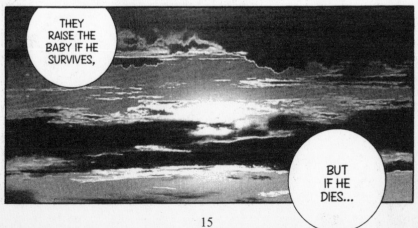

THEY RAISE THE BABY IF HE SURVIVES,

BUT IF HE DIES...

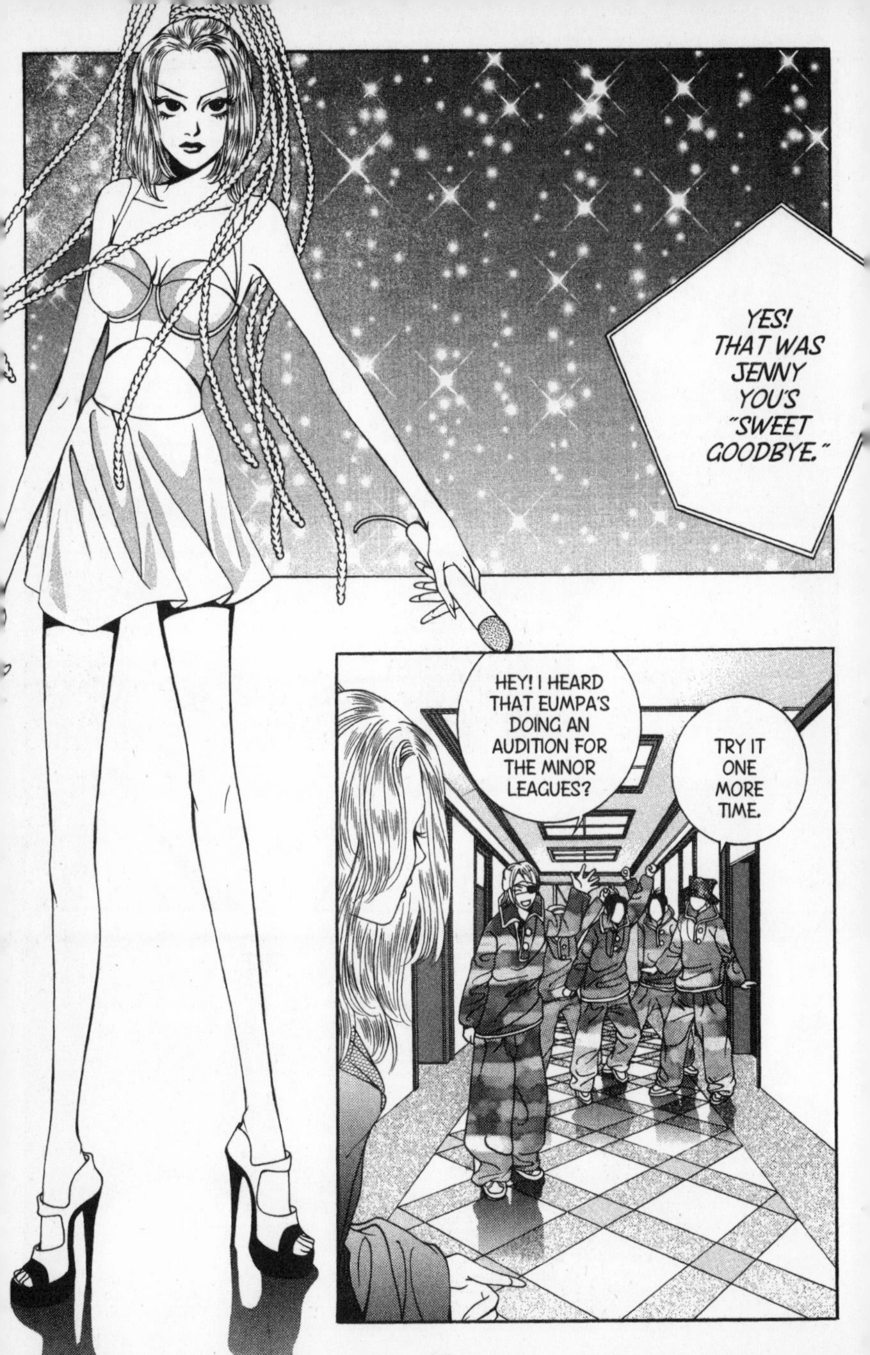
YES! THAT WAS JENNY YOU'S "SWEET GOODBYE."
HEY! I HEARD THAT EUMPA'S DOING AN AUDITION FOR THE MINOR LEAGUES?
TRY IT ONE MORE TIME.

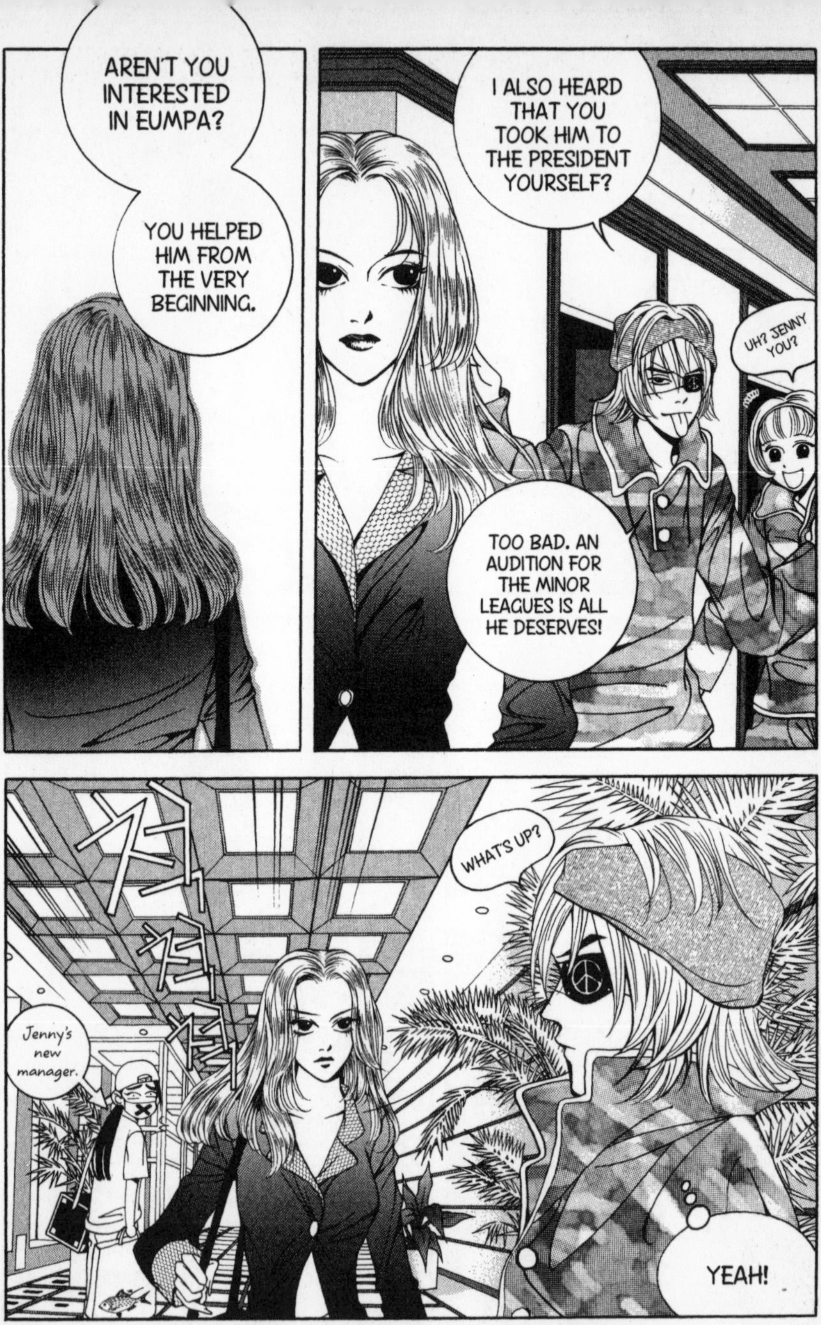

AREN'T YOU INTERESTED IN EUMPA?
YOU HELPED HIM FROM THE VERY BEGINNING.
I ALSO HEARD THAT YOU TOOK HIM TO THE PRESIDENT YOURSELF?
UH? JENNY YOU?
TOO BAD. AN AUDITION FOR THE MINOR LEAGUES IS ALL HE DESERVES!
Jenny's new manager.
WHAT'S UP?
YEAH!

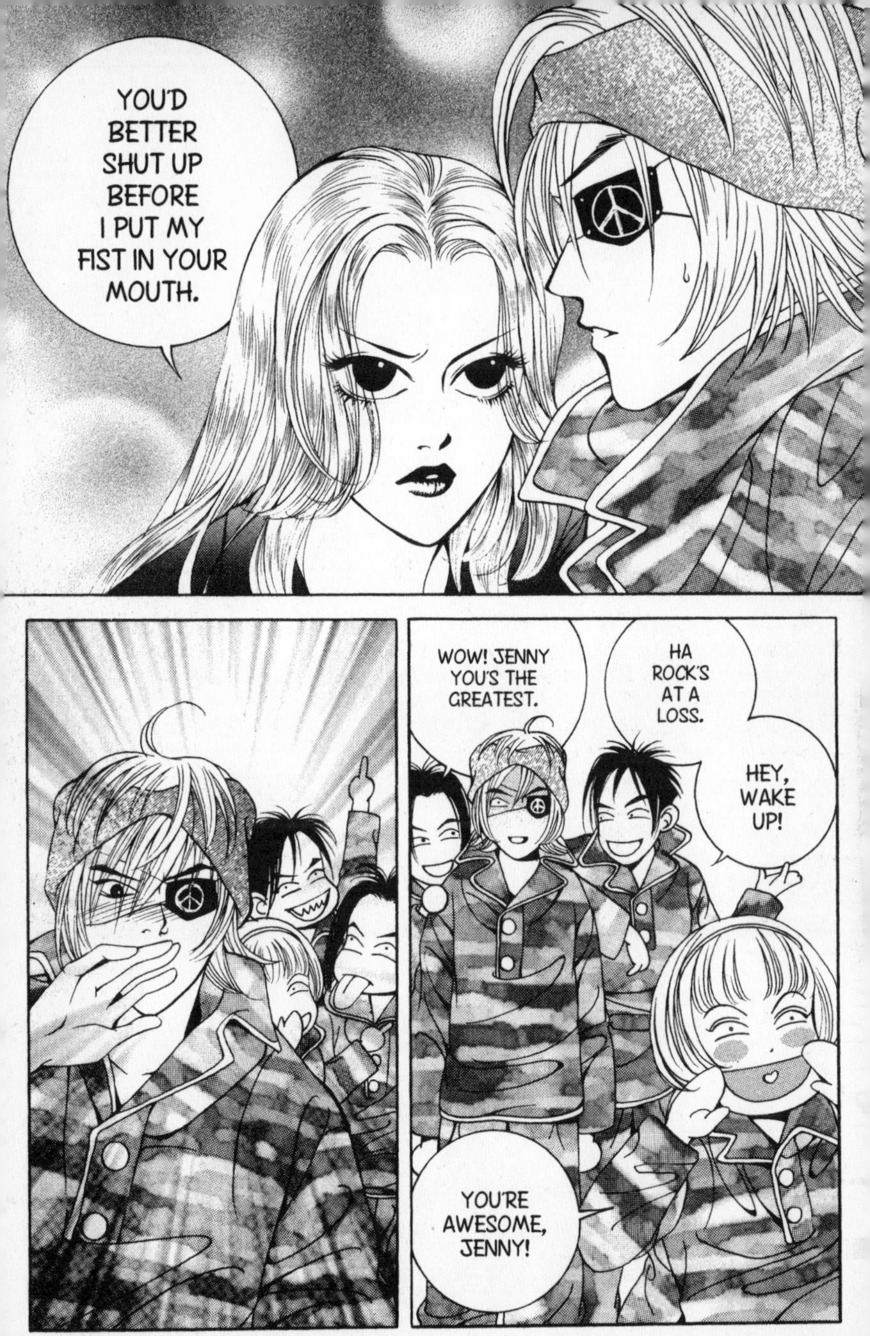
YOU'D BETTER SHUT UP BEFORE I PUT MY FIST IN YOUR MOUTH.
HA ROCK'S AT A LOSS.
WOW! JENNY YOU'S THE GREATEST.
HEY, WAKE UP!
YOU'RE AWESOME, JENNY!

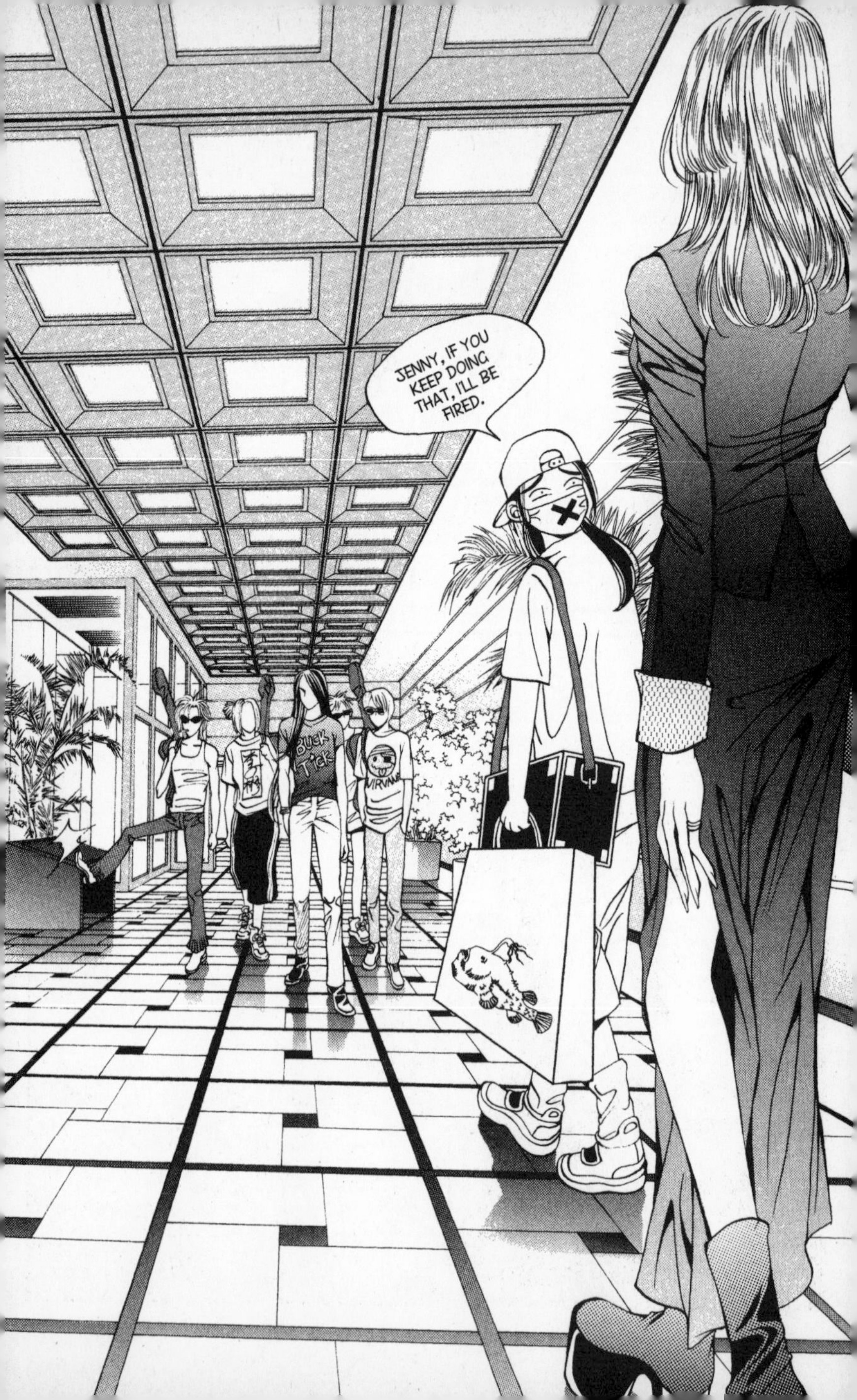
JENNY, IF YOU KEEP DOING THAT, I'LL BE FIRED.
Buck Tick

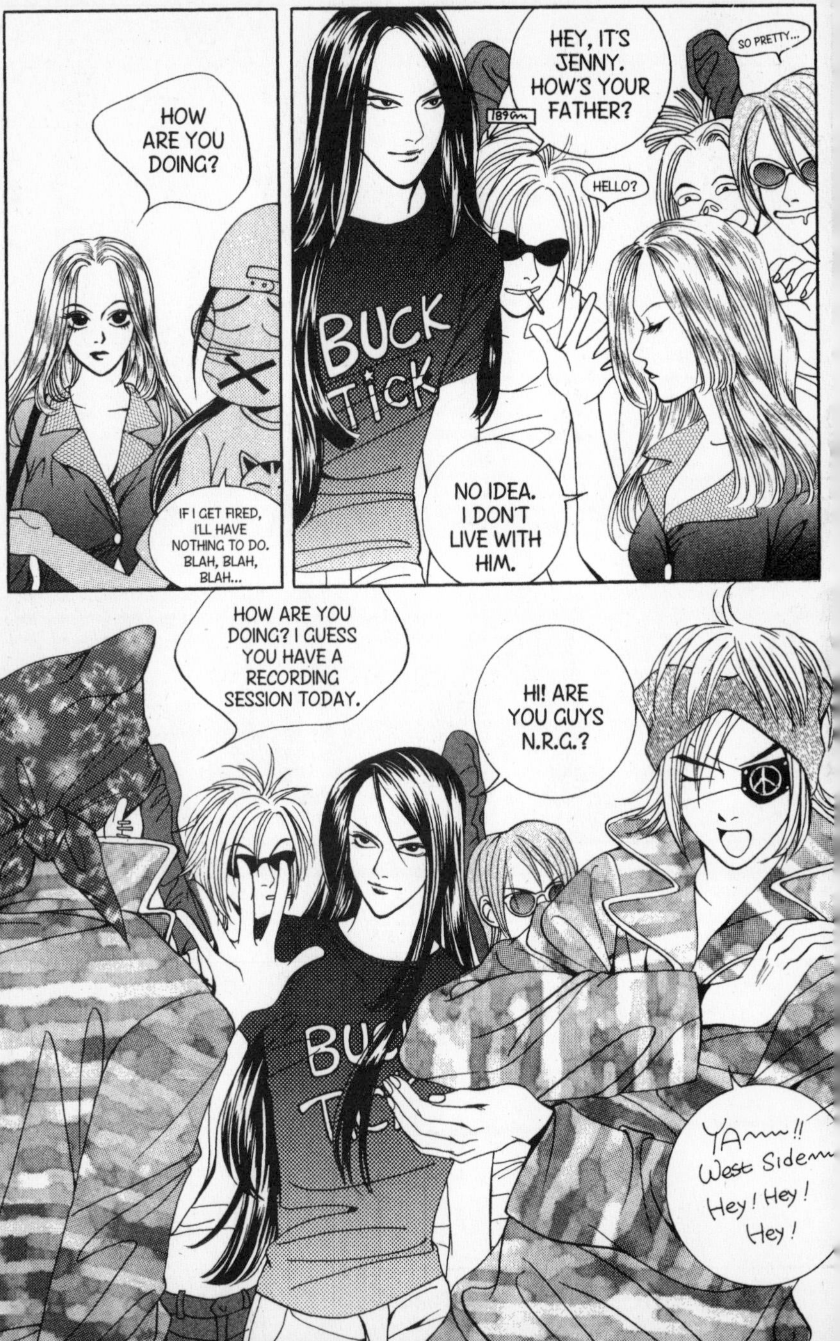
SO PRETTY...
HEY, IT'S JENNY. HOW'S YOUR FATHER?
189cm
HELLO?
NO IDEA. I DON'T LIVE WITH HIM.
HOW ARE YOU DOING?
IF I GET FIRED, I'LL HAVE NOTHING TO DO. BLAH, BLAH, BLAH...
HI! ARE YOU GUYS N.R.G.?
HOW ARE YOU DOING? I GUESS YOU HAVE A RECORDING SESSION TODAY.
YAm!! West Side Hey! Hey! Hey!

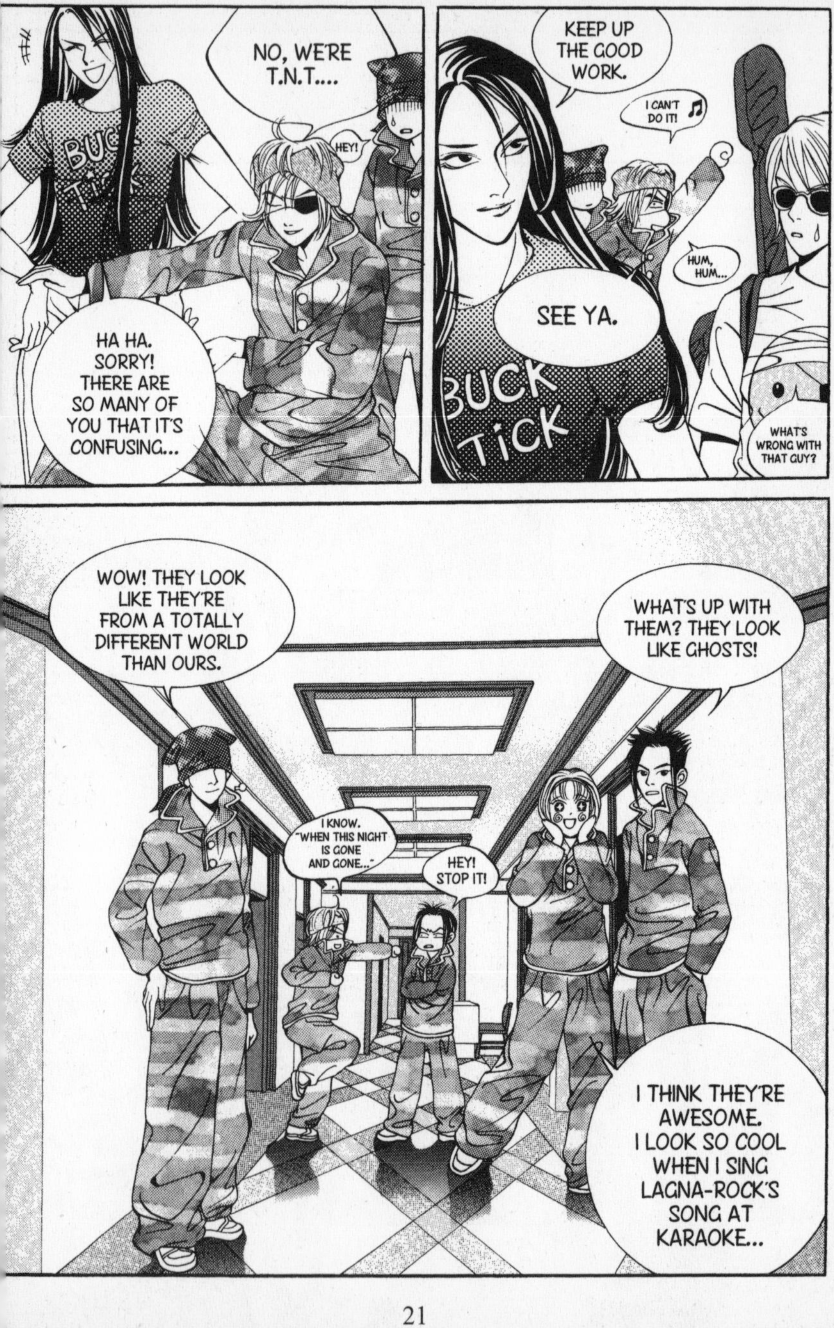
NO, WE'RE T.N.T....
HEY!
HA HA. SORRY! THERE ARE SO MANY OF YOU THAT IT'S CONFUSING...
KEEP UP THE GOOD WORK.
I CAN'T DO IT! ♫
HUM, HUM...
SEE YA.
WHAT'S WRONG WITH THAT GUY?
WOW! THEY LOOK LIKE THEY'RE FROM A TOTALLY DIFFERENT WORLD THAN OURS.
WHAT'S UP WITH THEM? THEY LOOK LIKE GHOSTS!
I KNOW. "WHEN THIS NIGHT IS GONE AND GONE..."
HEY! STOP IT!
I THINK THEY'RE AWESOME. I LOOK SO COOL WHEN I SING LAGNA-ROCK'S SONG AT KARAOKE...

Lagna-Rock

They're a 10-year-old veteran rock group. They earned fame in the club scene as an underground group, They were known as Six-Nine in the beginning. After making their debut in major markets, they changed their name to Lagna-Rock. They're the best rock group in Korea. Unlike other rock groups, they have a wide range of fans and critical support. Their psychedelic sound and strong charisma positioned them as a religion among rock fans.

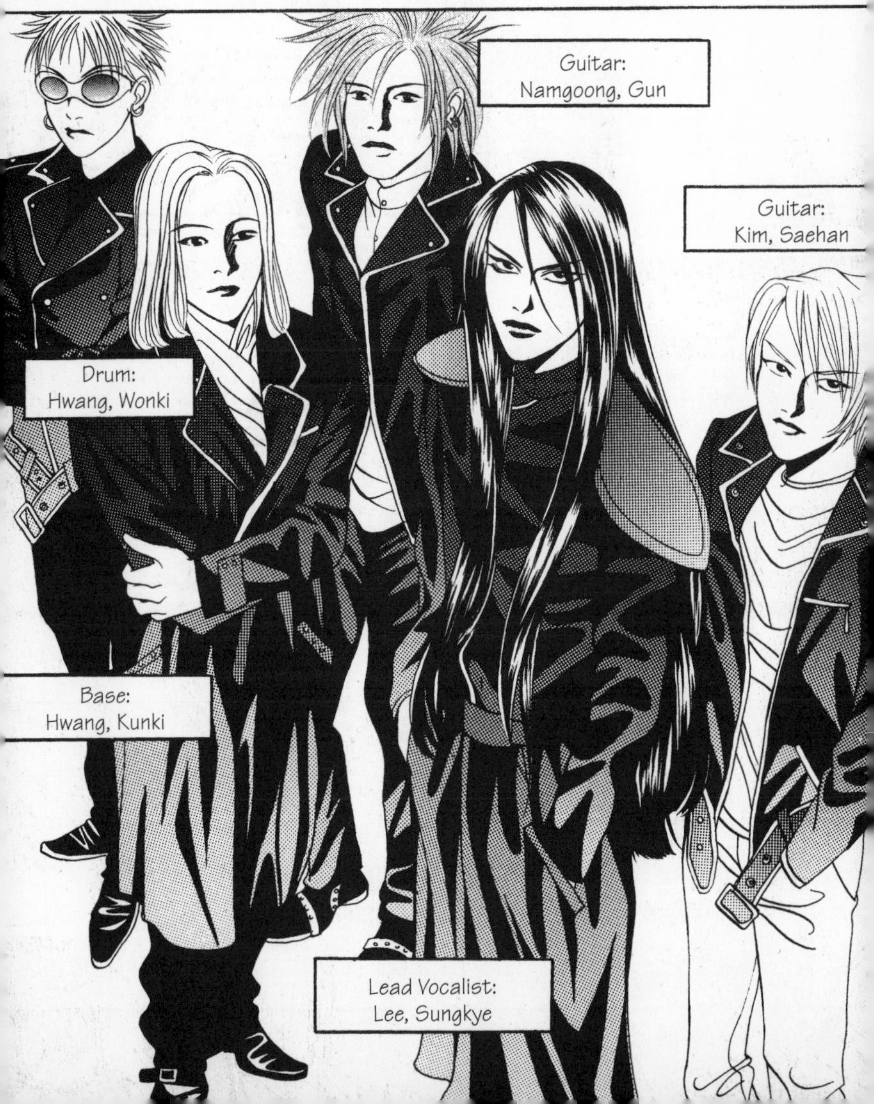
Guitar:
Namgoong, Gun
Guitar:
Kim, Saehan
Drum:
Hwang, Wonki
Base:
Hwang, Kunki
Lead Vocalist:
Lee, Sungkye

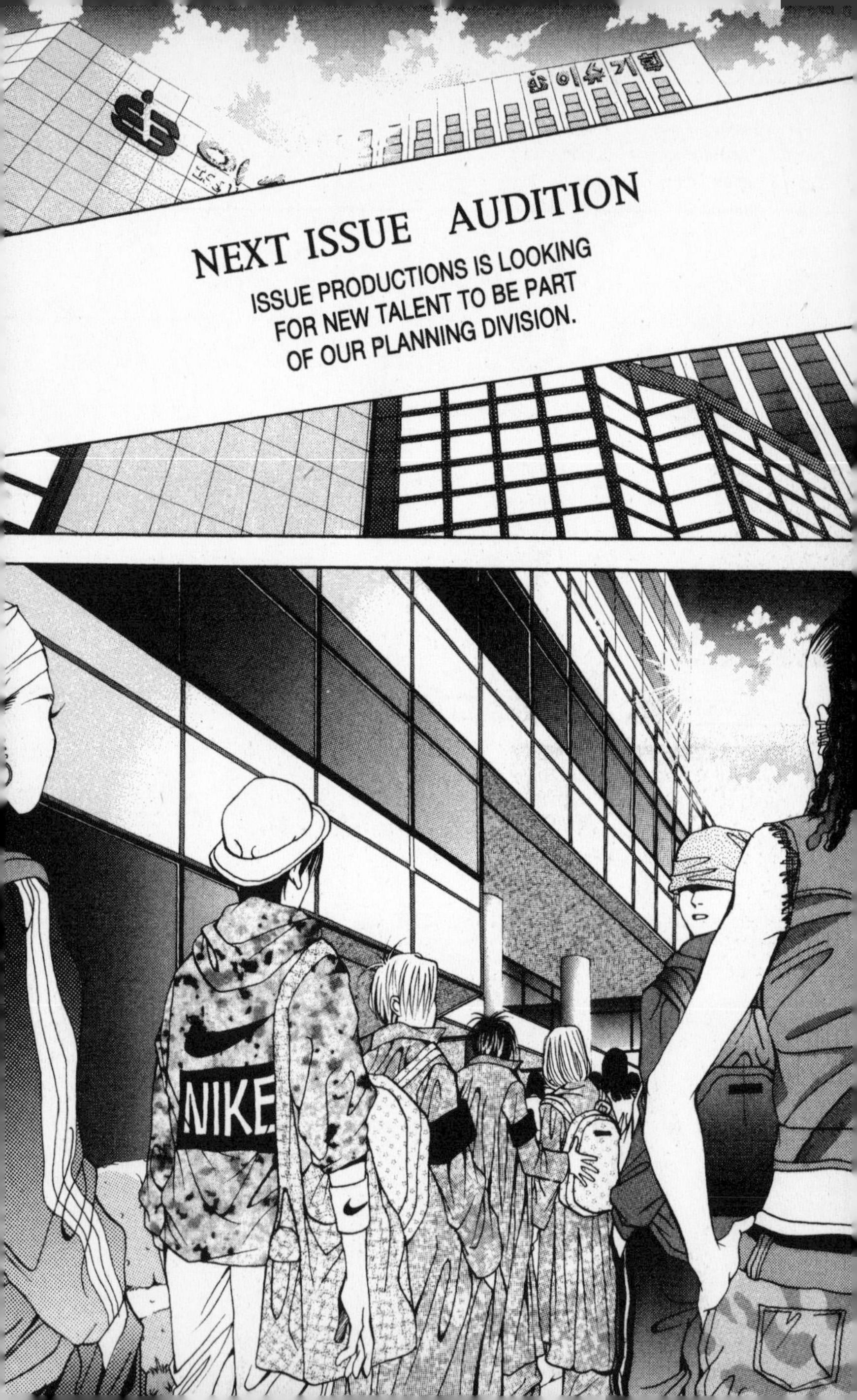
NEXT ISSUE AUDITION
ISSUE PRODUCTIONS IS LOOKING FOR NEW TALENT TO BE PART OF OUR PLANNING DIVISION.
NIKE

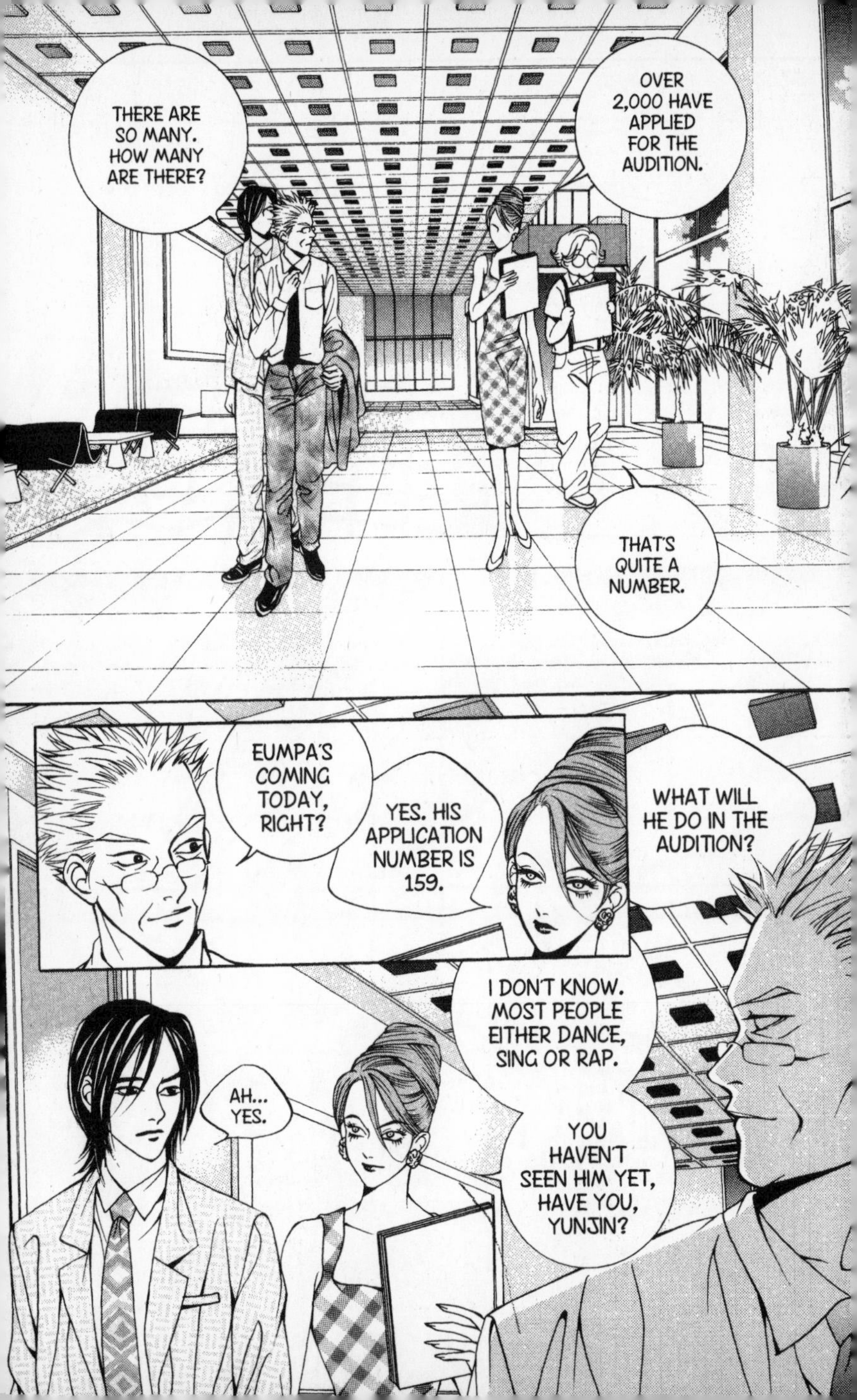
THERE ARE SO MANY. HOW MANY ARE THERE?
OVER 2,000 HAVE APPLIED FOR THE AUDITION.
THAT'S QUITE A NUMBER.
EUMPA'S COMING TODAY, RIGHT?
YES. HIS APPLICATION NUMBER IS 159.
WHAT WILL HE DO IN THE AUDITION?
I DON'T KNOW. MOST PEOPLE EITHER DANCE, SING OR RAP.
YOU HAVEN'T SEEN HIM YET, HAVE YOU, YUNJIN?
AH... YES.

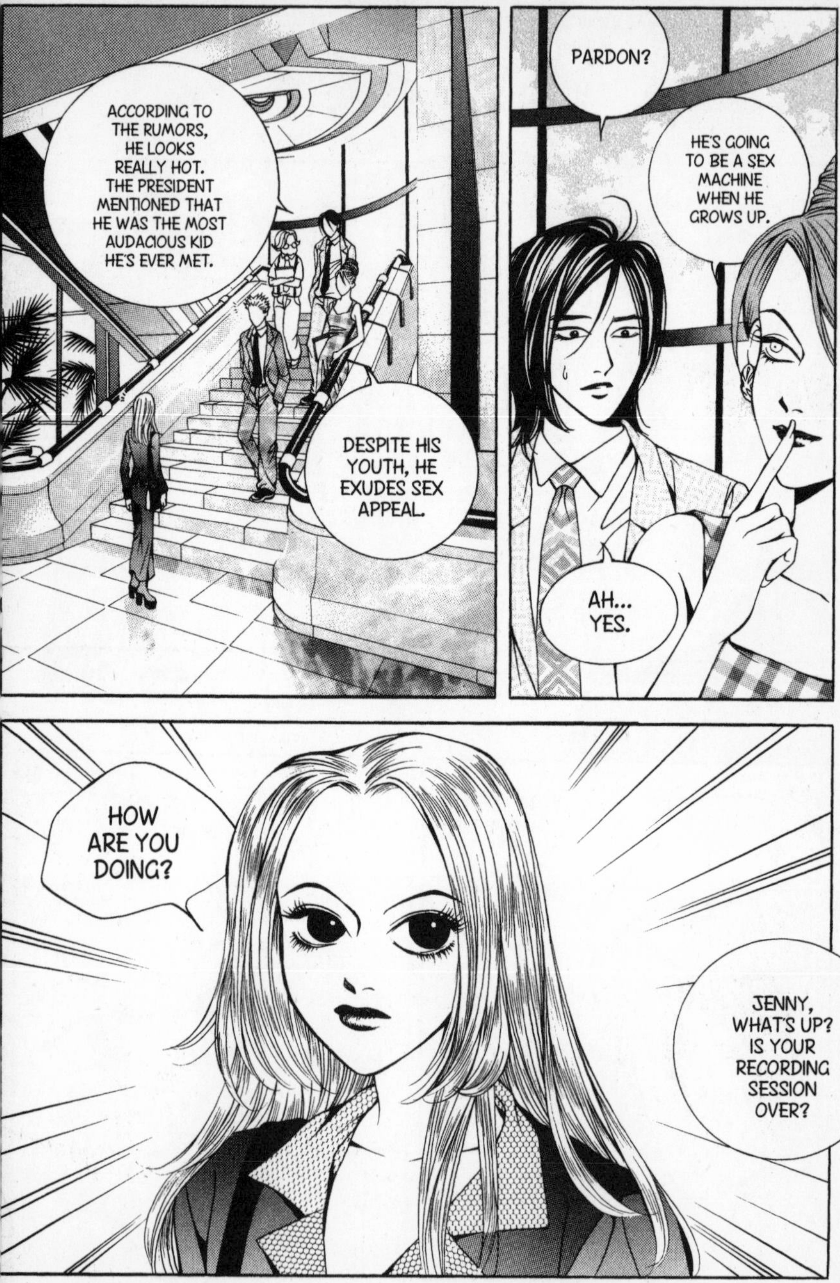
ACCORDING TO THE RUMORS, HE LOOKS REALLY HOT. THE PRESIDENT MENTIONED THAT HE WAS THE MOST AUDACIOUS KID HE'S EVER MET.
DESPITE HIS YOUTH, HE EXUDES SEX APPEAL.
PARDON?
HE'S GOING TO BE A SEX MACHINE WHEN HE GROWS UP.
AH... YES.
HOW ARE YOU DOING?
JENNY, WHAT'S UP? IS YOUR RECORDING SESSION OVER?

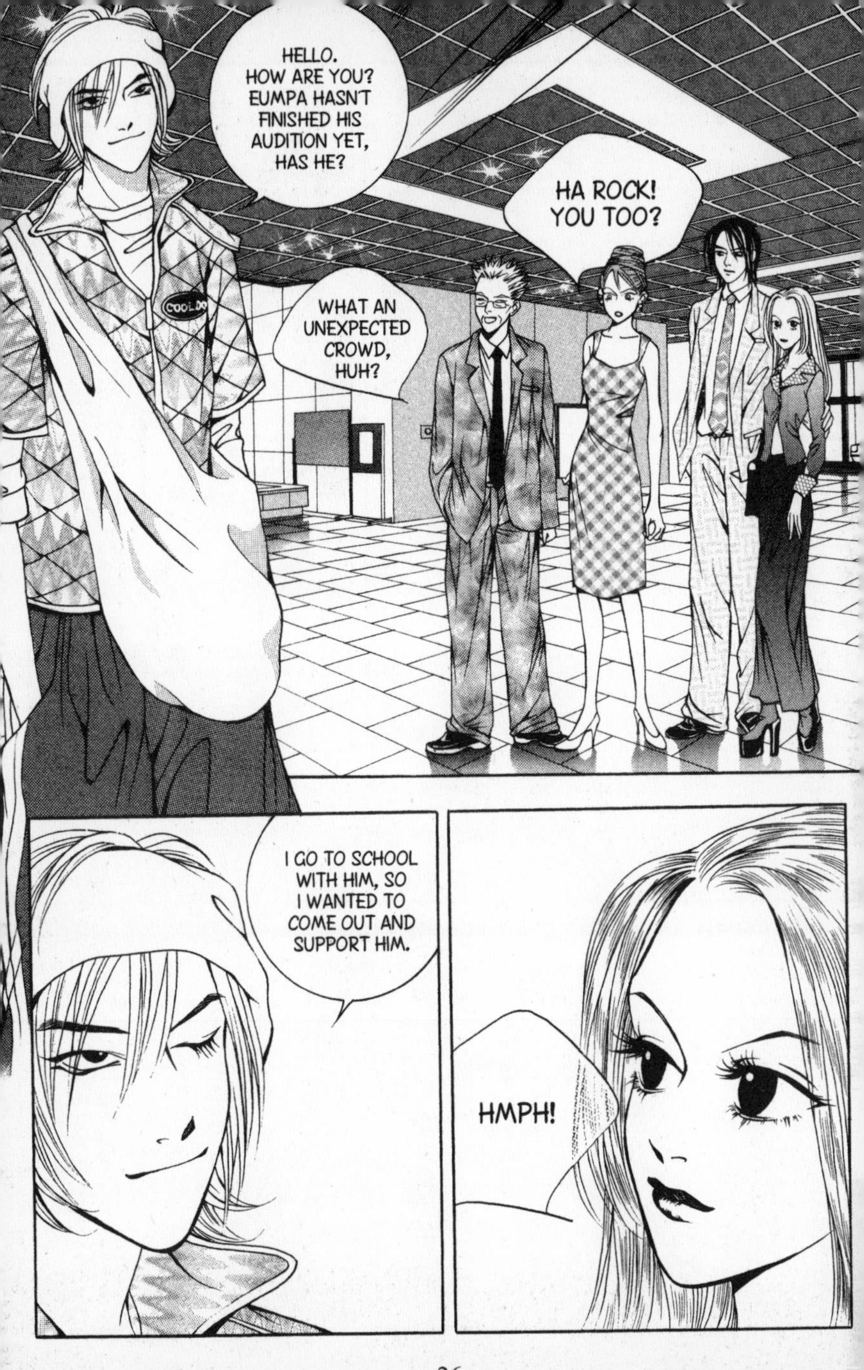
HELLO. HOW ARE YOU? EUMPA HASN'T FINISHED HIS AUDITION YET, HAS HE?
HA ROCK! YOU TOO?
WHAT AN UNEXPECTED CROWD, HUH?
COOL DO
I GO TO SCHOOL WITH HIM, SO I WANTED TO COME OUT AND SUPPORT HIM.
HMPH!

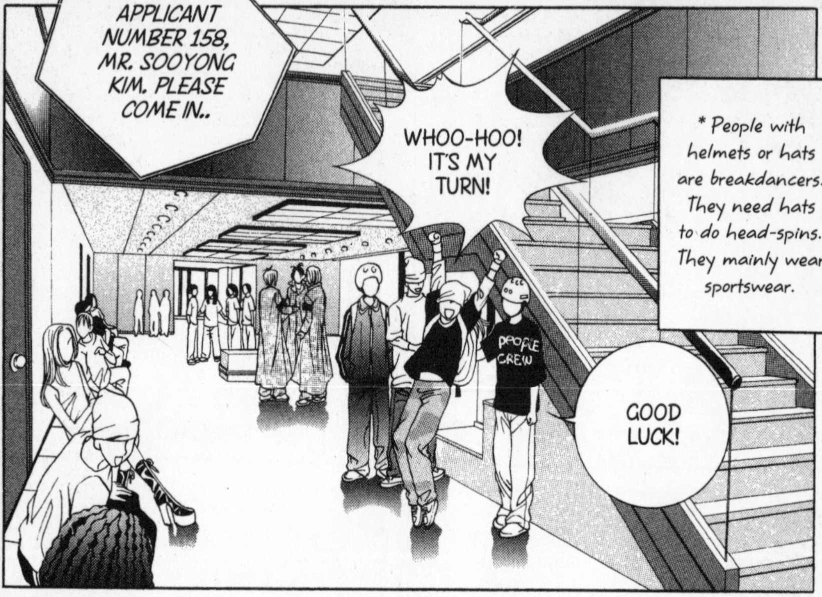
APPLICANT NUMBER 158, MR. SOOYONG KIM. PLEASE COME IN..
WHOO-HOO! IT'S MY TURN!
* People with helmets or hats are breakdancers. They need hats to do head-spins. They mainly wear sportswear.
PEOPLE CREW
GOOD LUCK!

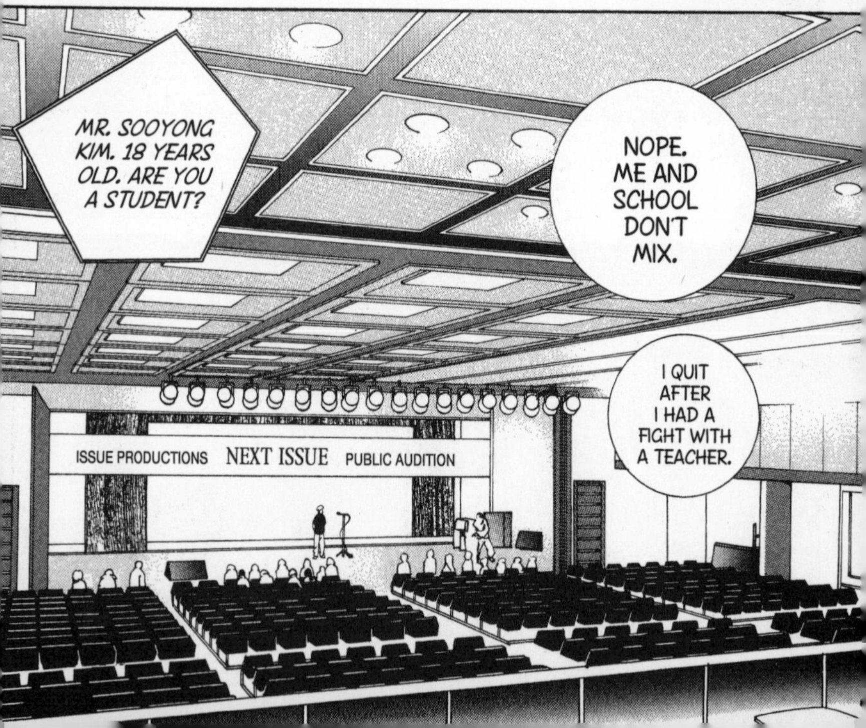
MR. SOOYONG KIM. 18 YEARS OLD. ARE YOU A STUDENT?
NOPE. ME AND SCHOOL DON'T MIX.
ISSUE PRODUCTIONS NEXT ISSUE PUBLIC AUDITION
I QUIT AFTER I HAD A FIGHT WITH A TEACHER.

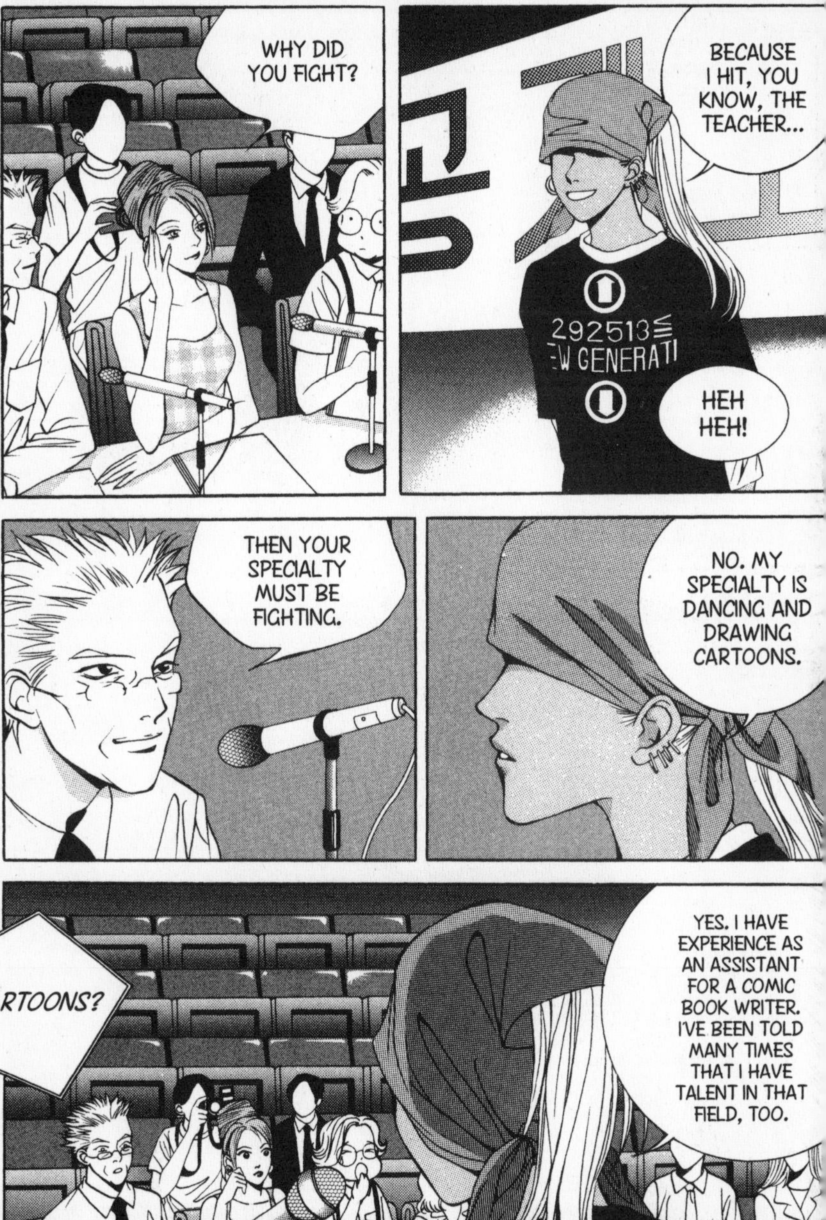
WHY DID YOU FIGHT?
BECAUSE I HIT, YOU KNOW, THE TEACHER...
292513 W GENERATI
HEH HEH!
THEN YOUR SPECIALTY MUST BE FIGHTING.
NO. MY SPECIALTY IS DANCING AND DRAWING CARTOONS.
CARTOONS?
YES. I HAVE EXPERIENCE AS AN ASSISTANT FOR A COMIC BOOK WRITER. I'VE BEEN TOLD MANY TIMES THAT I HAVE TALENT IN THAT FIELD, TOO.

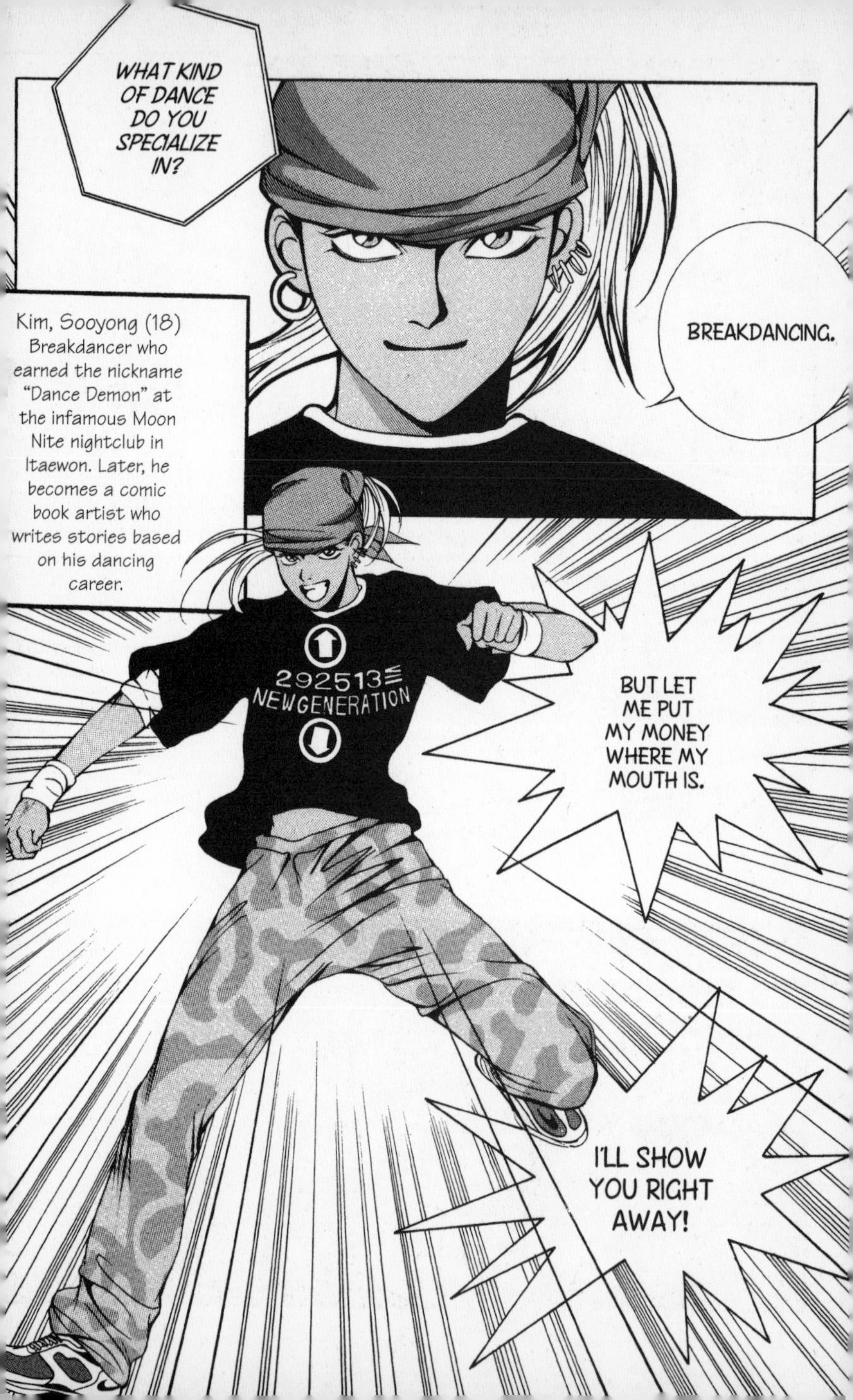
WHAT KIND OF DANCE DO YOU SPECIALIZE IN?
BREAKDANCING.
Kim, Sooyong (18) Breakdancer who earned the nickname "Dance Demon" at the infamous Moon Nite nightclub in Itaewon. Later, he becomes a comic book artist who writes stories based on his dancing career.
292513
NEWGENERATION
BUT LET ME PUT MY MONEY WHERE MY MOUTH IS.
I'LL SHOW YOU RIGHT AWAY!

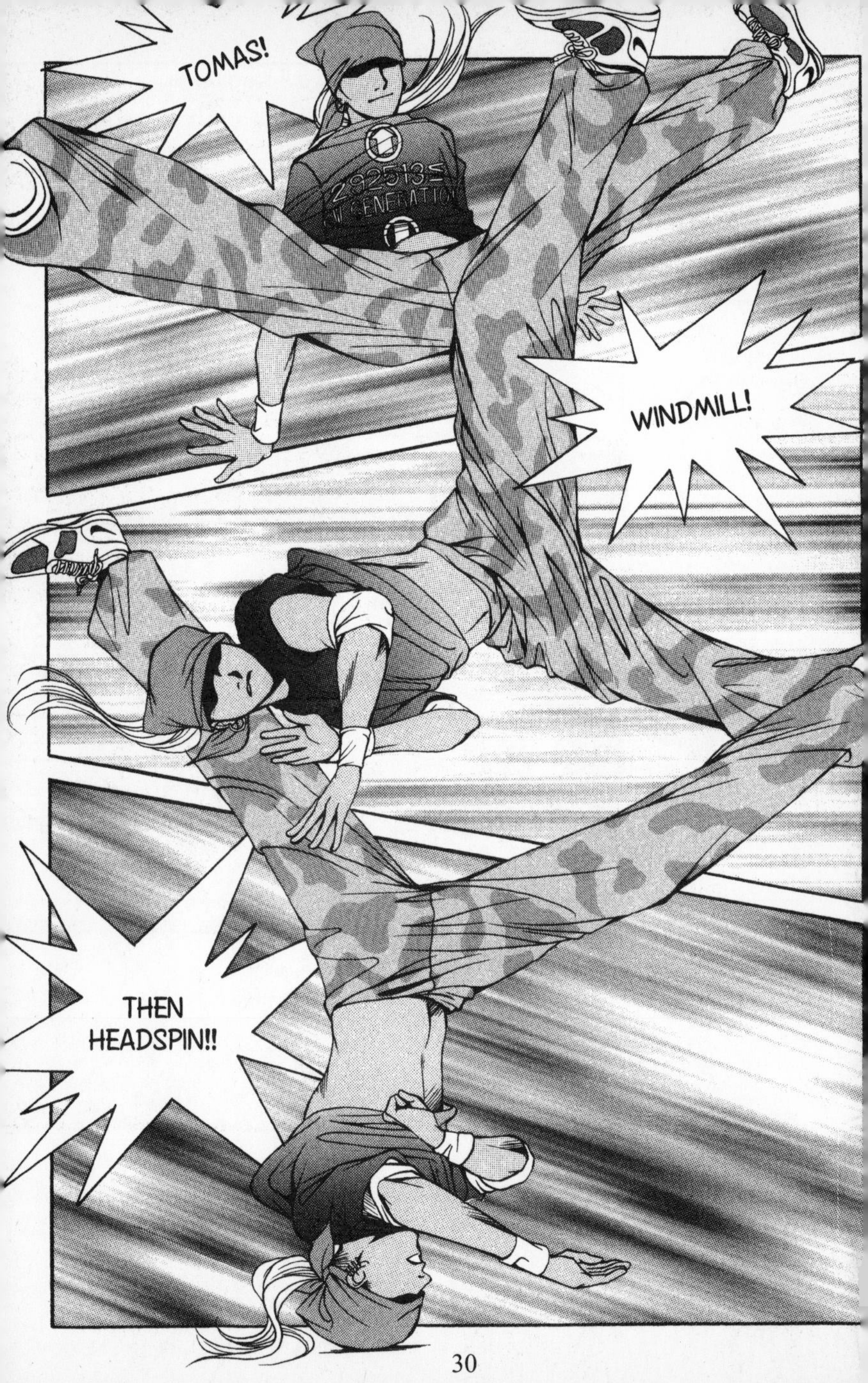
TOMAS!
WINDMILL!
THEN HEADSPIN!!

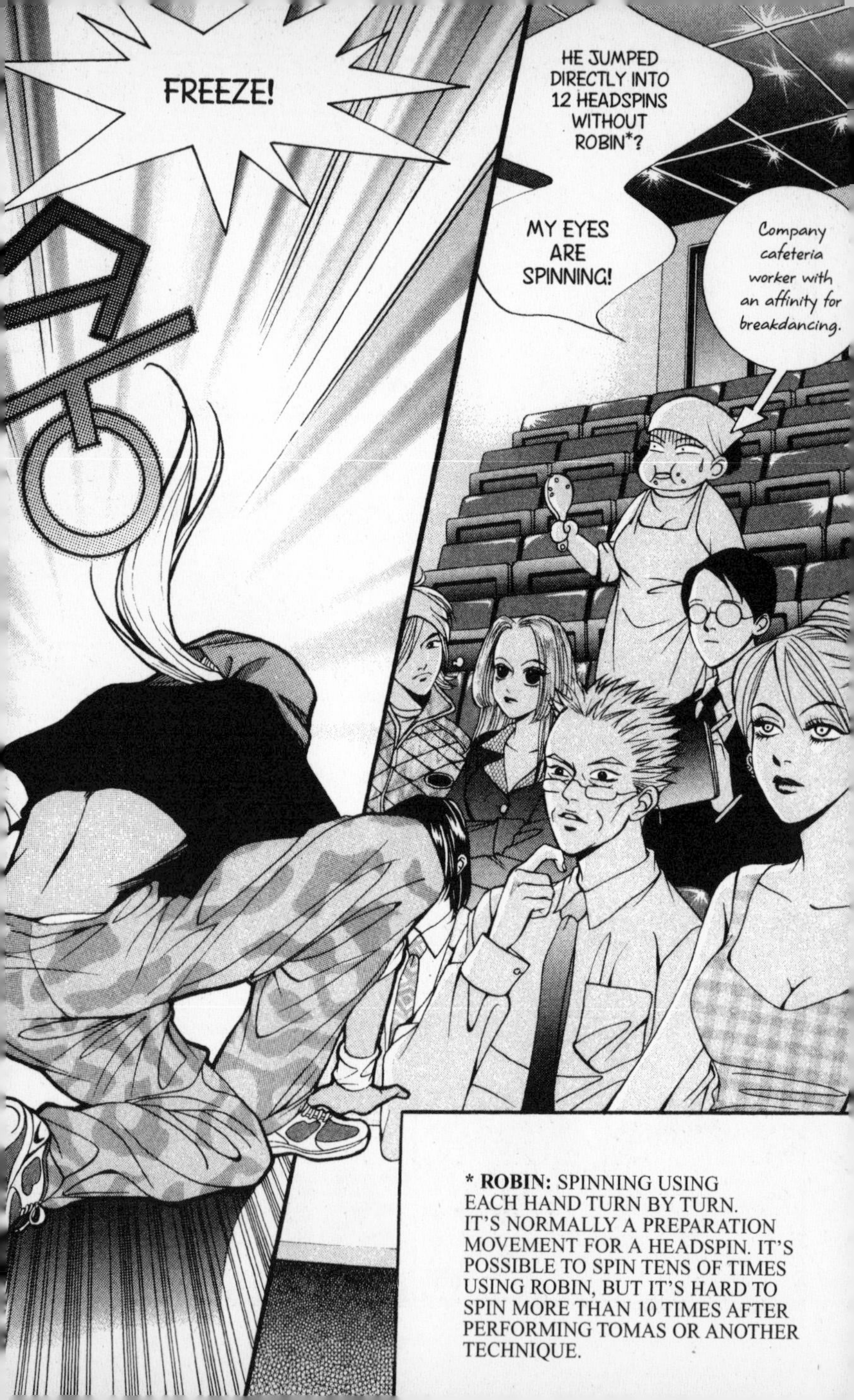
HE JUMPED DIRECTLY INTO 12 HEADSPINS WITHOUT ROBIN*?
MY EYES ARE SPINNING!
Company cafeteria worker with an affinity for breakdancing.
FREEZE!

* **ROBIN:** SPINNING USING EACH HAND TURN BY TURN. IT'S NORMALLY A PREPARATION MOVEMENT FOR A HEADSPIN. IT'S POSSIBLE TO SPIN TENS OF TIMES USING ROBIN, BUT IT'S HARD TO SPIN MORE THAN 10 TIMES AFTER PERFORMING TOMAS OR ANOTHER TECHNIQUE.

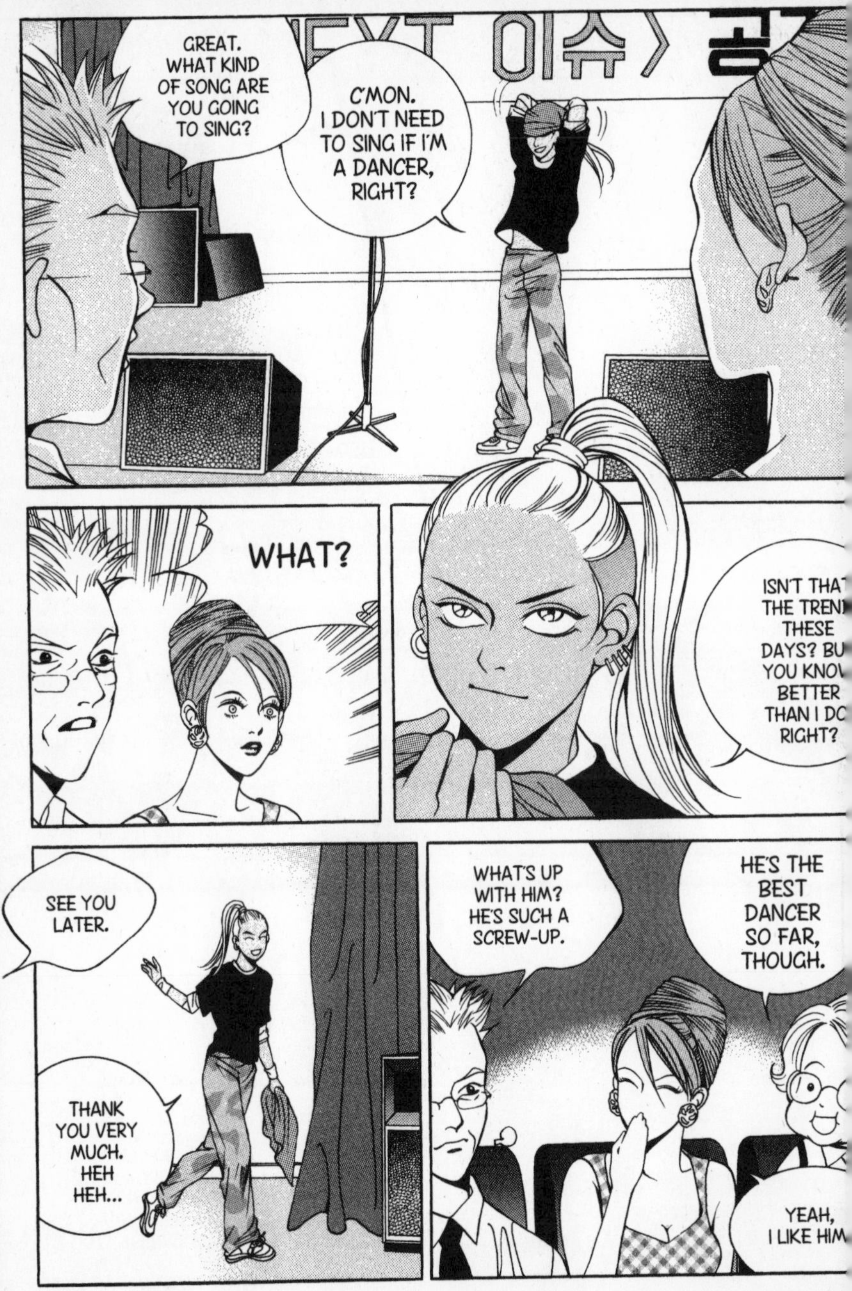
GREAT. WHAT KIND OF SONG ARE YOU GOING TO SING?
C'MON. I DON'T NEED TO SING IF I'M A DANCER, RIGHT?
WHAT?
ISN'T THAT THE TREN THESE DAYS? BU YOU KNOW BETTER THAN I DO RIGHT?
SEE YOU LATER.
THANK YOU VERY MUCH. HEH HEH...
WHAT'S UP WITH HIM? HE'S SUCH A SCREW-UP.
HE'S THE BEST DANCER SO FAR, THOUGH.
YEAH, I LIKE HIM

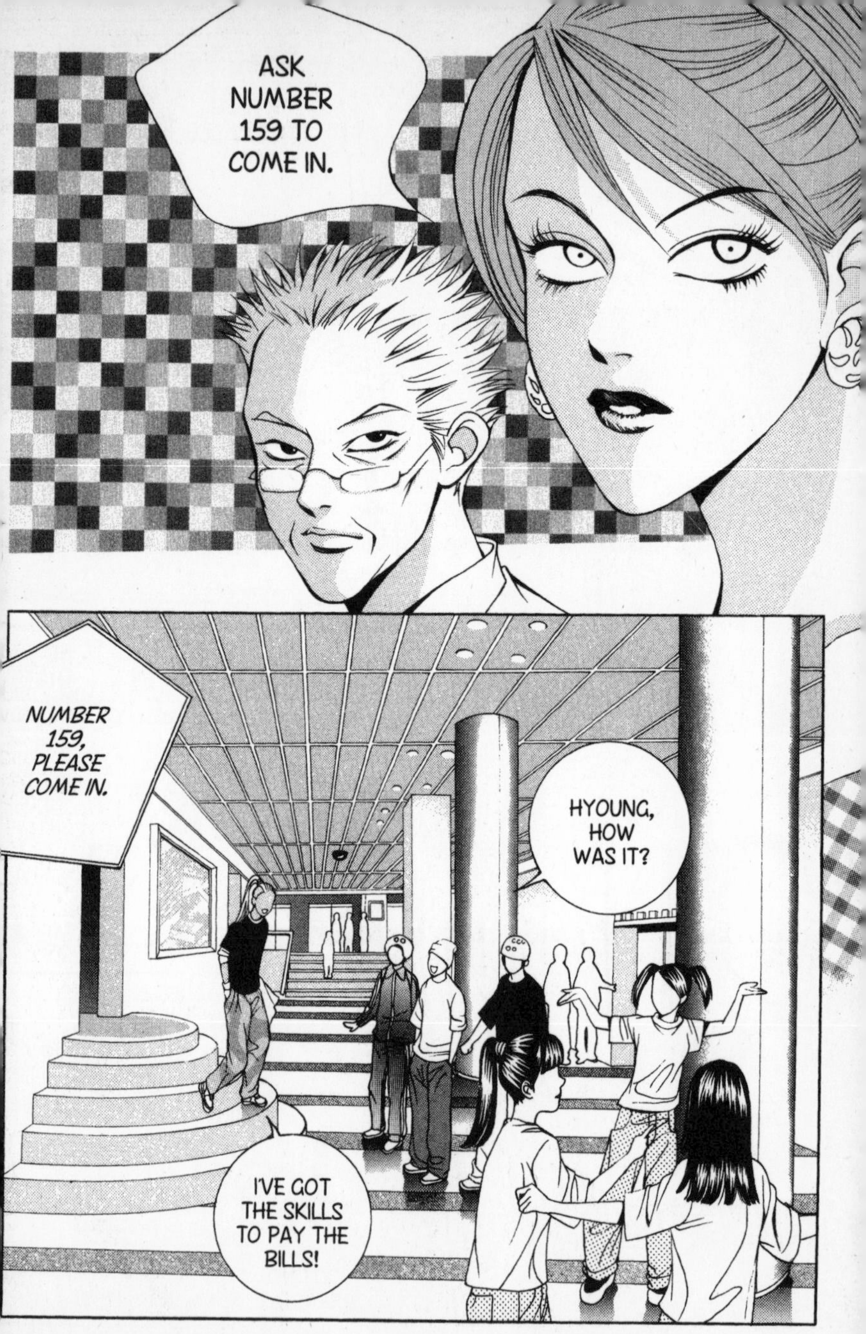
ASK NUMBER 159 TO COME IN.
NUMBER 159, PLEASE COME IN.
HYOUNG, HOW WAS IT?
I'VE GOT THE SKILLS TO PAY THE BILLS!

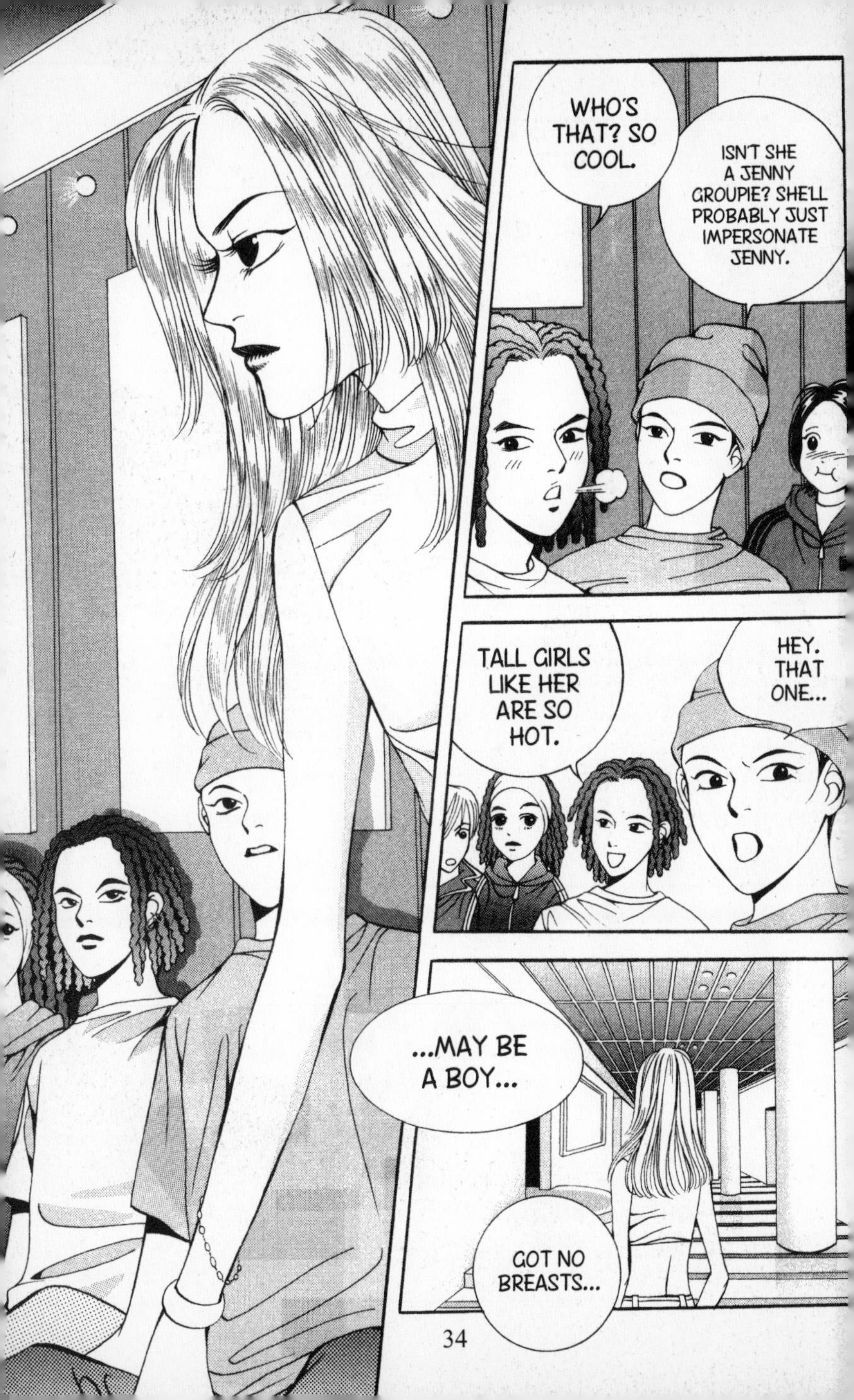
WHO'S THAT? SO COOL.
ISN'T SHE A JENNY GROUPIE? SHE'LL PROBABLY JUST IMPERSONATE JENNY.
TALL GIRLS LIKE HER ARE SO HOT.
HEY. THAT ONE...
...MAY BE A BOY...
GOT NO BREASTS...

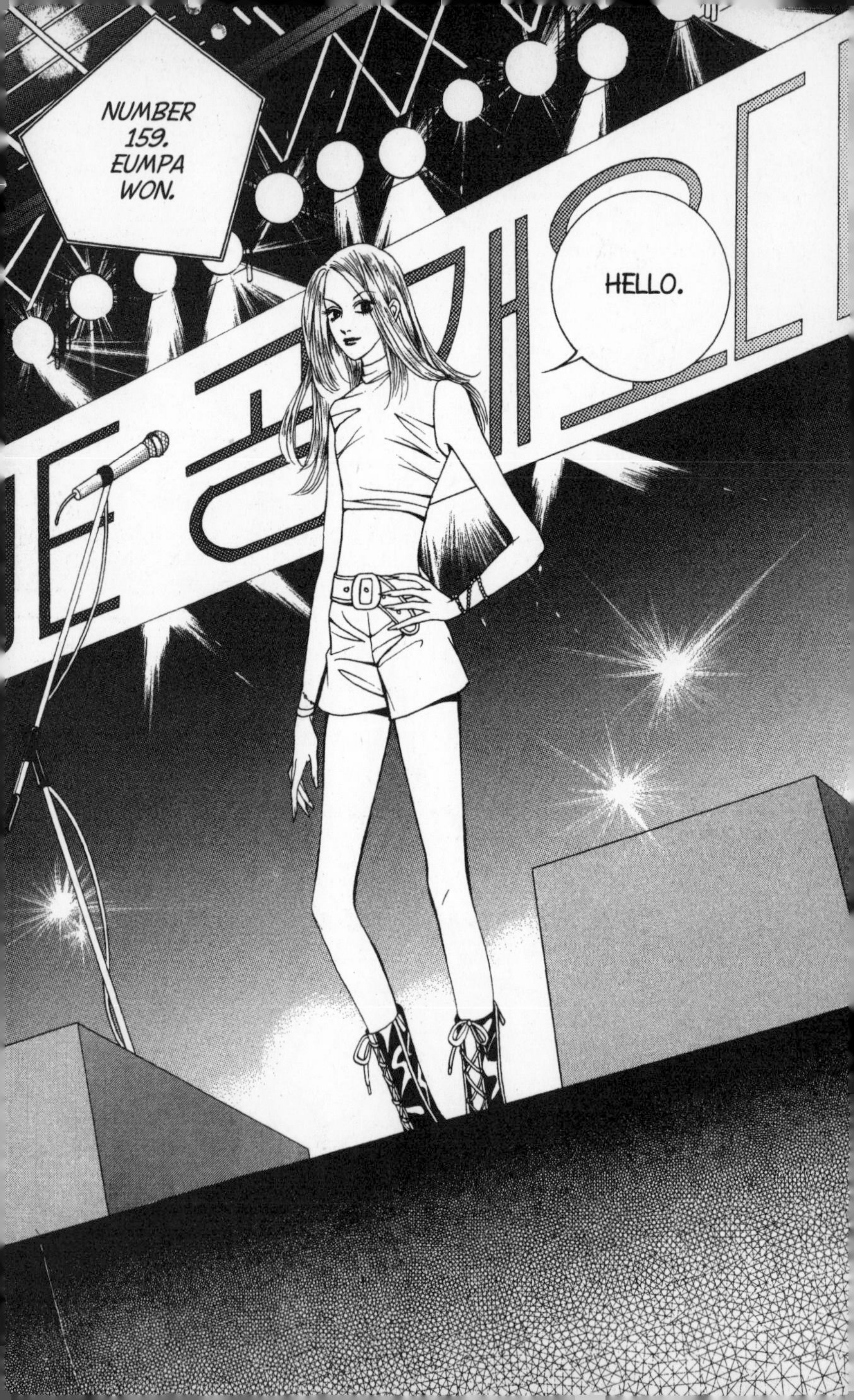
NUMBER 159. EUMPA WON.
HELLO.

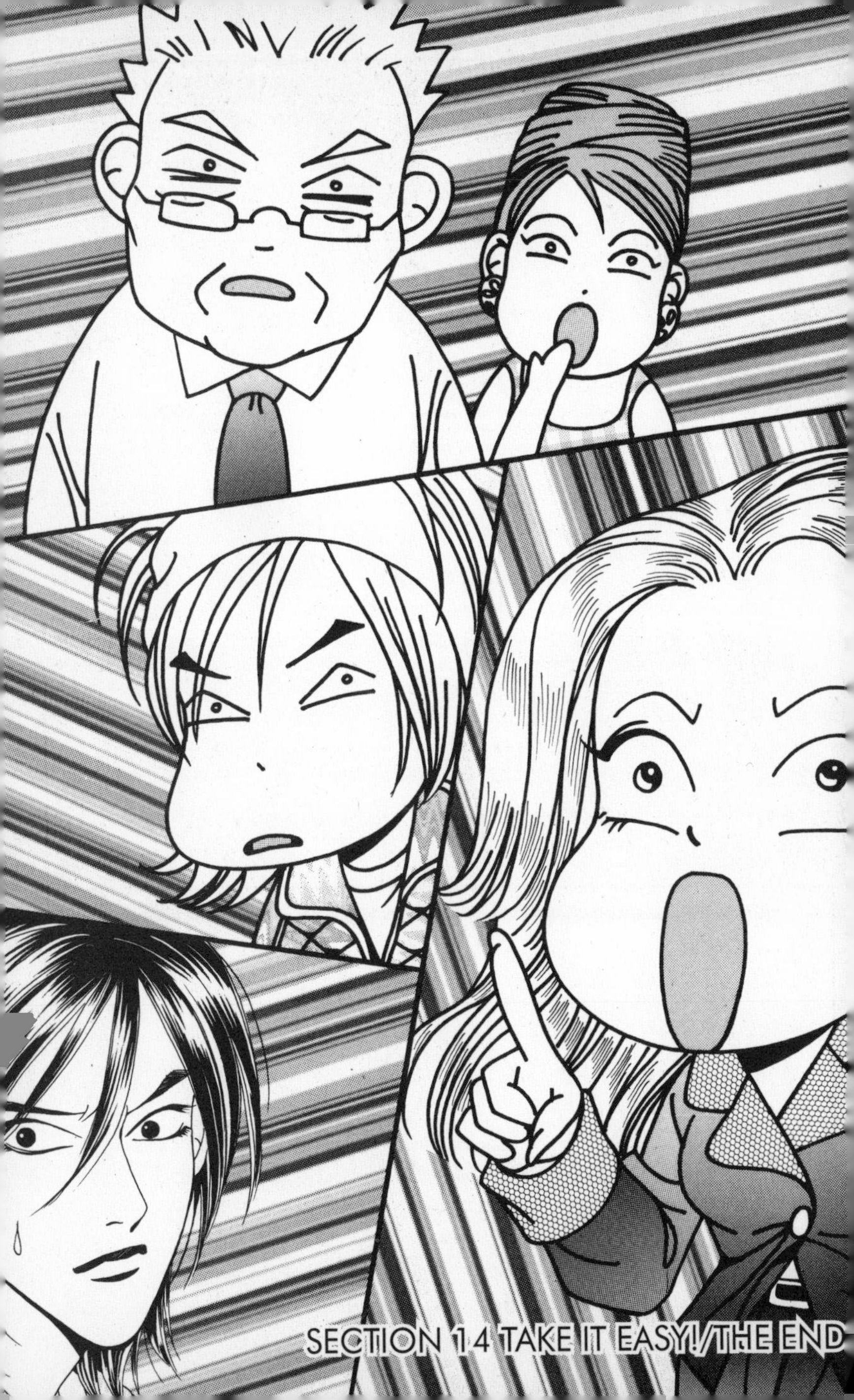
SECTION 14 TAKE IT EASY!/THE END

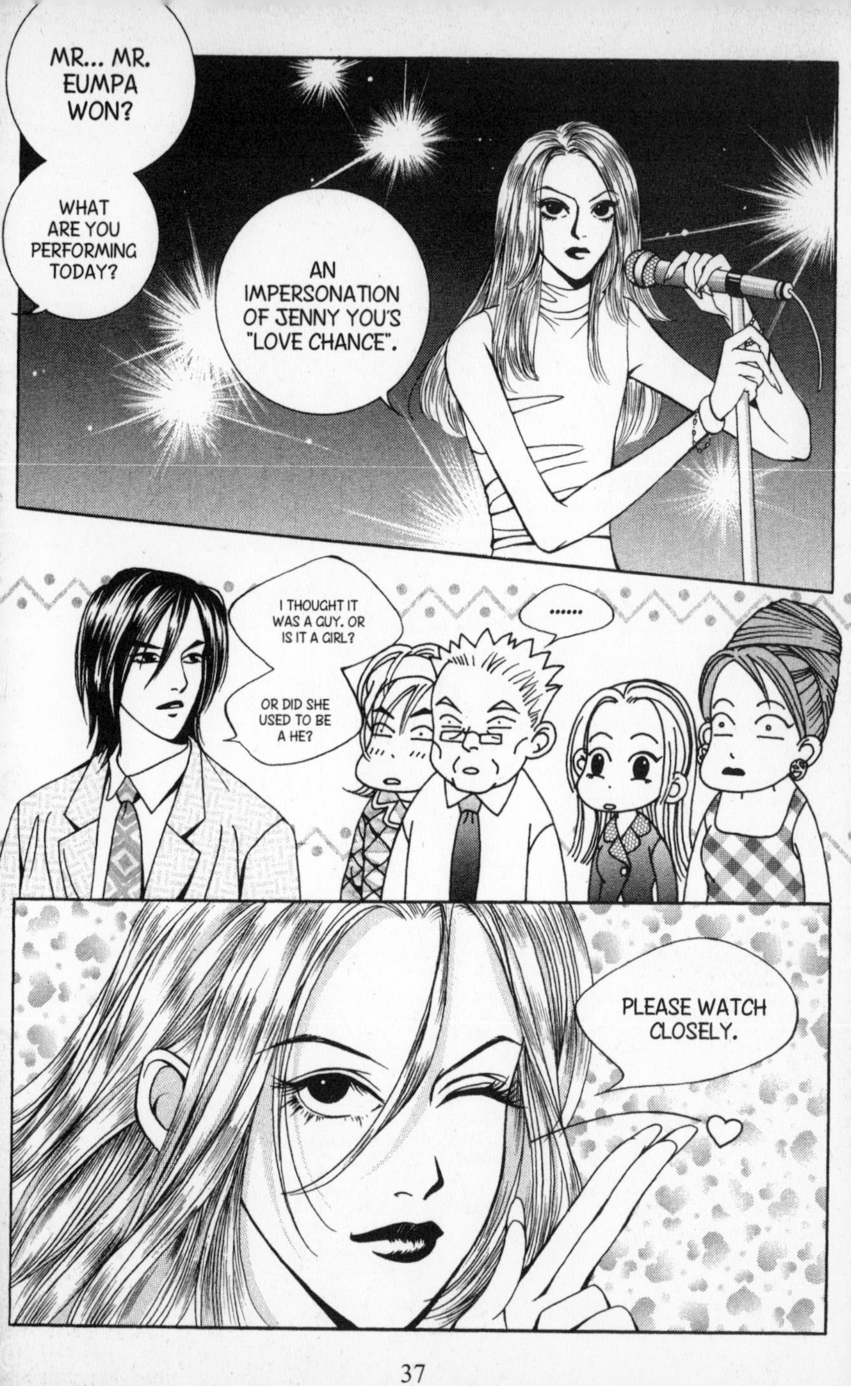
MR... MR. EUMPA WON?
WHAT ARE YOU PERFORMING TODAY?
AN IMPERSONATION OF JENNY YOU'S "LOVE CHANCE".
I THOUGHT IT WAS A GUY. OR IS IT A GIRL?
OR DID SHE USED TO BE A HE?
......
PLEASE WATCH CLOSELY.

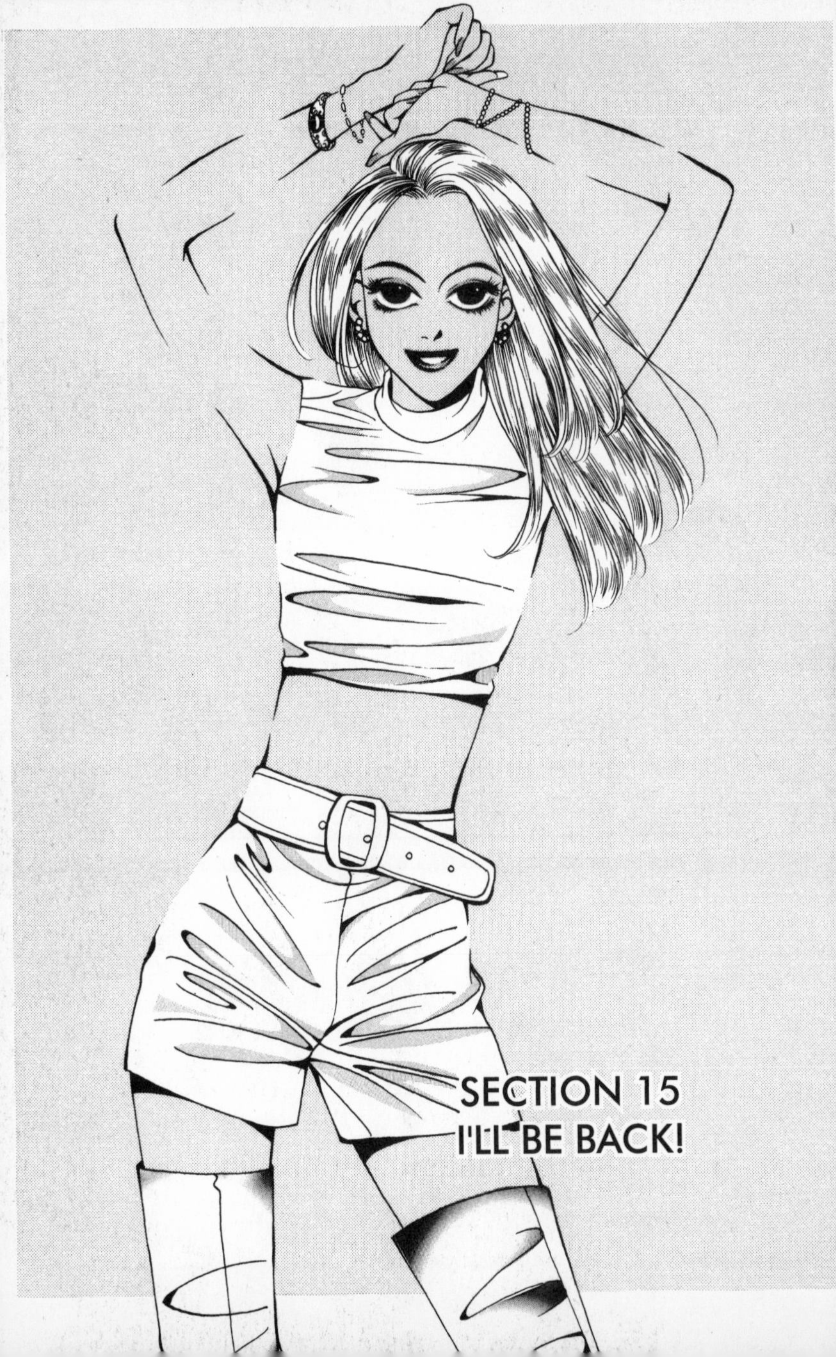
SECTION 15
I'LL BE BACK!

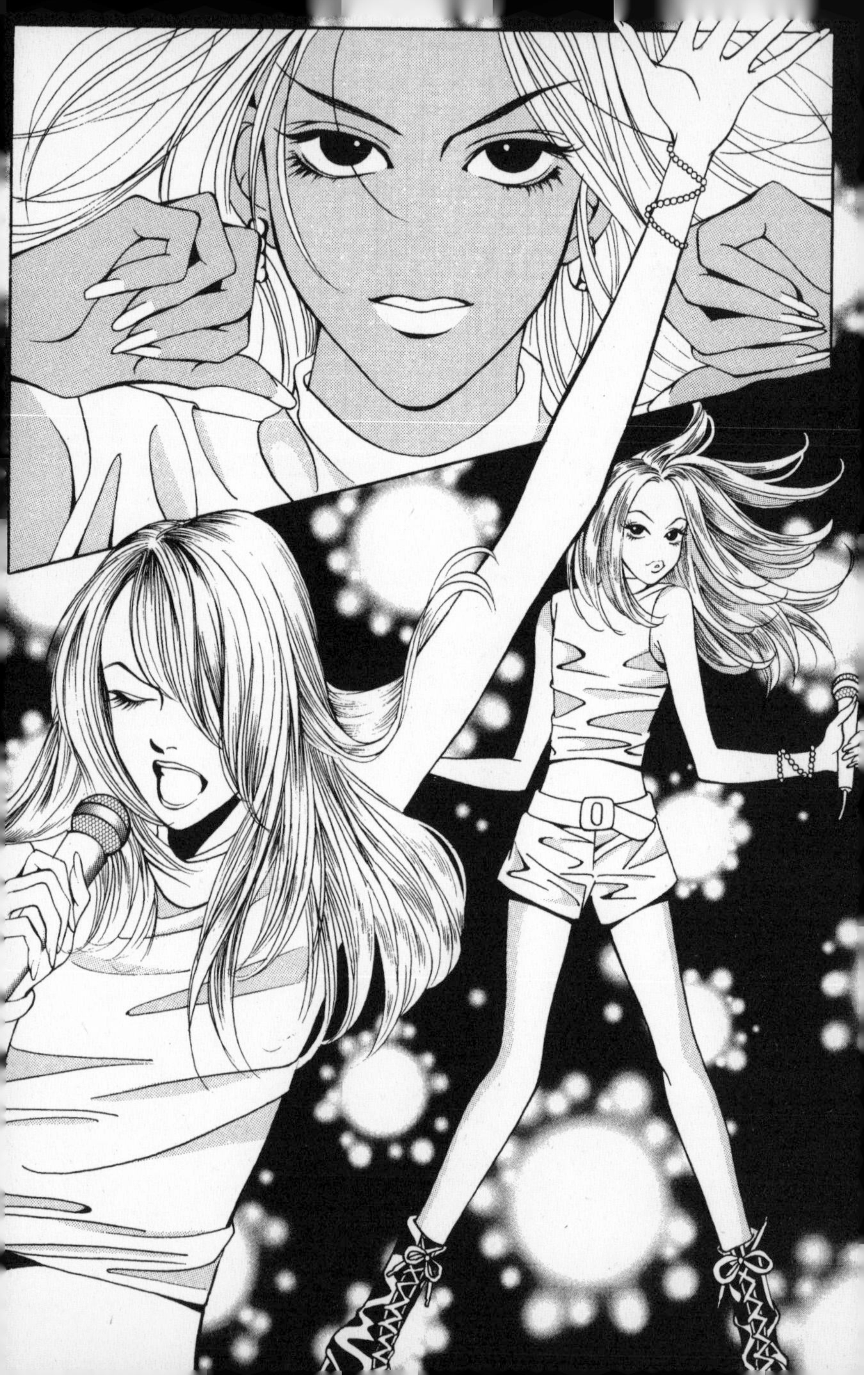

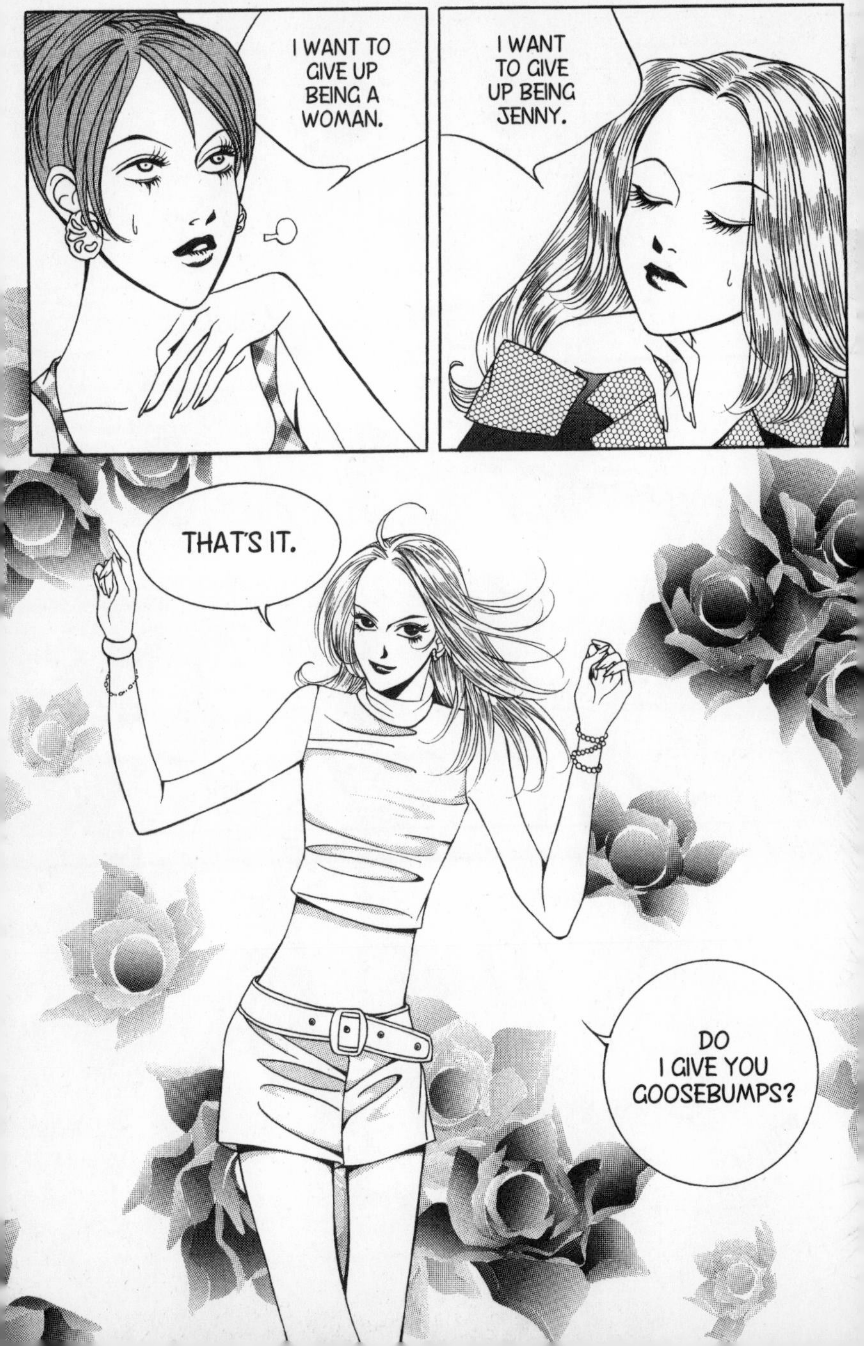
I WANT TO GIVE UP BEING JENNY.
I WANT TO GIVE UP BEING A WOMAN.
THAT'S IT.
DO I GIVE YOU GOOSEBUMPS?

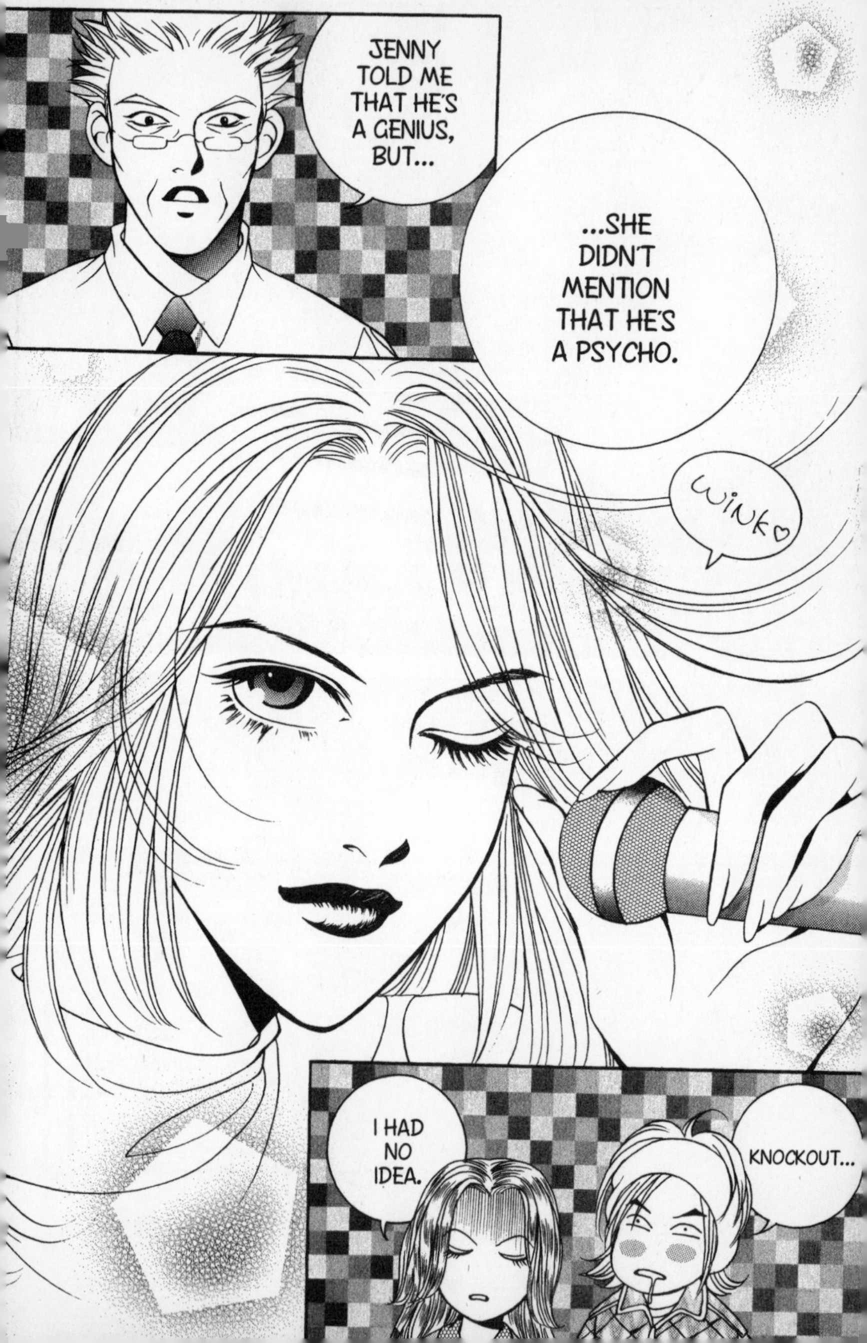
JENNY TOLD ME THAT HE'S A GENIUS, BUT...
...SHE DIDN'T MENTION THAT HE'S A PSYCHO.
wink♡
KNOCKOUT...
I HAD NO IDEA.

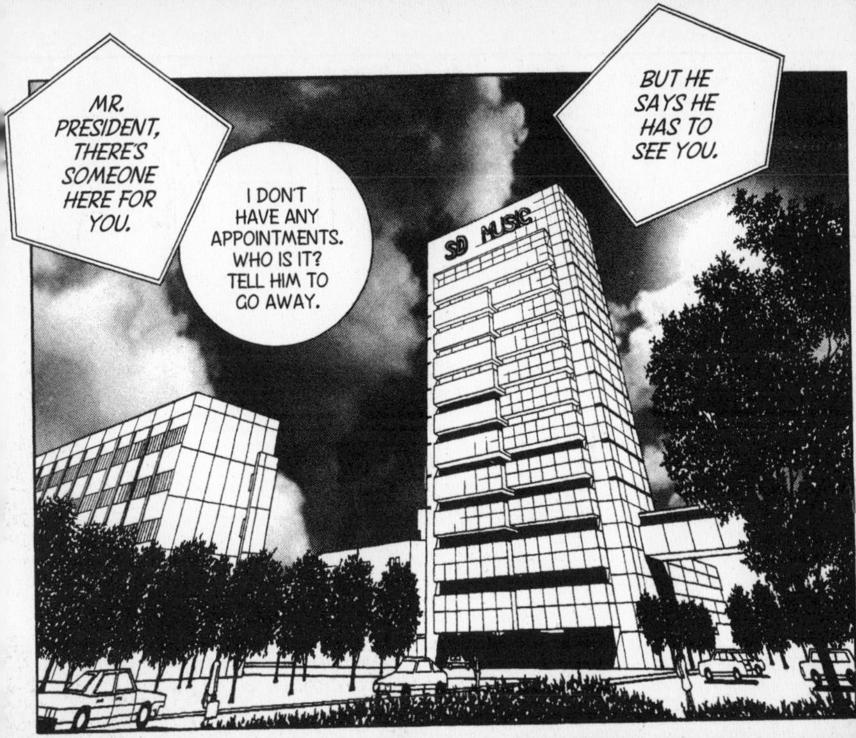
MR. PRESIDENT, THERE'S SOMEONE HERE FOR YOU.
I DON'T HAVE ANY APPOINTMENTS. WHO IS IT? TELL HIM TO GO AWAY.
BUT HE SAYS HE HAS TO SEE YOU.
SD MUSIC
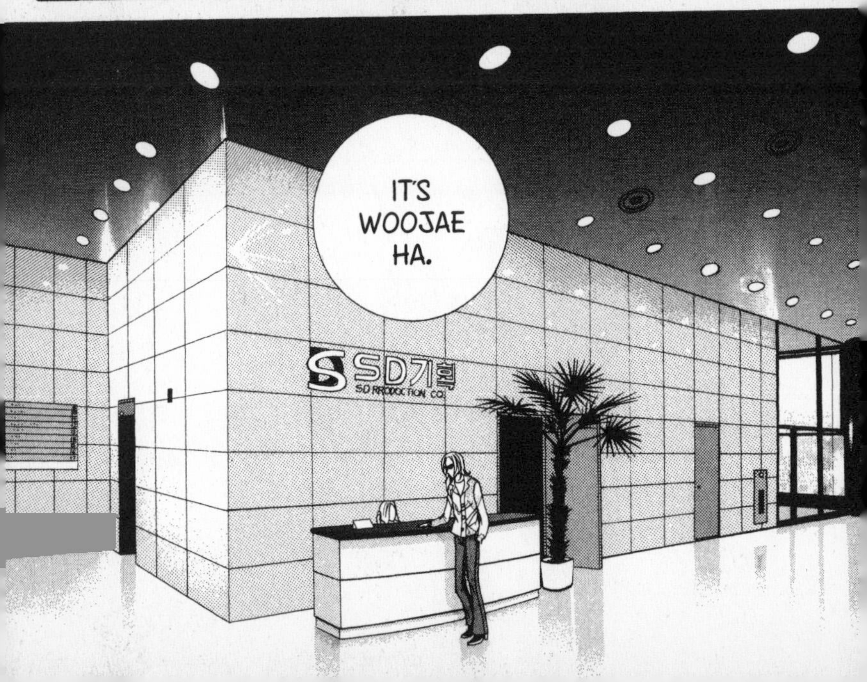
IT'S WOOJAE HA.
SD기획

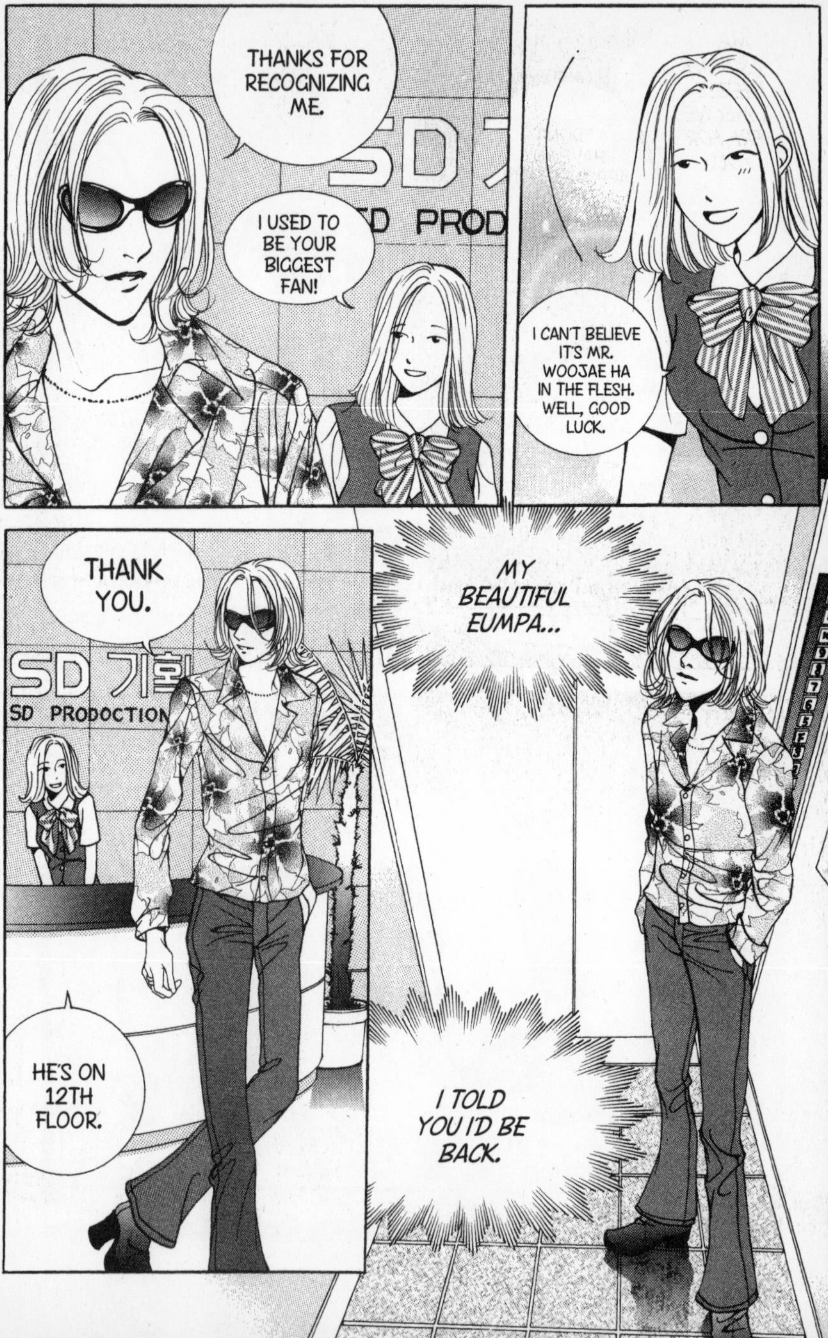
THANKS FOR RECOGNIZING ME.
SD 기획
SD PROD
I USED TO BE YOUR BIGGEST FAN!
I CAN'T BELIEVE IT'S MR. WOOJAE HA IN THE FLESH. WELL, GOOD LUCK.
THANK YOU.
SD 기획
SD PRODUCTION
HE'S ON 12TH FLOOR.
MY BEAUTIFUL EUMPA...
I TOLD YOU I'D BE BACK.

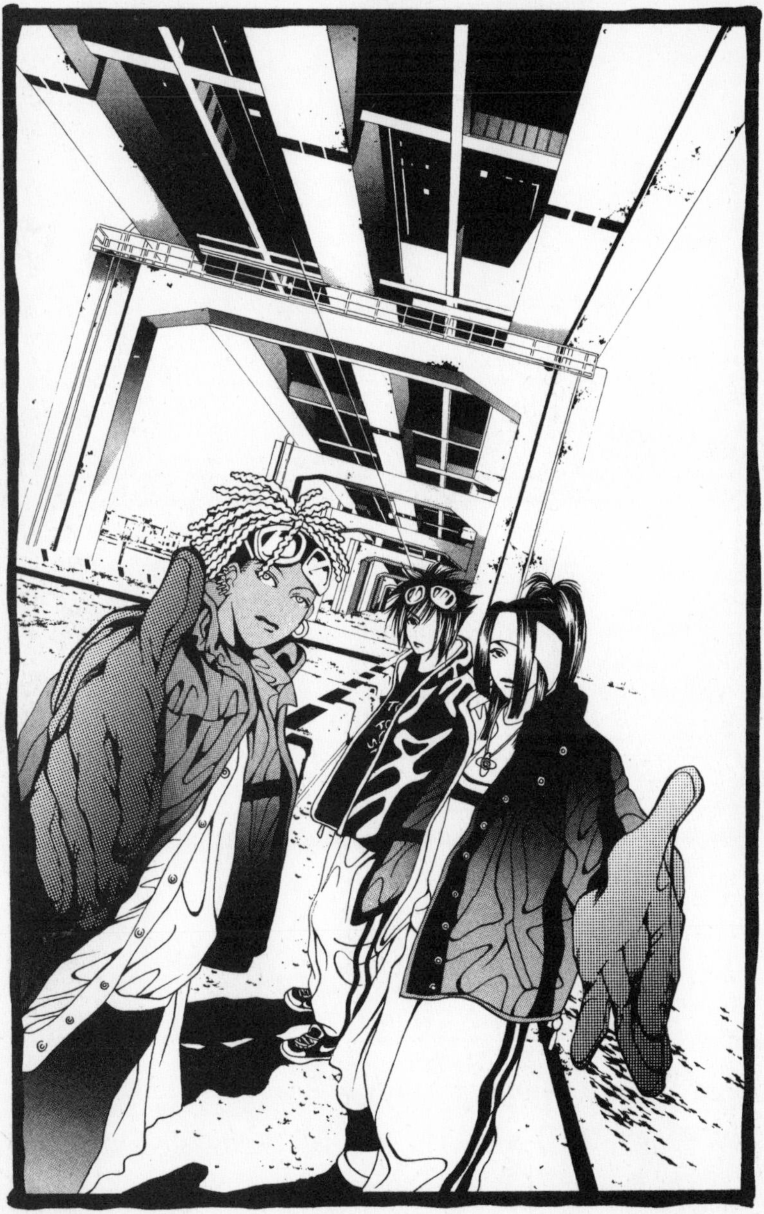

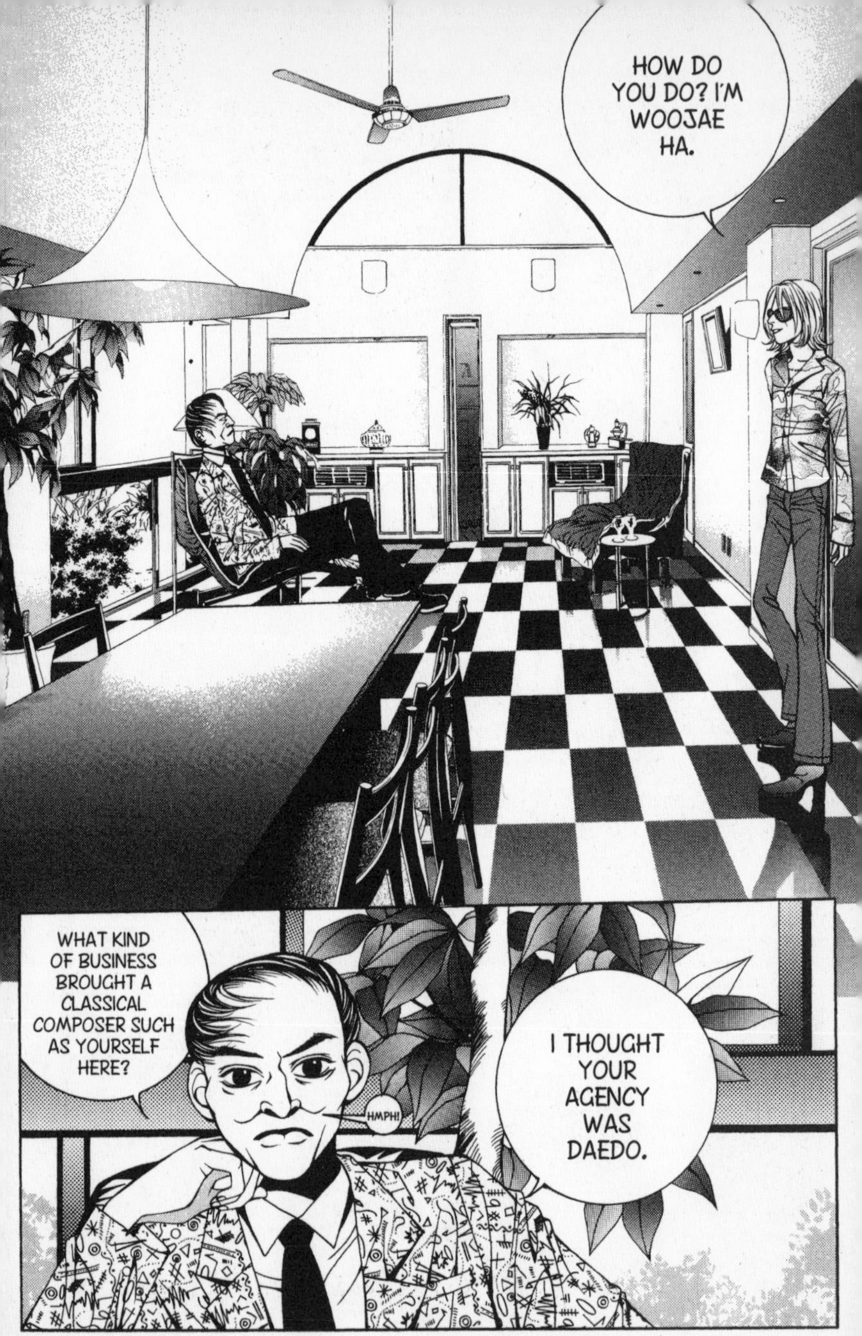
HOW DO YOU DO? I'M WOOJAE HA.
WHAT KIND OF BUSINESS BROUGHT A CLASSICAL COMPOSER SUCH AS YOURSELF HERE?
HMPH!
I THOUGHT YOUR AGENCY WAS DAEDO.

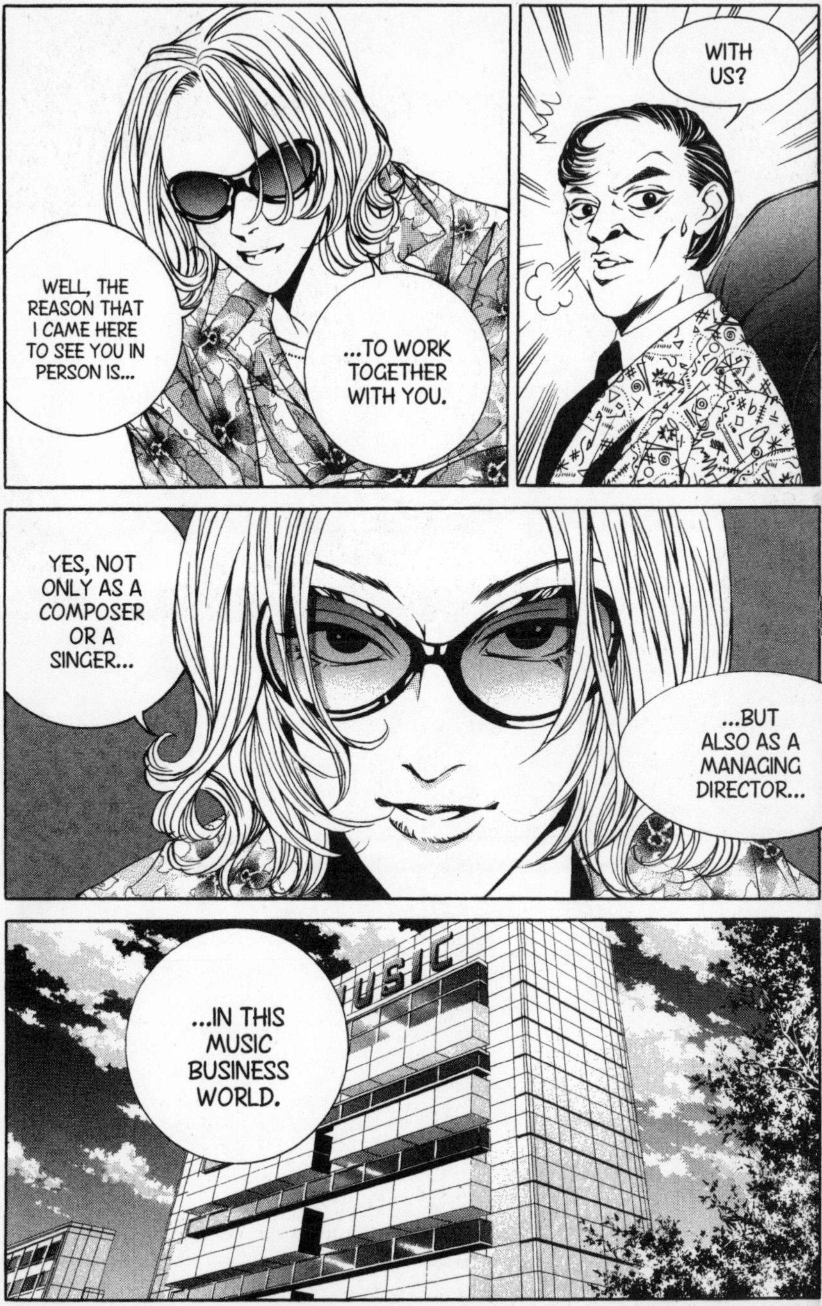
WELL, THE REASON THAT I CAME HERE TO SEE YOU IN PERSON IS...
...TO WORK TOGETHER WITH YOU.
WITH US?
YES, NOT ONLY AS A COMPOSER OR A SINGER...
...BUT ALSO AS A MANAGING DIRECTOR...
...IN THIS MUSIC BUSINESS WORLD.
MUSIC

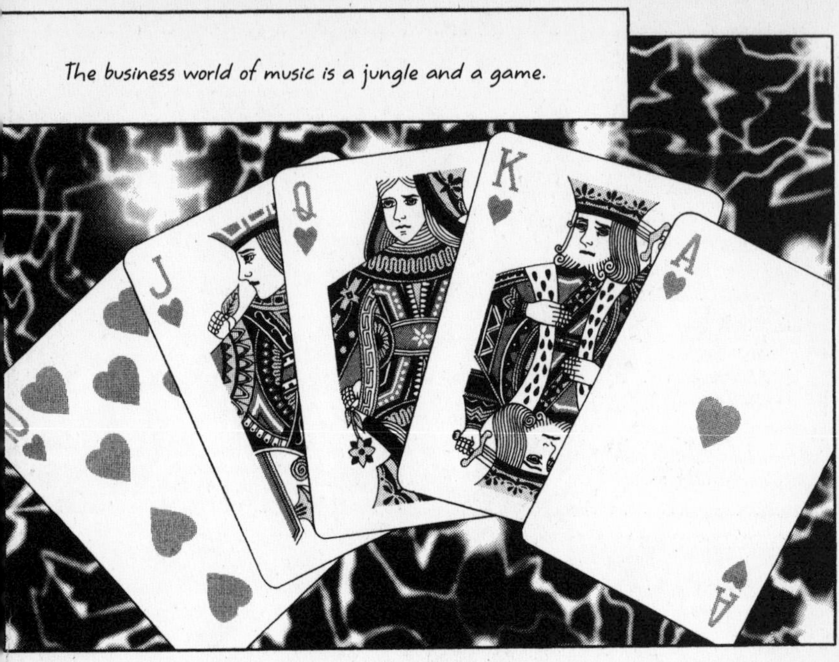
The business world of music is a jungle and a game.

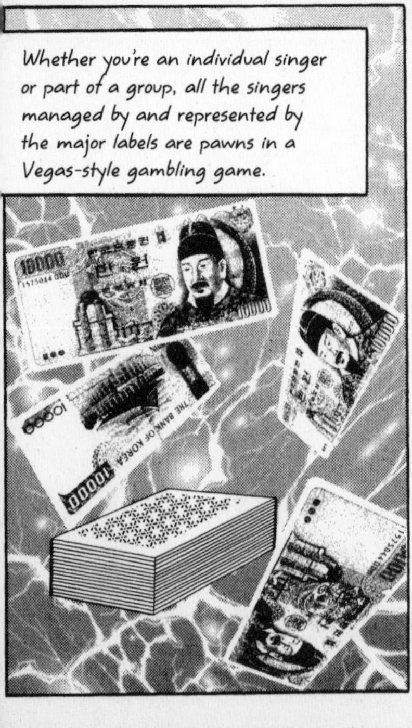
Whether you're an individual singer or part of a group, all the singers managed by and represented by the major labels are pawns in a Vegas-style gambling game.

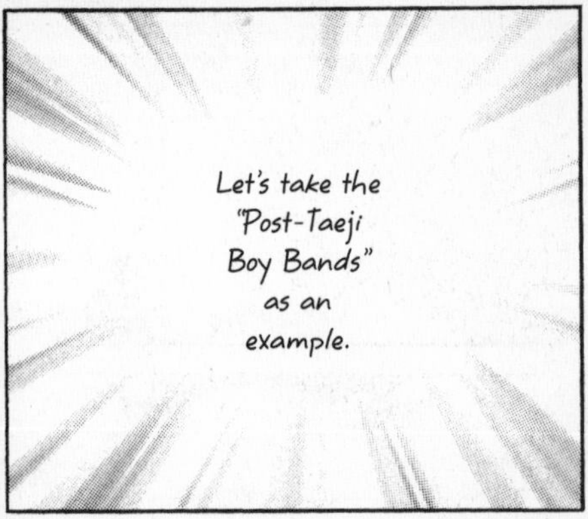
Let's take the "Post-Taeji Boy Bands" as an example.

* "Post-Taeji Boy Bands":
Dance groups who sprang out since Seo, Taeji and his boys hit the scene, imitating Taeji's planning strategies and practices. Most Korean groups except for Deux belong in this category. They always have a rapper, dancer, and vocalist, and produce songs mixed with rap and melody: faithful adaptations of "Taeji Boys" characteristics.

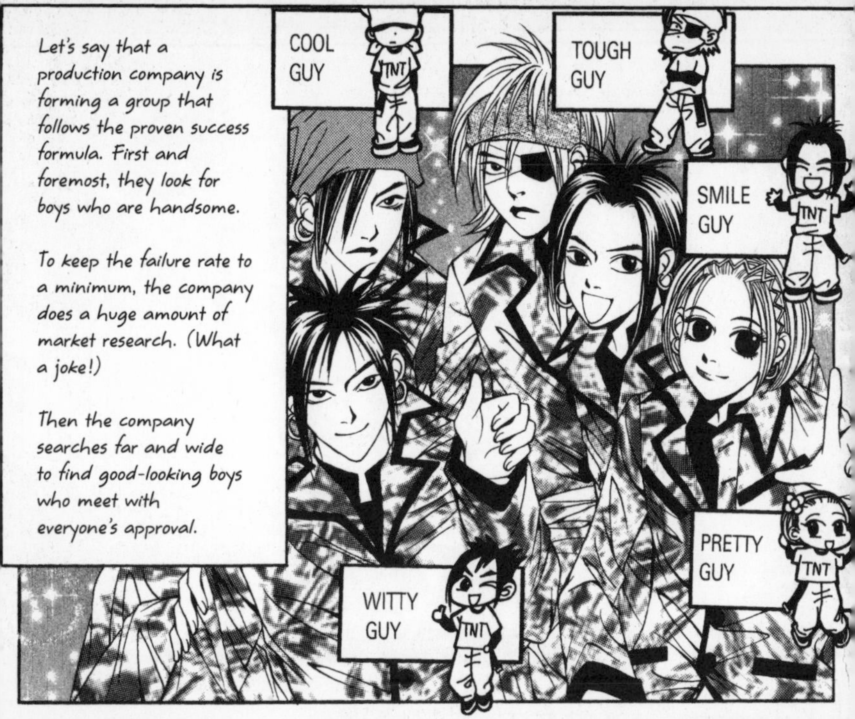
TOUGH GUY
COOL GUY
Let's say that a production company is forming a group that follows the proven success formula. First and foremost, they look for boys who are handsome.
To keep the failure rate to a minimum, the company does a huge amount of market research. (What a joke!)
Then the company searches far and wide to find good-looking boys who meet with everyone's approval.
SMILE GUY
PRETTY GUY
WITTY GUY

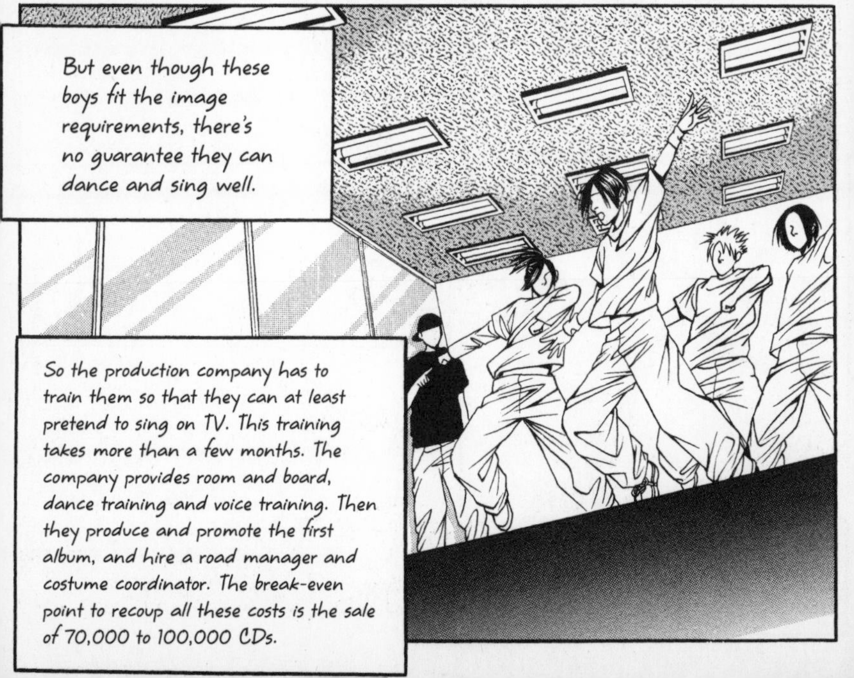
But even though these boys fit the image requirements, there's no guarantee they can dance and sing well.
So the production company has to train them so that they can at least pretend to sing on TV. This training takes more than a few months. The company provides room and board, dance training and voice training. Then they produce and promote the first album, and hire a road manager and costume coordinator. The break-even point to recoup all these costs is the sale of 70,000 to 100,000 CDs.

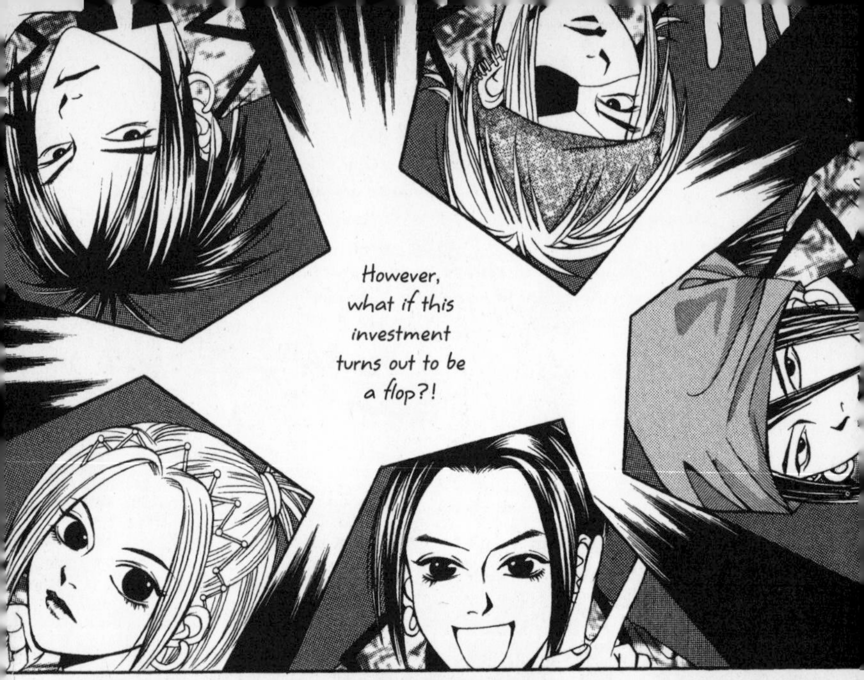
However, what if this investment turns out to be a flop?!

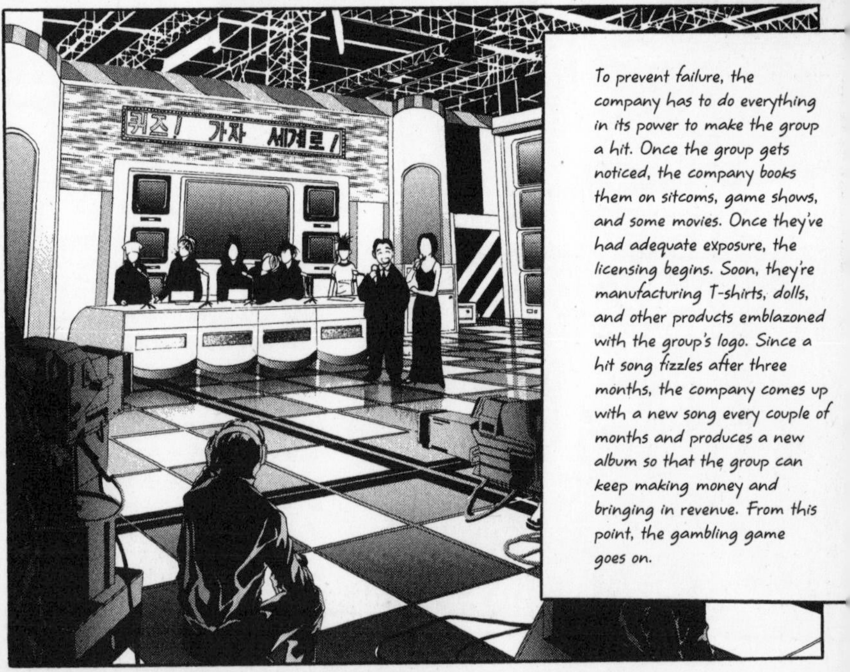
To prevent failure, the company has to do everything in its power to make the group a hit. Once the group gets noticed, the company books them on sitcoms, game shows, and some movies. Once they've had adequate exposure, the licensing begins. Soon, they're manufacturing T-shirts, dolls, and other products emblazoned with the group's logo. Since a hit song fizzles after three months, the company comes up with a new song every couple of months and produces a new album so that the group can keep making money and bringing in revenue. From this point, the gambling game goes on.
퀴즈! 가자 세계로!

There is definitely a successful "formula." But what the heck is a formula, anyway? Somebody must have come up with it!
In addition to the external formula—good looks and killer dance moves—there's another formula observed by major league dance groups. It's the development of music following the "rap-melody-rap-melody-interlude" style. It separates melody and rap completely, puts the easy-listening melody in the beginning, and inserts the rap part where the musical refrain comes, with a fast-beat background sound. Most contemporary dance groups produce their songs in accordance with this formula.

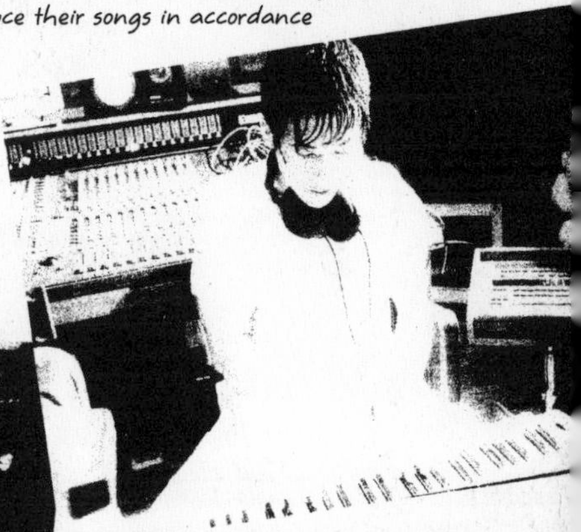

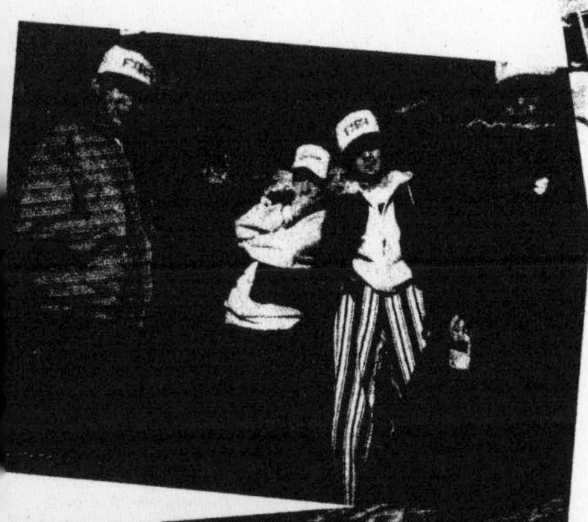

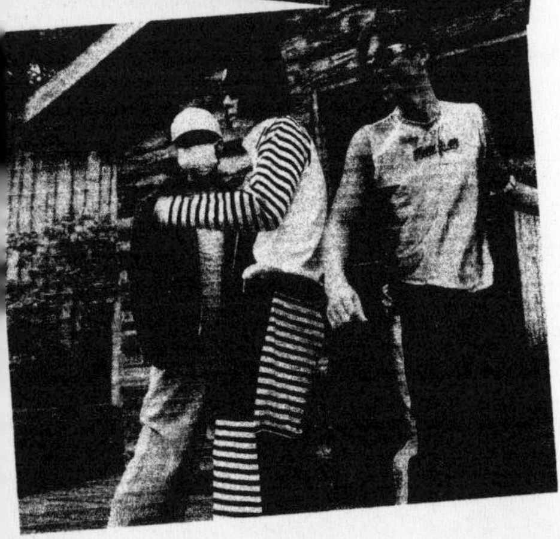

Well, this formula certainly did not exist before our time. In fact, the one who created this formula is Taeji Seo, of all people.
Rap used to be considered "mumbling," and was used for sitcoms only. Taeji Seo broke the "rap-impossible" theory, and established the firm foundation of rap in Korea. He restructured the hard-to-pronounce Korean words to make them easy to rap, and enhanced the mixing and engineering techniques. Soon, rap became a language and fashion trend among the young generation, and all his groups divided into three divisions: rapper-vocal-dancer. This then became the model of most up-and-coming groups.

Work Cited: Kang, Myoungseuk and Kim, Jinsung, Seo, Taeji and his boys. Since then, don't we have anyone?!

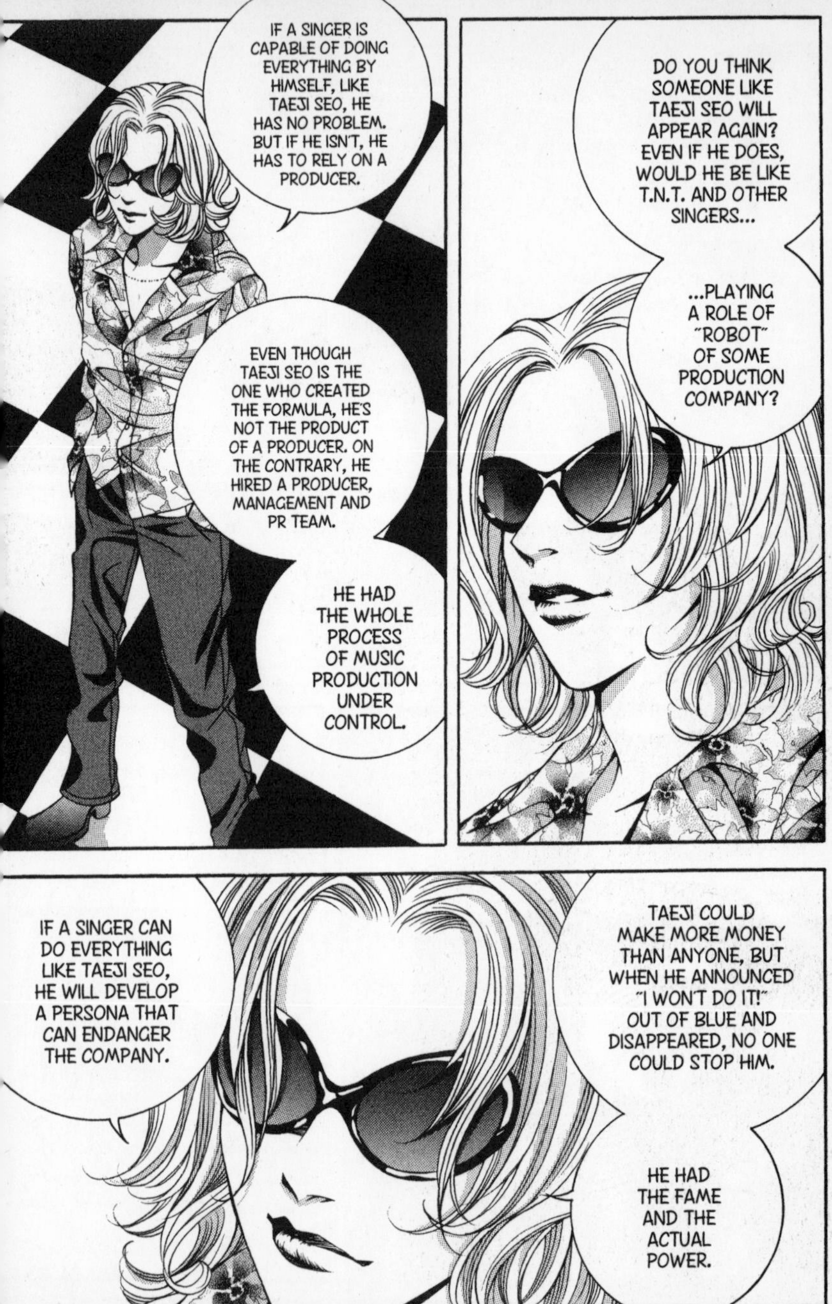
IF A SINGER IS CAPABLE OF DOING EVERYTHING BY HIMSELF, LIKE TAEJI SEO, HE HAS NO PROBLEM. BUT IF HE ISN'T, HE HAS TO RELY ON A PRODUCER.
EVEN THOUGH TAEJI SEO IS THE ONE WHO CREATED THE FORMULA, HE'S NOT THE PRODUCT OF A PRODUCER. ON THE CONTRARY, HE HIRED A PRODUCER, MANAGEMENT AND PR TEAM.
HE HAD THE WHOLE PROCESS OF MUSIC PRODUCTION UNDER CONTROL.
DO YOU THINK SOMEONE LIKE TAEJI SEO WILL APPEAR AGAIN? EVEN IF HE DOES, WOULD HE BE LIKE T.N.T. AND OTHER SINGERS...
...PLAYING A ROLE OF "ROBOT" OF SOME PRODUCTION COMPANY?
IF A SINGER CAN DO EVERYTHING LIKE TAEJI SEO, HE WILL DEVELOP A PERSONA THAT CAN ENDANGER THE COMPANY.
TAEJI COULD MAKE MORE MONEY THAN ANYONE, BUT WHEN HE ANNOUNCED "I WON'T DO IT!" OUT OF BLUE AND DISAPPEARED, NO ONE COULD STOP HIM.
HE HAD THE FAME AND THE ACTUAL POWER.

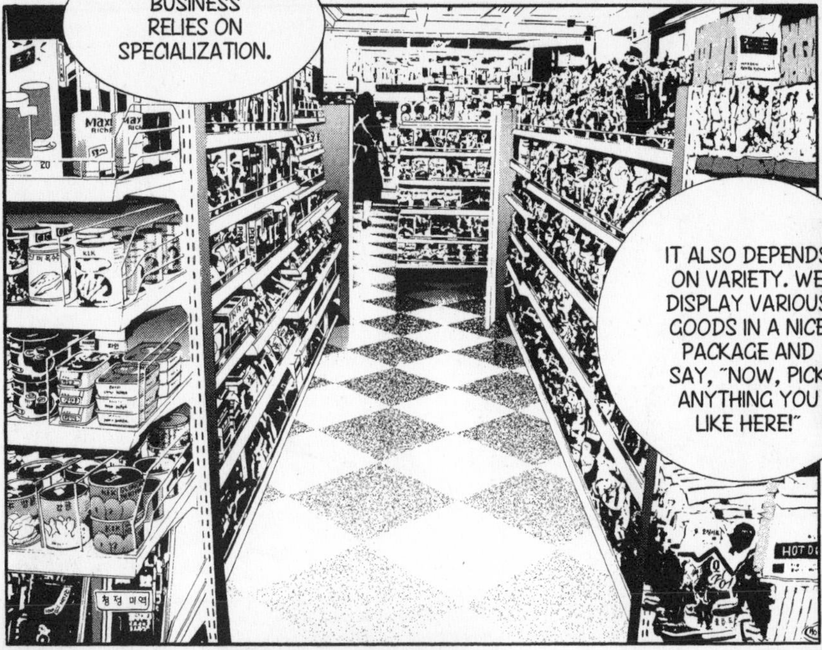
BUSINESS RELIES ON SPECIALIZATION.
청정 미역
IT ALSO DEPENDS ON VARIETY. WE DISPLAY VARIOUS GOODS IN A NICE PACKAGE AND SAY, "NOW, PICK ANYTHING YOU LIKE HERE!"
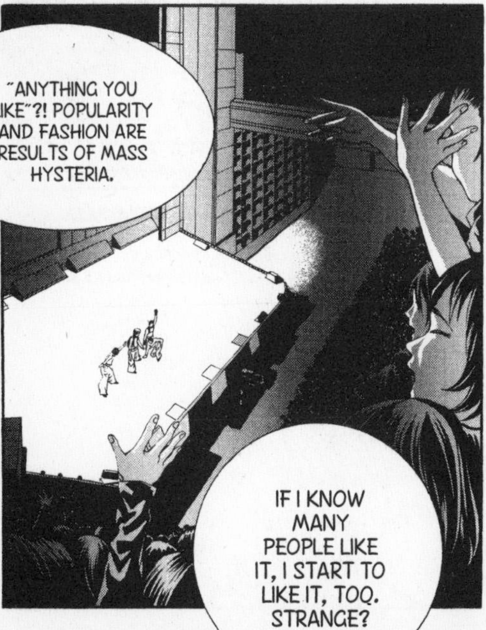
"ANYTHING YOU LIKE"?! POPULARITY AND FASHION ARE RESULTS OF MASS HYSTERIA.
IF I KNOW MANY PEOPLE LIKE IT, I START TO LIKE IT, TOO. STRANGE?
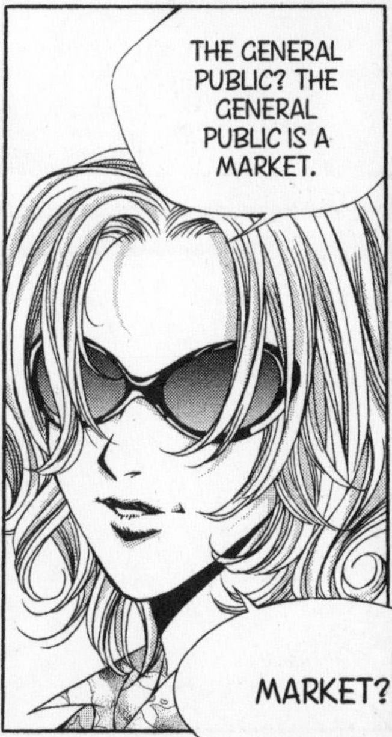
THE GENERAL PUBLIC? THE GENERAL PUBLIC IS A MARKET.
MARKET?

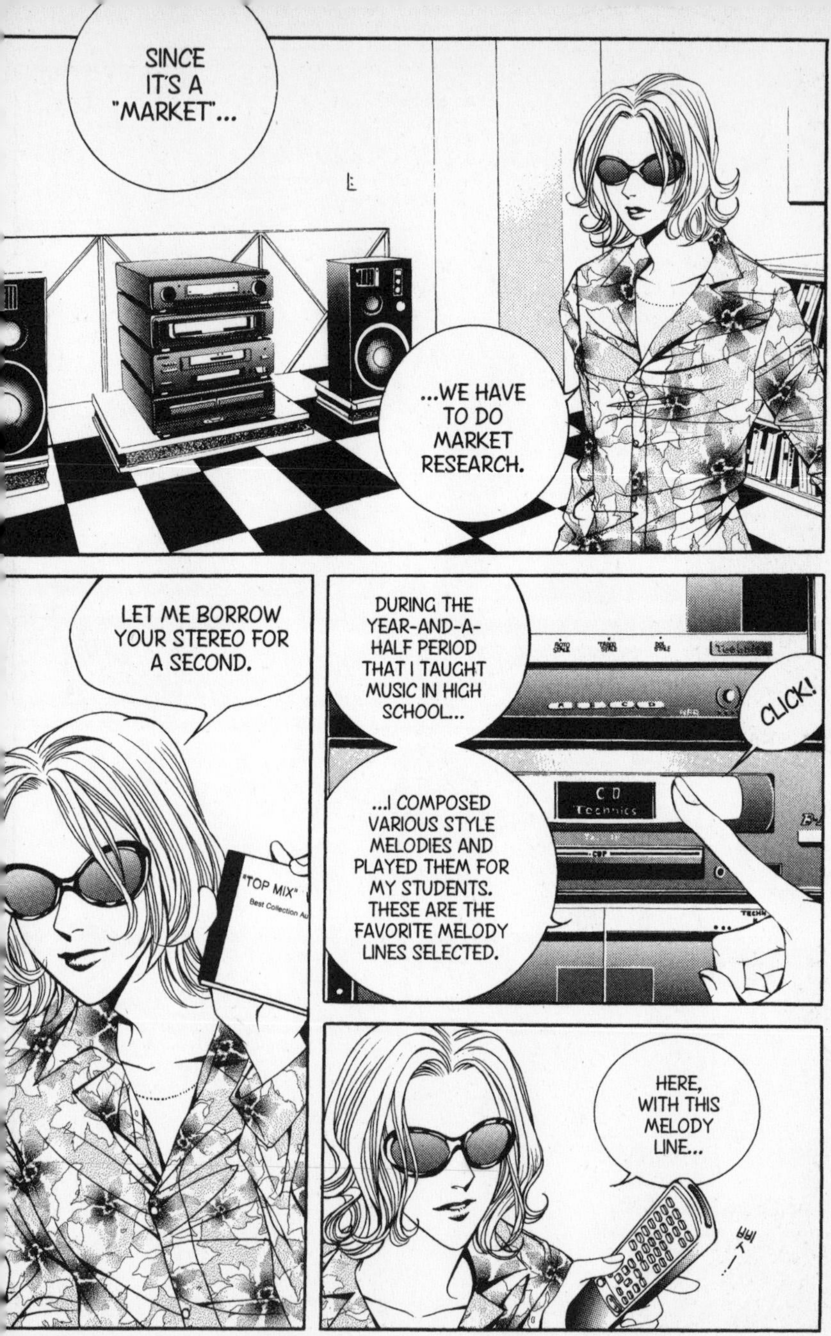
SINCE IT'S A "MARKET"...
...WE HAVE TO DO MARKET RESEARCH.
LET ME BORROW YOUR STEREO FOR A SECOND.
"TOP MIX"
DURING THE YEAR-AND-A-HALF PERIOD THAT I TAUGHT MUSIC IN HIGH SCHOOL...
CLICK!
...I COMPOSED VARIOUS STYLE MELODIES AND PLAYED THEM FOR MY STUDENTS. THESE ARE THE FAVORITE MELODY LINES SELECTED.
HERE, WITH THIS MELODY LINE...

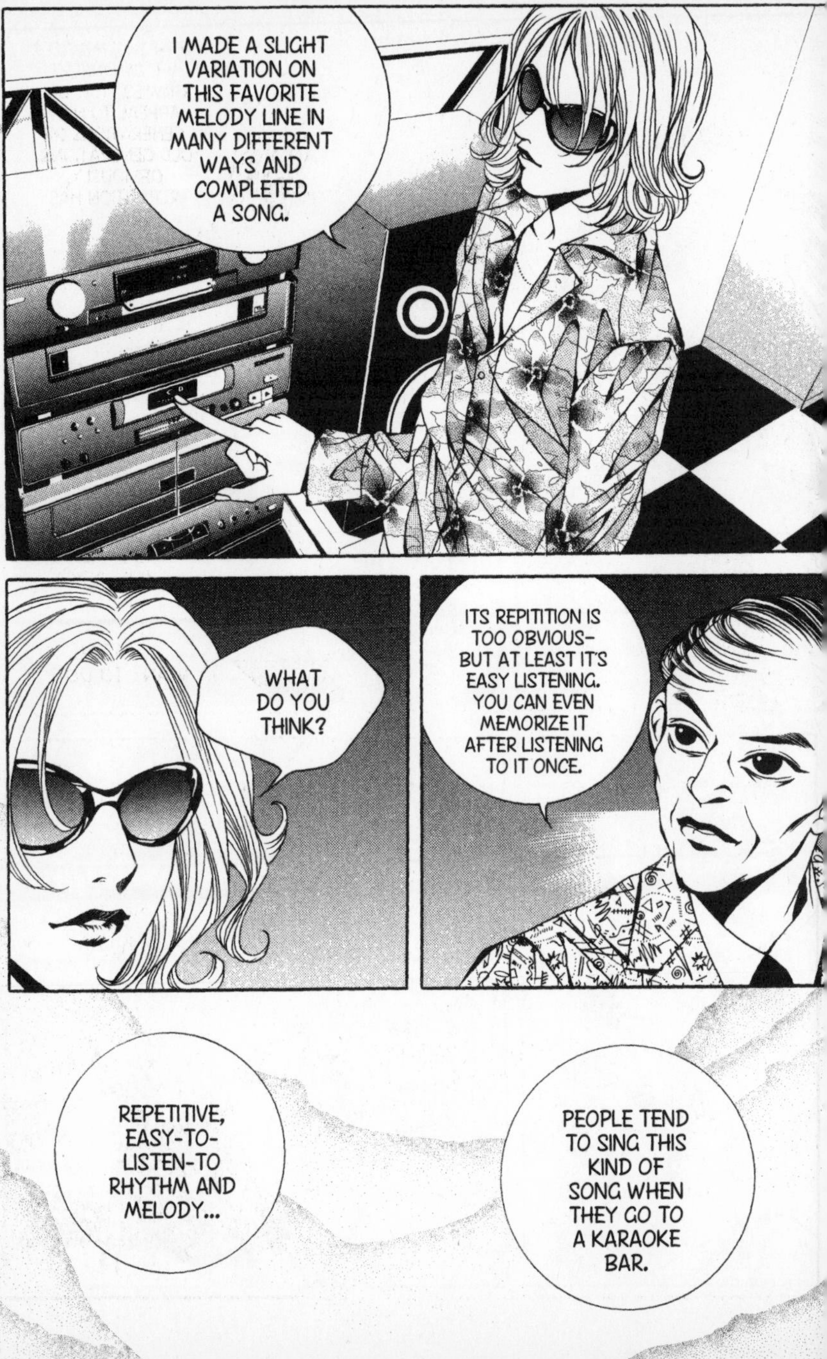
I MADE A SLIGHT VARIATION ON THIS FAVORITE MELODY LINE IN MANY DIFFERENT WAYS AND COMPLETED A SONG.
WHAT DO YOU THINK?
ITS REPITITION IS TOO OBVIOUS–BUT AT LEAST IT'S EASY LISTENING. YOU CAN EVEN MEMORIZE IT AFTER LISTENING TO IT ONCE.
REPETITIVE, EASY-TO-LISTEN-TO RHYTHM AND MELODY...
PEOPLE TEND TO SING THIS KIND OF SONG WHEN THEY GO TO A KARAOKE BAR.

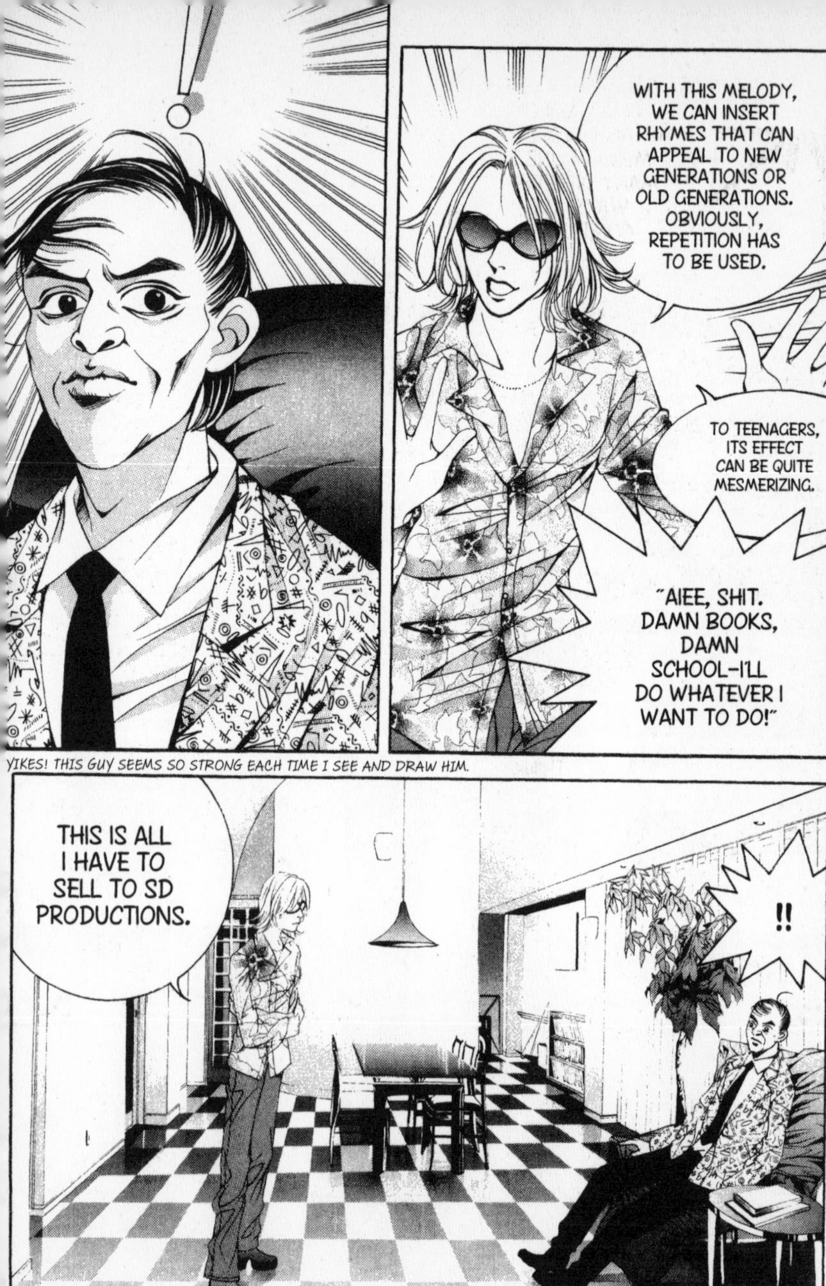
WITH THIS MELODY, WE CAN INSERT RHYMES THAT CAN APPEAL TO NEW GENERATIONS OR OLD GENERATIONS. OBVIOUSLY, REPETITION HAS TO BE USED.
TO TEENAGERS, ITS EFFECT CAN BE QUITE MESMERIZING.
"AIEE, SHIT. DAMN BOOKS, DAMN SCHOOL–I'LL DO WHATEVER I WANT TO DO!"
!
YIKES! THIS GUY SEEMS SO STRONG EACH TIME I SEE AND DRAW HIM.
THIS IS ALL I HAVE TO SELL TO SD PRODUCTIONS.
!!

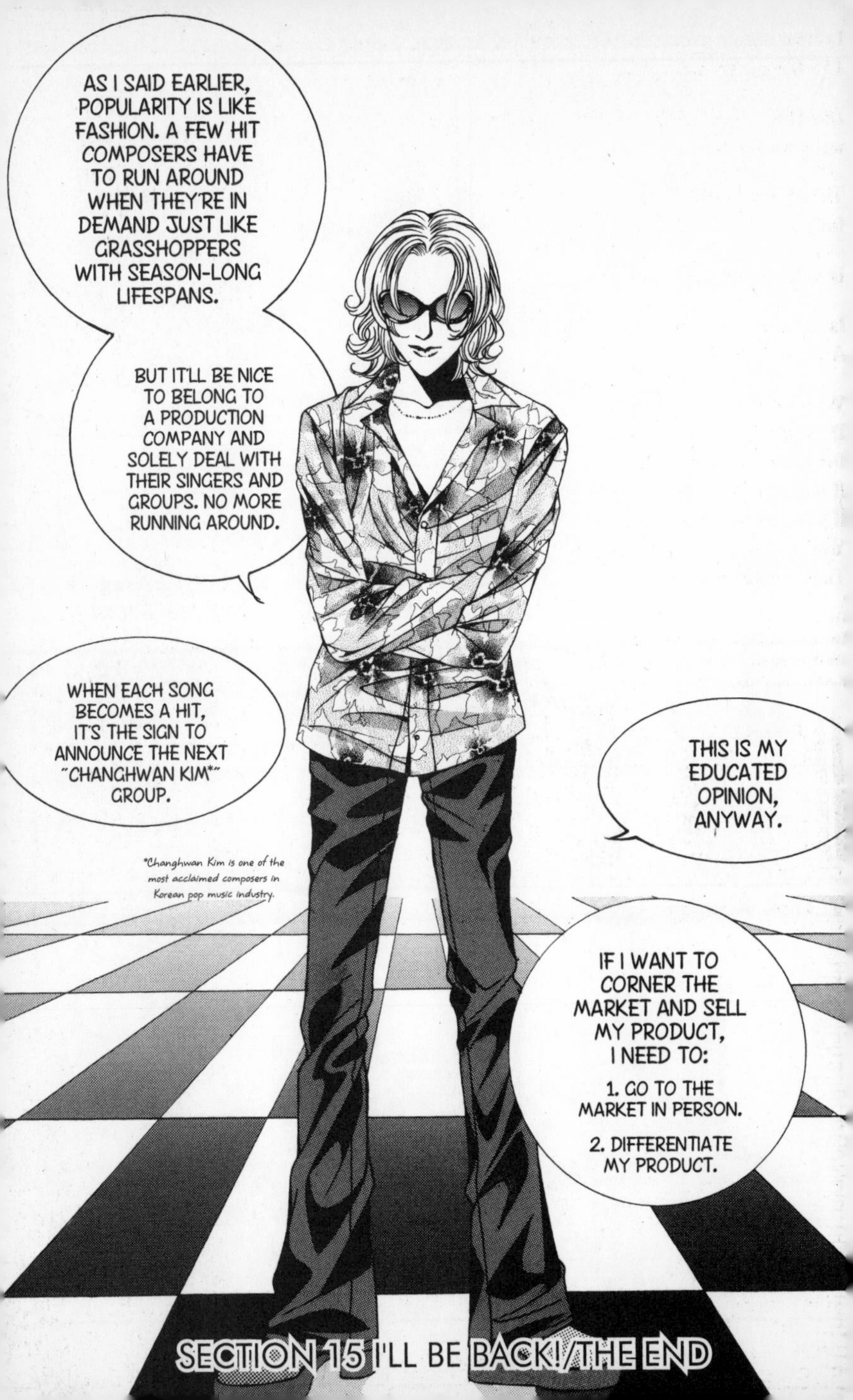
AS I SAID EARLIER, POPULARITY IS LIKE FASHION. A FEW HIT COMPOSERS HAVE TO RUN AROUND WHEN THEY'RE IN DEMAND JUST LIKE GRASSHOPPERS WITH SEASON-LONG LIFESPANS.
BUT IT'LL BE NICE TO BELONG TO A PRODUCTION COMPANY AND SOLELY DEAL WITH THEIR SINGERS AND GROUPS. NO MORE RUNNING AROUND.
WHEN EACH SONG BECOMES A HIT, IT'S THE SIGN TO ANNOUNCE THE NEXT "CHANGHWAN KIM*" GROUP.
*Changhwan Kim is one of the most acclaimed composers in Korean pop music industry.
THIS IS MY EDUCATED OPINION, ANYWAY.
IF I WANT TO CORNER THE MARKET AND SELL MY PRODUCT, I NEED TO:
1. GO TO THE MARKET IN PERSON.
2. DIFFERENTIATE MY PRODUCT.
SECTION 15 I'LL BE BACK!/THE END

Everyone's nervous. They're trembling. Looking around. Chattering around.

Like this–repeat the same thing, and repeat the things that make no sense.

They know nothing about nothing. But still making a fuss.

Is music a joke, toy, moneymaker.

Is the music industry where you guys really belong? Are you kidding?

What do you sing music for?
Do you really love music?
Do you even know what music means?
If you're handsome, you're a singer.
If you can dance, you're a singer.
You are a singer, I am a singer.
Then we all are singers.

From Victory.
Produced by Kunhyoung Ryu.
Written, composed, and arranged by Kunhyoung Ryu.

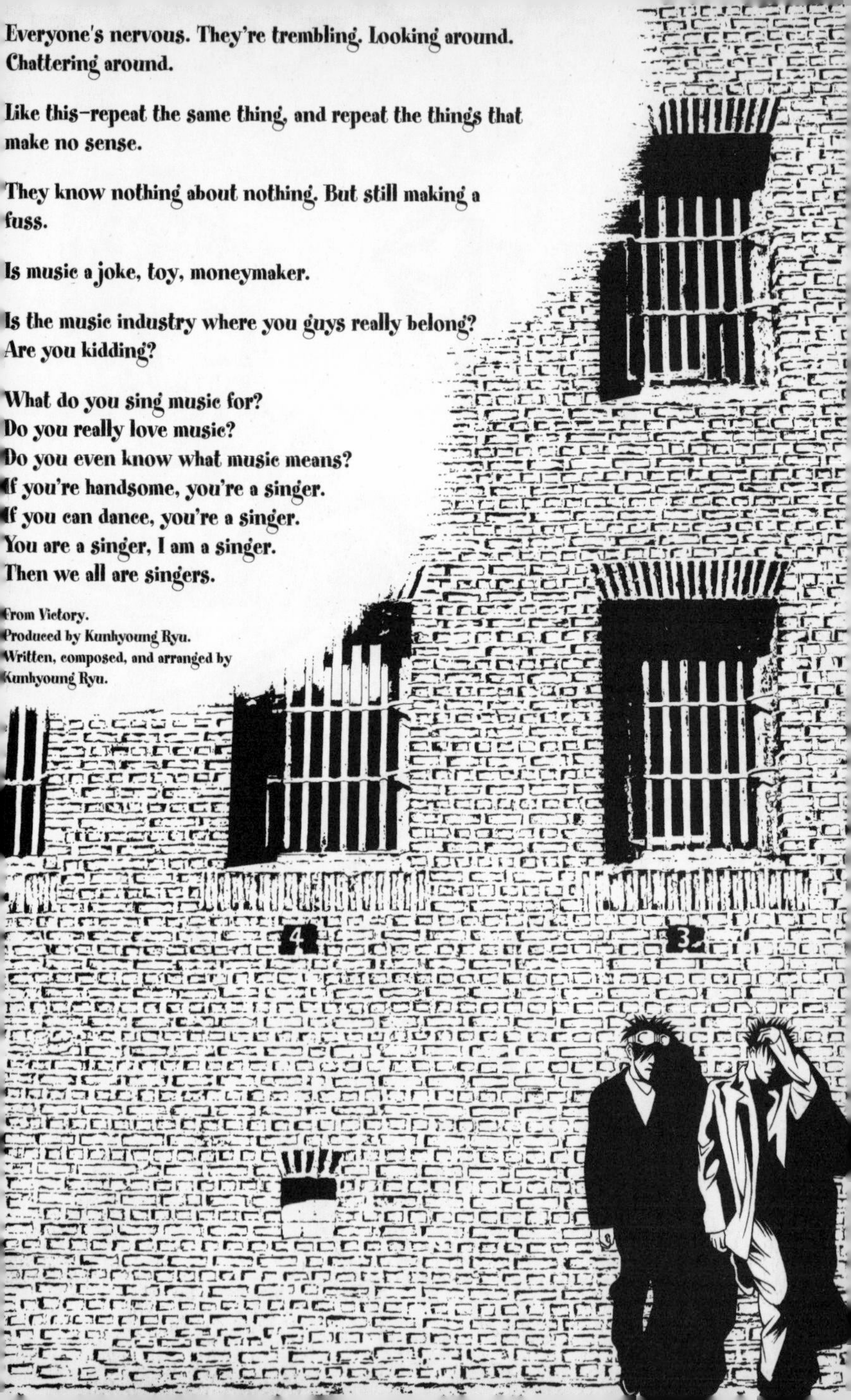

4
3

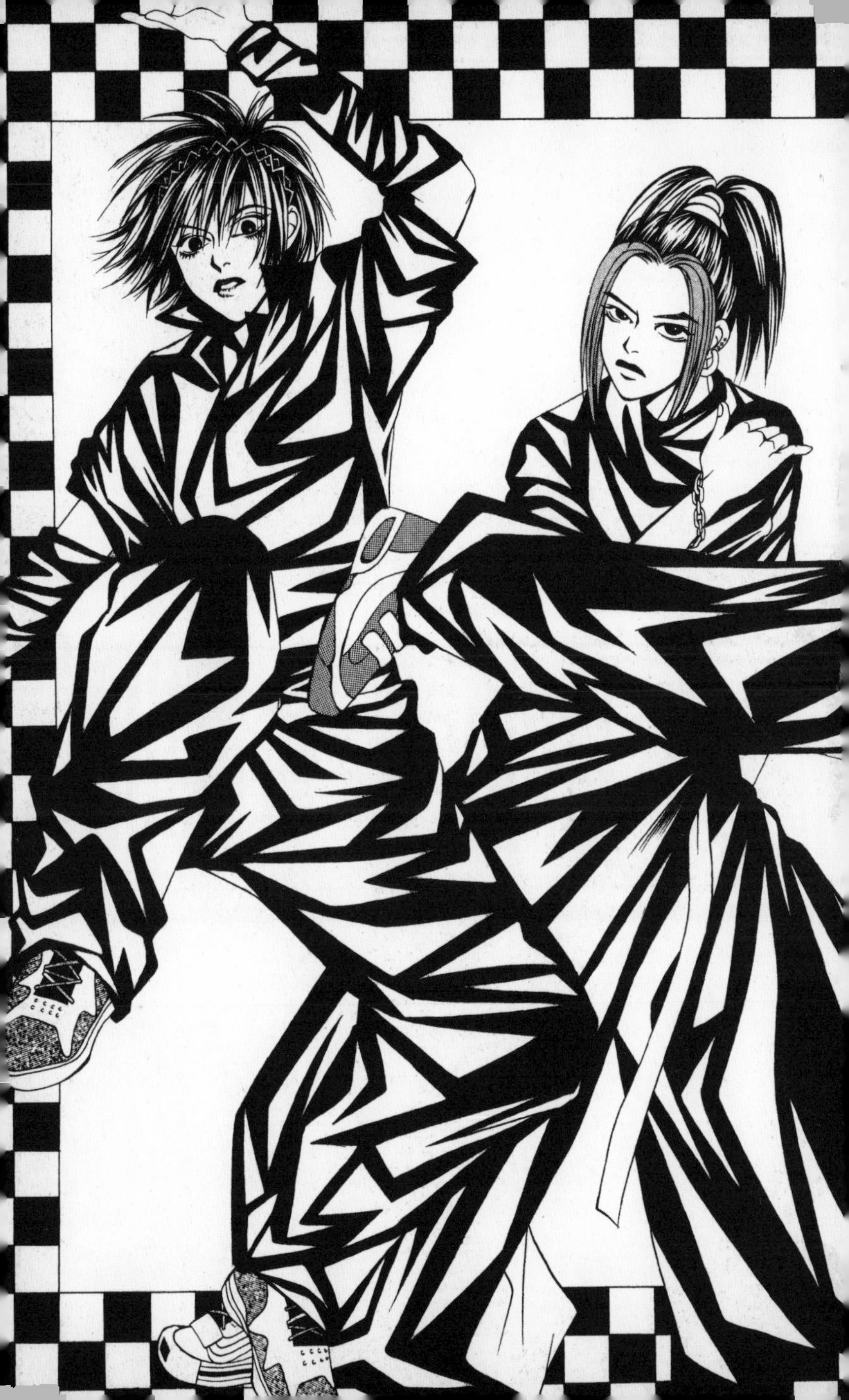

SECTION 16
SHUT UP AND DANCE!

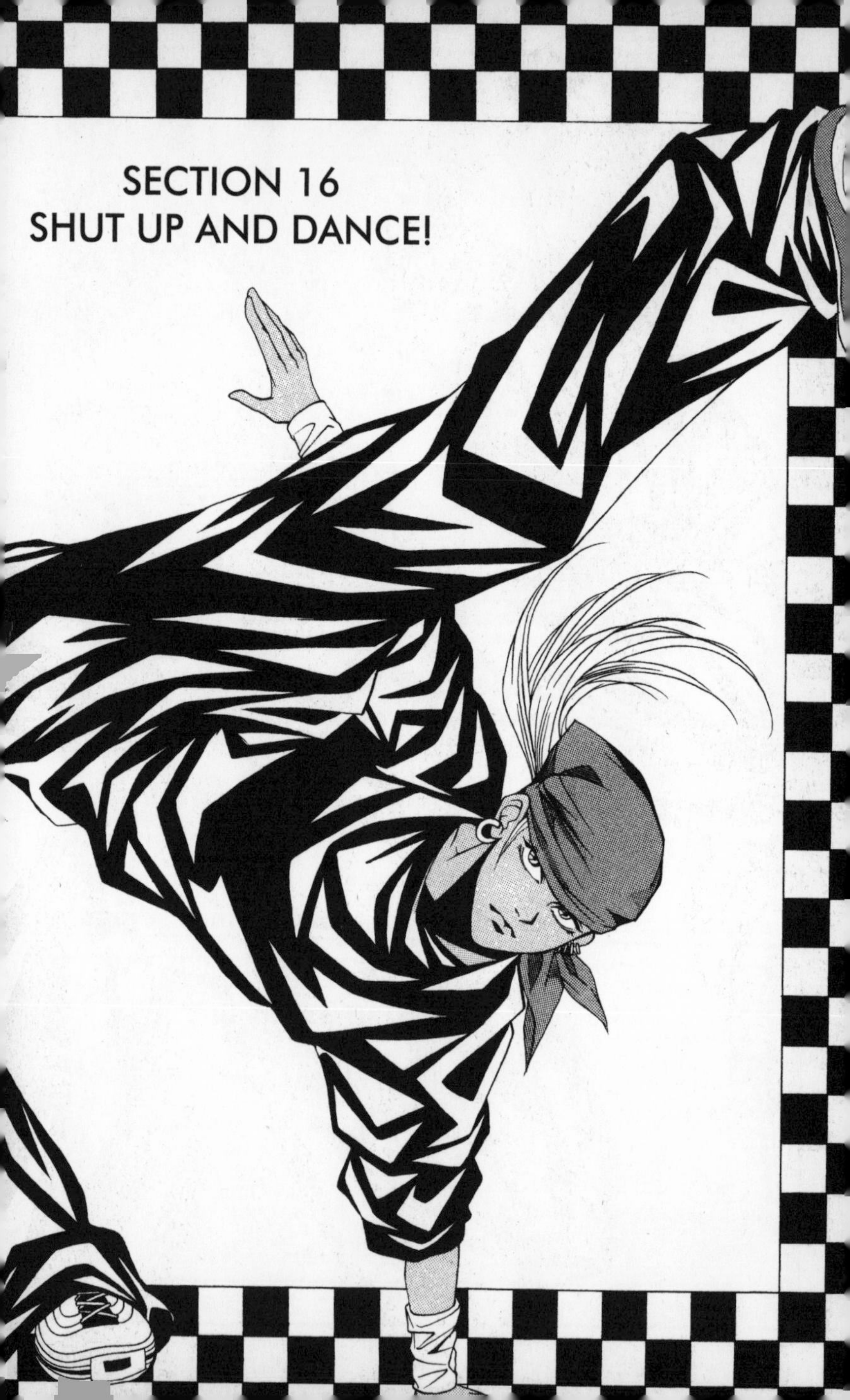

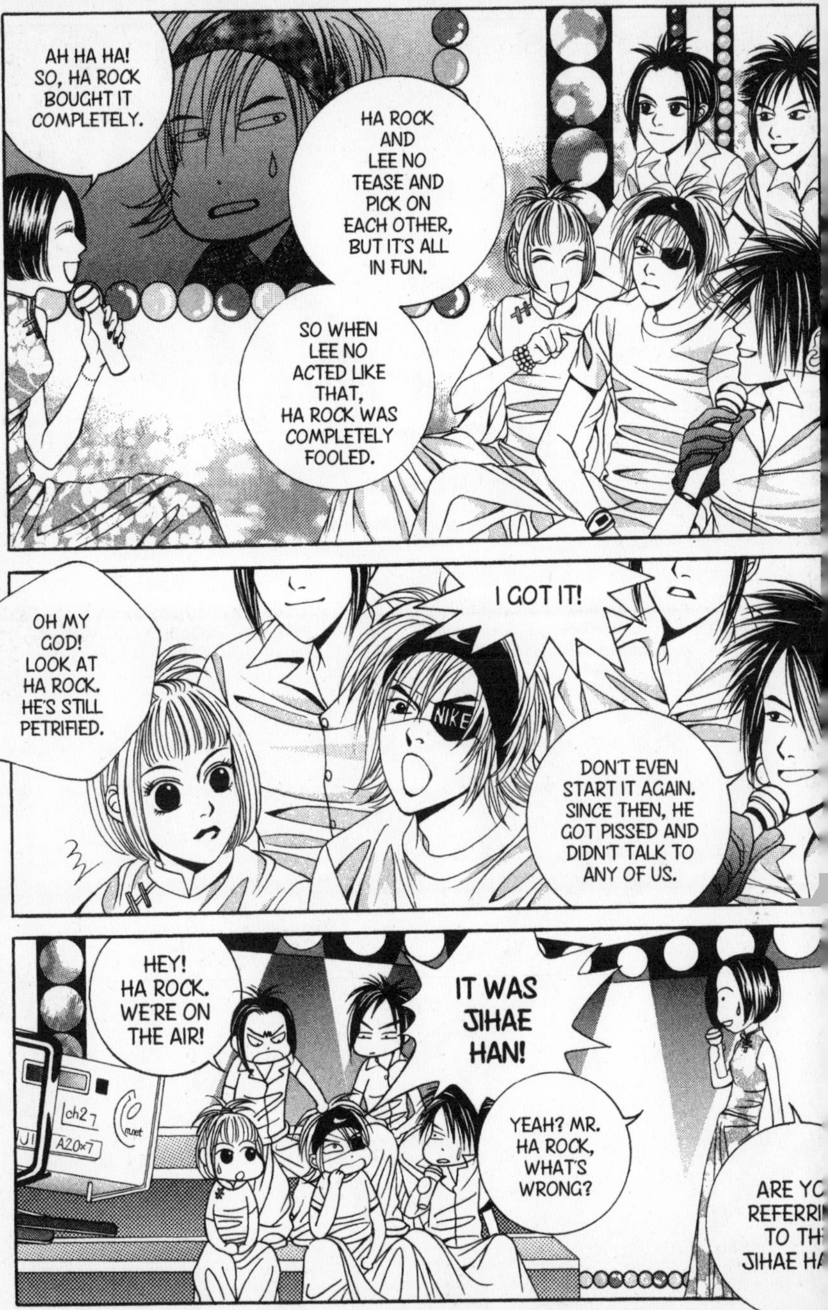
AH HA HA! SO, HA ROCK BOUGHT IT COMPLETELY.
HA ROCK AND LEE NO TEASE AND PICK ON EACH OTHER, BUT IT'S ALL IN FUN.
SO WHEN LEE NO ACTED LIKE THAT, HA ROCK WAS COMPLETELY FOOLED.
OH MY GOD! LOOK AT HA ROCK. HE'S STILL PETRIFIED.
DON'T EVEN START IT AGAIN. SINCE THEN, HE GOT PISSED AND DIDN'T TALK TO ANY OF US.
I GOT IT!
NIKE
IT WAS JIHAE HAN!
HEY! HA ROCK. WE'RE ON THE AIR!
ch2
A20×7
m.net
YEAH? MR. HA ROCK, WHAT'S WRONG?
ARE YO REFERRI TO TH JIHAE HA

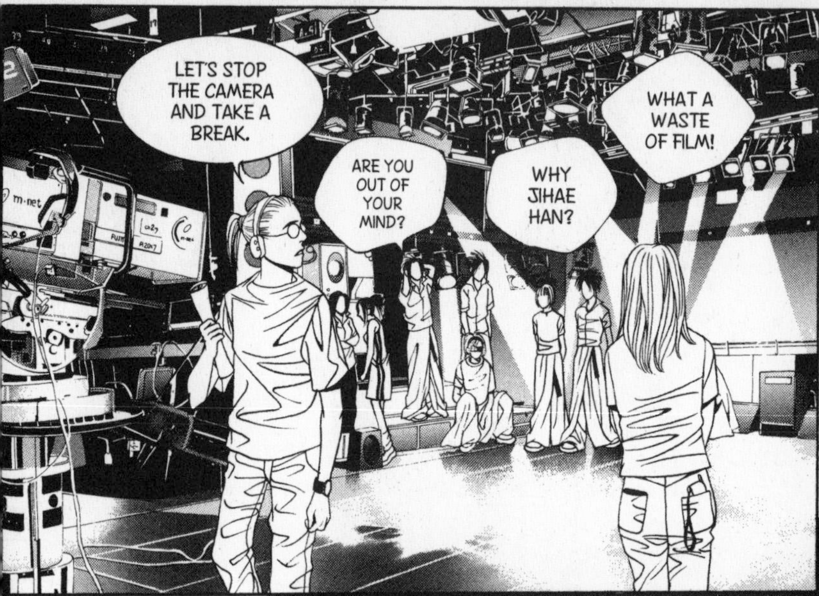
LET'S STOP THE CAMERA AND TAKE A BREAK.
ARE YOU OUT OF YOUR MIND?
WHY JIHAE HAN?
WHAT A WASTE OF FILM!

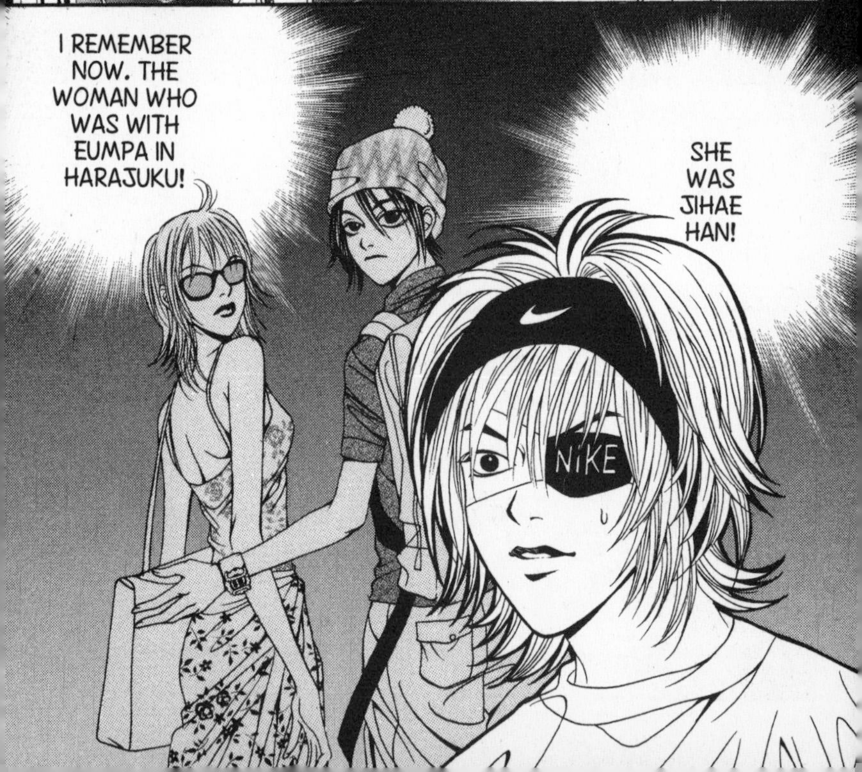
I REMEMBER NOW. THE WOMAN WHO WAS WITH EUMPA IN HARAJUKU!
SHE WAS JIHAE HAN!
NIKE

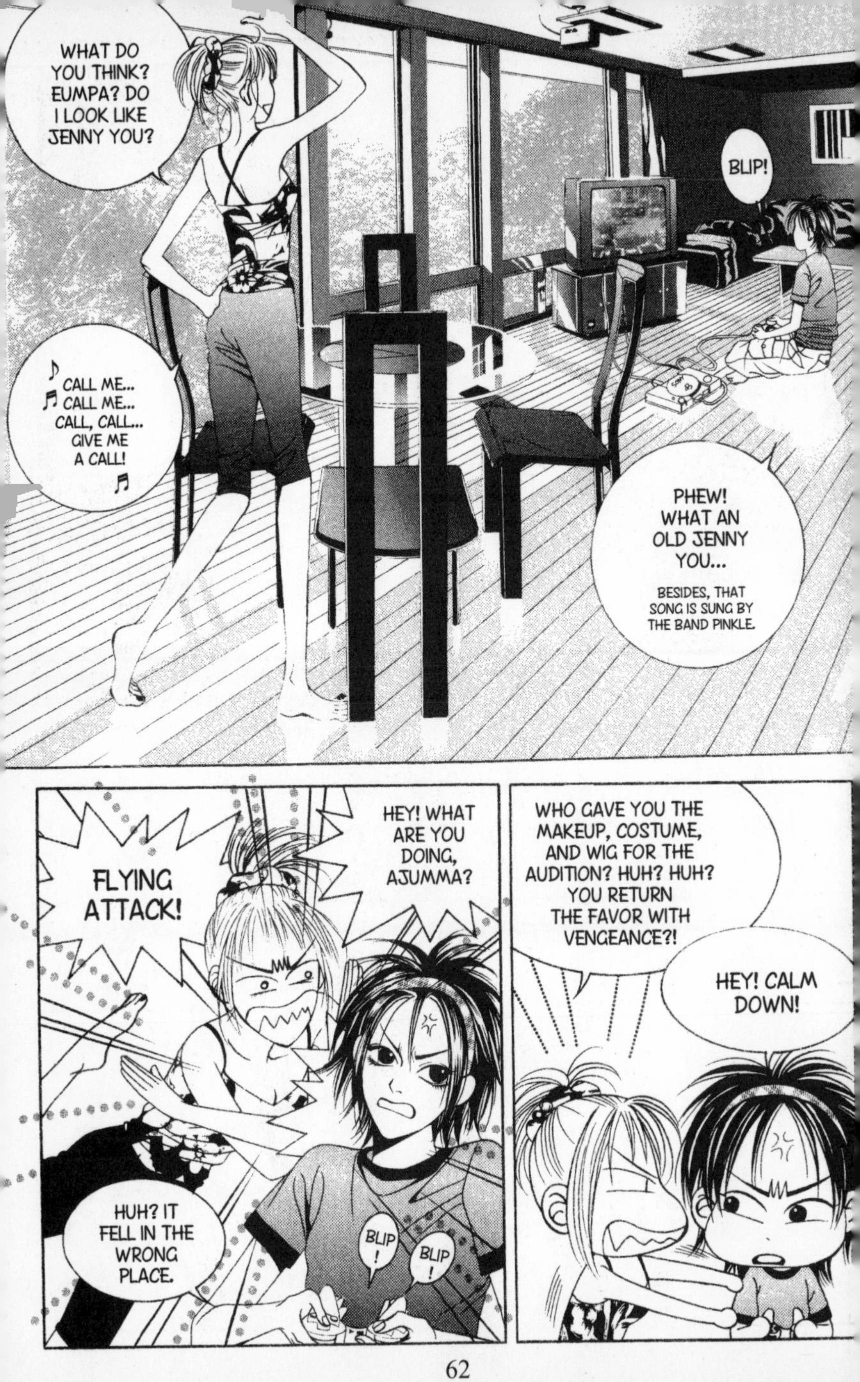
WHAT DO YOU THINK? EUMPA? DO I LOOK LIKE JENNY YOU?
♪ CALL ME... ♬ CALL ME... CALL, CALL... GIVE ME A CALL! ♬
BLIP!
PHEW! WHAT AN OLD JENNY YOU...
BESIDES, THAT SONG IS SUNG BY THE BAND PINKLE.
FLYING ATTACK!
HEY! WHAT ARE YOU DOING, AJUMMA?
BLIP!
BLIP!
HUH? IT FELL IN THE WRONG PLACE.
WHO GAVE YOU THE MAKEUP, COSTUME, AND WIG FOR THE AUDITION? HUH? HUH? YOU RETURN THE FAVOR WITH VENGEANCE?!
HEY! CALM DOWN!

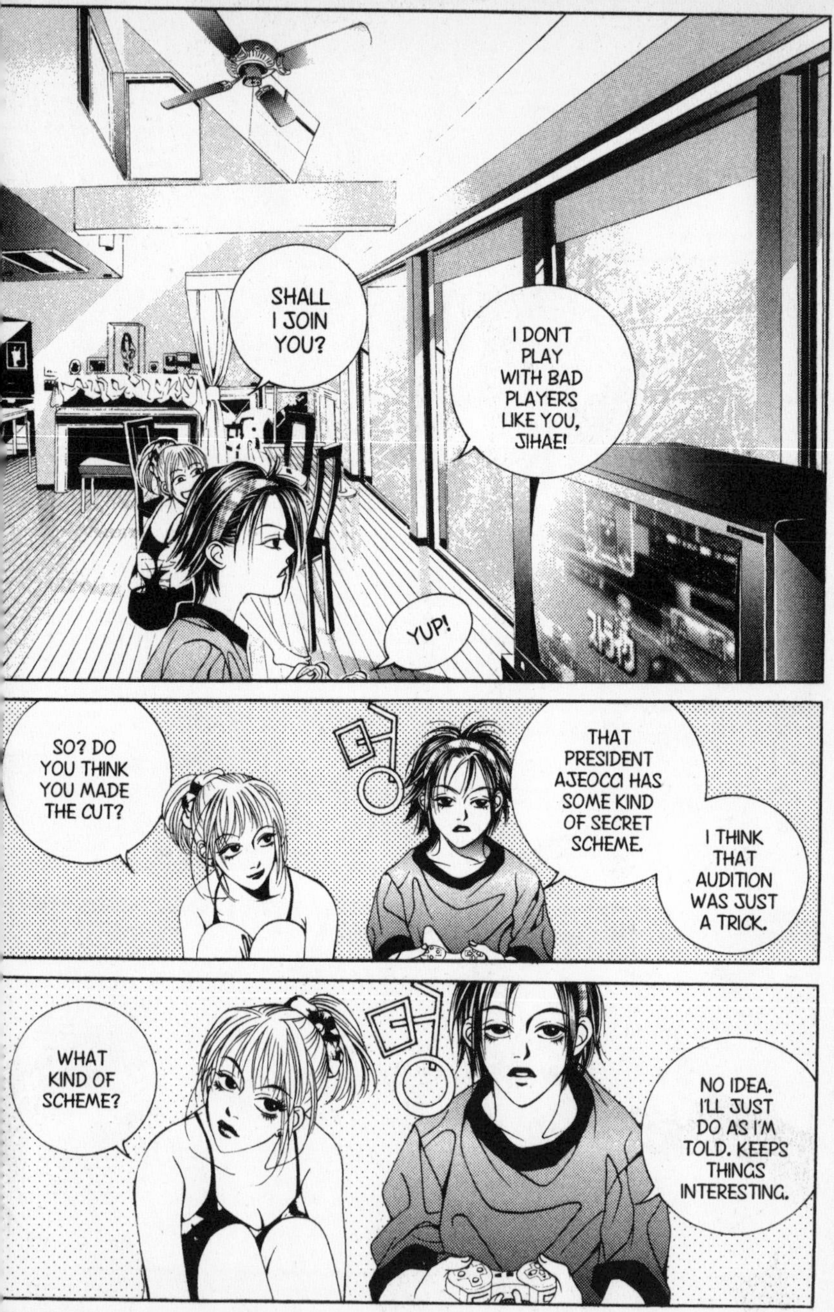
SHALL I JOIN YOU?
I DON'T PLAY WITH BAD PLAYERS LIKE YOU, JIHAE!
YUP!
SO? DO YOU THINK YOU MADE THE CUT?
THAT PRESIDENT AJEOCCI HAS SOME KIND OF SECRET SCHEME.
I THINK THAT AUDITION WAS JUST A TRICK.
WHAT KIND OF SCHEME?
NO IDEA. I'LL JUST DO AS I'M TOLD. KEEPS THINGS INTERESTING.

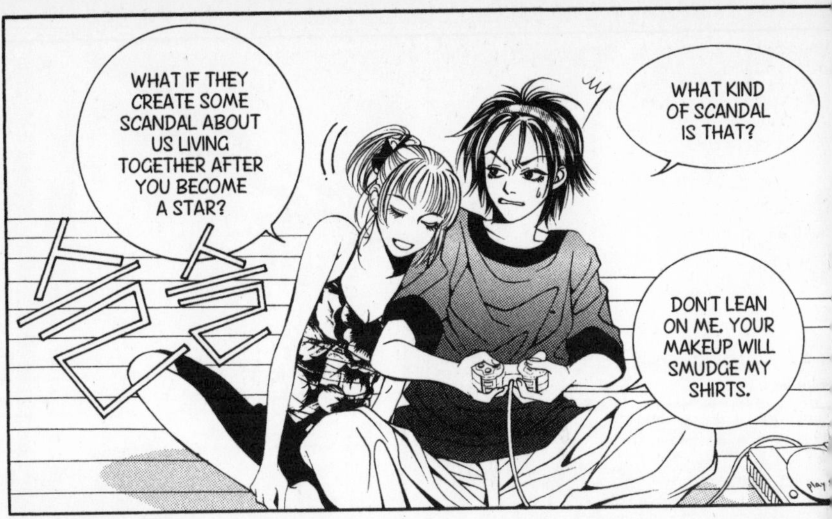
WHAT IF THEY CREATE SOME SCANDAL ABOUT US LIVING TOGETHER AFTER YOU BECOME A STAR?
WHAT KIND OF SCANDAL IS THAT?
DON'T LEAN ON ME. YOUR MAKEUP WILL SMUDGE MY SHIRTS.

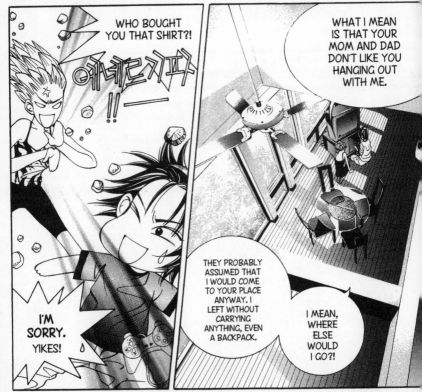

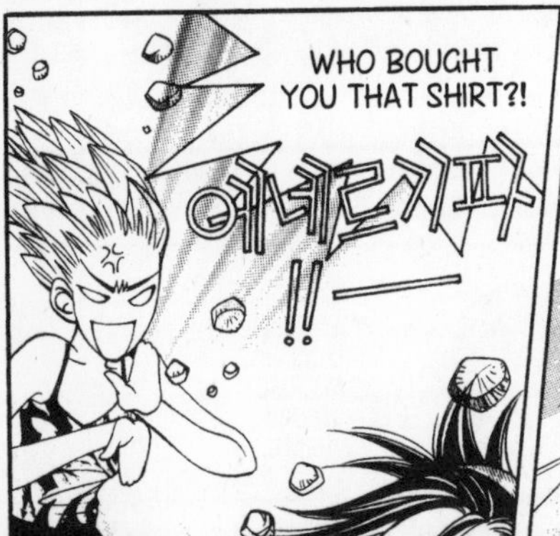
WHO BOUGHT YOU THAT SHIRT?!
I'M SORRY.
YIKES!

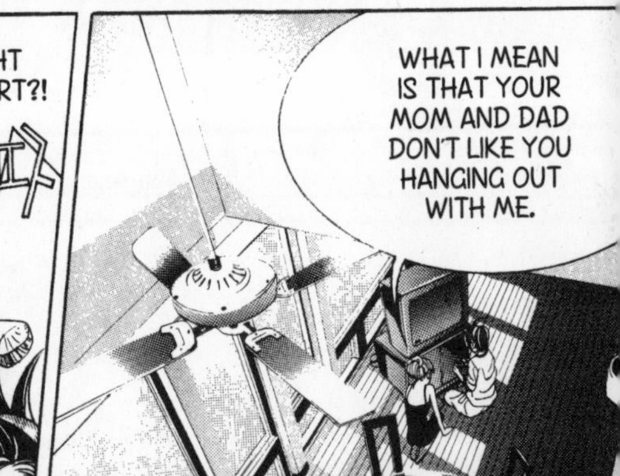
WHAT I MEAN IS THAT YOUR MOM AND DAD DON'T LIKE YOU HANGING OUT WITH ME.
THEY PROBABLY ASSUMED THAT I WOULD COME TO YOUR PLACE ANYWAY. I LEFT WITHOUT CARRYING ANYTHING, EVEN A BACKPACK.
I MEAN, WHERE ELSE WOULD I GO?!

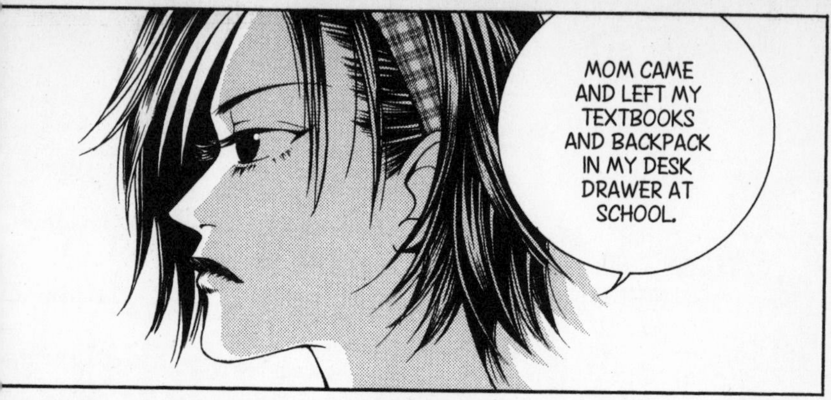
MOM CAME AND LEFT MY TEXTBOOKS AND BACKPACK IN MY DESK DRAWER AT SCHOOL.

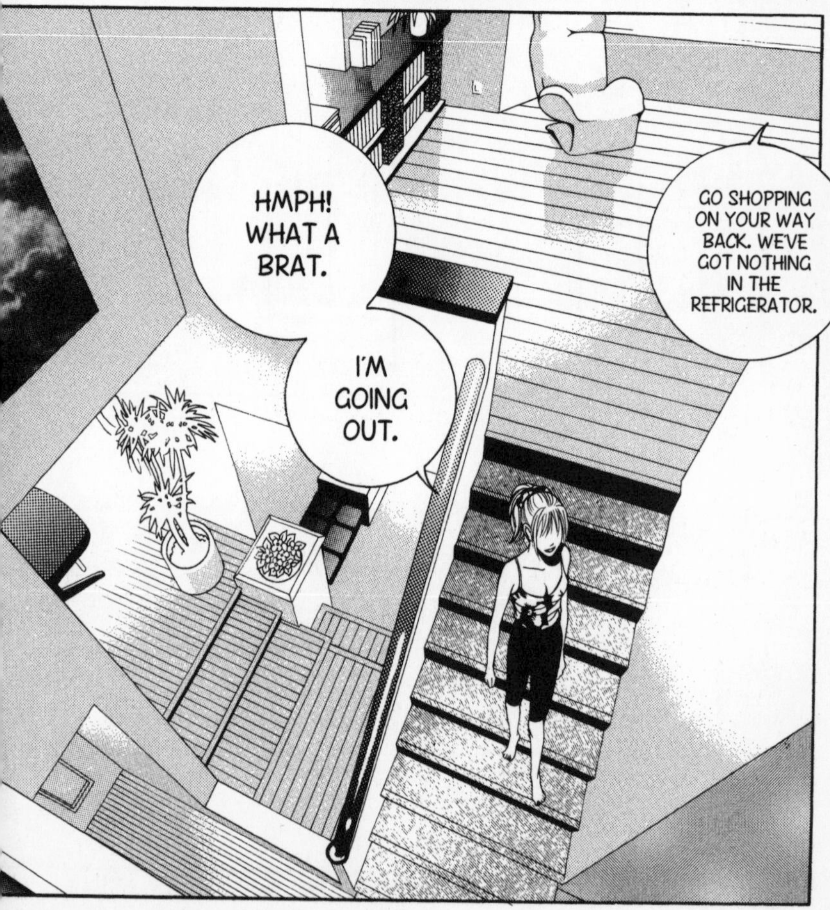
GO SHOPPING ON YOUR WAY BACK. WE'VE GOT NOTHING IN THE REFRIGERATOR.
HMPH! WHAT A BRAT.
I'M GOING OUT.

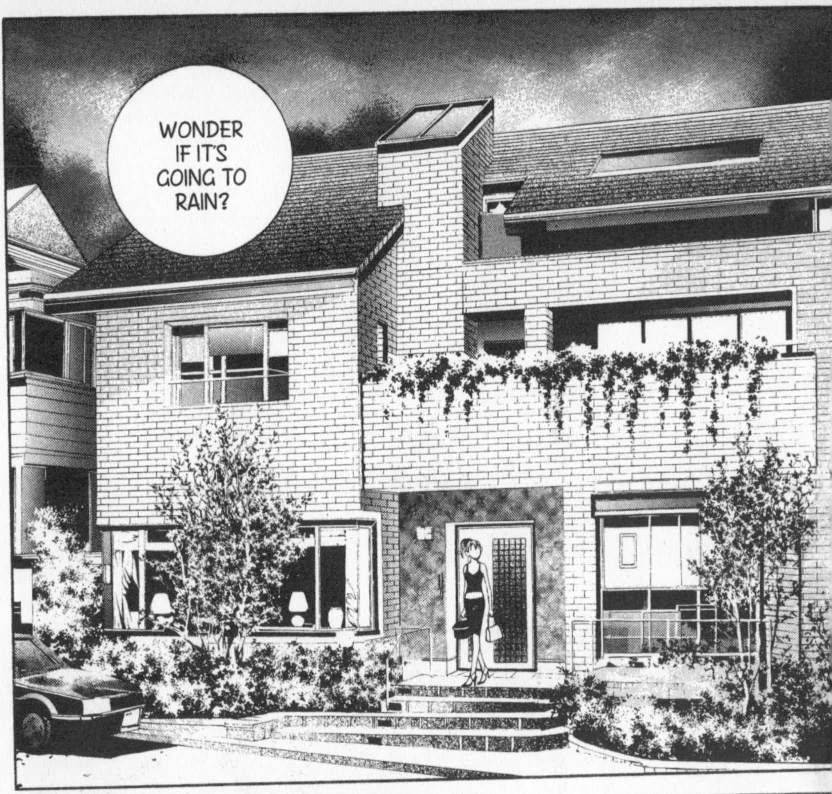
WONDER IF IT'S GOING TO RAIN?
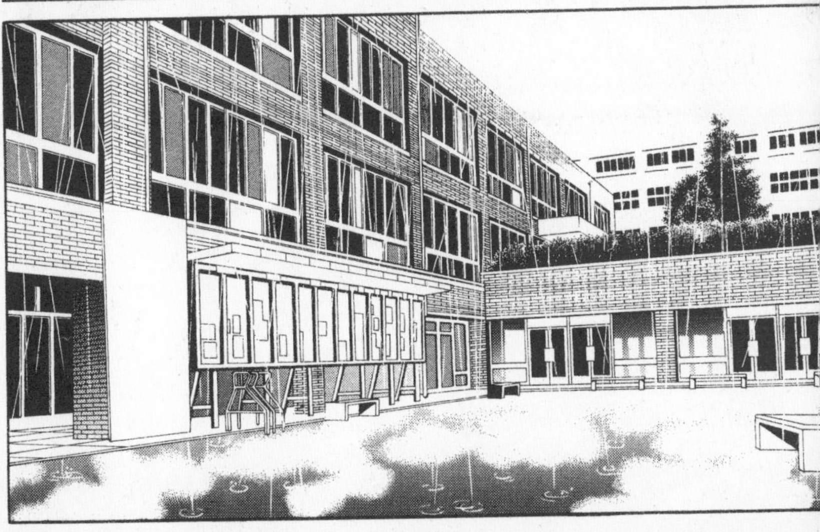

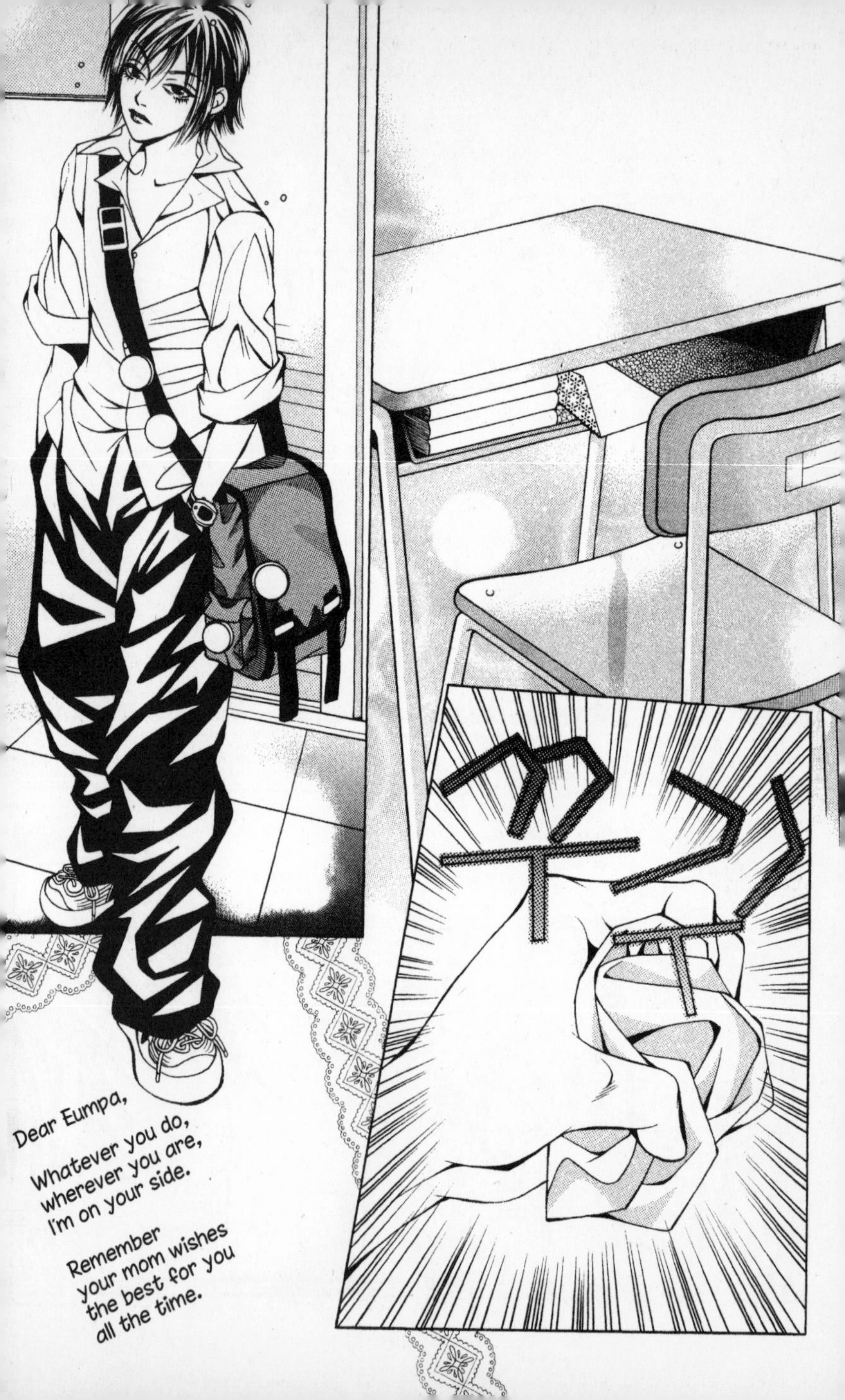
Dear Eumpa,
Whatever you do,
wherever you are,
I'm on your side.
Remember
your mom wishes
the best for you
all the time.

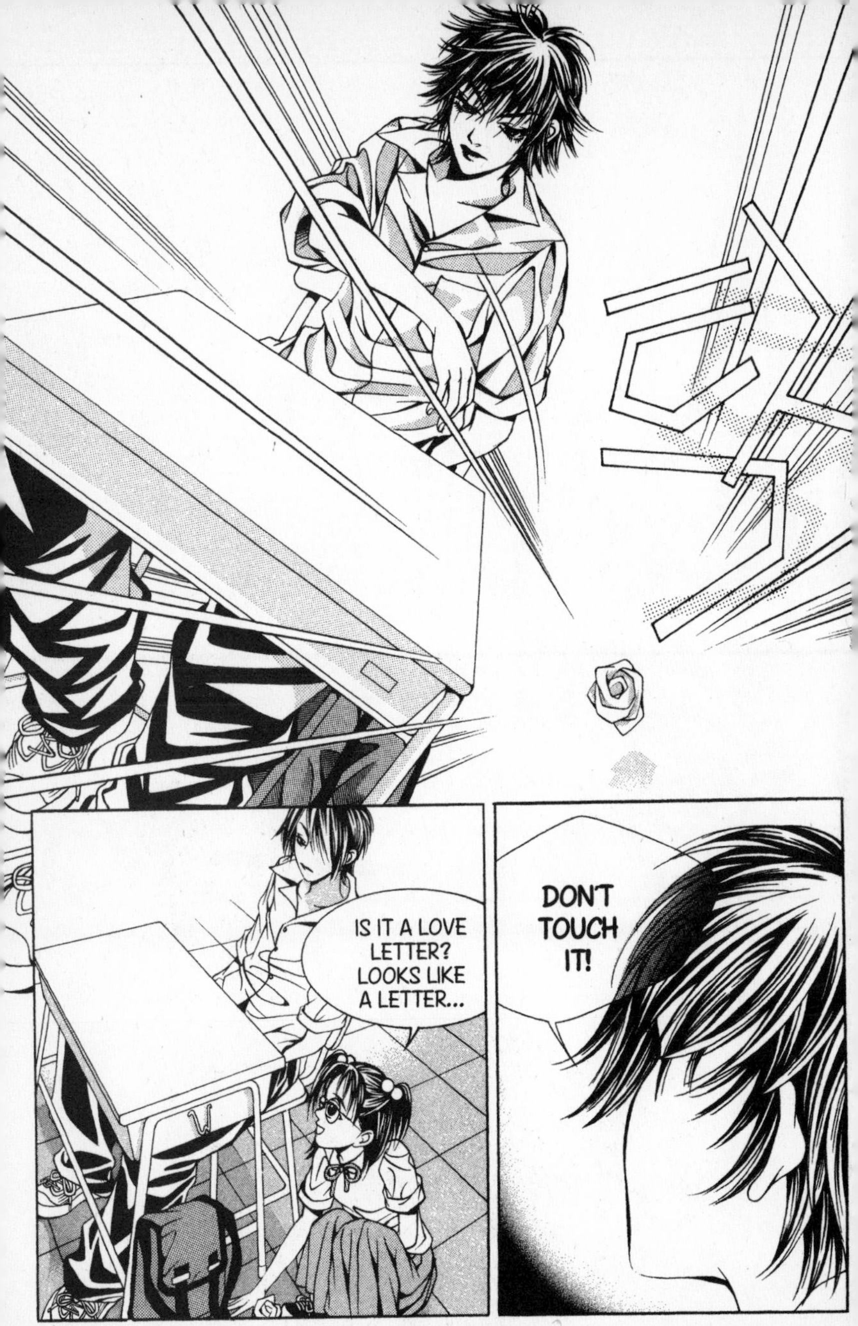
IS IT A LOVE LETTER? LOOKS LIKE A LETTER...
DON'T TOUCH IT!

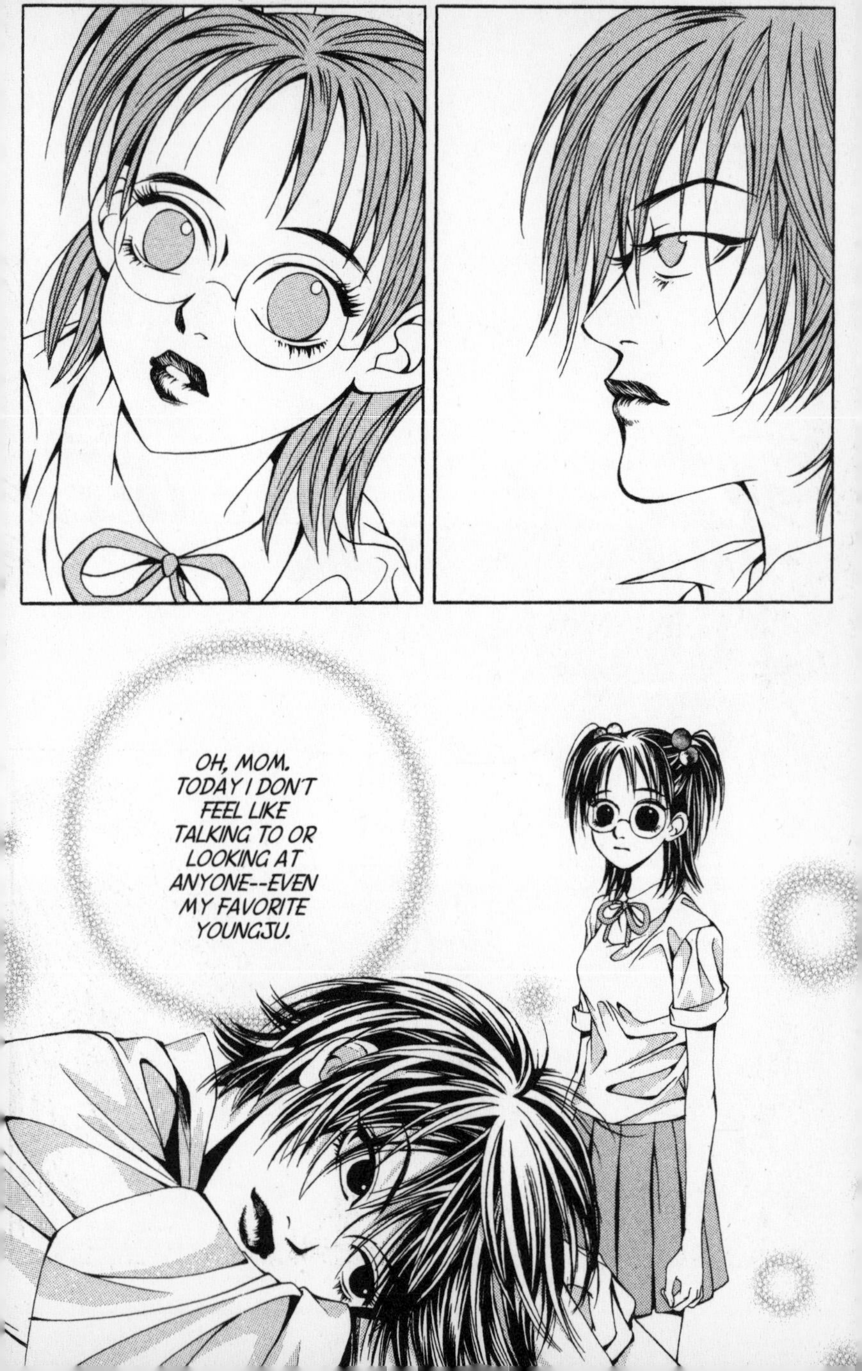
OH, MOM. TODAY I DON'T FEEL LIKE TALKING TO OR LOOKING AT ANYONE--EVEN MY FAVORITE YOUNGJU.

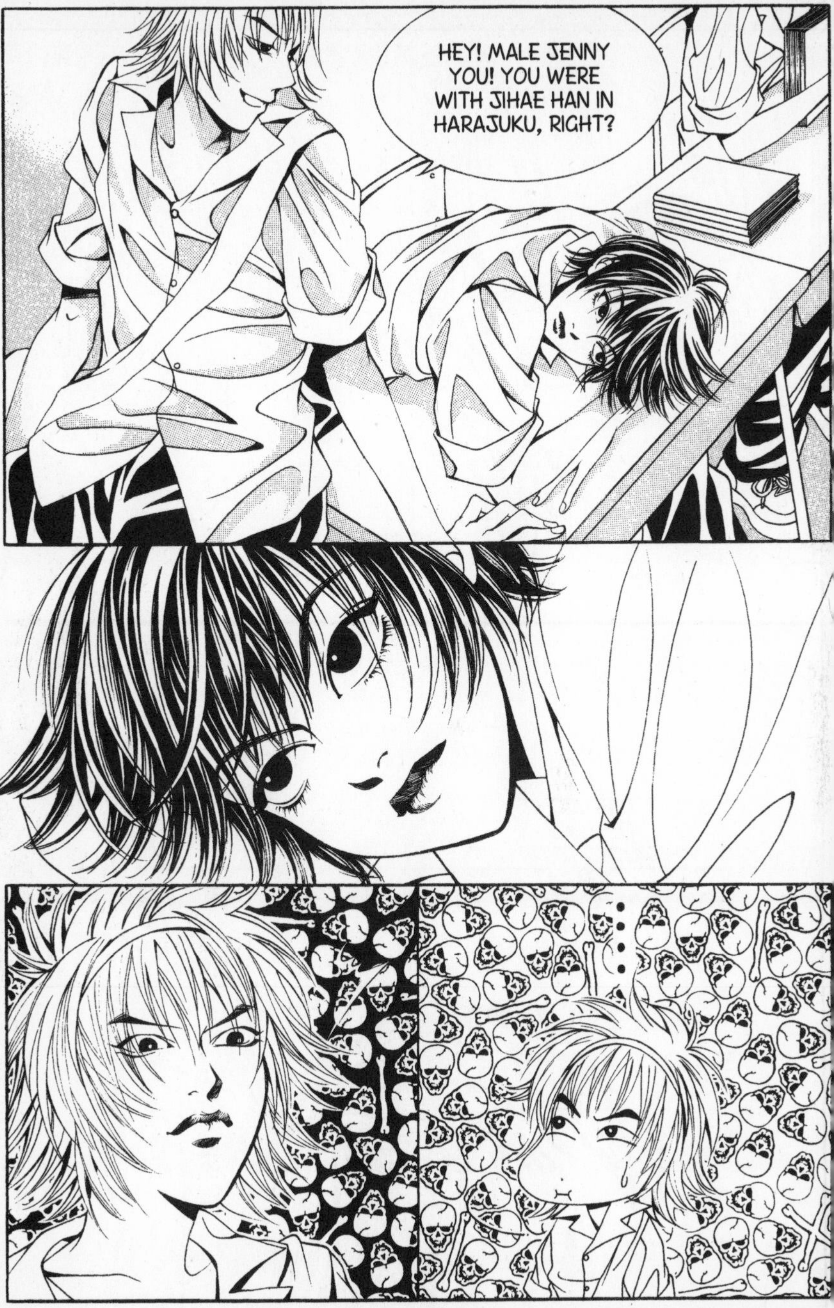
HEY! MALE JENNY YOU! YOU WERE WITH JIHAE HAN IN HARAJUKU, RIGHT?

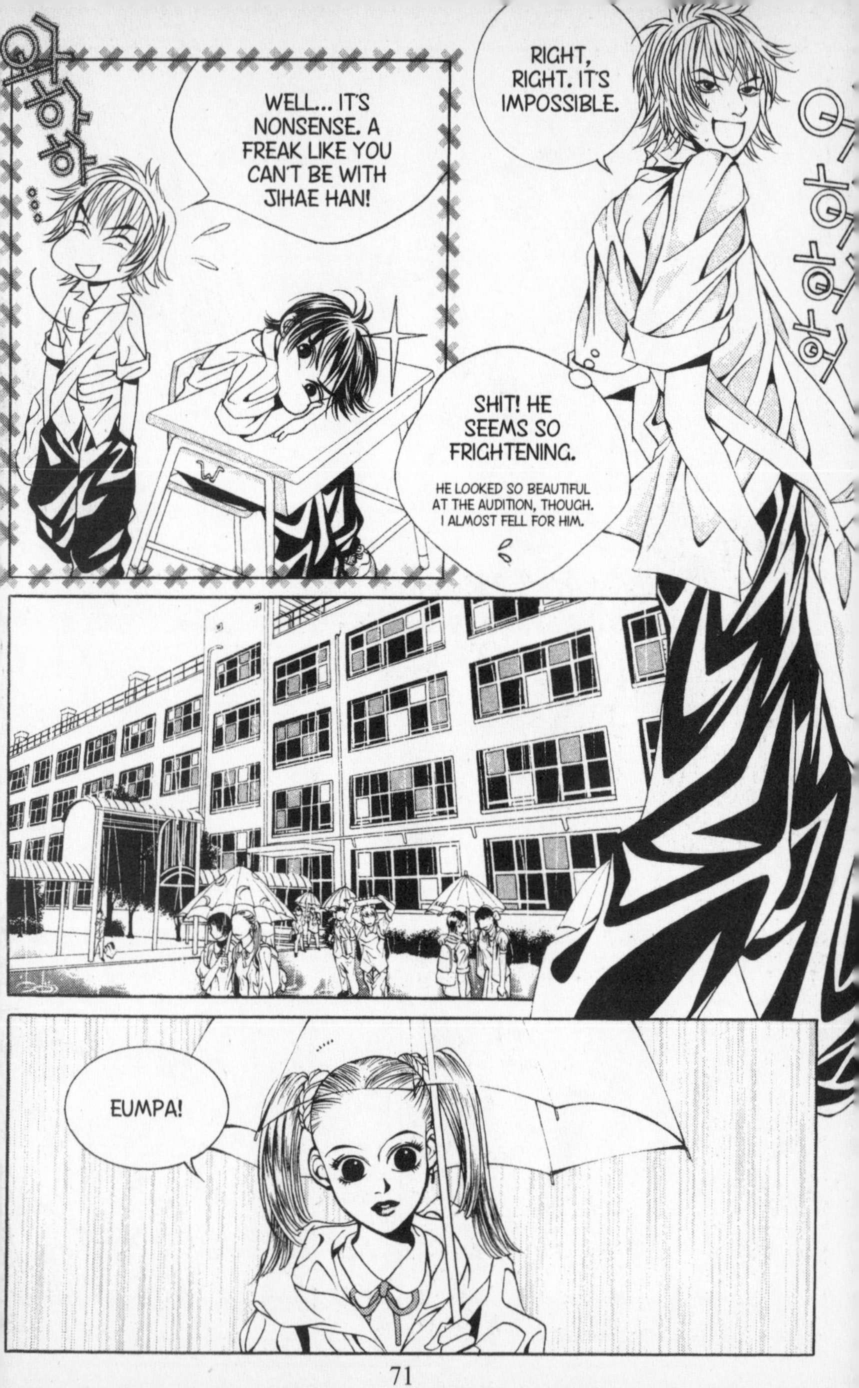
WELL... IT'S NONSENSE. A FREAK LIKE YOU CAN'T BE WITH JIHAE HAN!
RIGHT, RIGHT. IT'S IMPOSSIBLE.
SHIT! HE SEEMS SO FRIGHTENING.
HE LOOKED SO BEAUTIFUL AT THE AUDITION, THOUGH. I ALMOST FELL FOR HIM.
EUMPA!

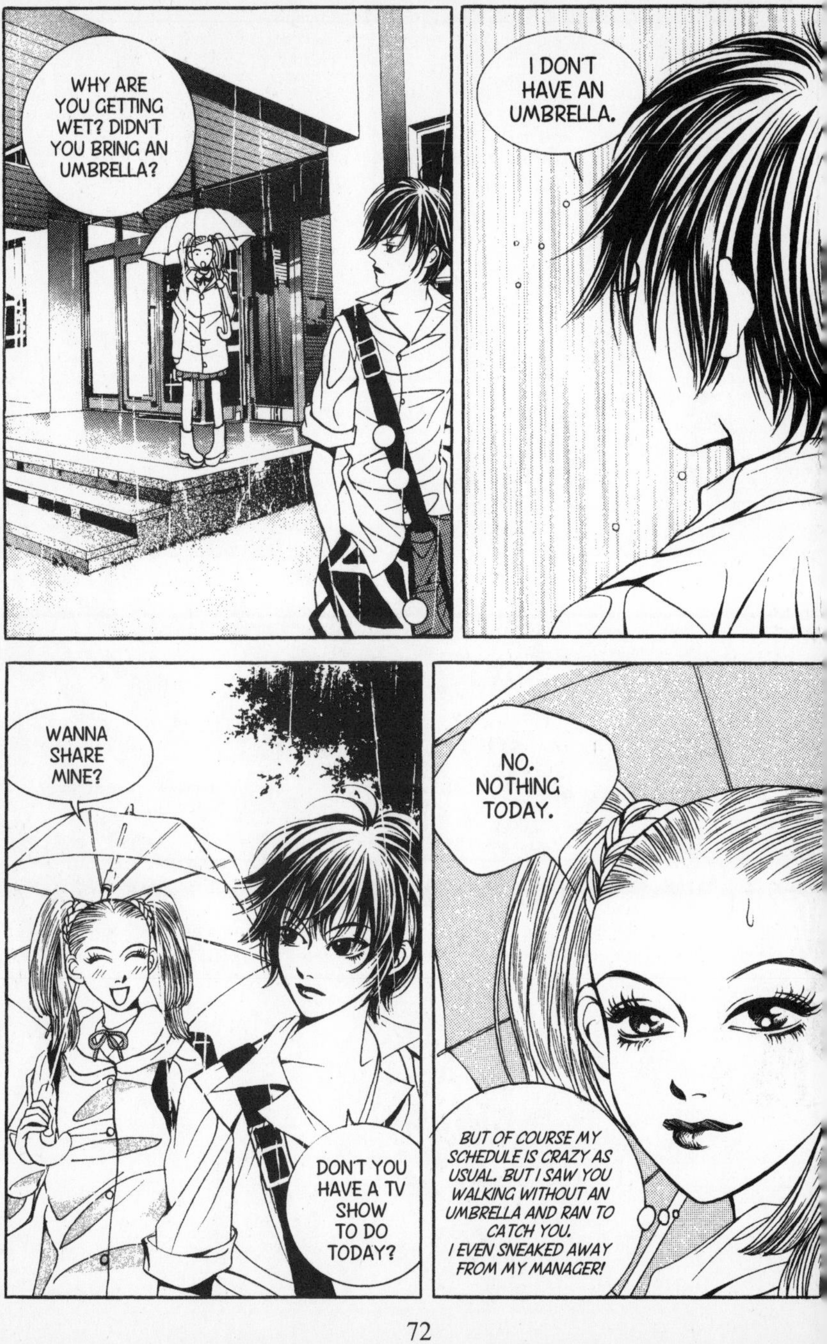
WHY ARE YOU GETTING WET? DIDN'T YOU BRING AN UMBRELLA?
I DON'T HAVE AN UMBRELLA.
WANNA SHARE MINE?
DON'T YOU HAVE A TV SHOW TO DO TODAY?
NO. NOTHING TODAY.
BUT OF COURSE MY SCHEDULE IS CRAZY AS USUAL. BUT I SAW YOU WALKING WITHOUT AN UMBRELLA AND RAN TO CATCH YOU. I EVEN SNEAKED AWAY FROM MY MANAGER!

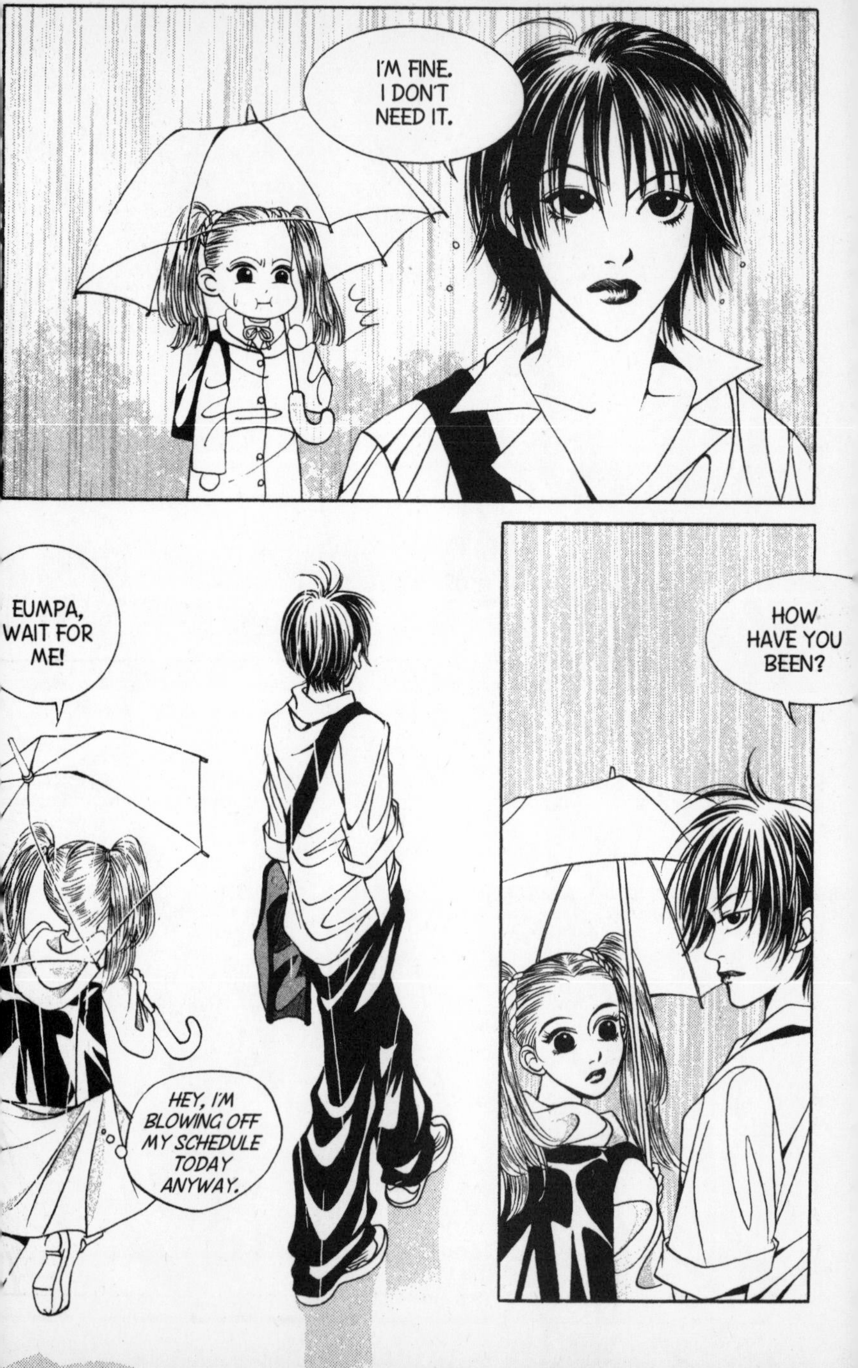
I'M FINE. I DON'T NEED IT.
EUMPA, WAIT FOR ME!
HEY, I'M BLOWING OFF MY SCHEDULE TODAY ANYWAY.
HOW HAVE YOU BEEN?

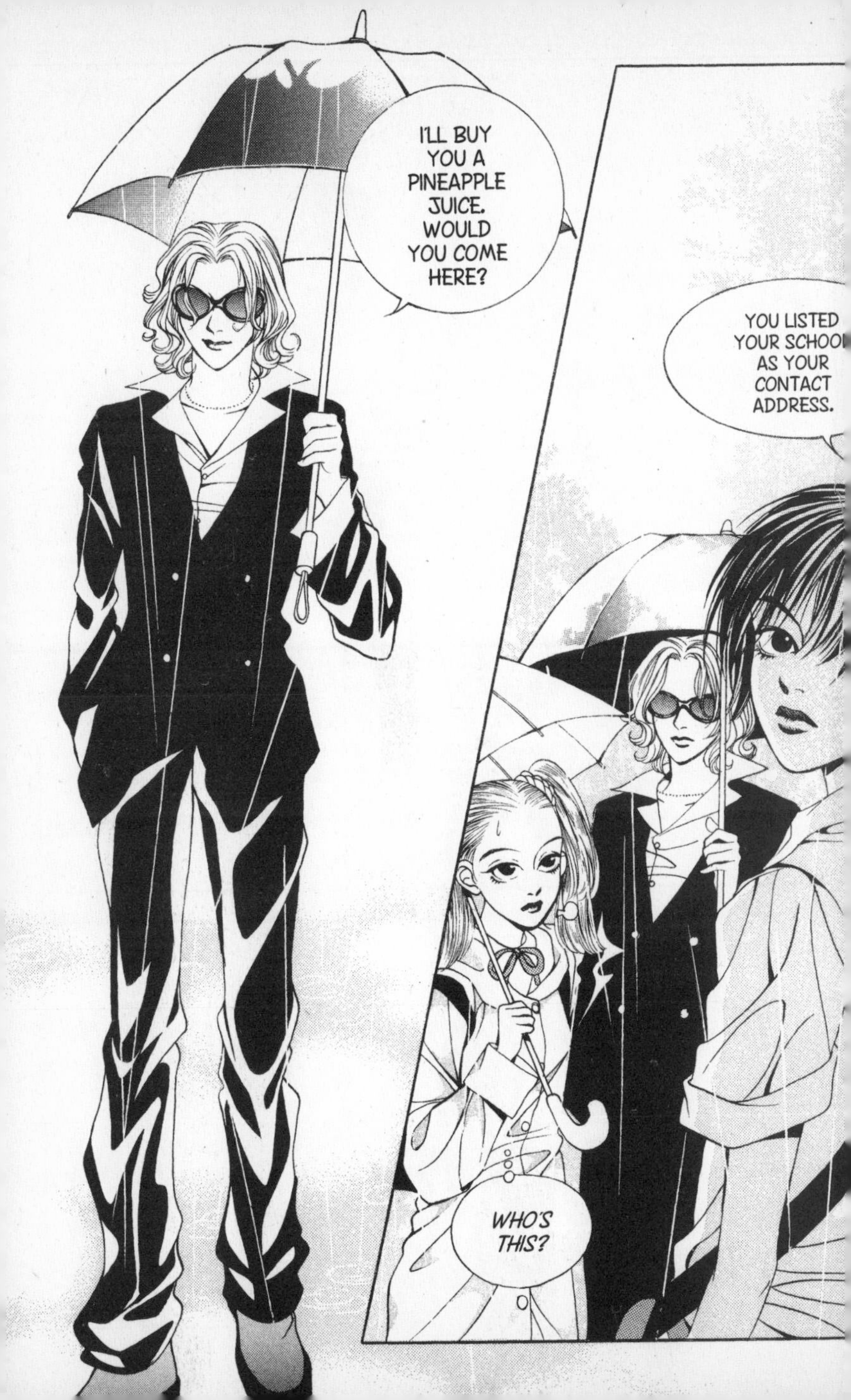
YOU LISTED YOUR SCHOOL AS YOUR CONTACT ADDRESS.
WHO'S THIS?
I'LL BUY YOU A PINEAPPLE JUICE. WOULD YOU COME HERE?

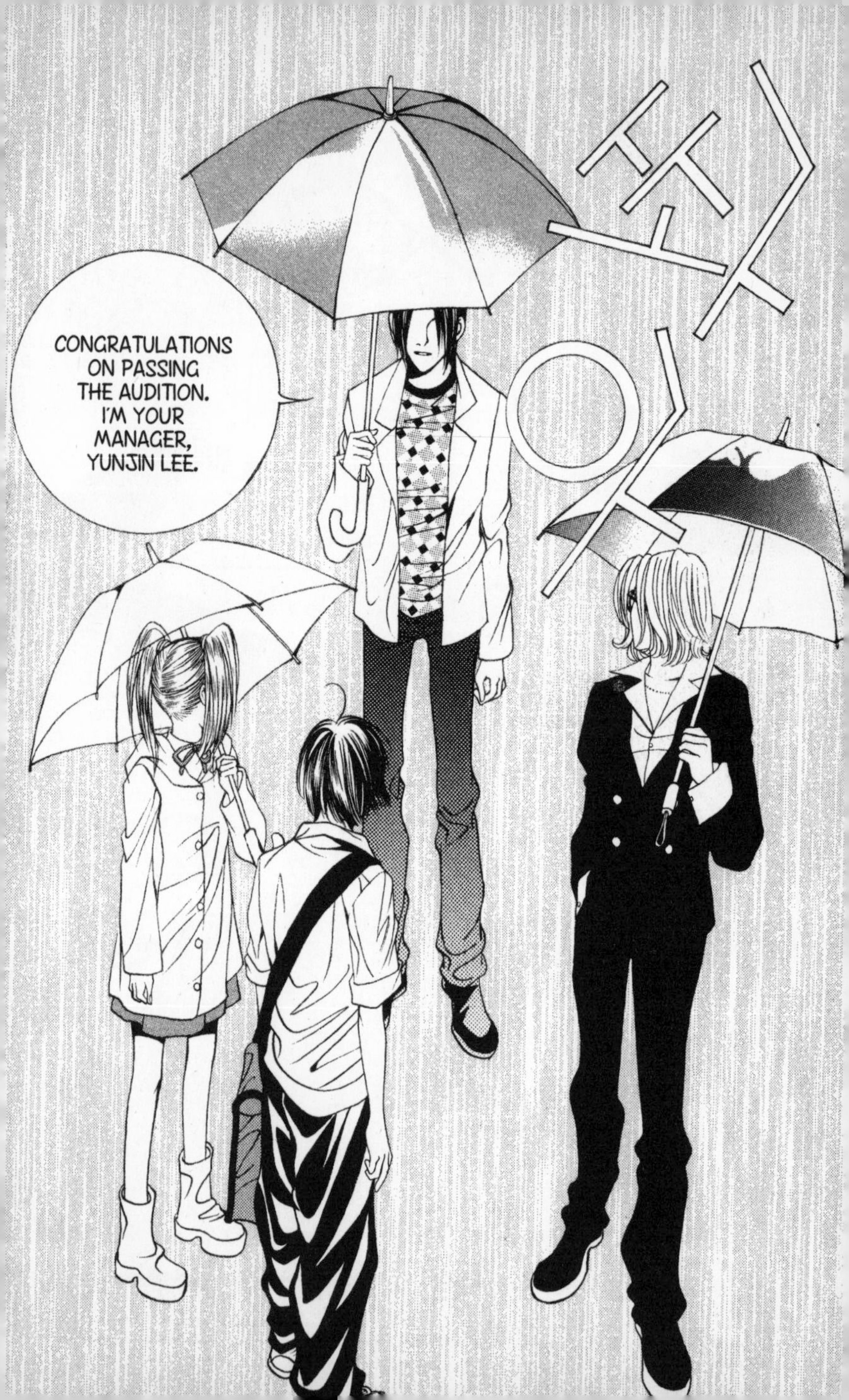
CONGRATULATIONS ON PASSING THE AUDITION. I'M YOUR MANAGER, YUNJIN LEE.

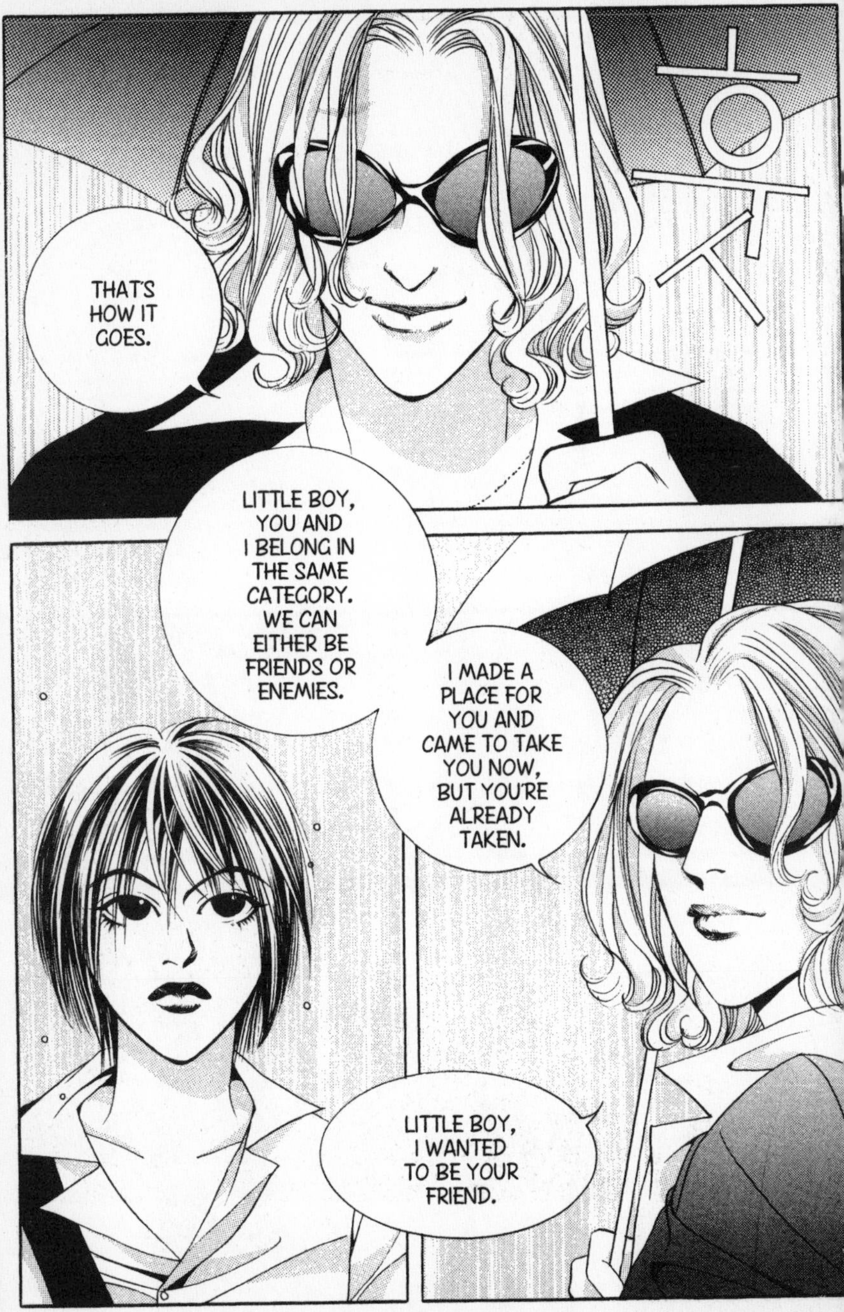
헛
THAT'S HOW IT GOES.
LITTLE BOY, YOU AND I BELONG IN THE SAME CATEGORY. WE CAN EITHER BE FRIENDS OR ENEMIES.
I MADE A PLACE FOR YOU AND CAME TO TAKE YOU NOW, BUT YOU'RE ALREADY TAKEN.
LITTLE BOY, I WANTED TO BE YOUR FRIEND.

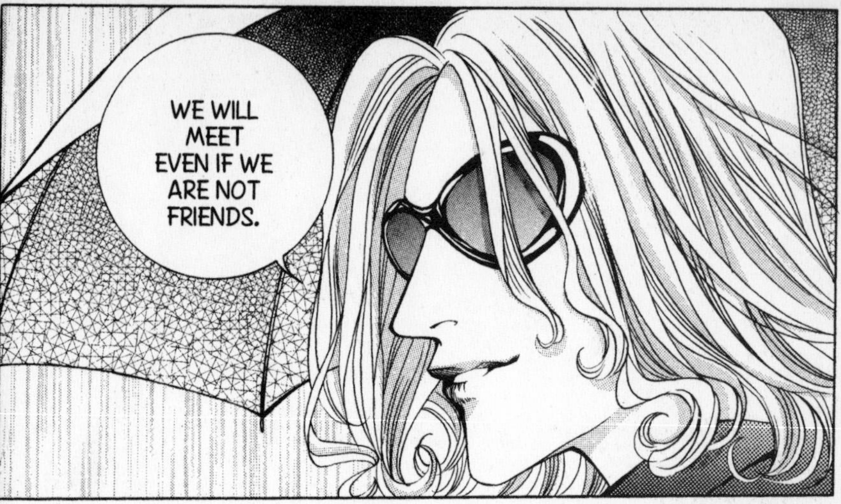
WE WILL MEET EVEN IF WE ARE NOT FRIENDS.

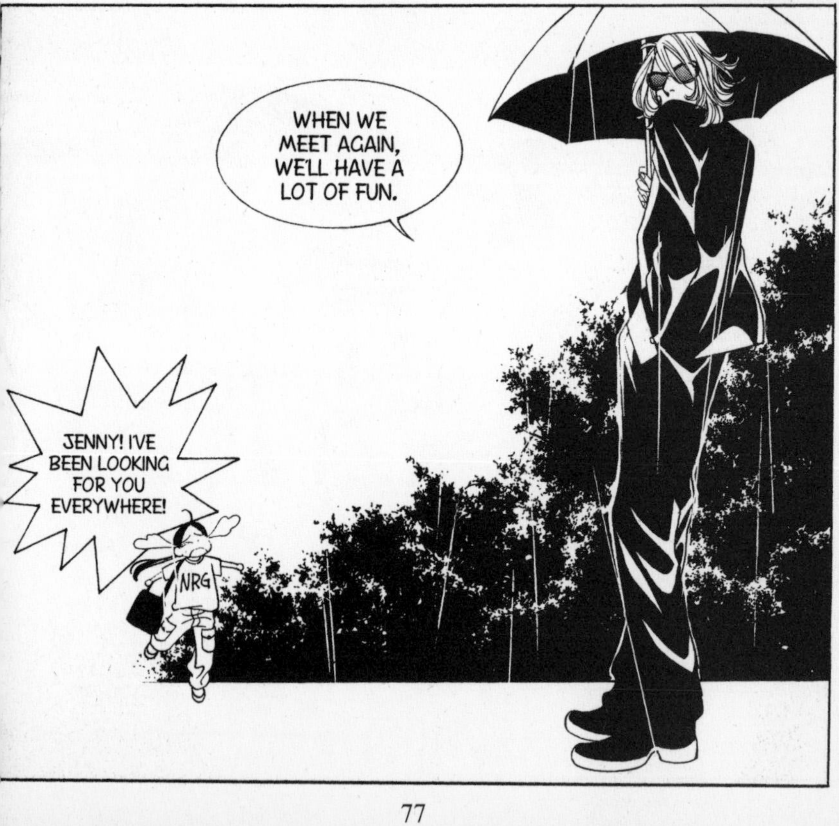
WHEN WE MEET AGAIN, WE'LL HAVE A LOT OF FUN.
JENNY! I'VE BEEN LOOKING FOR YOU EVERYWHERE!
NRG

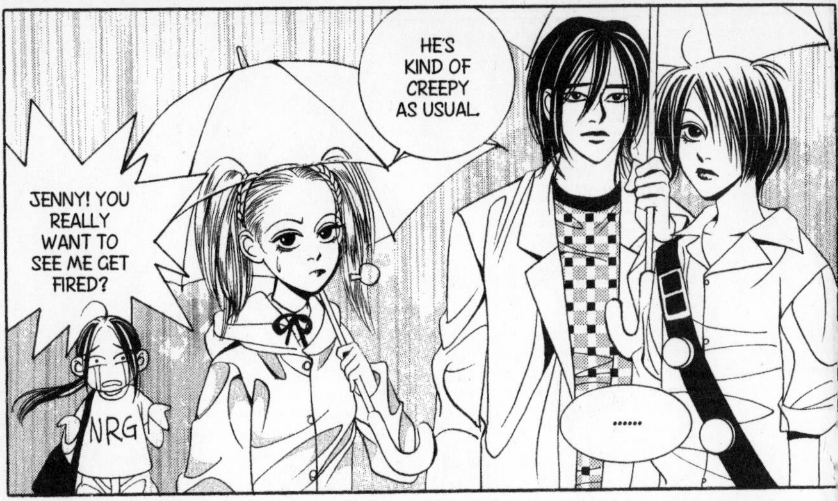
HE'S KIND OF CREEPY AS USUAL.
......
JENNY! YOU REALLY WANT TO SEE ME GET FIRED?

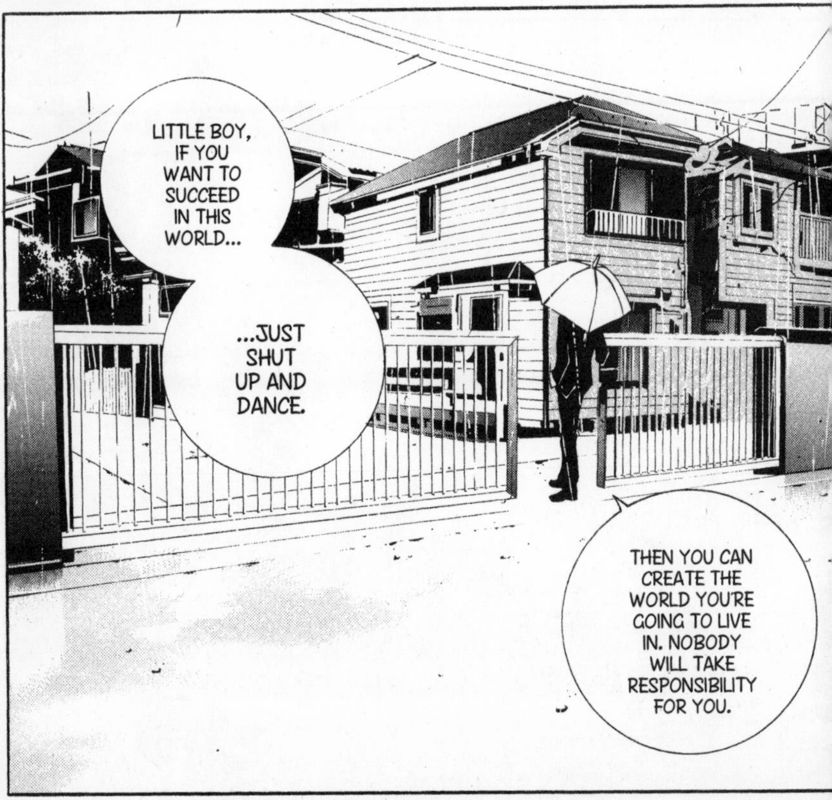
LITTLE BOY, IF YOU WANT TO SUCCEED IN THIS WORLD...
...JUST SHUT UP AND DANCE.
THEN YOU CAN CREATE THE WORLD YOU'RE GOING TO LIVE IN. NOBODY WILL TAKE RESPONSIBILITY FOR YOU.

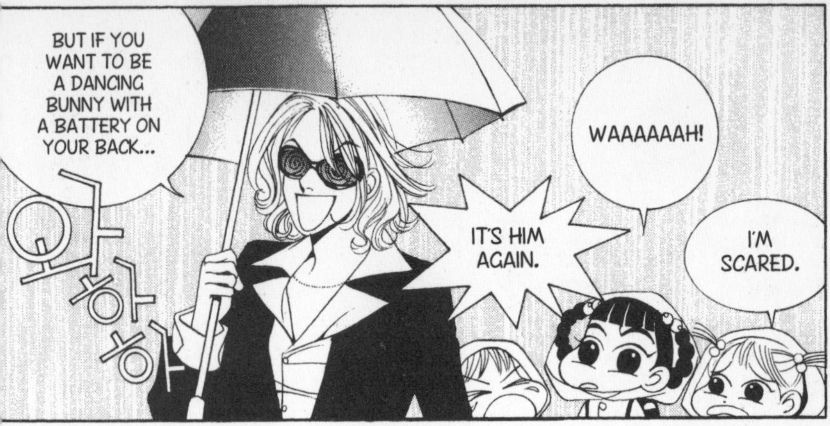
BUT IF YOU WANT TO BE A DANCING BUNNY WITH A BATTERY ON YOUR BACK...
와하하
IT'S HIM AGAIN.
WAAAAAAH!
I'M SCARED.

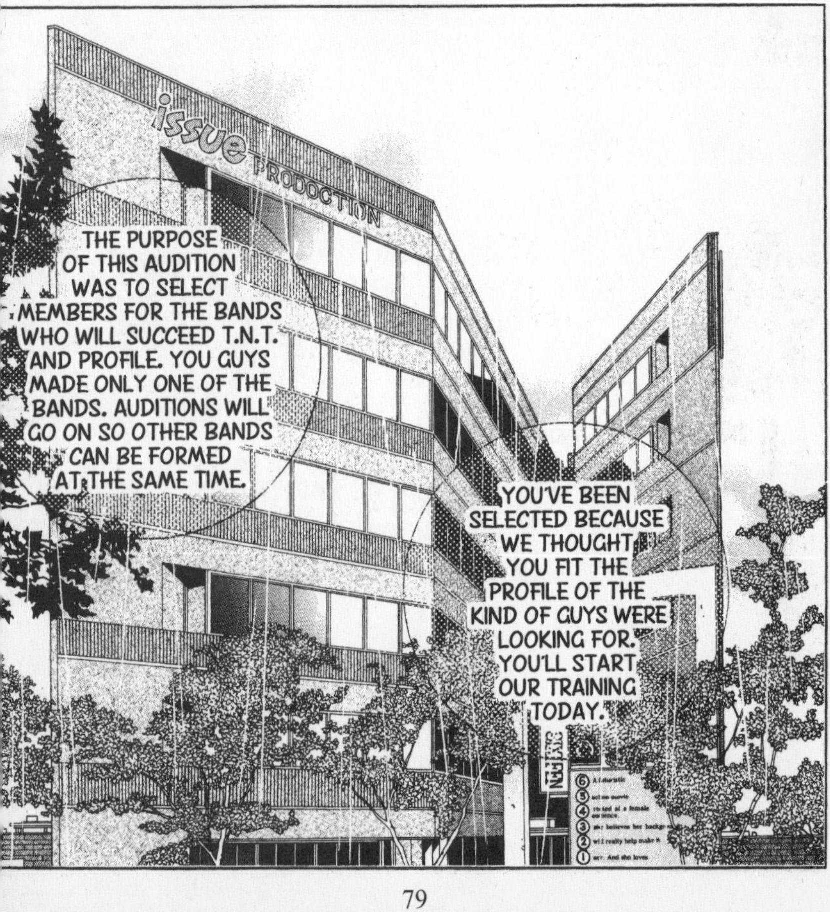
issue PRODUCTION
THE PURPOSE OF THIS AUDITION WAS TO SELECT MEMBERS FOR THE BANDS WHO WILL SUCCEED T.N.T. AND PROFILE. YOU GUYS MADE ONLY ONE OF THE BANDS. AUDITIONS WILL GO ON SO OTHER BANDS CAN BE FORMED AT THE SAME TIME.
YOU'VE BEEN SELECTED BECAUSE WE THOUGHT YOU FIT THE PROFILE OF THE KIND OF GUYS WERE LOOKING FOR. YOU'LL START OUR TRAINING TODAY.

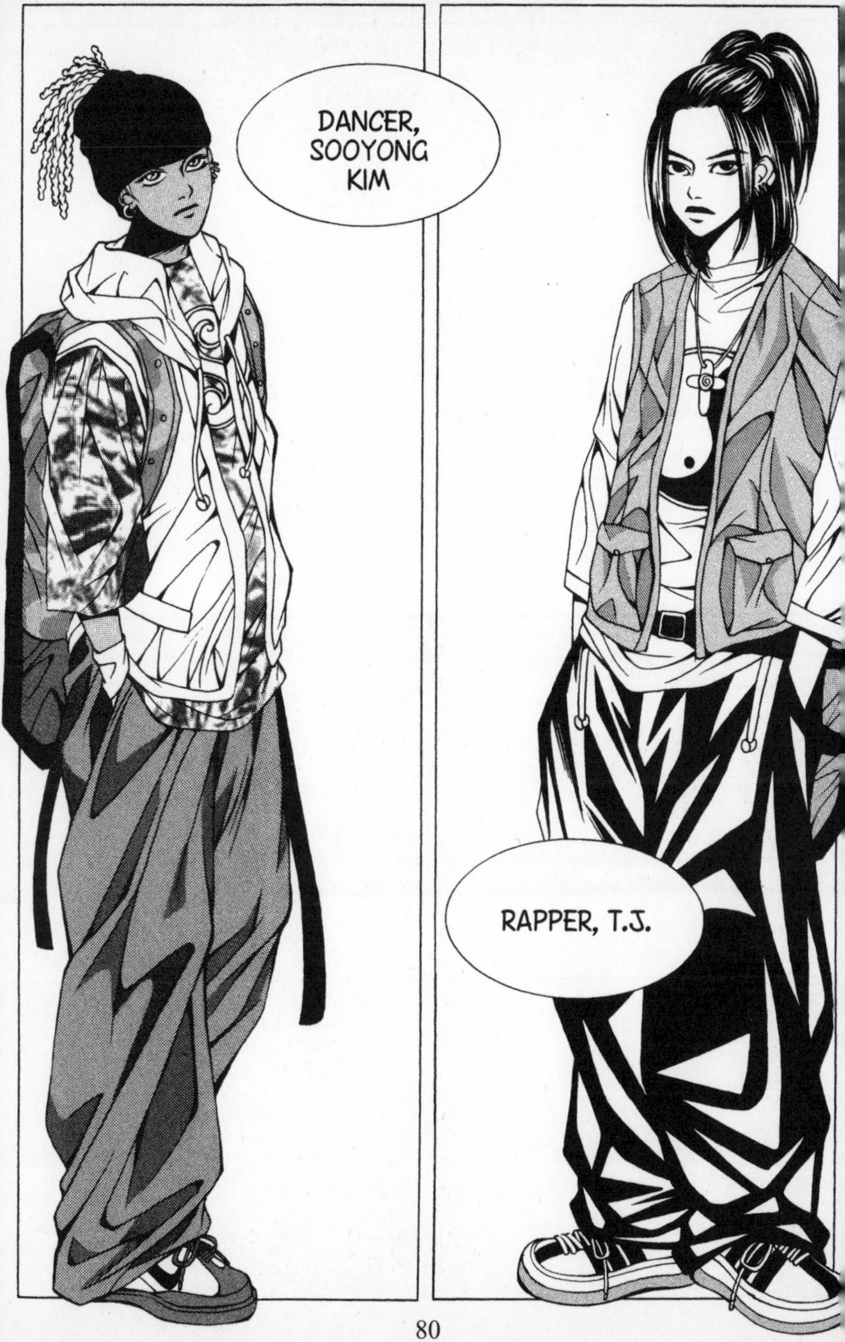
DANCER, SOOYONG KIM
RAPPER, T.J.

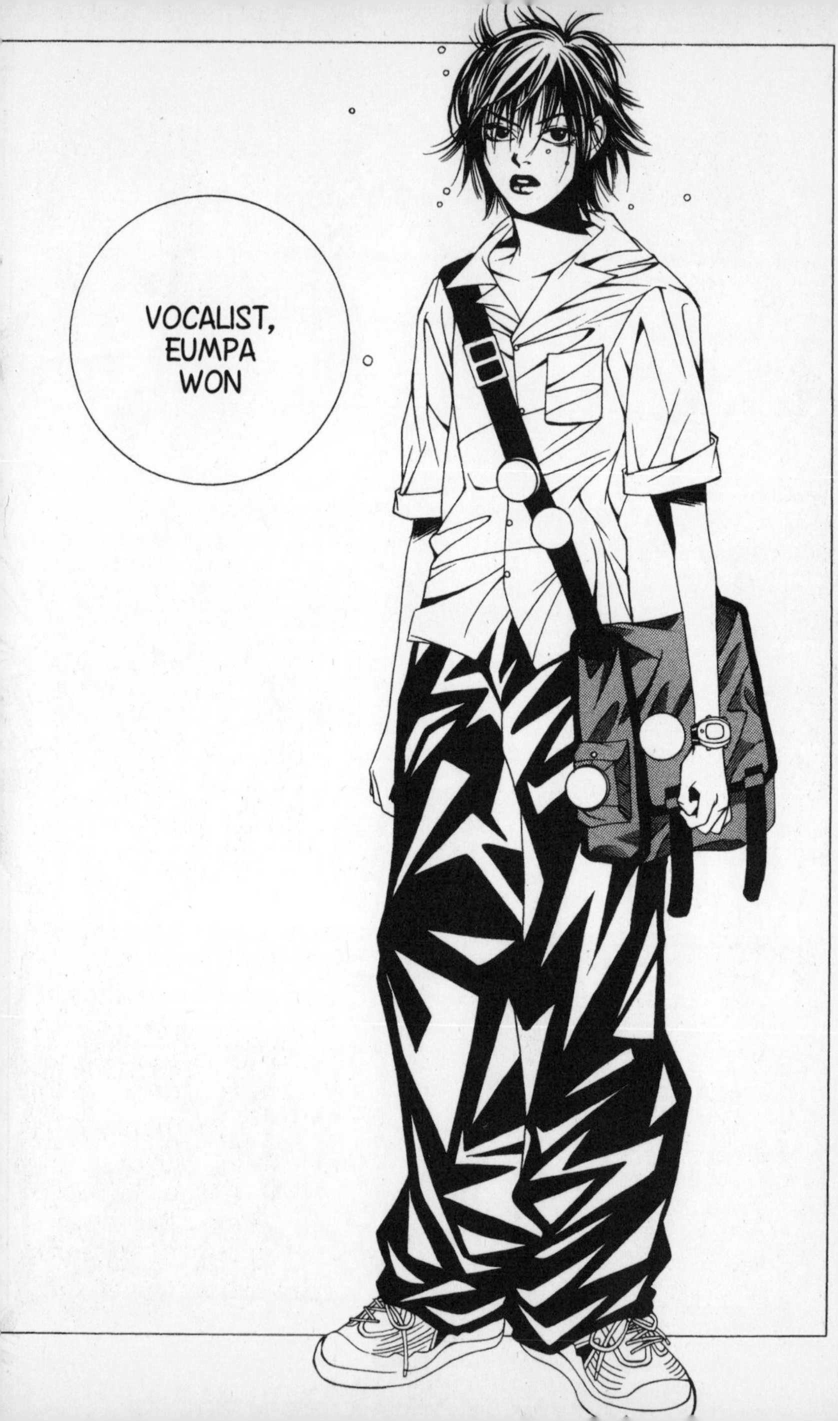
VOCALIST, EUMPA WON

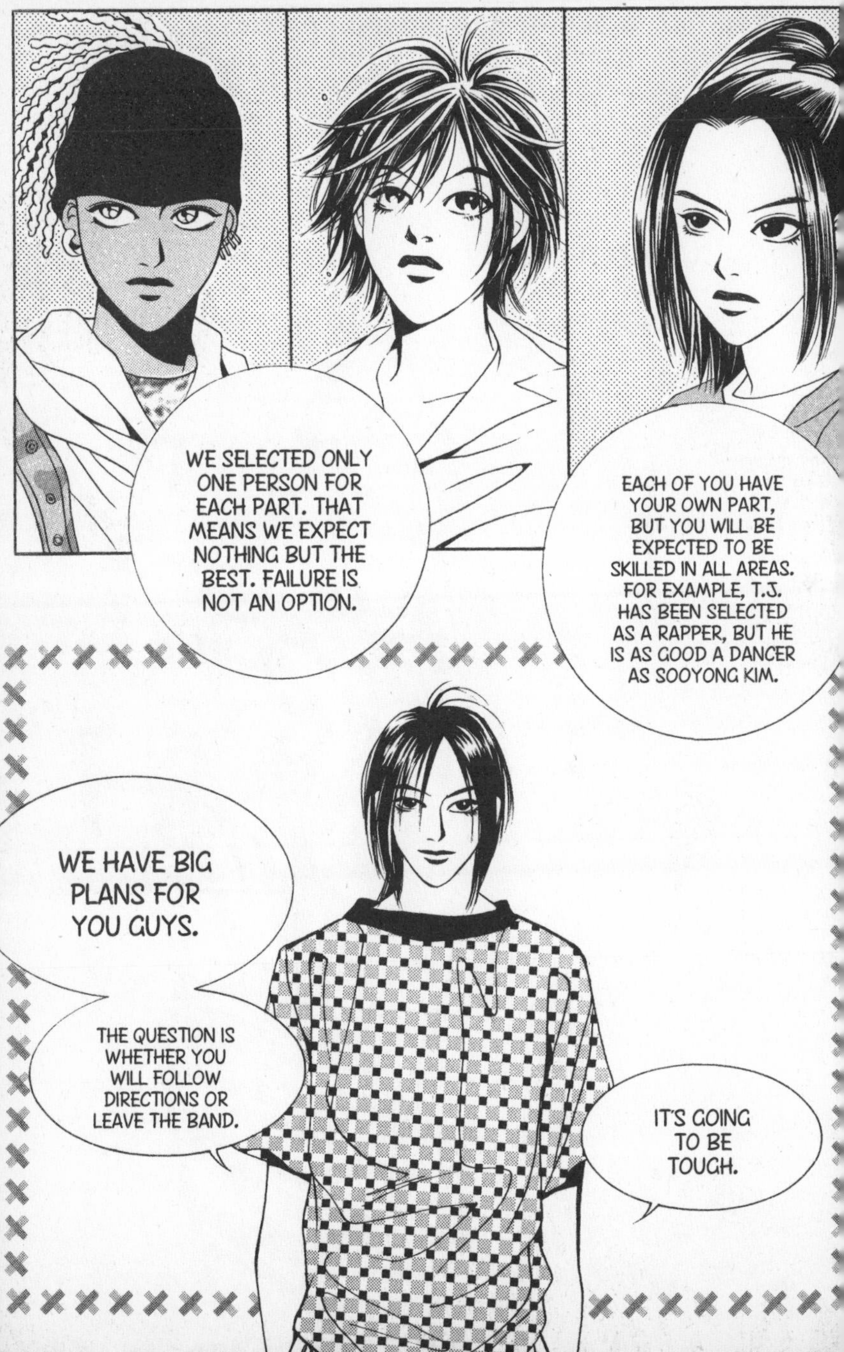
WE SELECTED ONLY ONE PERSON FOR EACH PART. THAT MEANS WE EXPECT NOTHING BUT THE BEST. FAILURE IS NOT AN OPTION.
EACH OF YOU HAVE YOUR OWN PART, BUT YOU WILL BE EXPECTED TO BE SKILLED IN ALL AREAS. FOR EXAMPLE, T.J. HAS BEEN SELECTED AS A RAPPER, BUT HE IS AS GOOD A DANCER AS SOOYONG KIM.
WE HAVE BIG PLANS FOR YOU GUYS.
THE QUESTION IS WHETHER YOU WILL FOLLOW DIRECTIONS OR LEAVE THE BAND.
IT'S GOING TO BE TOUGH.

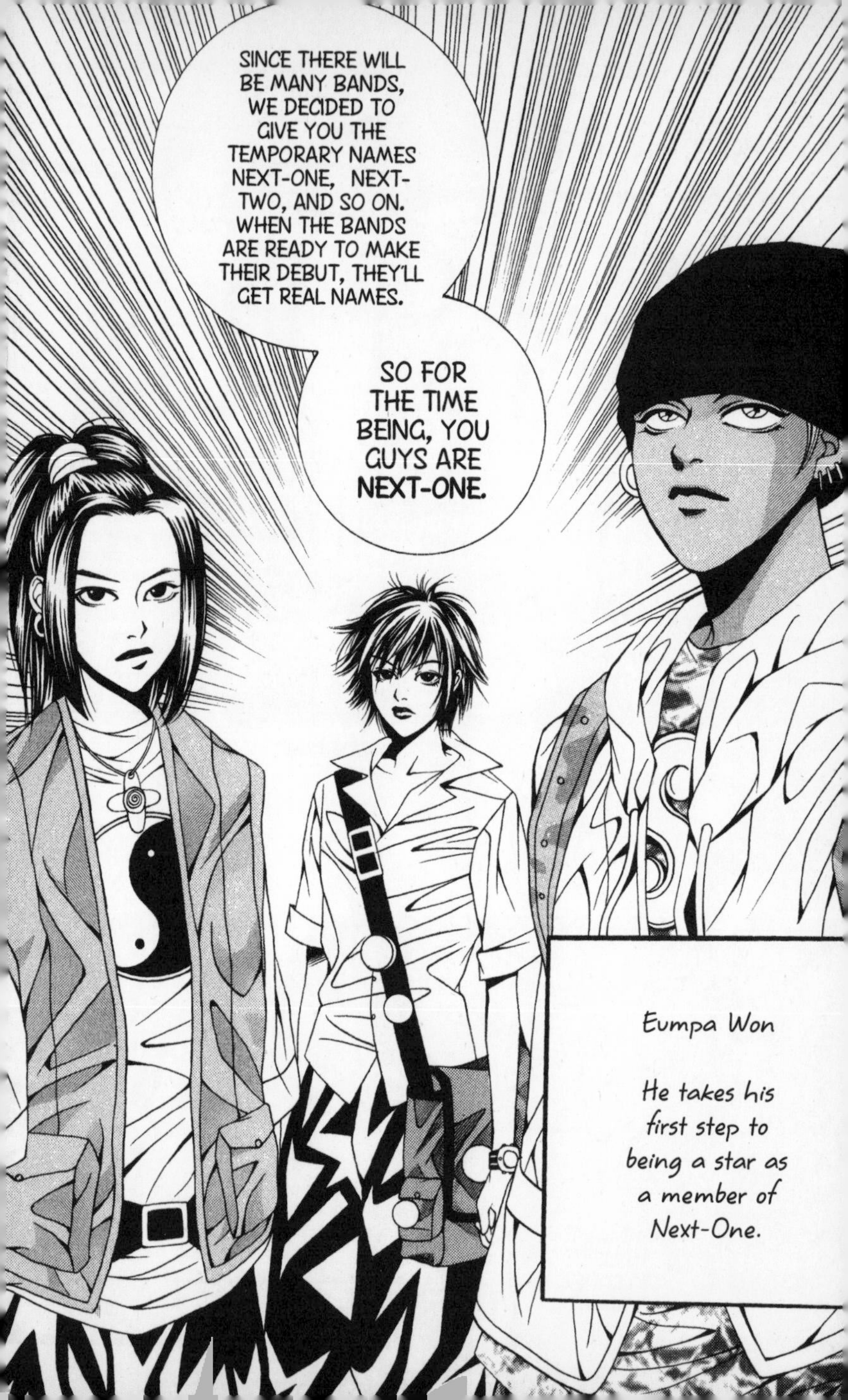
SINCE THERE WILL BE MANY BANDS, WE DECIDED TO GIVE YOU THE TEMPORARY NAMES NEXT-ONE, NEXT-TWO, AND SO ON. WHEN THE BANDS ARE READY TO MAKE THEIR DEBUT, THEY'LL GET REAL NAMES.
SO FOR THE TIME BEING, YOU GUYS ARE NEXT-ONE.
Eumpa Won
He takes his first step to being a star as a member of Next-One.

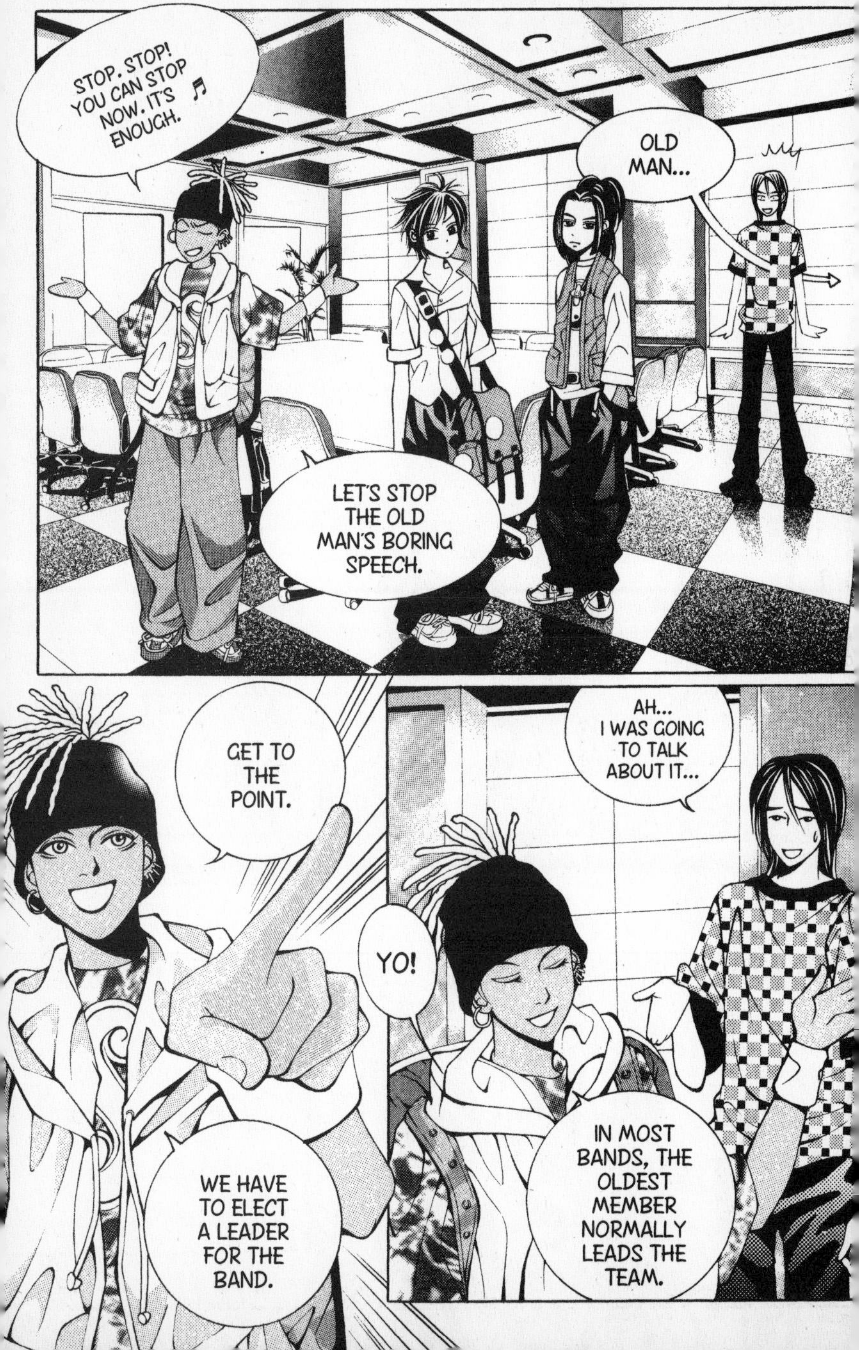
STOP. STOP! YOU CAN STOP NOW. IT'S ENOUGH.
OLD MAN...
LET'S STOP THE OLD MAN'S BORING SPEECH.
GET TO THE POINT.
WE HAVE TO ELECT A LEADER FOR THE BAND.
AH... I WAS GOING TO TALK ABOUT IT...
YO!
IN MOST BANDS, THE OLDEST MEMBER NORMALLY LEADS THE TEAM.

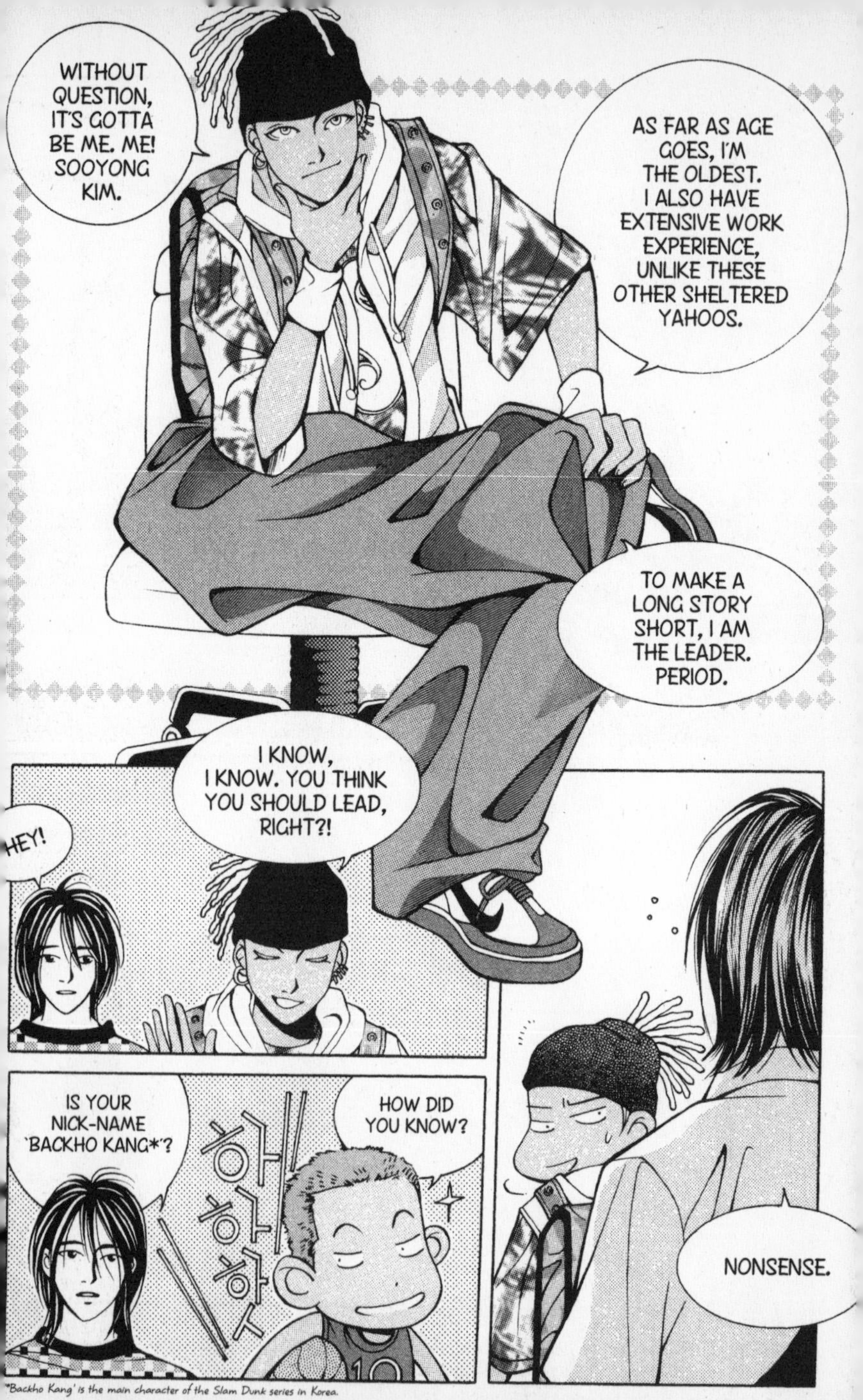
WITHOUT QUESTION, IT'S GOTTA BE ME. ME! SOOYONG KIM.
AS FAR AS AGE GOES, I'M THE OLDEST. I ALSO HAVE EXTENSIVE WORK EXPERIENCE, UNLIKE THESE OTHER SHELTERED YAHOOS.
TO MAKE A LONG STORY SHORT, I AM THE LEADER. PERIOD.
HEY!
I KNOW, I KNOW. YOU THINK YOU SHOULD LEAD, RIGHT?!
NONSENSE.
IS YOUR NICK-NAME 'BACKHO KANG*'?
HOW DID YOU KNOW?

*'Backho Kang' is the main character of the Slam Dunk series in Korea.

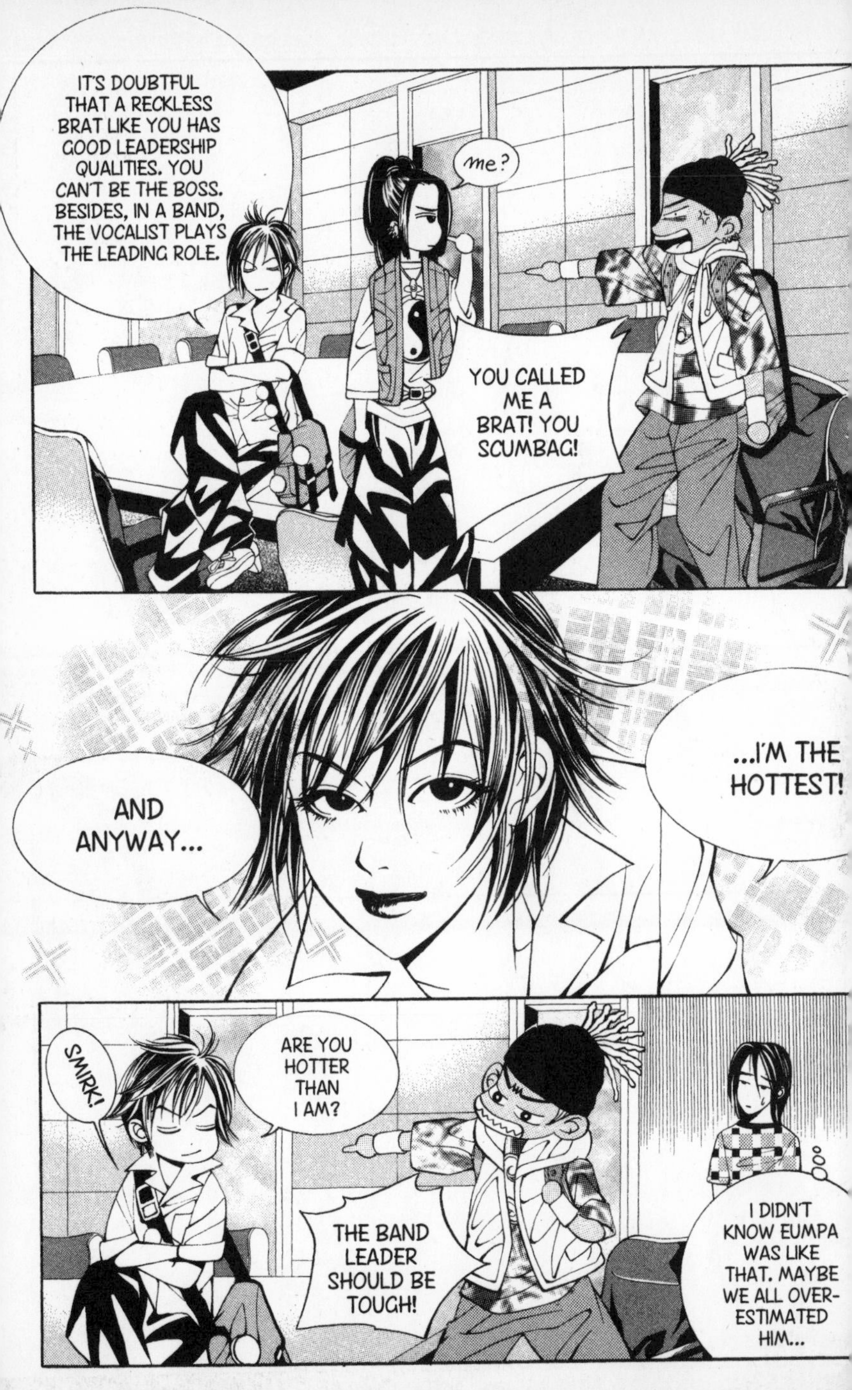
IT'S DOUBTFUL THAT A RECKLESS BRAT LIKE YOU HAS GOOD LEADERSHIP QUALITIES. YOU CAN'T BE THE BOSS. BESIDES, IN A BAND, THE VOCALIST PLAYS THE LEADING ROLE.
me?
YOU CALLED ME A BRAT! YOU SCUMBAG!
AND ANYWAY...
...I'M THE HOTTEST!
SMIRK!
ARE YOU HOTTER THAN I AM?
THE BAND LEADER SHOULD BE TOUGH!
I DIDN'T KNOW EUMPA WAS LIKE THAT. MAYBE WE ALL OVER-ESTIMATED HIM...

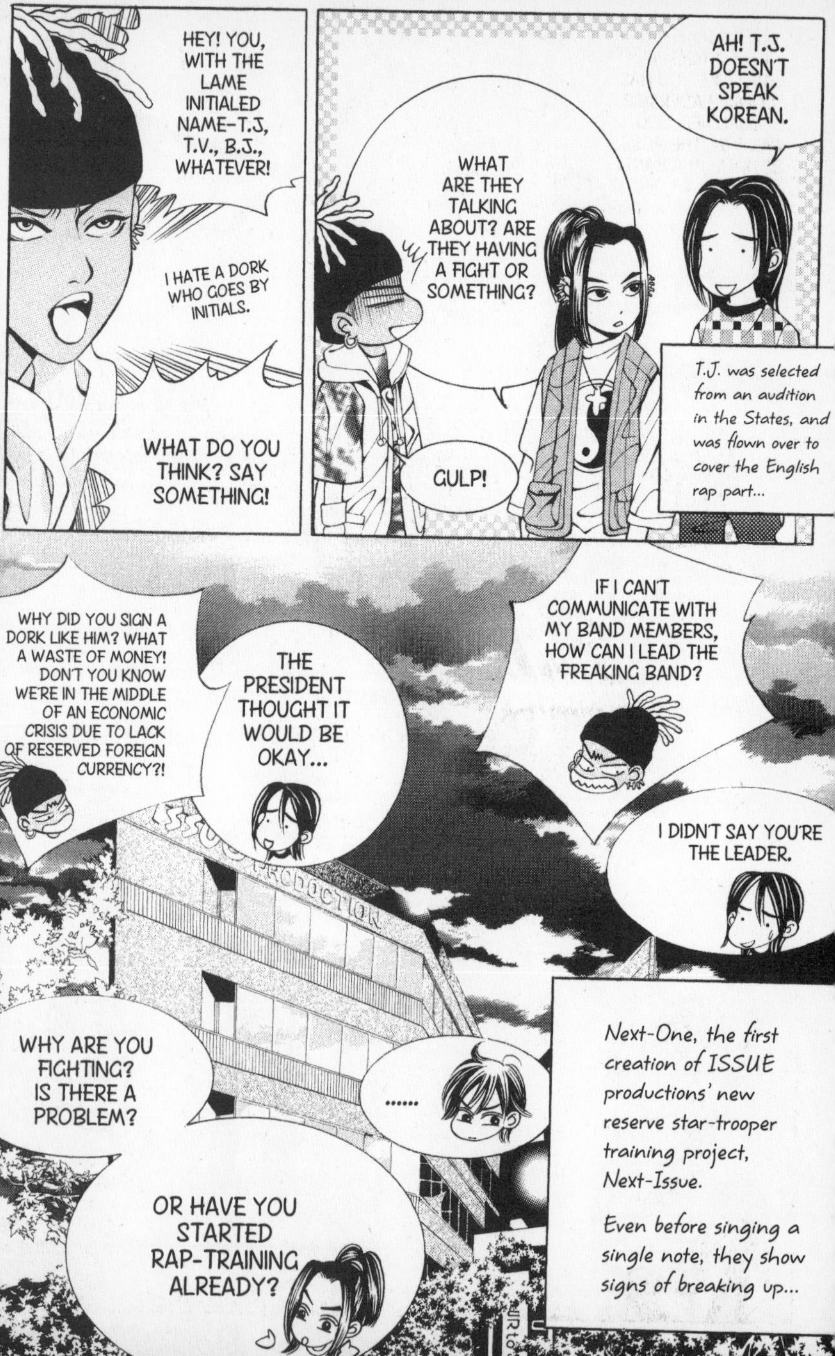
HEY! YOU, WITH THE LAME INITIALED NAME–T.J, T.V., B.J., WHATEVER!
I HATE A DORK WHO GOES BY INITIALS.
WHAT DO YOU THINK? SAY SOMETHING!
WHAT ARE THEY TALKING ABOUT? ARE THEY HAVING A FIGHT OR SOMETHING?
GULP!
AH! T.J. DOESN'T SPEAK KOREAN.
T.J. was selected from an audition in the States, and was flown over to cover the English rap part...
WHY DID YOU SIGN A DORK LIKE HIM? WHAT A WASTE OF MONEY! DON'T YOU KNOW WE'RE IN THE MIDDLE OF AN ECONOMIC CRISIS DUE TO LACK OF RESERVED FOREIGN CURRENCY?!
THE PRESIDENT THOUGHT IT WOULD BE OKAY...
IF I CAN'T COMMUNICATE WITH MY BAND MEMBERS, HOW CAN I LEAD THE FREAKING BAND?
I DIDN'T SAY YOU'RE THE LEADER.
PRODUCTION
WHY ARE YOU FIGHTING? IS THERE A PROBLEM?
......
OR HAVE YOU STARTED RAP-TRAINING ALREADY?
Next-One, the first creation of ISSUE productions' new reserve star-trooper training project, Next-Issue.
Even before singing a single note, they show signs of breaking up...

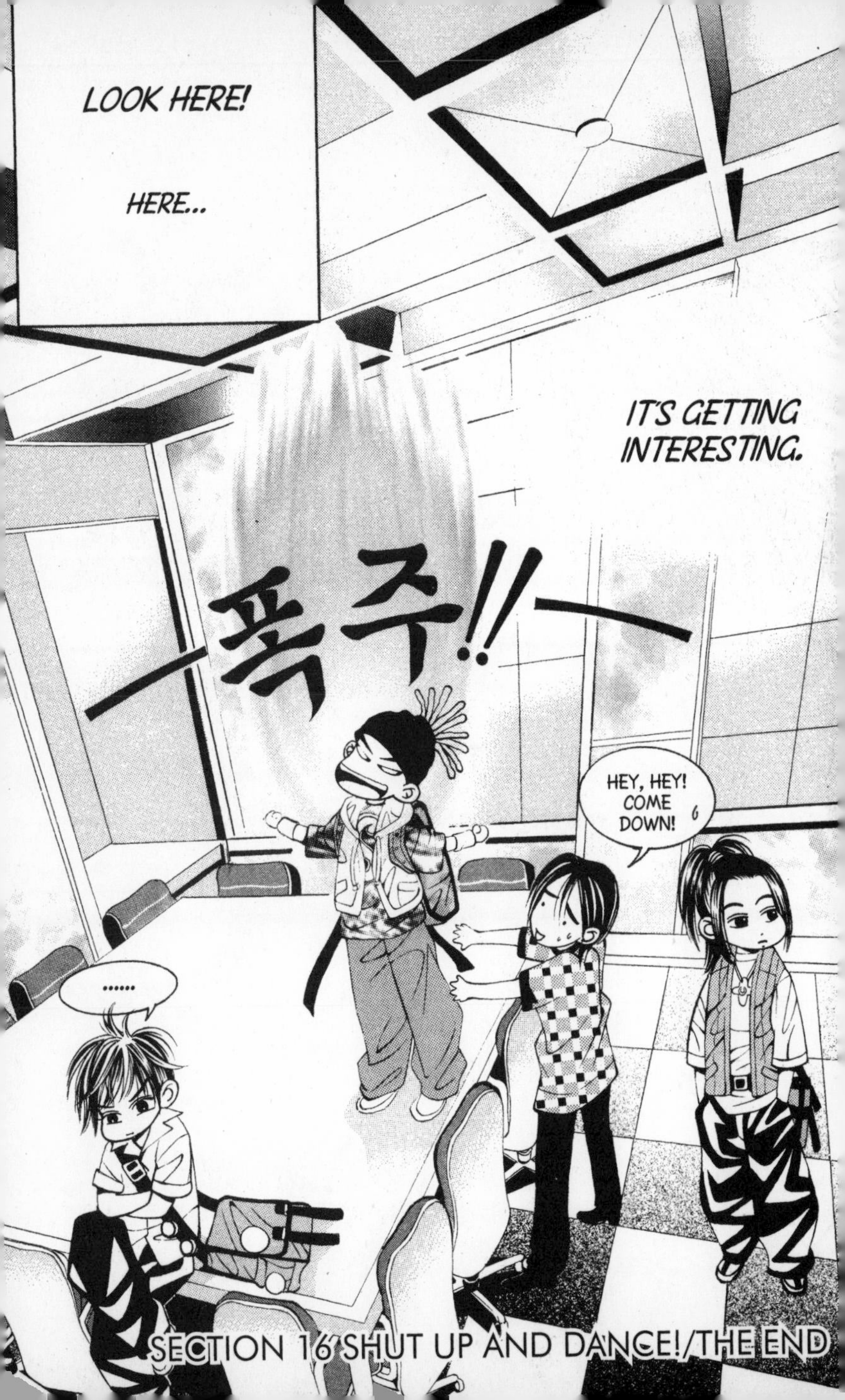
LOOK HERE!
HERE...
IT'S GETTING INTERESTING.
폭주!!
HEY, HEY! COME DOWN!
......
SECTION 16 SHUT UP AND DANCE!/THE END

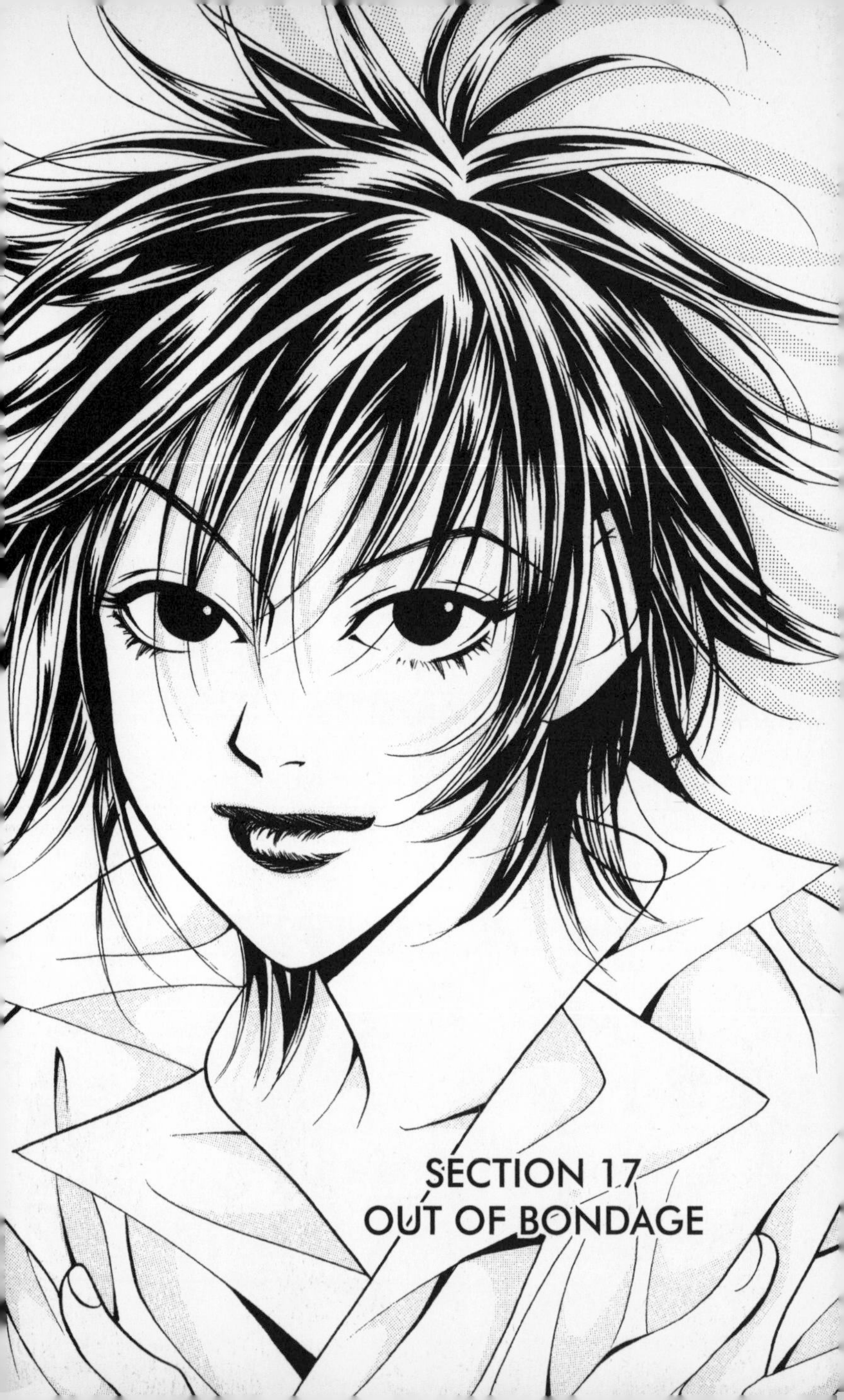
SECTION 17
OUT OF BONDAGE

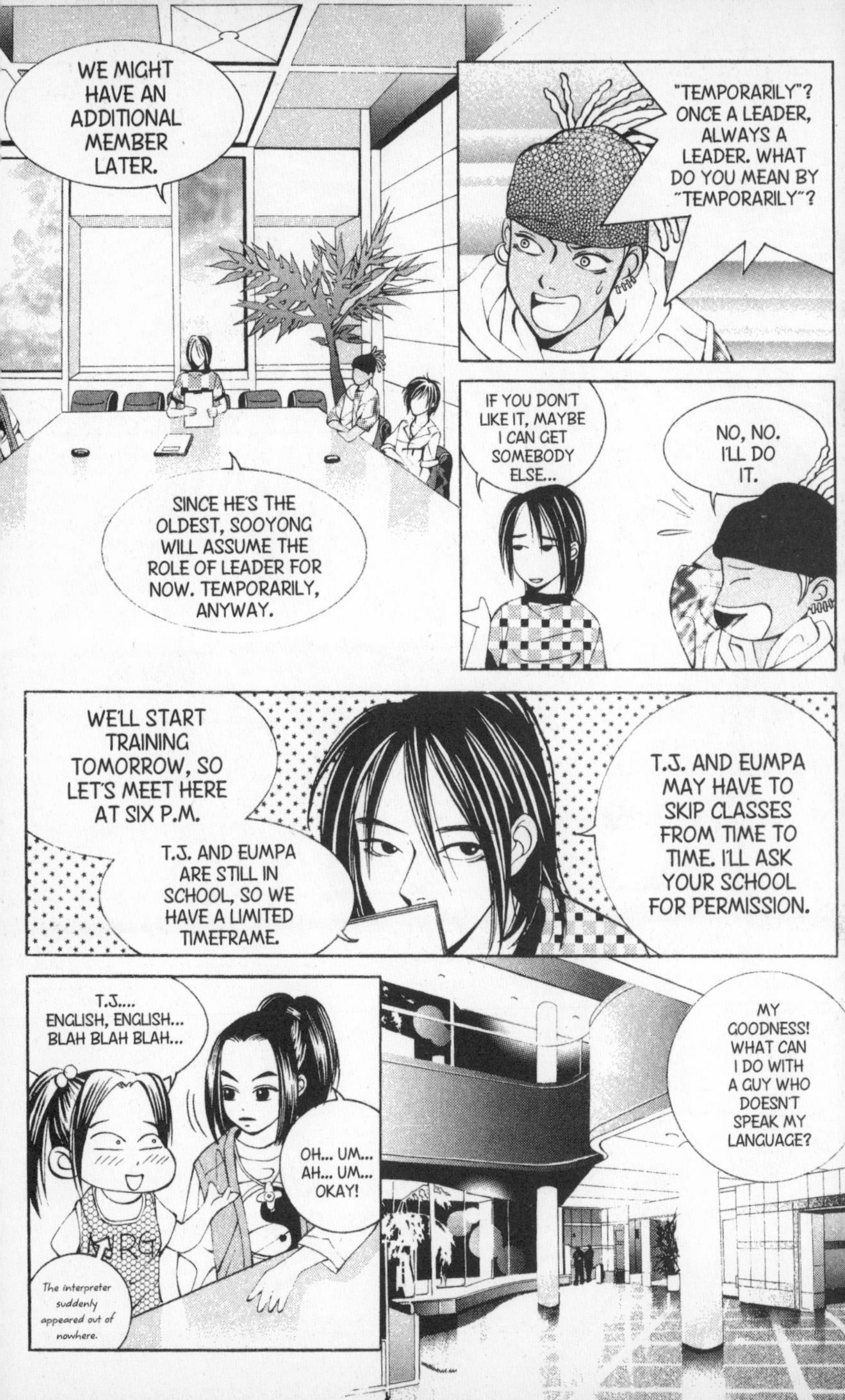
WE MIGHT HAVE AN ADDITIONAL MEMBER LATER.
SINCE HE'S THE OLDEST, SOOYONG WILL ASSUME THE ROLE OF LEADER FOR NOW. TEMPORARILY, ANYWAY.
"TEMPORARILY"? ONCE A LEADER, ALWAYS A LEADER. WHAT DO YOU MEAN BY "TEMPORARILY"?
IF YOU DON'T LIKE IT, MAYBE I CAN GET SOMEBODY ELSE...
NO, NO. I'LL DO IT.
WE'LL START TRAINING TOMORROW, SO LET'S MEET HERE AT SIX P.M.
T.J. AND EUMPA ARE STILL IN SCHOOL, SO WE HAVE A LIMITED TIMEFRAME.
T.J. AND EUMPA MAY HAVE TO SKIP CLASSES FROM TIME TO TIME. I'LL ASK YOUR SCHOOL FOR PERMISSION.
T.J.... ENGLISH, ENGLISH... BLAH BLAH BLAH...
OH... UM... AH... UM... OKAY!
The interpreter suddenly appeared out of nowhere.
MY GOODNESS! WHAT CAN I DO WITH A GUY WHO DOESN'T SPEAK MY LANGUAGE?

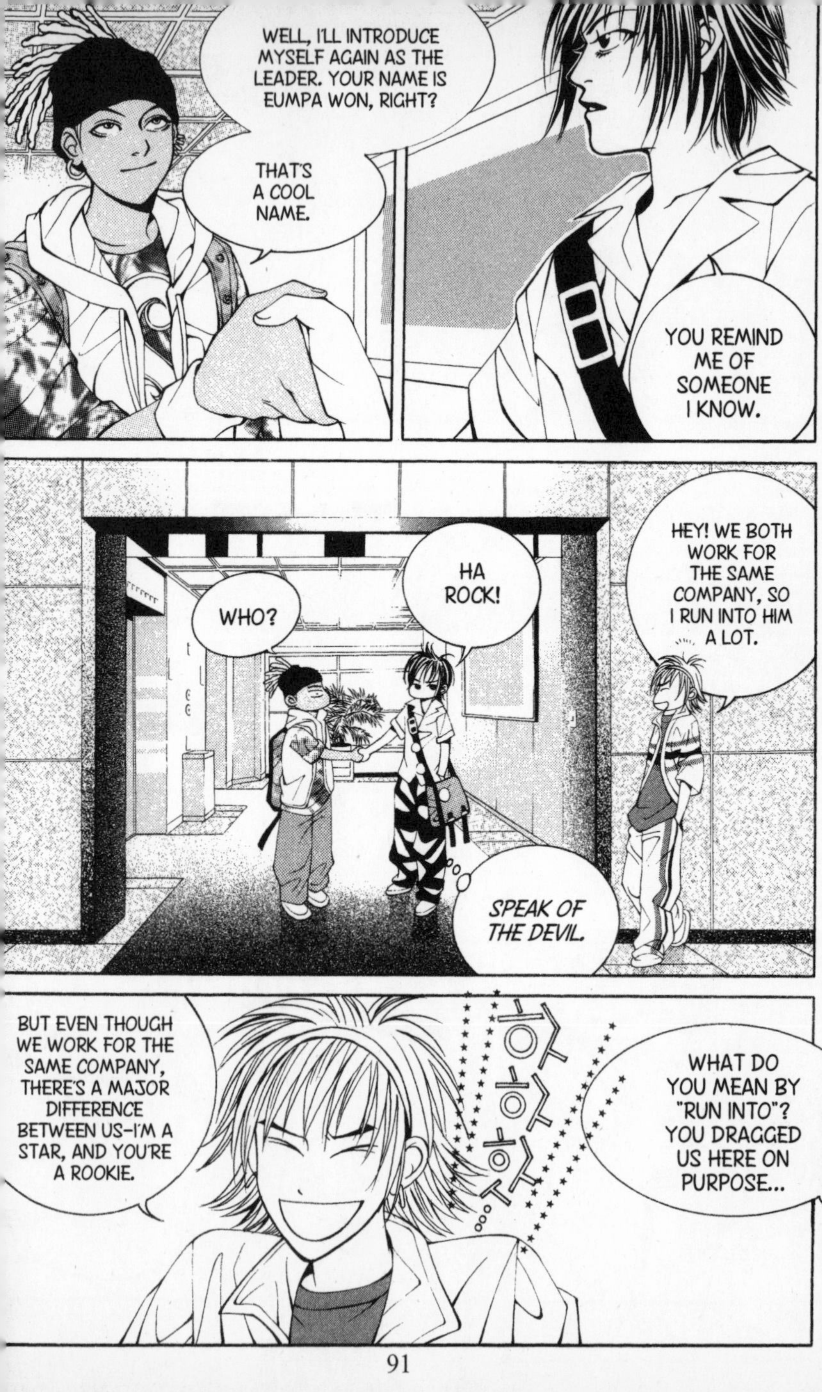
WELL, I'LL INTRODUCE MYSELF AGAIN AS THE LEADER. YOUR NAME IS EUMPA WON, RIGHT?
THAT'S A COOL NAME.
YOU REMIND ME OF SOMEONE I KNOW.
WHO?
HA ROCK!
HEY! WE BOTH WORK FOR THE SAME COMPANY, SO I RUN INTO HIM A LOT.
SPEAK OF THE DEVIL.
BUT EVEN THOUGH WE WORK FOR THE SAME COMPANY, THERE'S A MAJOR DIFFERENCE BETWEEN US–I'M A STAR, AND YOU'RE A ROOKIE.
WHAT DO YOU MEAN BY "RUN INTO"? YOU DRAGGED US HERE ON PURPOSE...

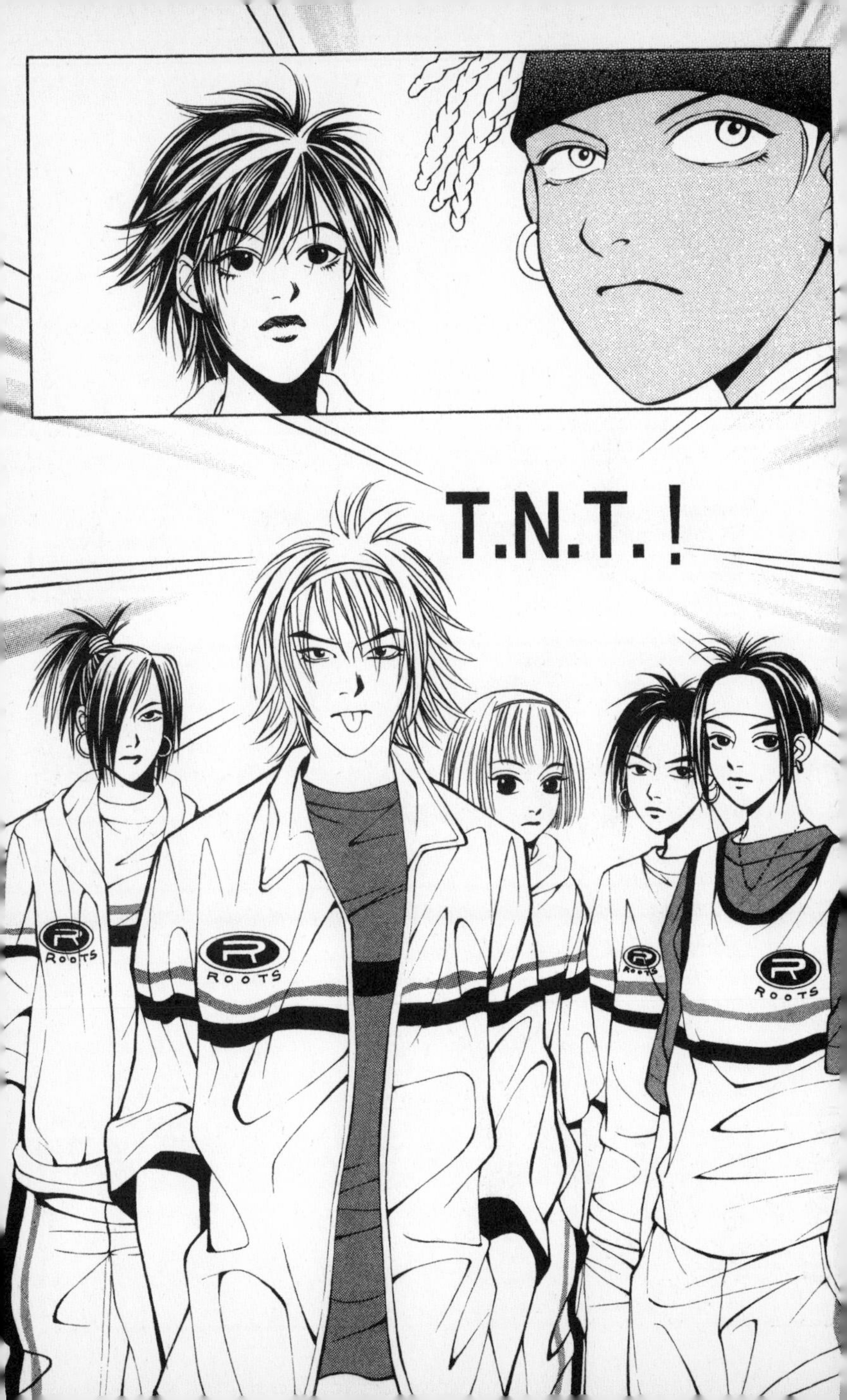
T.N.T. !
ROOTS
ROOTS
ROOTS
ROOTS

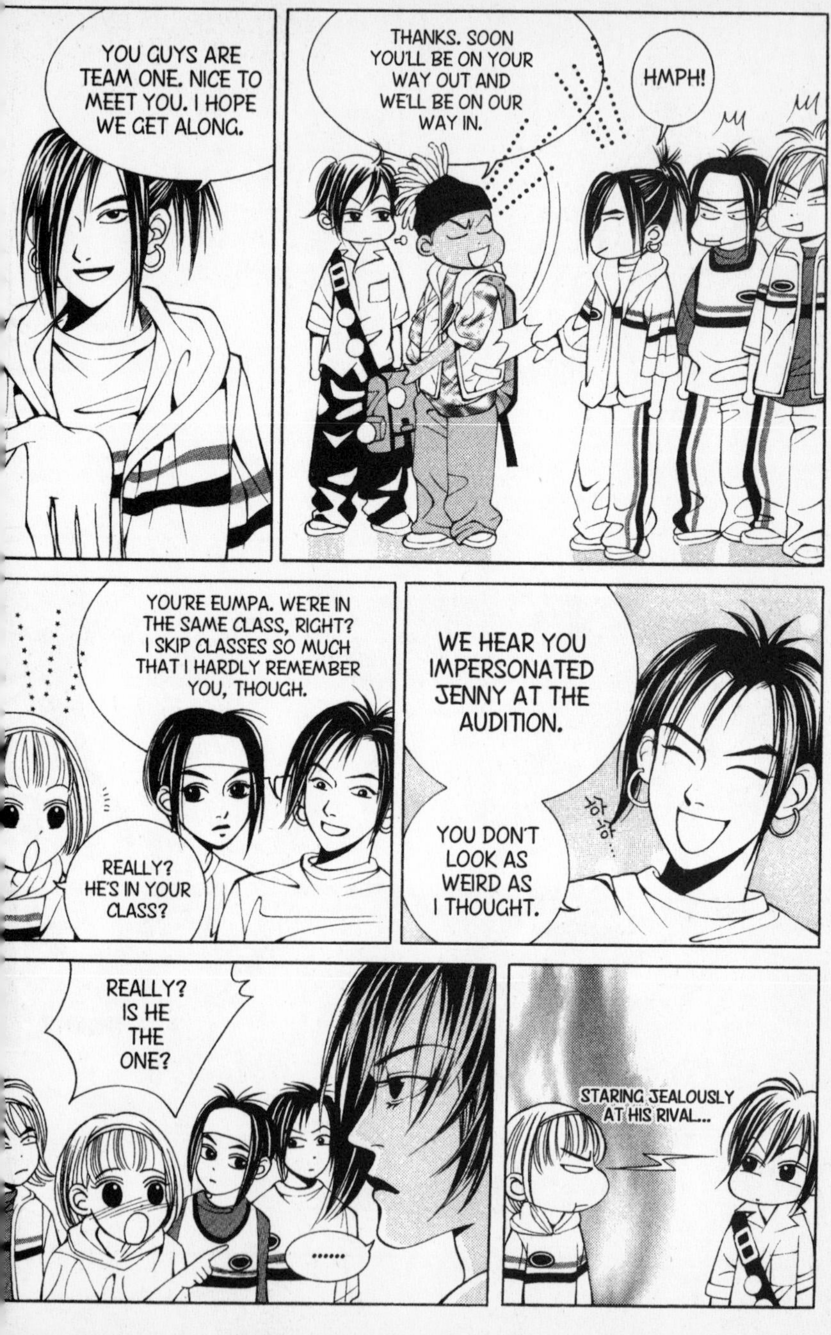
YOU GUYS ARE TEAM ONE. NICE TO MEET YOU. I HOPE WE GET ALONG.
THANKS. SOON YOU'LL BE ON YOUR WAY OUT AND WE'LL BE ON OUR WAY IN.
HMPH!
YOU'RE EUMPA. WE'RE IN THE SAME CLASS, RIGHT? I SKIP CLASSES SO MUCH THAT I HARDLY REMEMBER YOU, THOUGH.
REALLY? HE'S IN YOUR CLASS?
WE HEAR YOU IMPERSONATED JENNY AT THE AUDITION.
하하...
YOU DON'T LOOK AS WEIRD AS I THOUGHT.
REALLY? IS HE THE ONE?
......
STARING JEALOUSLY AT HIS RIVAL...

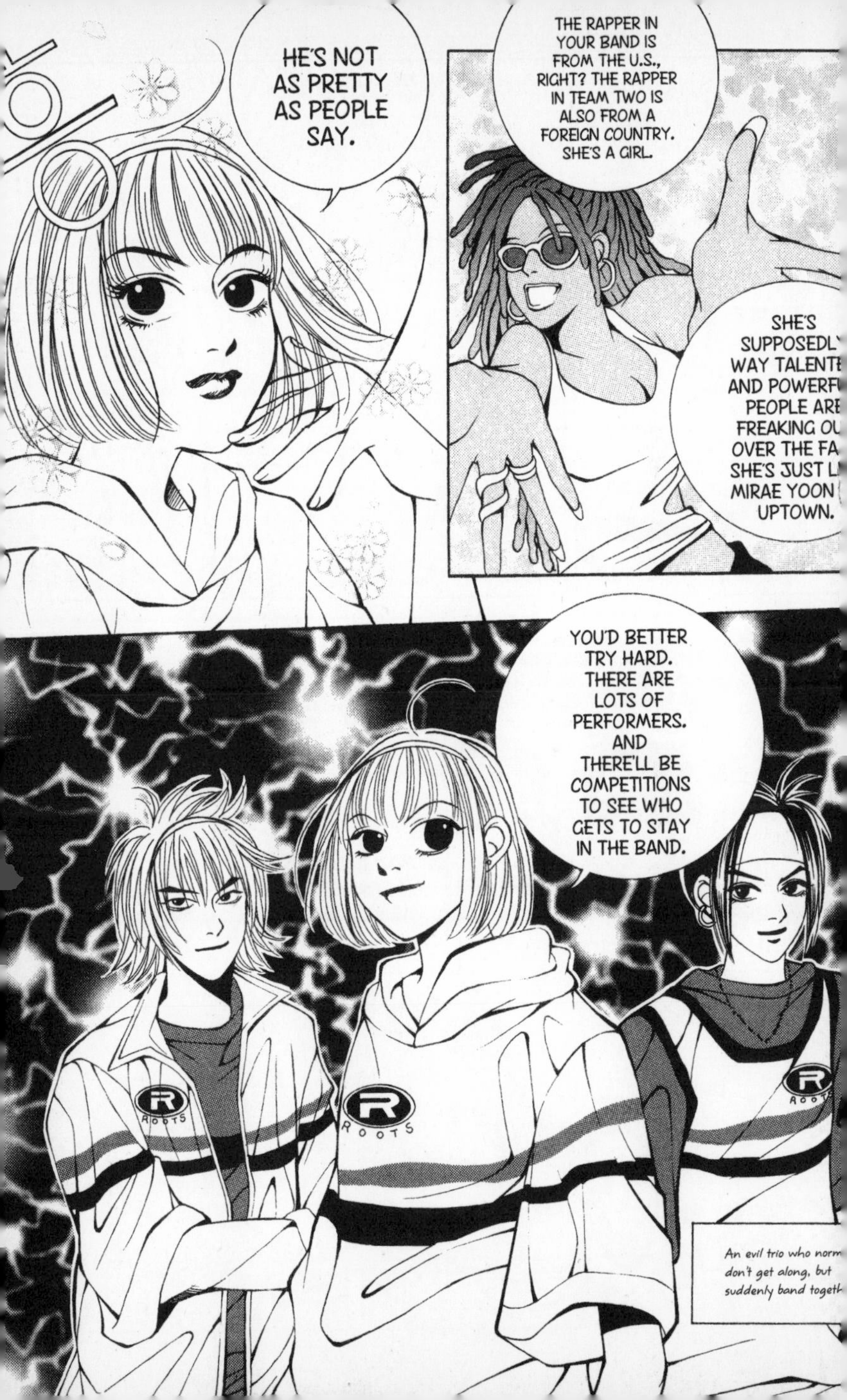
HE'S NOT AS PRETTY AS PEOPLE SAY.
THE RAPPER IN YOUR BAND IS FROM THE U.S., RIGHT? THE RAPPER IN TEAM TWO IS ALSO FROM A FOREIGN COUNTRY. SHE'S A GIRL.
SHE'S SUPPOSEDL WAY TALENTE AND POWERF PEOPLE ARE FREAKING OU OVER THE FA SHE'S JUST L MIRAE YOON UPTOWN.
YOU'D BETTER TRY HARD. THERE ARE LOTS OF PERFORMERS. AND THERE'LL BE COMPETITIONS TO SEE WHO GETS TO STAY IN THE BAND.
ROOTS
ROOTS
ROOTS
An evil trio who norm don't get along, but suddenly band togeth

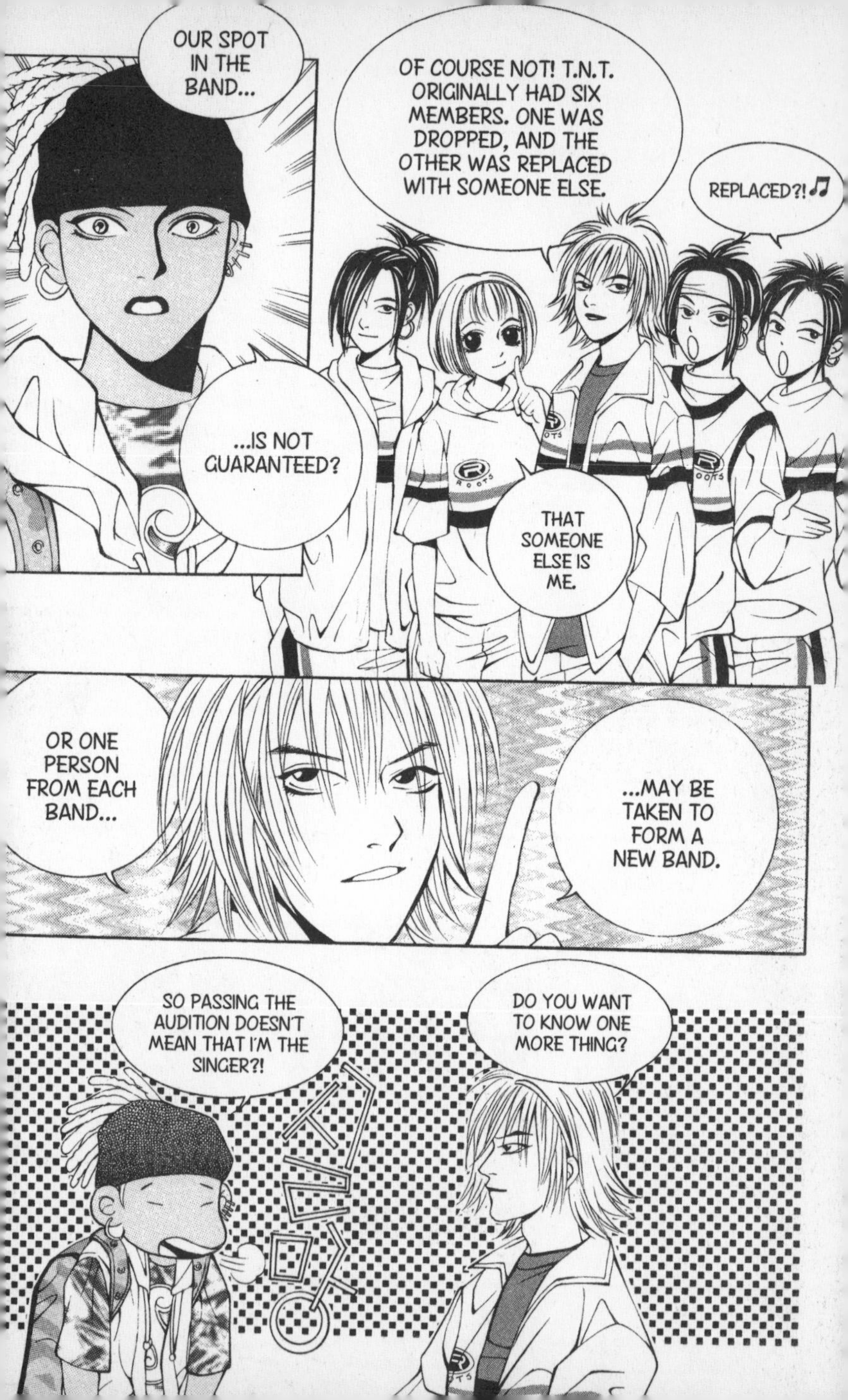
OUR SPOT IN THE BAND...
...IS NOT GUARANTEED?
OF COURSE NOT! T.N.T. ORIGINALLY HAD SIX MEMBERS. ONE WAS DROPPED, AND THE OTHER WAS REPLACED WITH SOMEONE ELSE.
REPLACED?! ♫
THAT SOMEONE ELSE IS ME.
OR ONE PERSON FROM EACH BAND...
...MAY BE TAKEN TO FORM A NEW BAND.
SO PASSING THE AUDITION DOESN'T MEAN THAT I'M THE SINGER?!
DO YOU WANT TO KNOW ONE MORE THING?

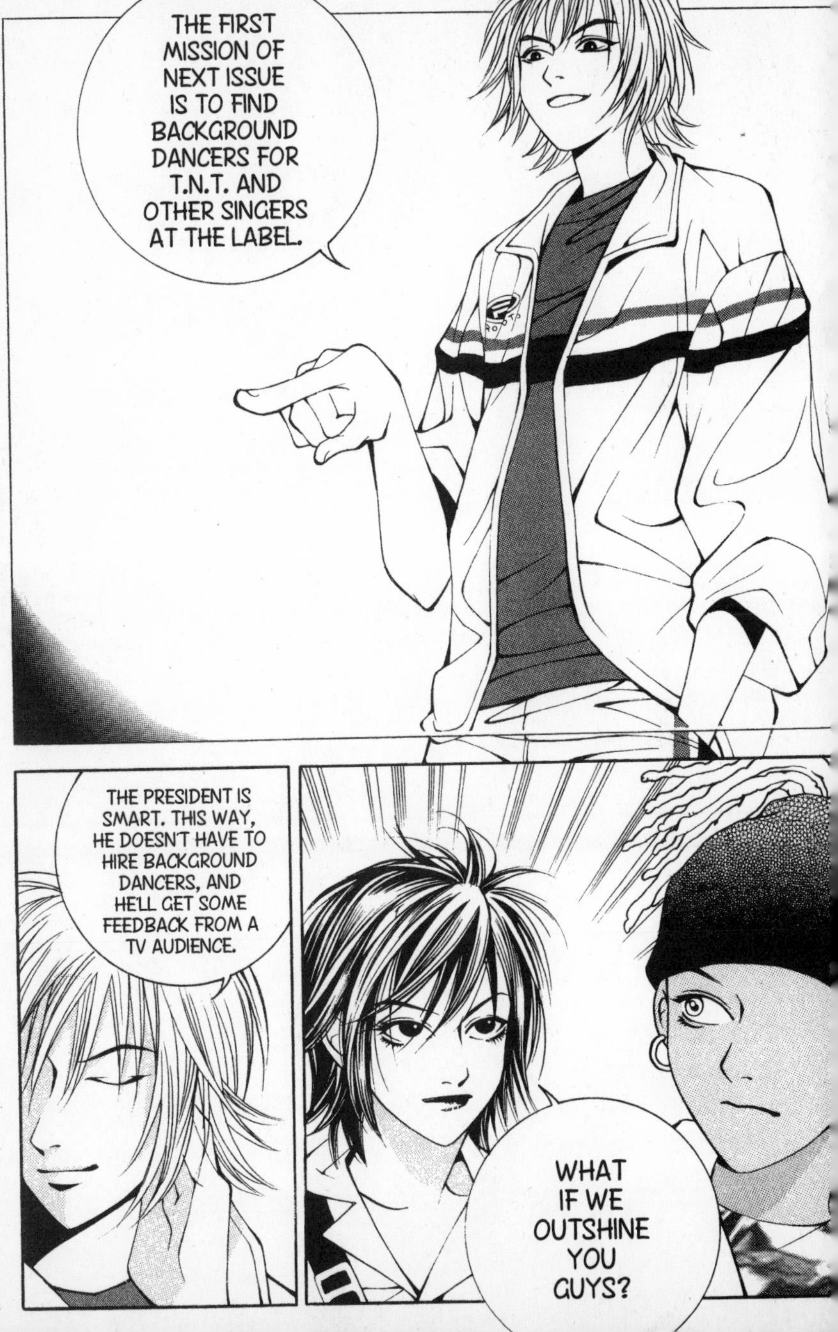
THE FIRST MISSION OF NEXT ISSUE IS TO FIND BACKGROUND DANCERS FOR T.N.T. AND OTHER SINGERS AT THE LABEL.
THE PRESIDENT IS SMART. THIS WAY, HE DOESN'T HAVE TO HIRE BACKGROUND DANCERS, AND HE'LL GET SOME FEEDBACK FROM A TV AUDIENCE.
WHAT IF WE OUTSHINE YOU GUYS?

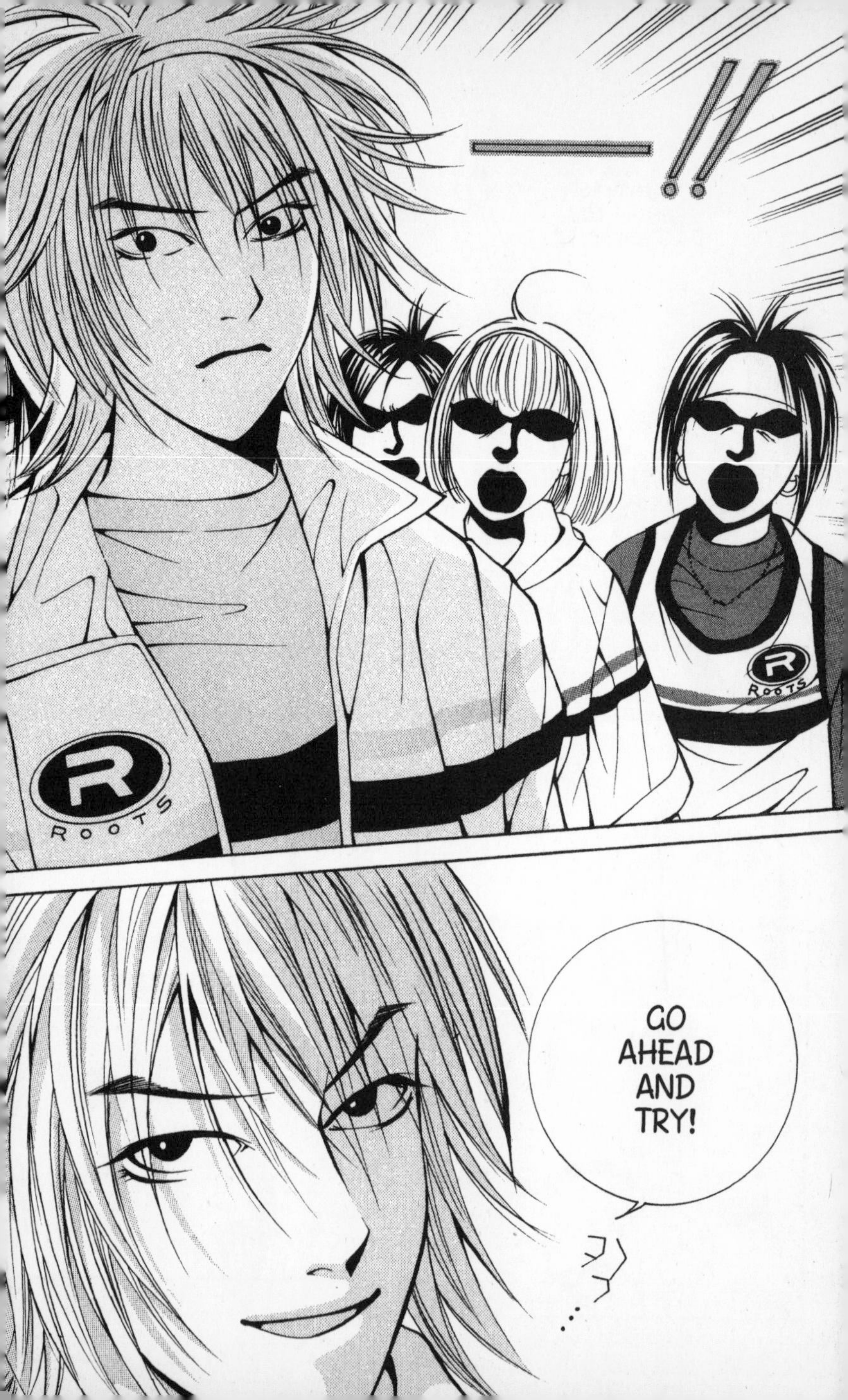
GO AHEAD AND TRY!

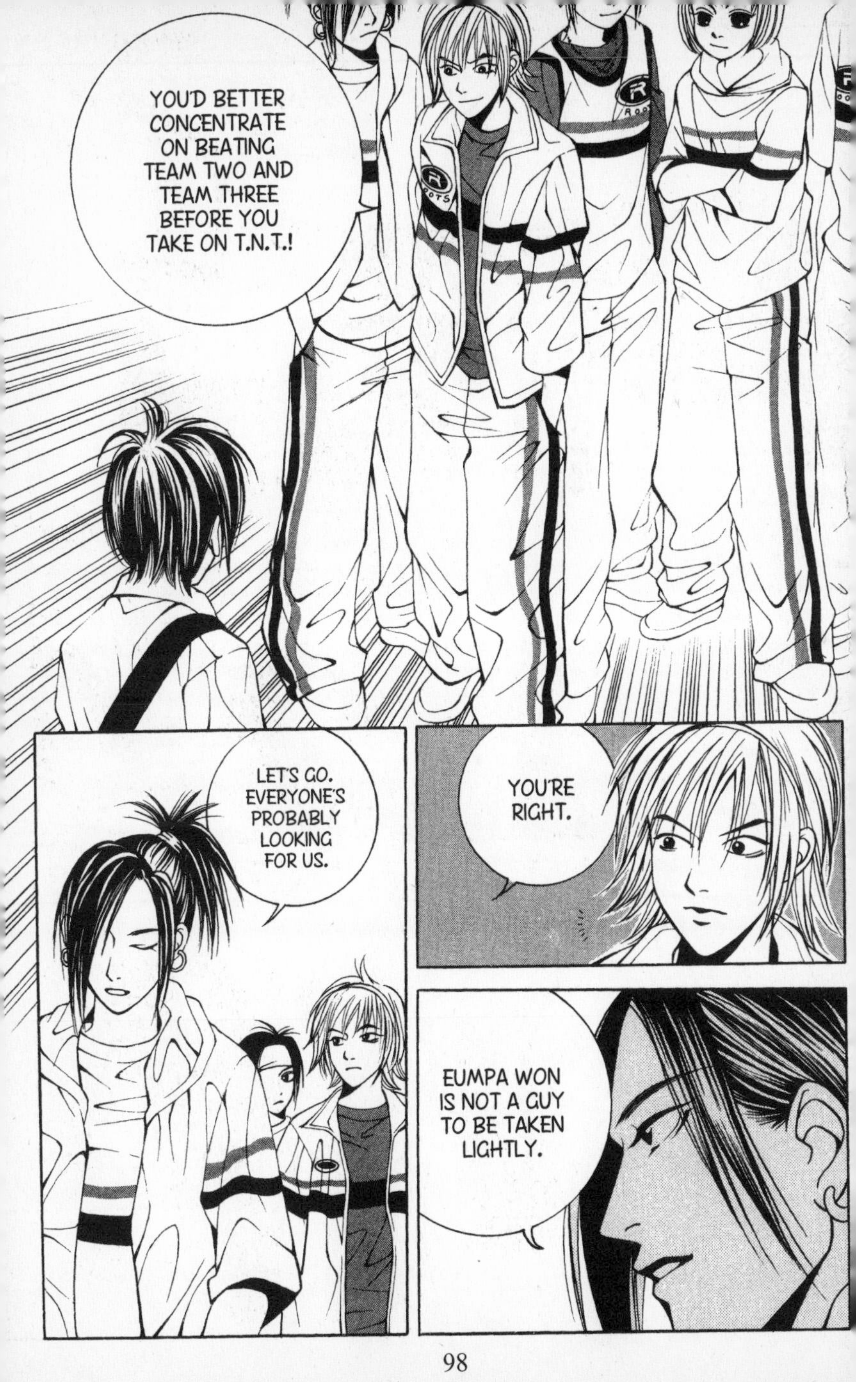
YOU'D BETTER CONCENTRATE ON BEATING TEAM TWO AND TEAM THREE BEFORE YOU TAKE ON T.N.T.!
LET'S GO. EVERYONE'S PROBABLY LOOKING FOR US.
YOU'RE RIGHT.
EUMPA WON IS NOT A GUY TO BE TAKEN LIGHTLY.

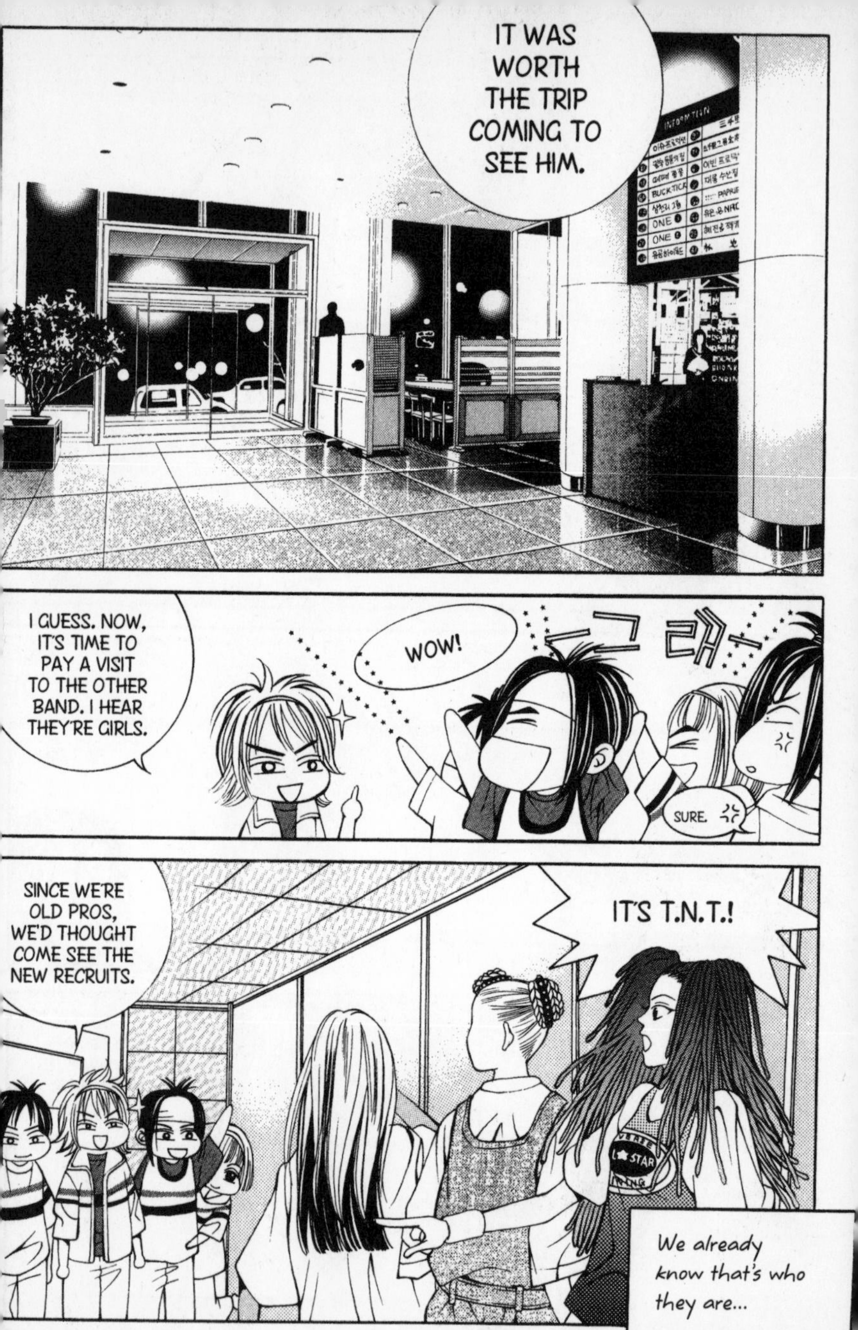
IT WAS WORTH THE TRIP COMING TO SEE HIM.
I GUESS. NOW, IT'S TIME TO PAY A VISIT TO THE OTHER BAND. I HEAR THEY'RE GIRLS.
WOW!
그래~
SURE.
SINCE WE'RE OLD PROS, WE'D THOUGHT COME SEE THE NEW RECRUITS.
IT'S T.N.T.!
We already know that's who they are...

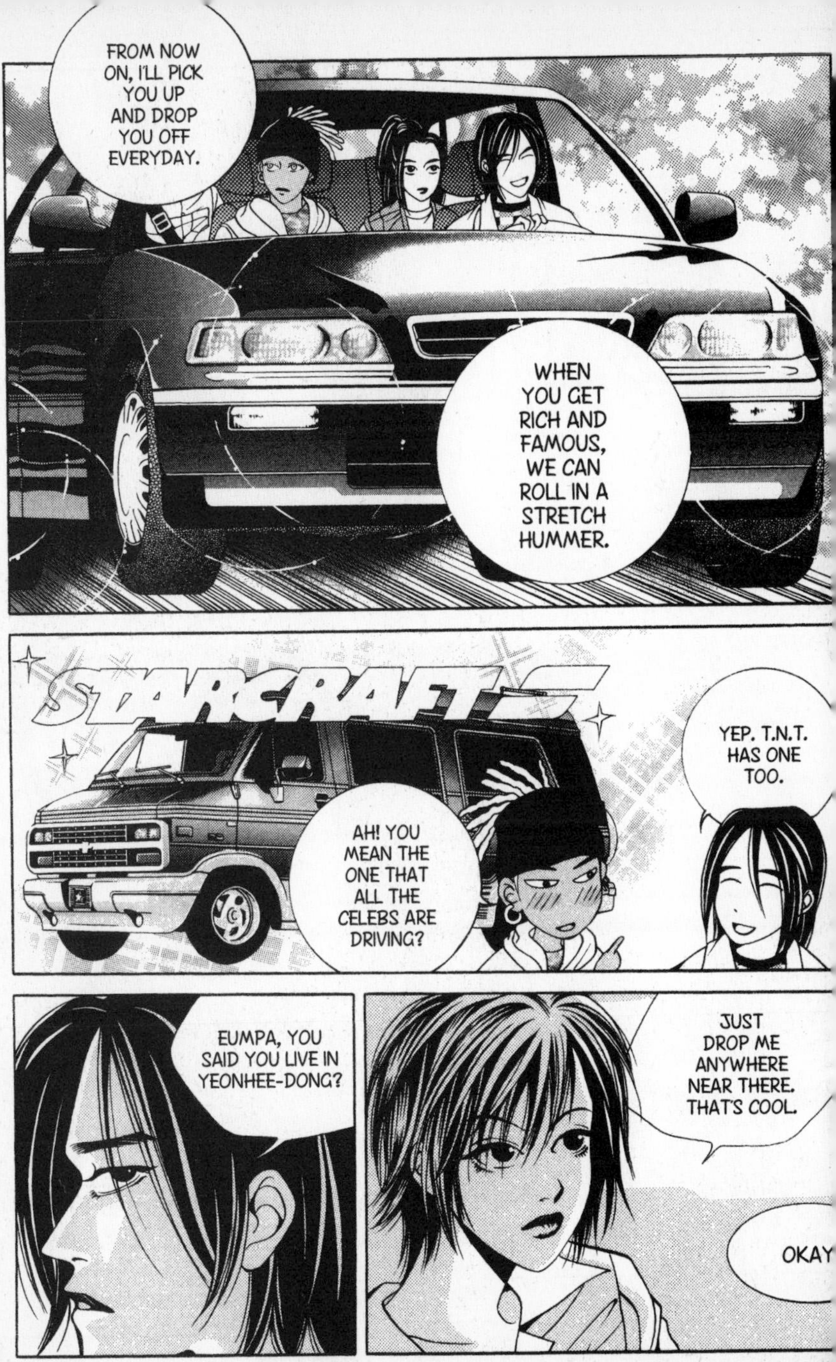
FROM NOW ON, I'LL PICK YOU UP AND DROP YOU OFF EVERYDAY.
WHEN YOU GET RICH AND FAMOUS, WE CAN ROLL IN A STRETCH HUMMER.
STARCRAFT'S
AH! YOU MEAN THE ONE THAT ALL THE CELEBS ARE DRIVING?
YEP. T.N.T. HAS ONE TOO.
EUMPA, YOU SAID YOU LIVE IN YEONHEE-DONG?
JUST DROP ME ANYWHERE NEAR THERE. THAT'S COOL.
OKAY

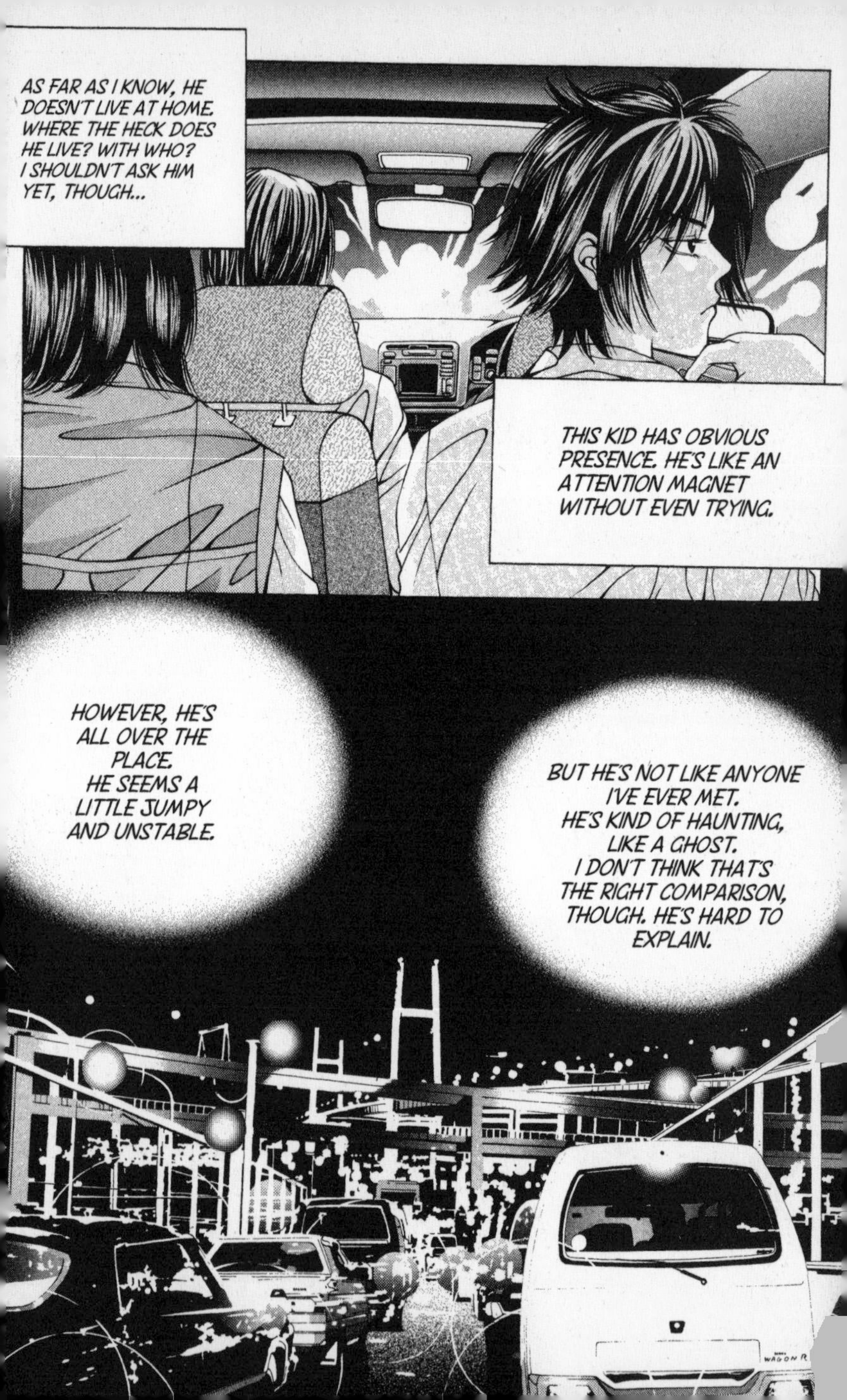
AS FAR AS I KNOW, HE DOESN'T LIVE AT HOME. WHERE THE HECK DOES HE LIVE? WITH WHO? I SHOULDN'T ASK HIM YET, THOUGH...
THIS KID HAS OBVIOUS PRESENCE. HE'S LIKE AN ATTENTION MAGNET WITHOUT EVEN TRYING.
HOWEVER, HE'S ALL OVER THE PLACE. HE SEEMS A LITTLE JUMPY AND UNSTABLE.
BUT HE'S NOT LIKE ANYONE I'VE EVER MET. HE'S KIND OF HAUNTING, LIKE A GHOST. I DON'T THINK THAT'S THE RIGHT COMPARISON, THOUGH. HE'S HARD TO EXPLAIN.
WAGON R

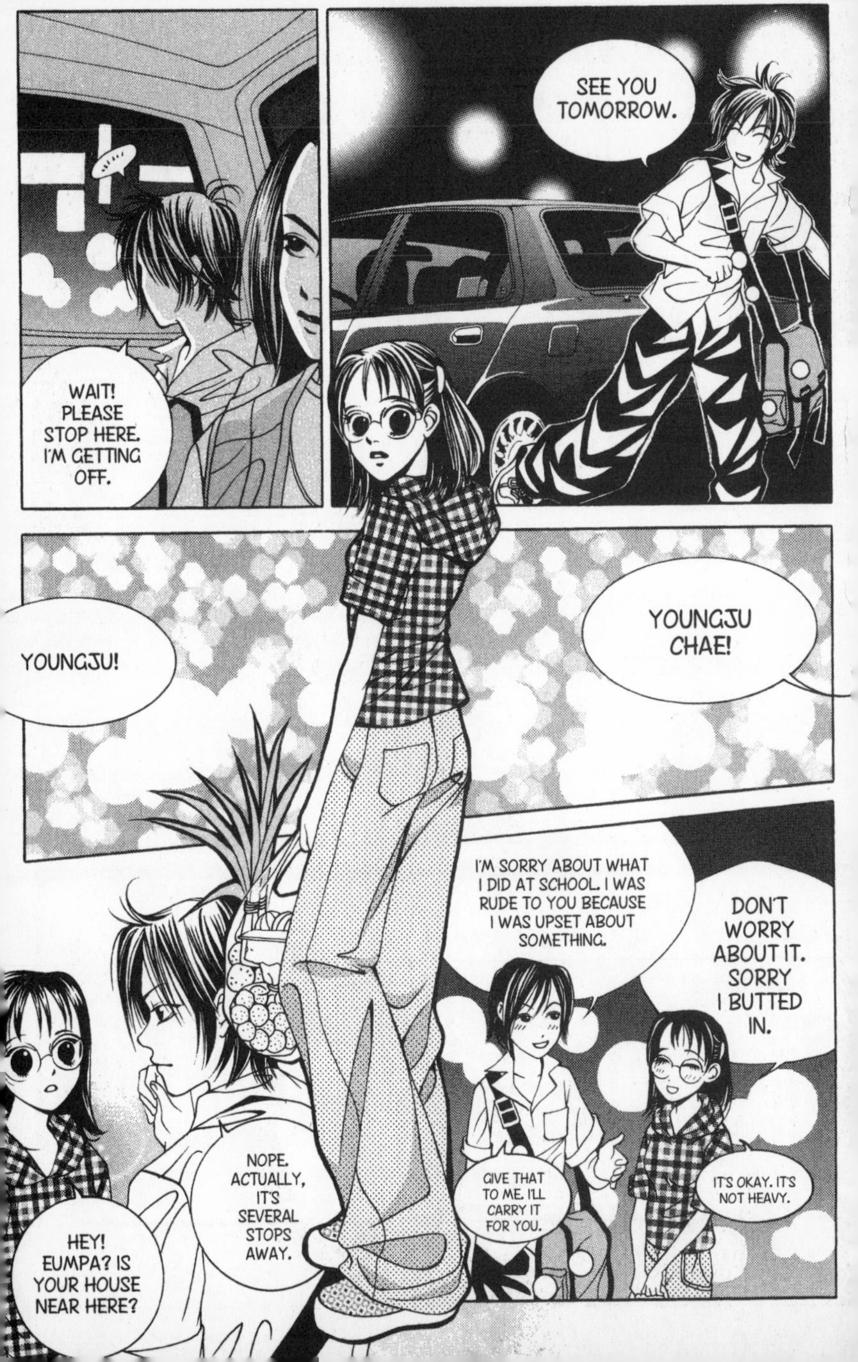
WAIT! PLEASE STOP HERE. I'M GETTING OFF.
SEE YOU TOMORROW.
YOUNGJU!
YOUNGJU CHAE!
HEY! EUMPA? IS YOUR HOUSE NEAR HERE?
NOPE. ACTUALLY, IT'S SEVERAL STOPS AWAY.
I'M SORRY ABOUT WHAT I DID AT SCHOOL. I WAS RUDE TO YOU BECAUSE I WAS UPSET ABOUT SOMETHING.
DON'T WORRY ABOUT IT. SORRY I BUTTED IN.
GIVE THAT TO ME. I'LL CARRY IT FOR YOU.
IT'S OKAY. IT'S NOT HEAVY.

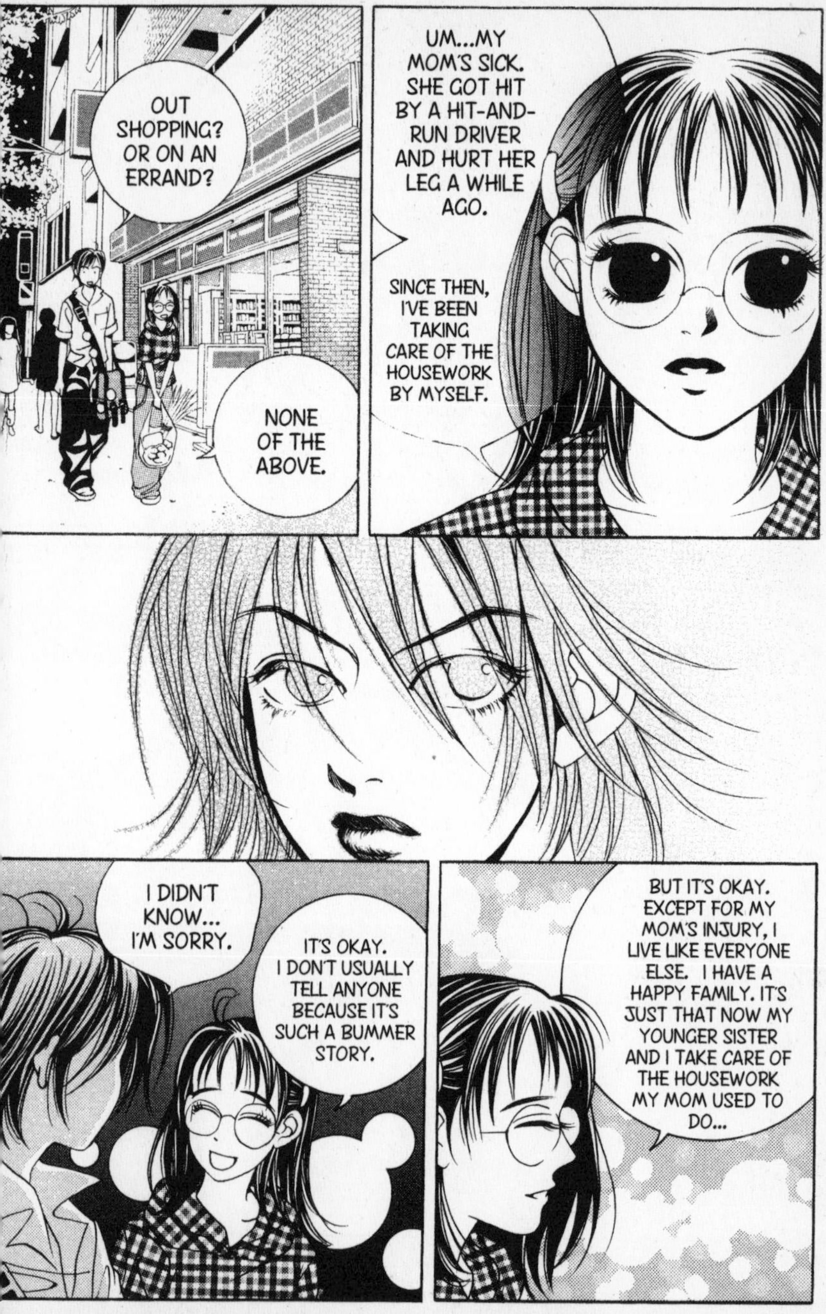
OUT SHOPPING? OR ON AN ERRAND?
NONE OF THE ABOVE.
UM...MY MOM'S SICK. SHE GOT HIT BY A HIT-AND-RUN DRIVER AND HURT HER LEG A WHILE AGO.
SINCE THEN, I'VE BEEN TAKING CARE OF THE HOUSEWORK BY MYSELF.
I DIDN'T KNOW... I'M SORRY.
IT'S OKAY. I DON'T USUALLY TELL ANYONE BECAUSE IT'S SUCH A BUMMER STORY.
BUT IT'S OKAY. EXCEPT FOR MY MOM'S INJURY, I LIVE LIKE EVERYONE ELSE. I HAVE A HAPPY FAMILY. IT'S JUST THAT NOW MY YOUNGER SISTER AND I TAKE CARE OF THE HOUSEWORK MY MOM USED TO DO...

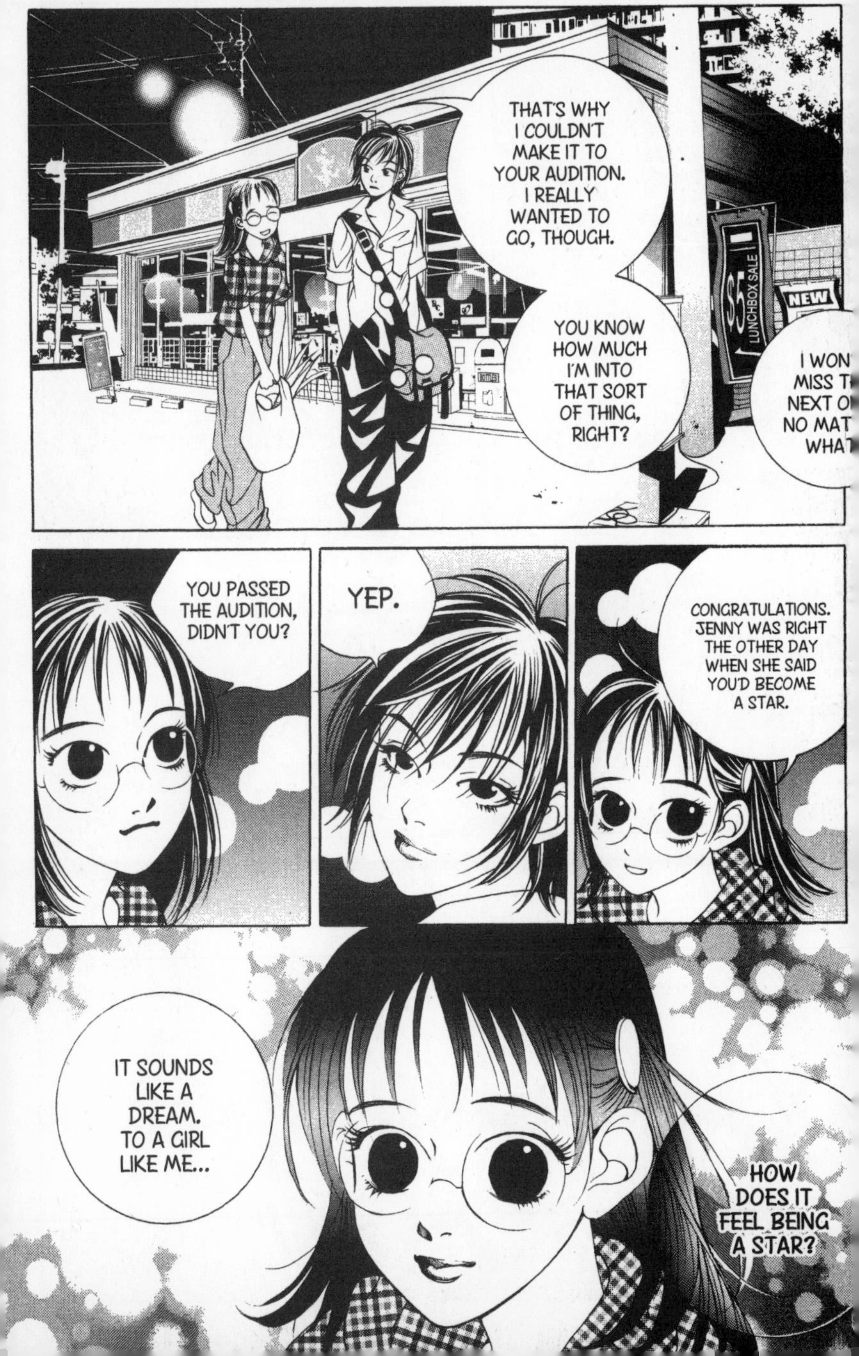
THAT'S WHY I COULDN'T MAKE IT TO YOUR AUDITION. I REALLY WANTED TO GO, THOUGH.
YOU KNOW HOW MUCH I'M INTO THAT SORT OF THING, RIGHT?
I WON MISS T NEXT O NO MAT WHAT
YOU PASSED THE AUDITION, DIDN'T YOU?
YEP.
CONGRATULATIONS. JENNY WAS RIGHT THE OTHER DAY WHEN SHE SAID YOU'D BECOME A STAR.
IT SOUNDS LIKE A DREAM. TO A GIRL LIKE ME...
HOW DOES IT FEEL BEING A STAR?

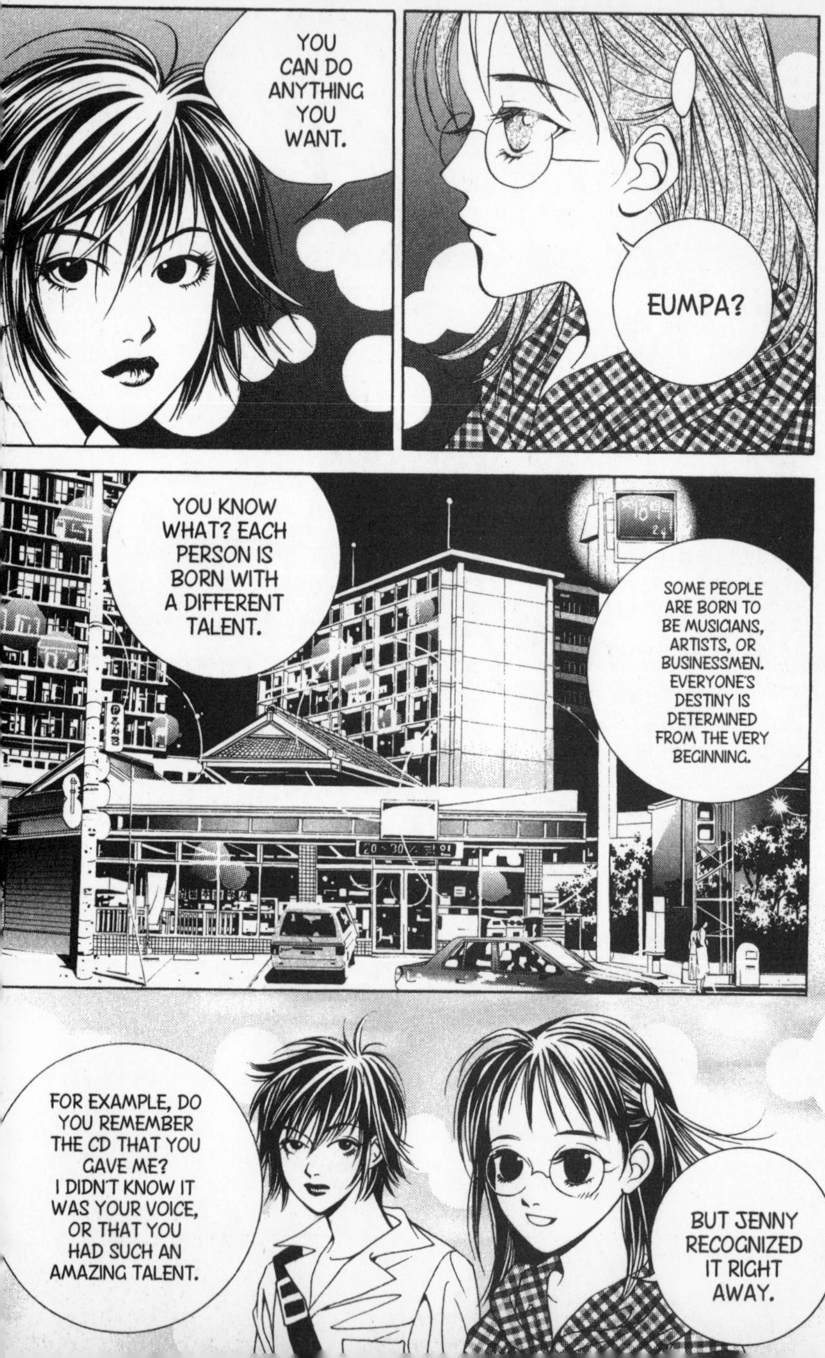
YOU CAN DO ANYTHING YOU WANT.
EUMPA?
YOU KNOW WHAT? EACH PERSON IS BORN WITH A DIFFERENT TALENT.
SOME PEOPLE ARE BORN TO BE MUSICIANS, ARTISTS, OR BUSINESSMEN. EVERYONE'S DESTINY IS DETERMINED FROM THE VERY BEGINNING.
FOR EXAMPLE, DO YOU REMEMBER THE CD THAT YOU GAVE ME? I DIDN'T KNOW IT WAS YOUR VOICE, OR THAT YOU HAD SUCH AN AMAZING TALENT.
BUT JENNY RECOGNIZED IT RIGHT AWAY.

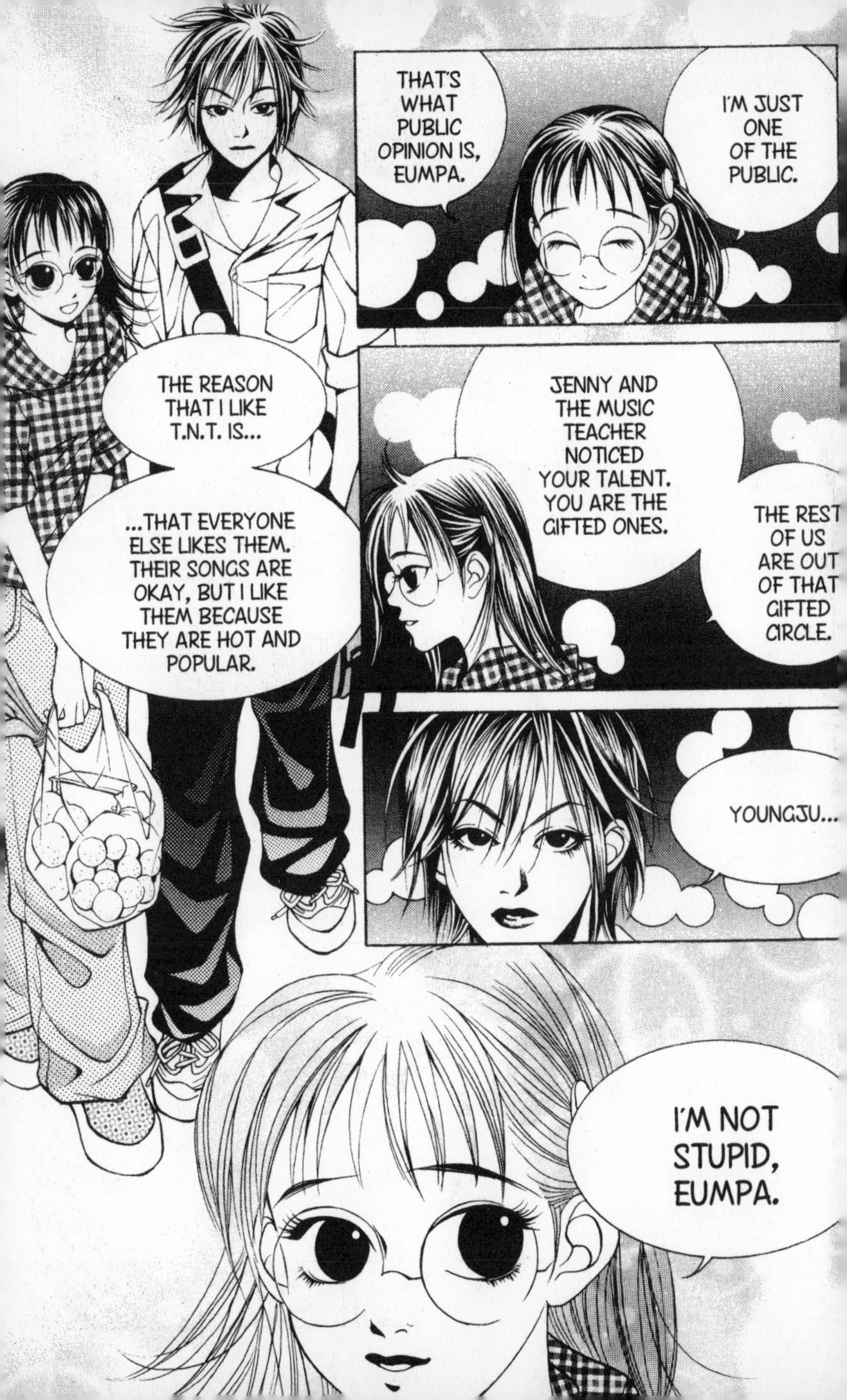
THE REASON THAT I LIKE T.N.T. IS...
...THAT EVERYONE ELSE LIKES THEM. THEIR SONGS ARE OKAY, BUT I LIKE THEM BECAUSE THEY ARE HOT AND POPULAR.
THAT'S WHAT PUBLIC OPINION IS, EUMPA.
I'M JUST ONE OF THE PUBLIC.
JENNY AND THE MUSIC TEACHER NOTICED YOUR TALENT. YOU ARE THE GIFTED ONES.
THE REST OF US ARE OUT OF THAT GIFTED CIRCLE.
YOUNGJU...
I'M NOT STUPID, EUMPA.

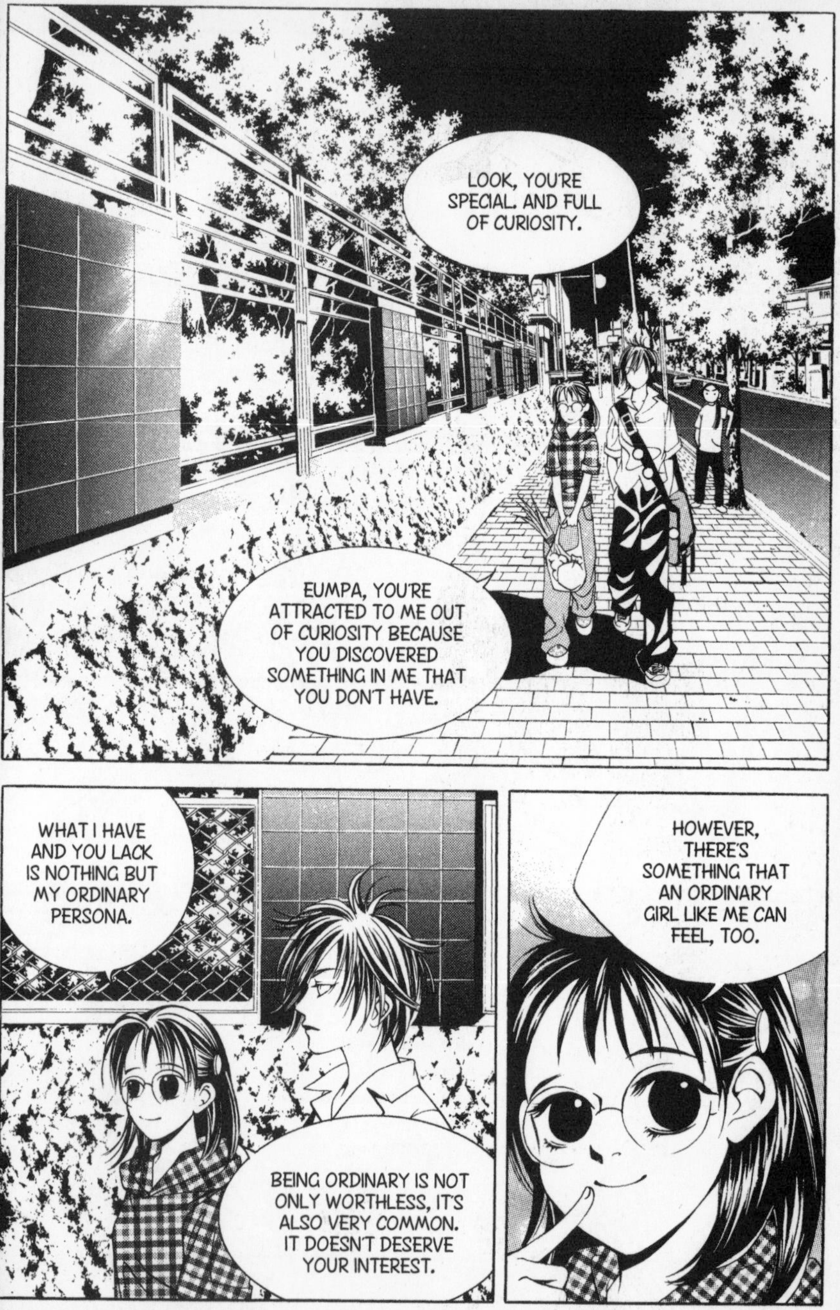
LOOK, YOU'RE SPECIAL. AND FULL OF CURIOSITY.
EUMPA, YOU'RE ATTRACTED TO ME OUT OF CURIOSITY BECAUSE YOU DISCOVERED SOMETHING IN ME THAT YOU DON'T HAVE.
WHAT I HAVE AND YOU LACK IS NOTHING BUT MY ORDINARY PERSONA.
BEING ORDINARY IS NOT ONLY WORTHLESS, IT'S ALSO VERY COMMON. IT DOESN'T DESERVE YOUR INTEREST.
HOWEVER, THERE'S SOMETHING THAT AN ORDINARY GIRL LIKE ME CAN FEEL, TOO.

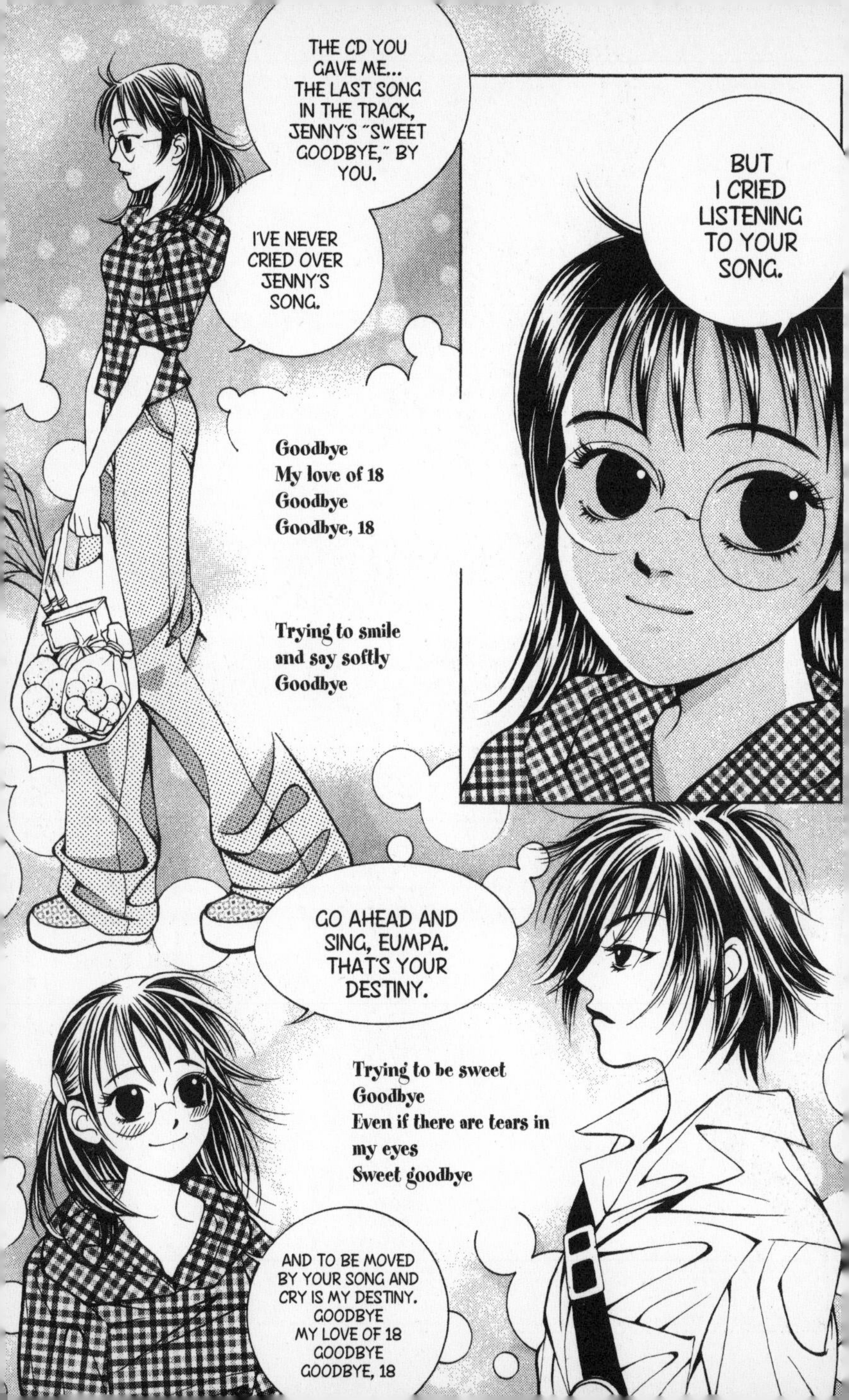
THE CD YOU GAVE ME... THE LAST SONG IN THE TRACK, JENNY'S "SWEET GOODBYE," BY YOU.
I'VE NEVER CRIED OVER JENNY'S SONG.
BUT I CRIED LISTENING TO YOUR SONG.
Goodbye
My love of 18
Goodbye
Goodbye, 18
Trying to smile
and say softly
Goodbye
GO AHEAD AND SING, EUMPA. THAT'S YOUR DESTINY.
Trying to be sweet
Goodbye
Even if there are tears in my eyes
Sweet goodbye
AND TO BE MOVED BY YOUR SONG AND CRY IS MY DESTINY. GOODBYE MY LOVE OF 18 GOODBYE GOODBYE, 18

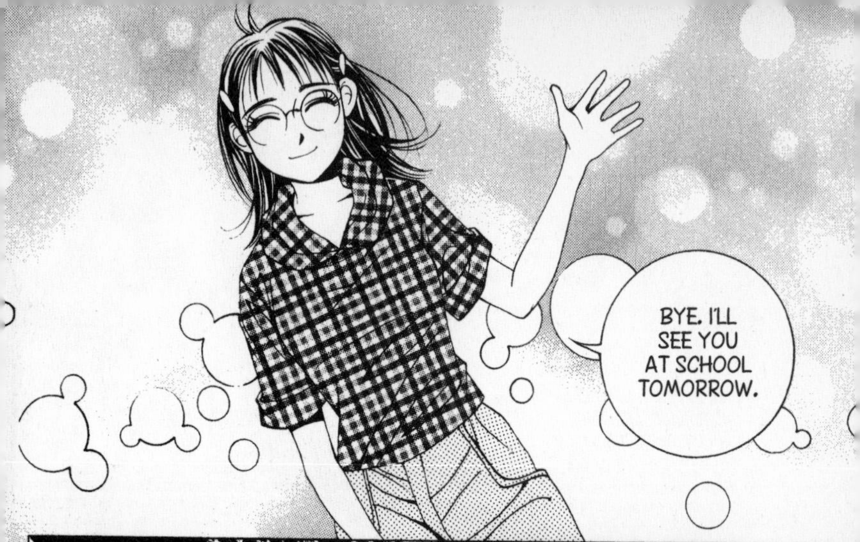
BYE. I'LL SEE YOU AT SCHOOL TOMORROW.

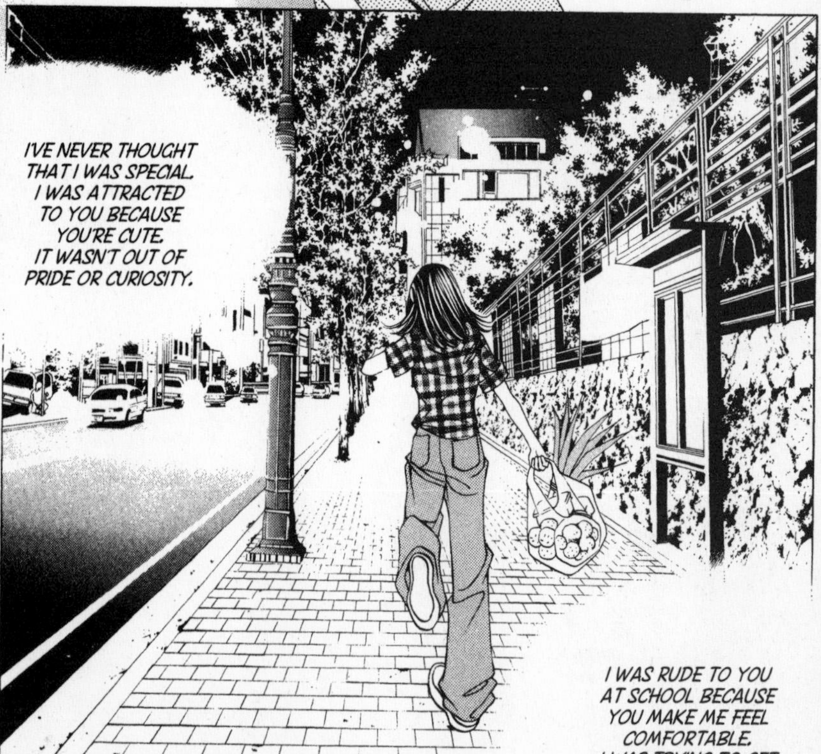
I'VE NEVER THOUGHT THAT I WAS SPECIAL. I WAS ATTRACTED TO YOU BECAUSE YOU'RE CUTE. IT WASN'T OUT OF PRIDE OR CURIOSITY.
I WAS RUDE TO YOU AT SCHOOL BECAUSE YOU MAKE ME FEEL COMFORTABLE. I WAS TRYING TO GET YOUR ATTENTION.

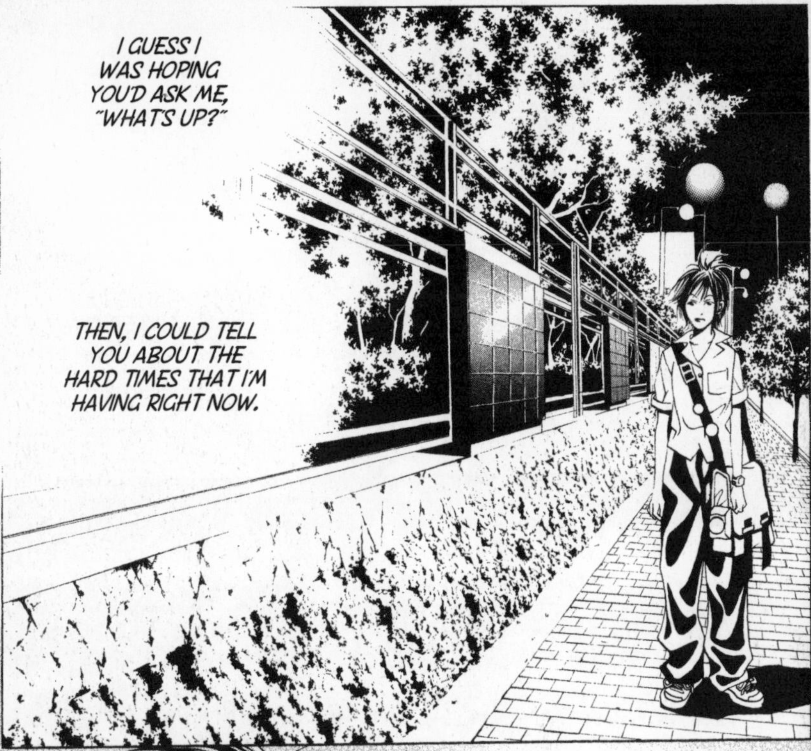
I GUESS I WAS HOPING YOU'D ASK ME, "WHAT'S UP?"
THEN, I COULD TELL YOU ABOUT THE HARD TIMES THAT I'M HAVING RIGHT NOW.

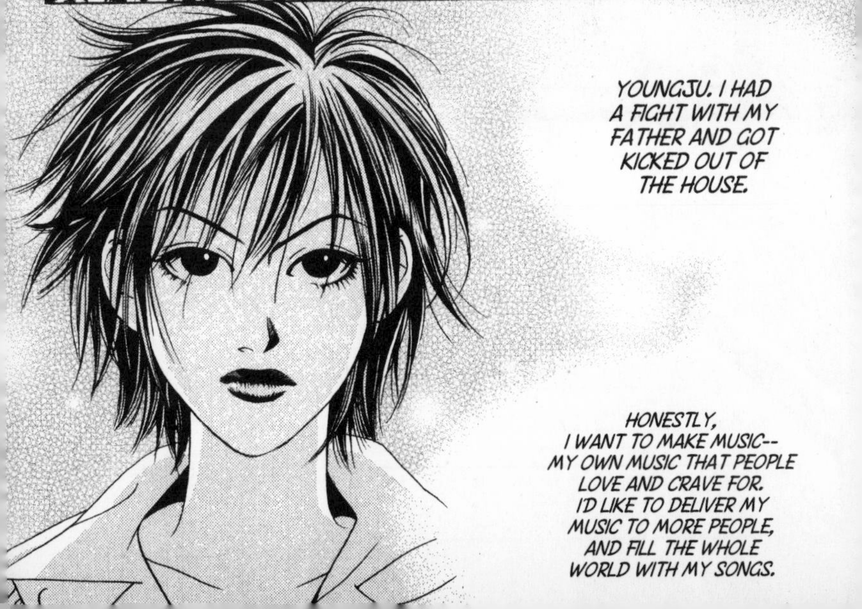
YOUNGJU. I HAD A FIGHT WITH MY FATHER AND GOT KICKED OUT OF THE HOUSE.
HONESTLY, I WANT TO MAKE MUSIC-- MY OWN MUSIC THAT PEOPLE LOVE AND CRAVE FOR. I'D LIKE TO DELIVER MY MUSIC TO MORE PEOPLE, AND FILL THE WHOLE WORLD WITH MY SONGS.

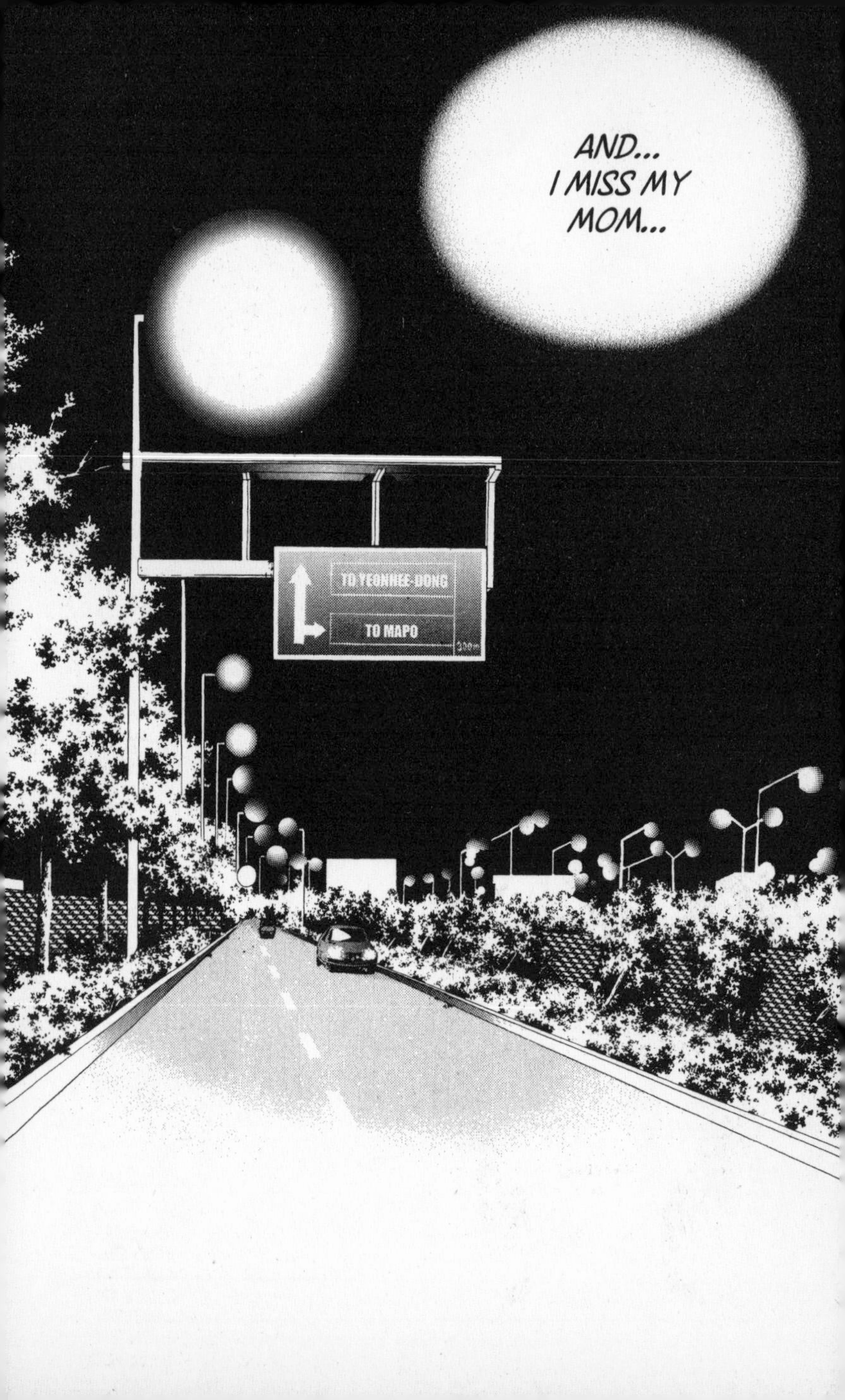
AND... I MISS MY MOM...
TO YEONHEE-DONG
TO MAPO

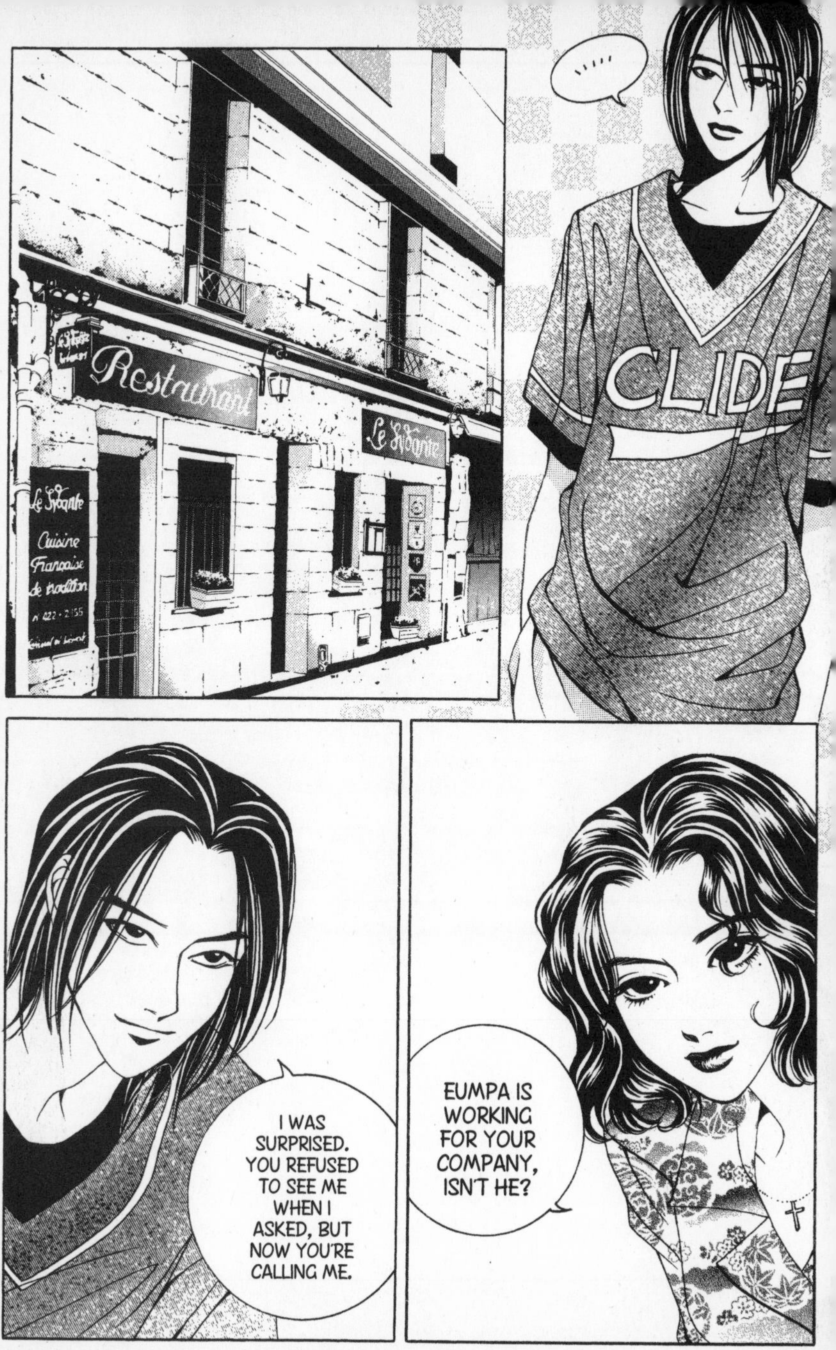
Restaurant
Cuisine Française de tradition
....
CLIDE
I WAS SURPRISED. YOU REFUSED TO SEE ME WHEN I ASKED, BUT NOW YOU'RE CALLING ME.
EUMPA IS WORKING FOR YOUR COMPANY, ISN'T HE?

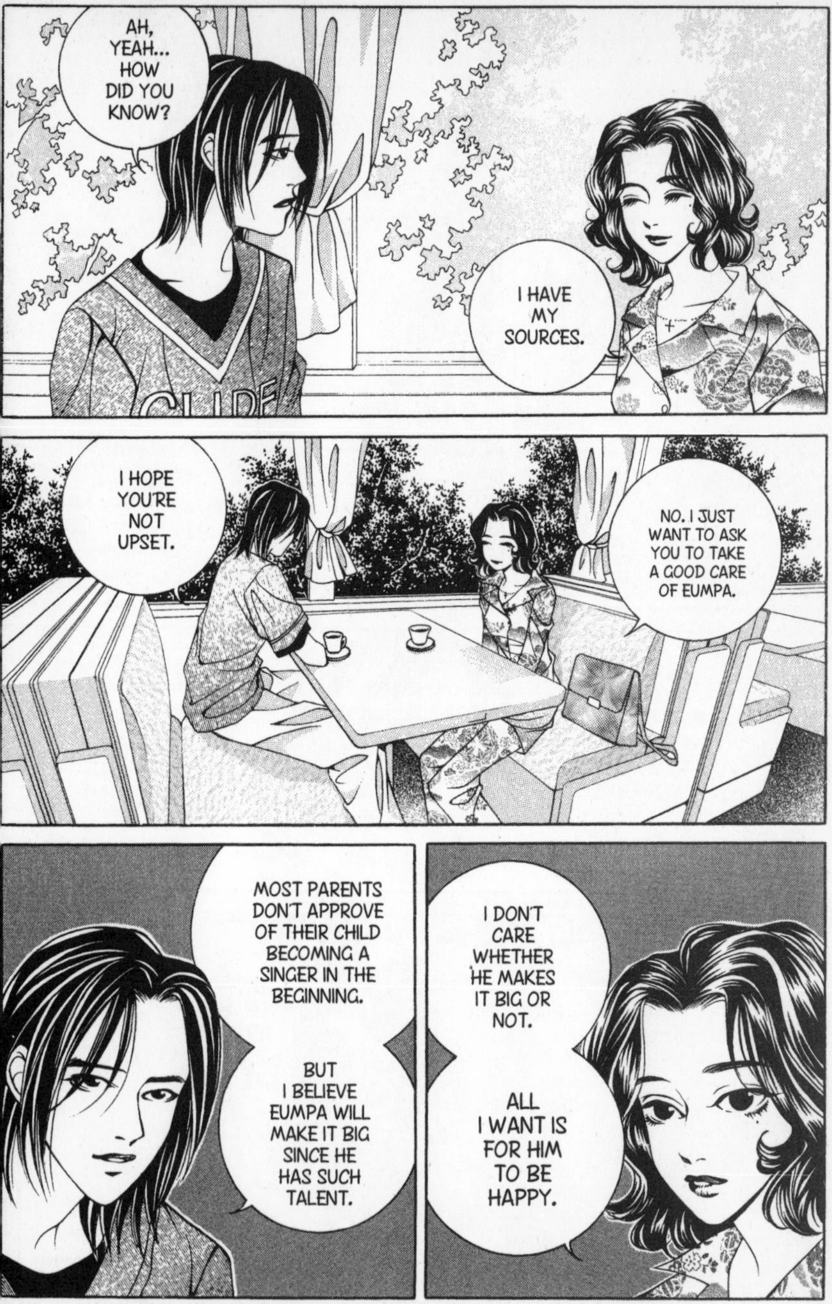
AH, YEAH... HOW DID YOU KNOW?
I HAVE MY SOURCES.
I HOPE YOU'RE NOT UPSET.
NO. I JUST WANT TO ASK YOU TO TAKE A GOOD CARE OF EUMPA.
MOST PARENTS DON'T APPROVE OF THEIR CHILD BECOMING A SINGER IN THE BEGINNING.
BUT I BELIEVE EUMPA WILL MAKE IT BIG SINCE HE HAS SUCH TALENT.
I DON'T CARE WHETHER HE MAKES IT BIG OR NOT.
ALL I WANT IS FOR HIM TO BE HAPPY.

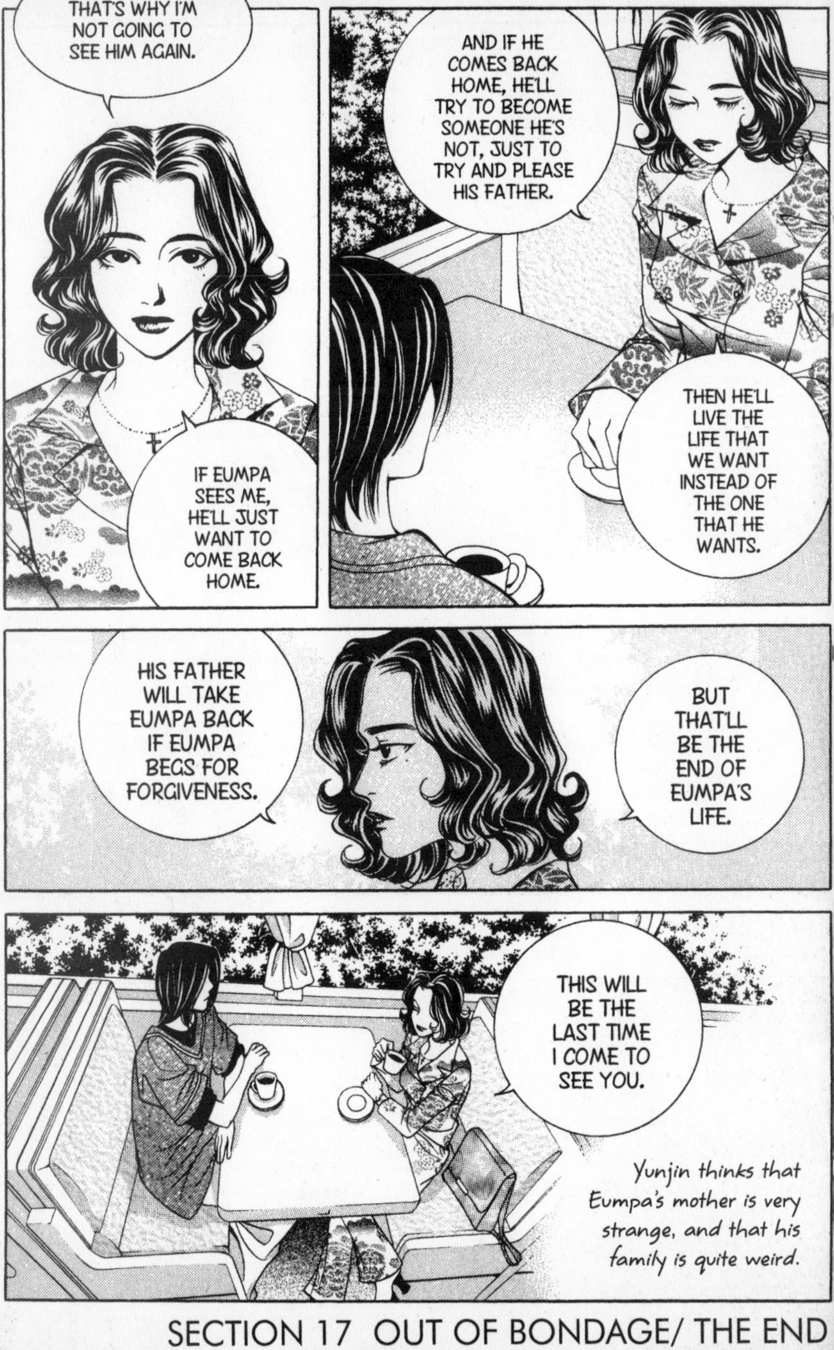
THAT'S WHY I'M NOT GOING TO SEE HIM AGAIN.
IF EUMPA SEES ME, HE'LL JUST WANT TO COME BACK HOME.
AND IF HE COMES BACK HOME, HE'LL TRY TO BECOME SOMEONE HE'S NOT, JUST TO TRY AND PLEASE HIS FATHER.
THEN HE'LL LIVE THE LIFE THAT WE WANT INSTEAD OF THE ONE THAT HE WANTS.
HIS FATHER WILL TAKE EUMPA BACK IF EUMPA BEGS FOR FORGIVENESS.
BUT THAT'LL BE THE END OF EUMPA'S LIFE.
THIS WILL BE THE LAST TIME I COME TO SEE YOU.
Yunjin thinks that Eumpa's mother is very strange, and that his family is quite weird.

SECTION 17 OUT OF BONDAGE/ THE END

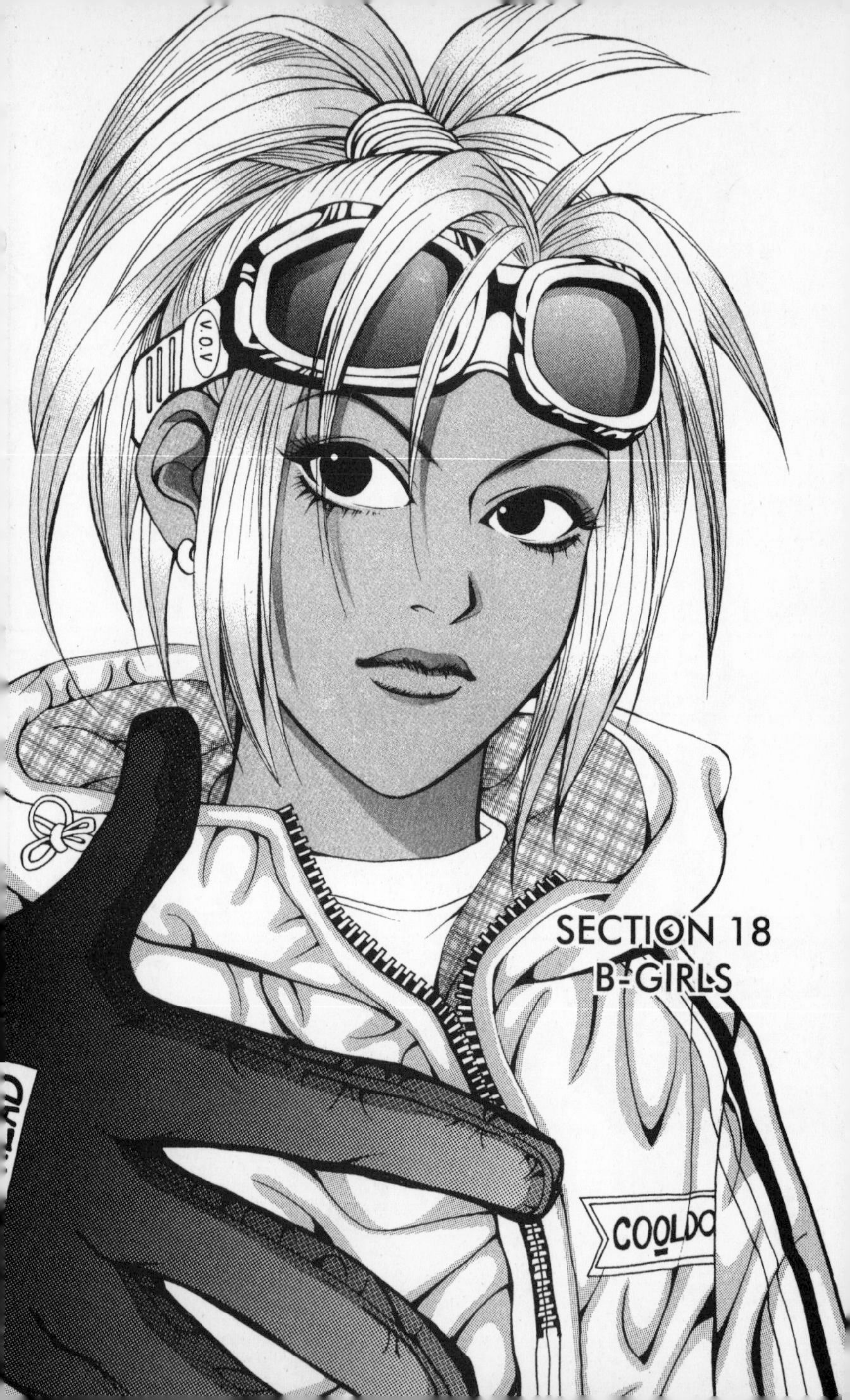
SECTION 18
B-GIRLS
V.O.V
COOLDO

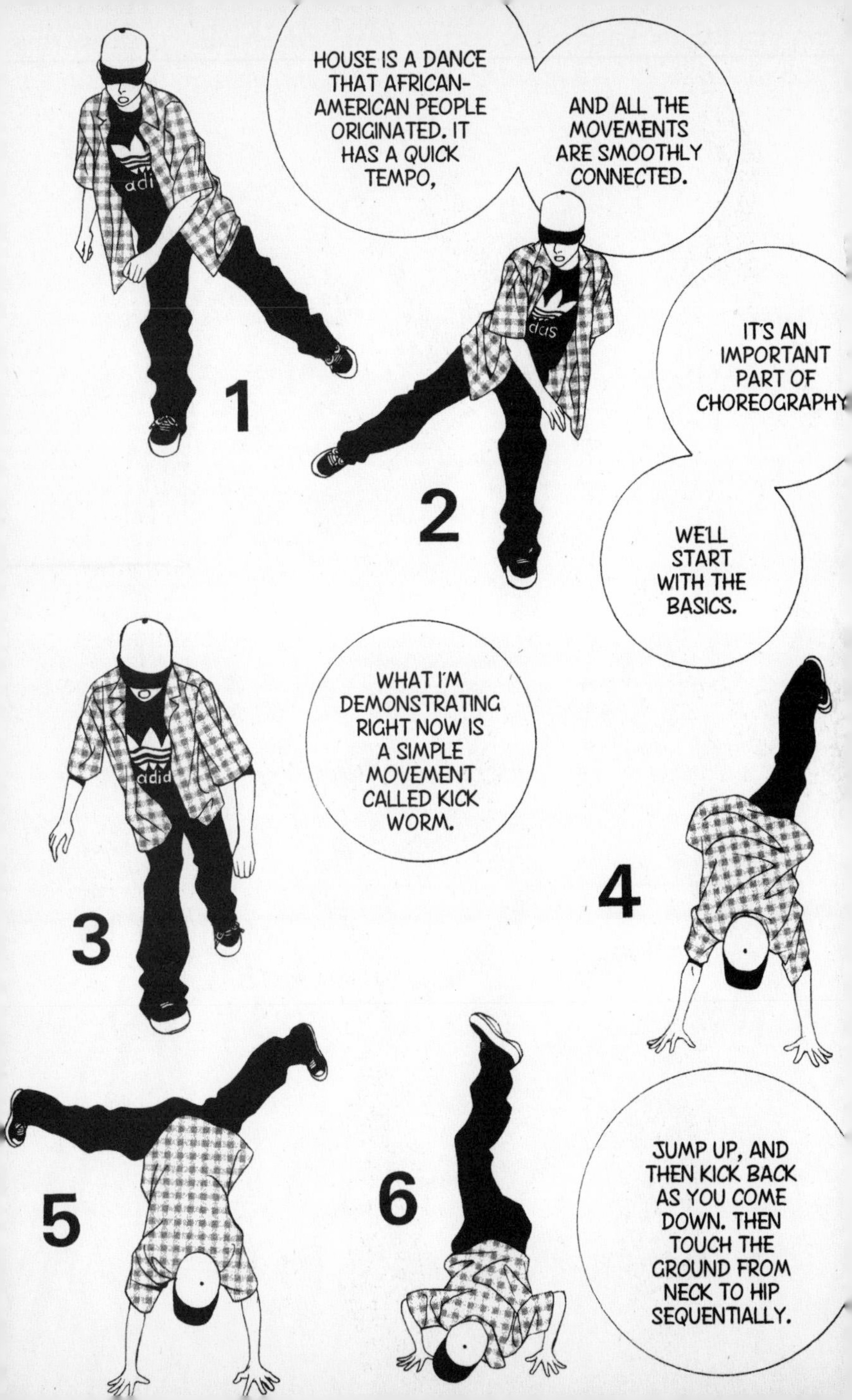
HOUSE IS A DANCE THAT AFRICAN-AMERICAN PEOPLE ORIGINATED. IT HAS A QUICK TEMPO,
AND ALL THE MOVEMENTS ARE SMOOTHLY CONNECTED.
IT'S AN IMPORTANT PART OF CHOREOGRAPHY
WE'LL START WITH THE BASICS.
WHAT I'M DEMONSTRATING RIGHT NOW IS A SIMPLE MOVEMENT CALLED KICK WORM.
JUMP UP, AND THEN KICK BACK AS YOU COME DOWN. THEN TOUCH THE GROUND FROM NECK TO HIP SEQUENTIALLY.
1
2
3
4
5
6

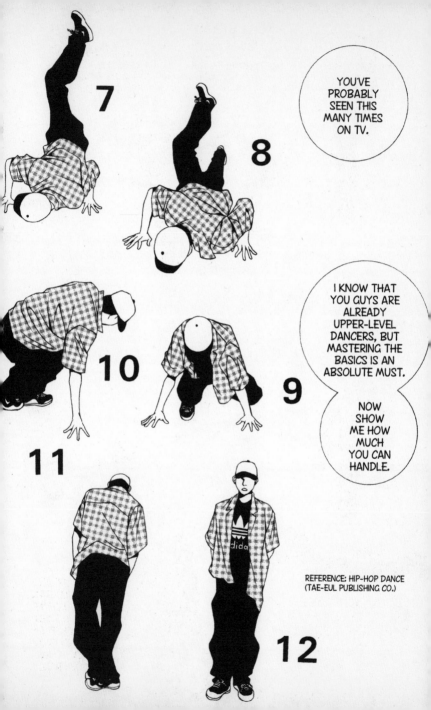

YOU'VE PROBABLY SEEN THIS MANY TIMES ON TV.

I KNOW THAT YOU GUYS ARE ALREADY UPPER-LEVEL DANCERS, BUT MASTERING THE BASICS IS AN ABSOLUTE MUST.

NOW SHOW ME HOW MUCH YOU CAN HANDLE.

REFERENCE: HIP-HOP DANCE
(TAE-EUL PUBLISHING CO.)

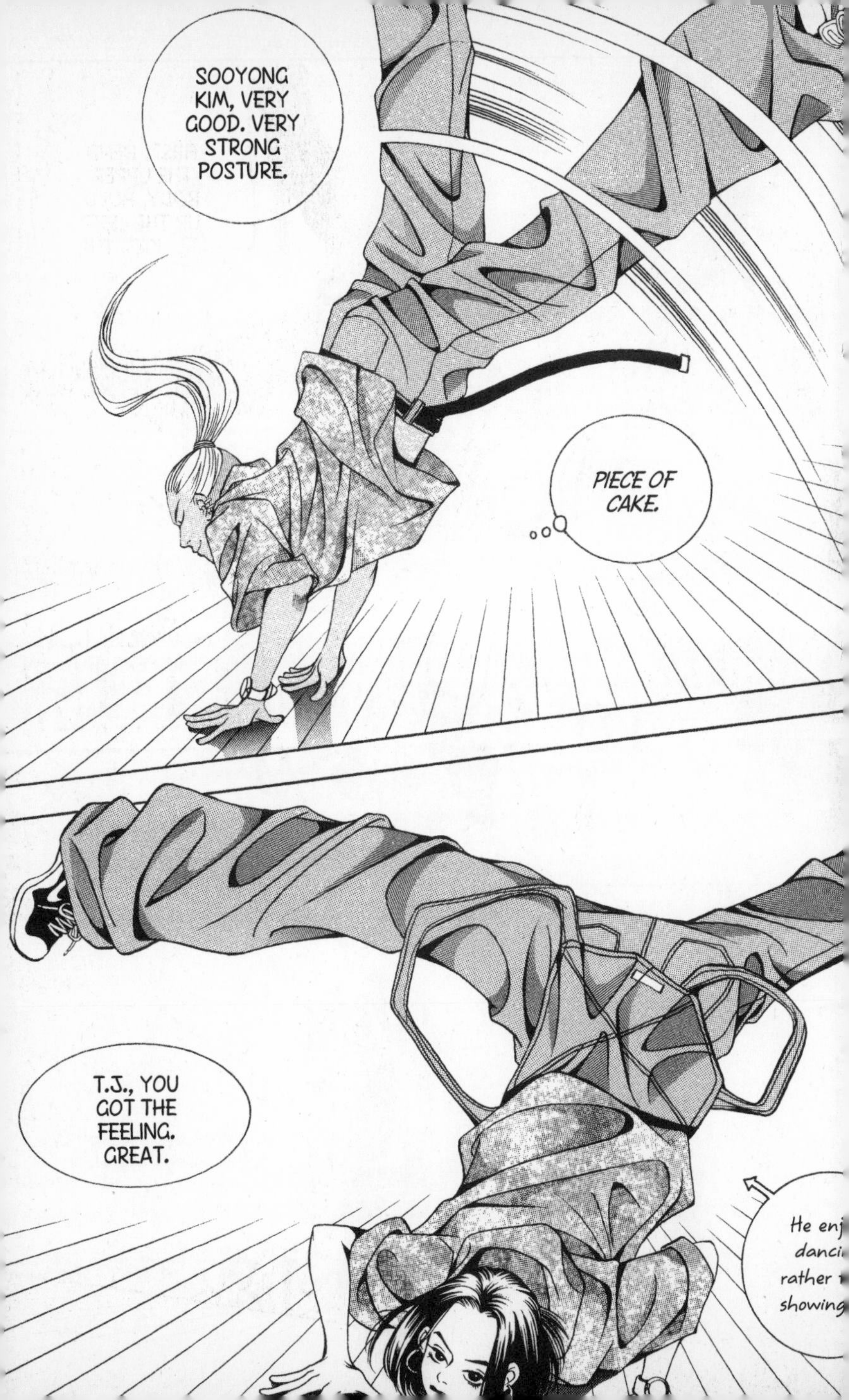
SOOYONG KIM, VERY GOOD. VERY STRONG POSTURE.
PIECE OF CAKE.
T.J., YOU GOT THE FEELING. GREAT.

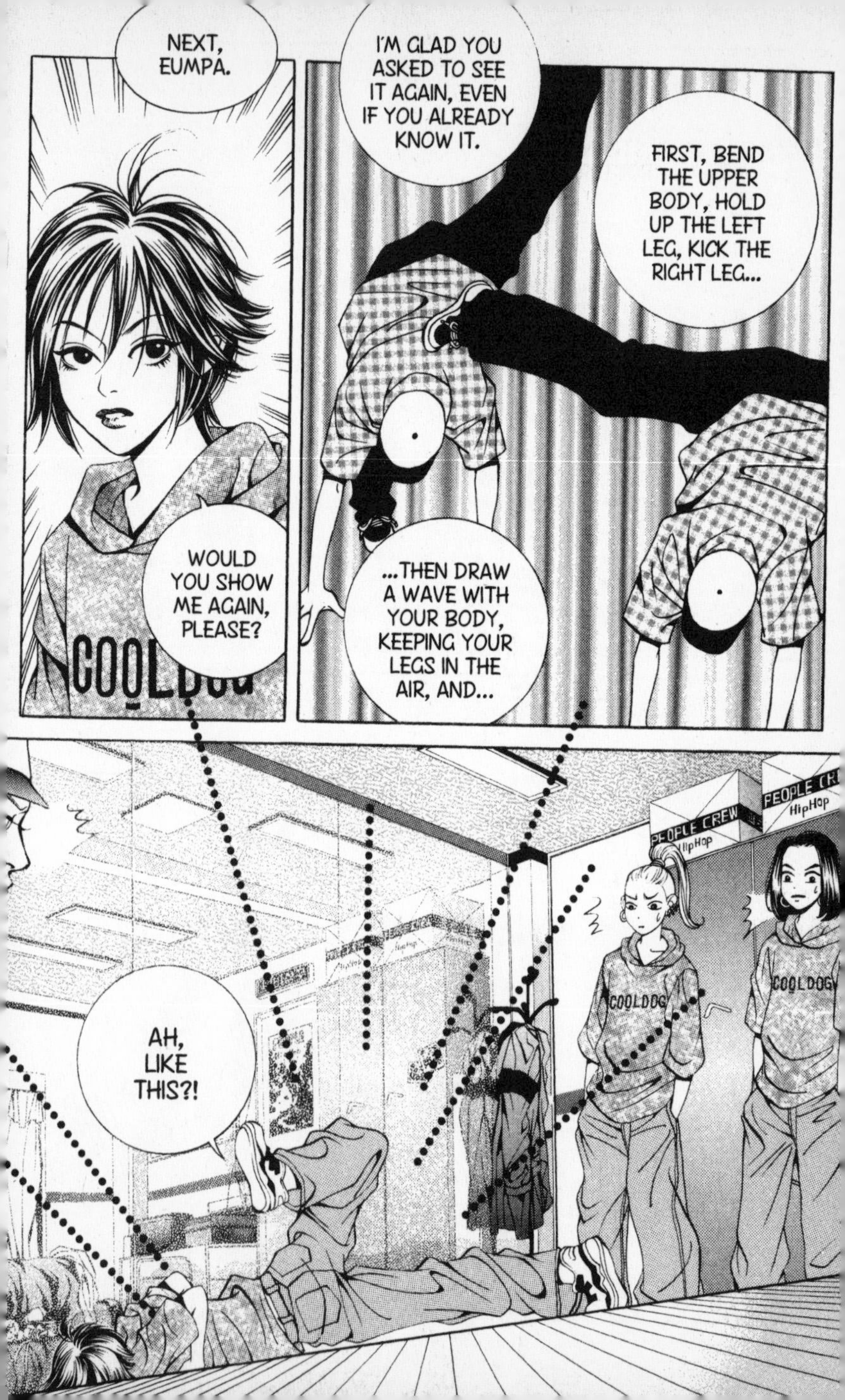
NEXT, EUMPA.
WOULD YOU SHOW ME AGAIN, PLEASE?
COOLDOG
I'M GLAD YOU ASKED TO SEE IT AGAIN, EVEN IF YOU ALREADY KNOW IT.
FIRST, BEND THE UPPER BODY, HOLD UP THE LEFT LEG, KICK THE RIGHT LEG...
...THEN DRAW A WAVE WITH YOUR BODY, KEEPING YOUR LEGS IN THE AIR, AND...
PEOPLE CREW
HipHop
AH, LIKE THIS?!
COOLDOG
COOLDOG

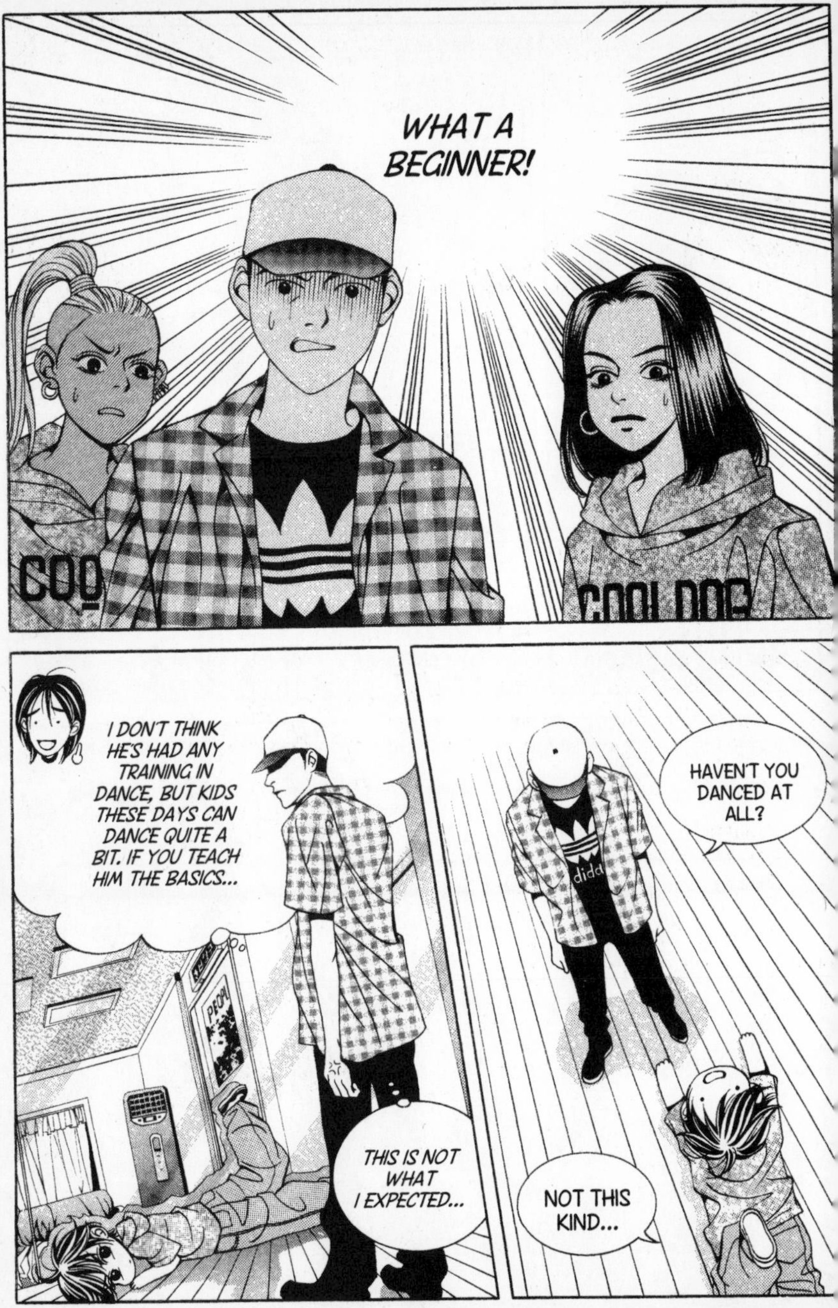
WHAT A BEGINNER!
HAVEN'T YOU DANCED AT ALL?
NOT THIS KIND...
I DON'T THINK HE'S HAD ANY TRAINING IN DANCE, BUT KIDS THESE DAYS CAN DANCE QUITE A BIT. IF YOU TEACH HIM THE BASICS...
THIS IS NOT WHAT I EXPECTED...

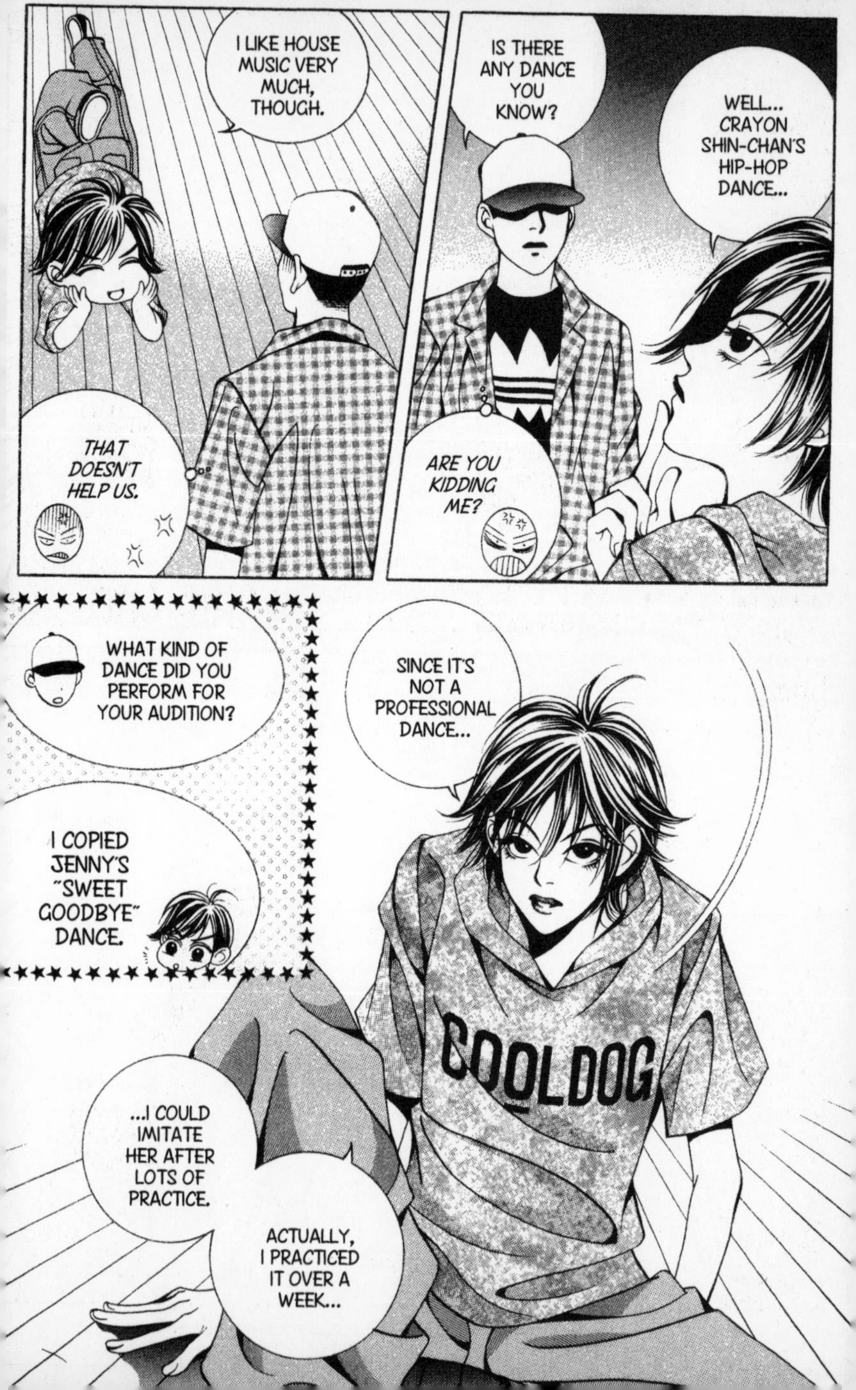
IS THERE ANY DANCE YOU KNOW?
WELL... CRAYON SHIN-CHAN'S HIP-HOP DANCE...
ARE YOU KIDDING ME?
I LIKE HOUSE MUSIC VERY MUCH, THOUGH.
THAT DOESN'T HELP US.
WHAT KIND OF DANCE DID YOU PERFORM FOR YOUR AUDITION?
I COPIED JENNY'S "SWEET GOODBYE" DANCE.
SINCE IT'S NOT A PROFESSIONAL DANCE...
...I COULD IMITATE HER AFTER LOTS OF PRACTICE.
ACTUALLY, I PRACTICED IT OVER A WEEK...
COOLDOG

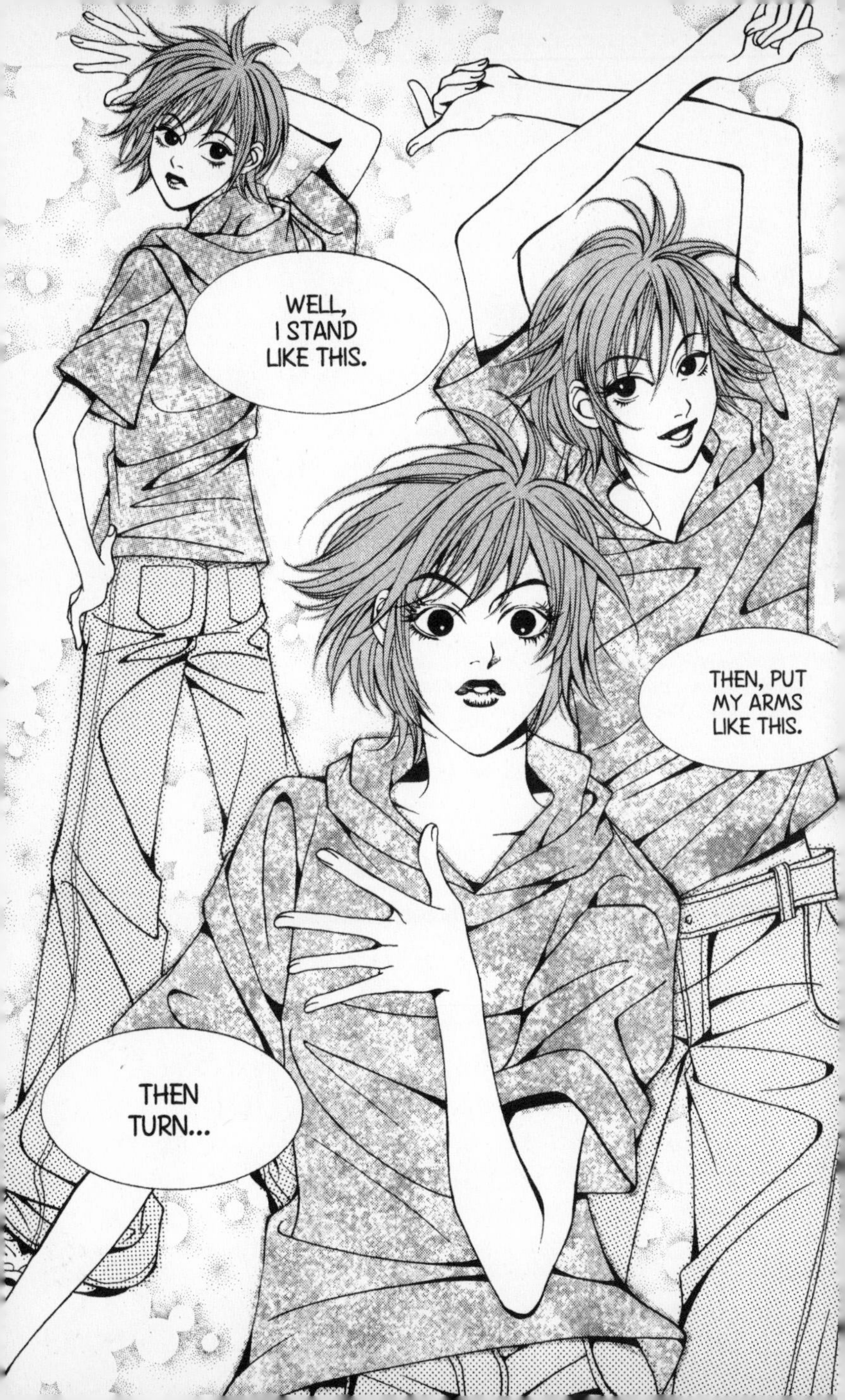
WELL, I STAND LIKE THIS.
THEN, PUT MY ARMS LIKE THIS.
THEN TURN...

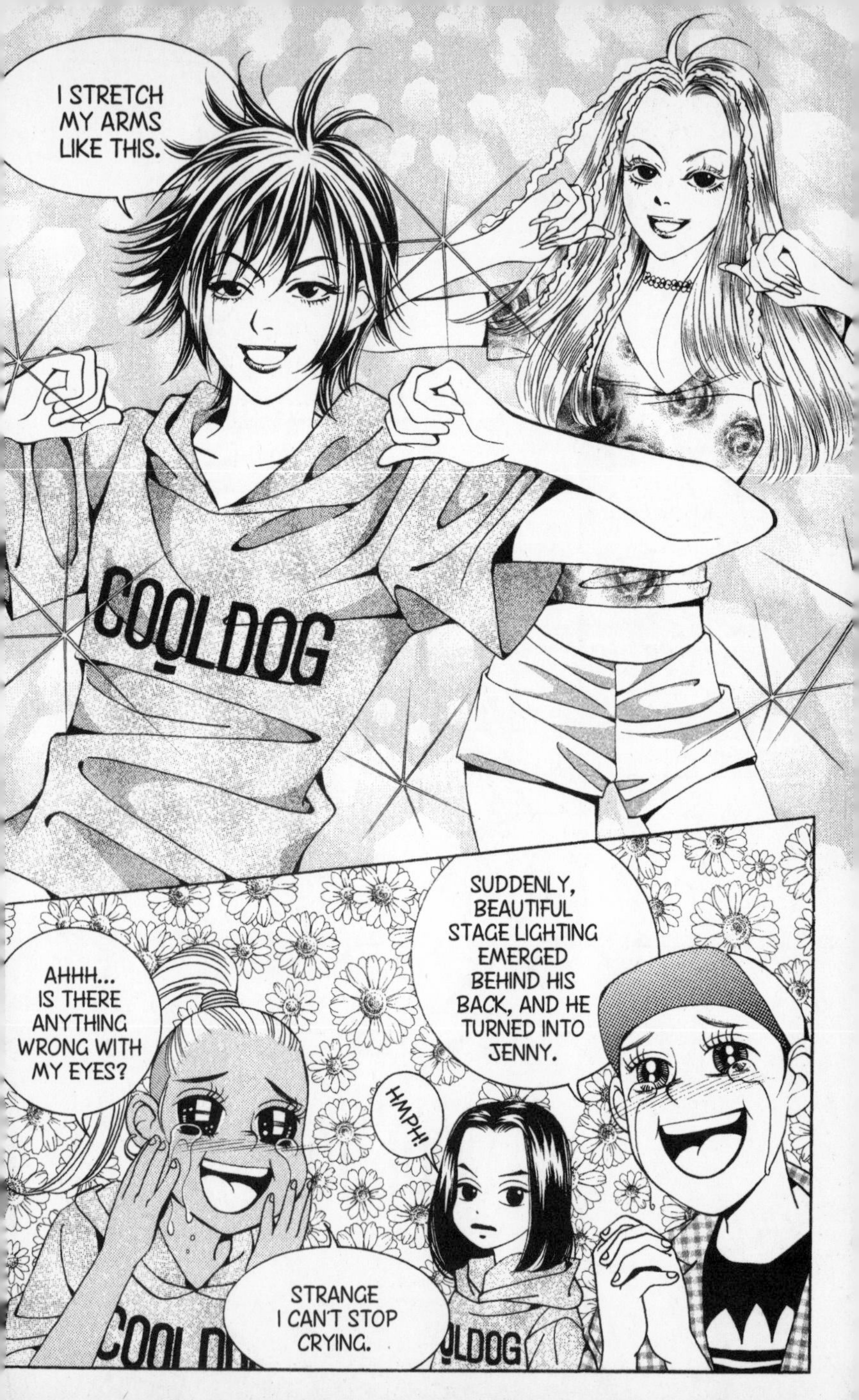
I STRETCH MY ARMS LIKE THIS.
COOLDOG
SUDDENLY, BEAUTIFUL STAGE LIGHTING EMERGED BEHIND HIS BACK, AND HE TURNED INTO JENNY.
HMPH!
AHHH... IS THERE ANYTHING WRONG WITH MY EYES?
STRANGE I CAN'T STOP CRYING.

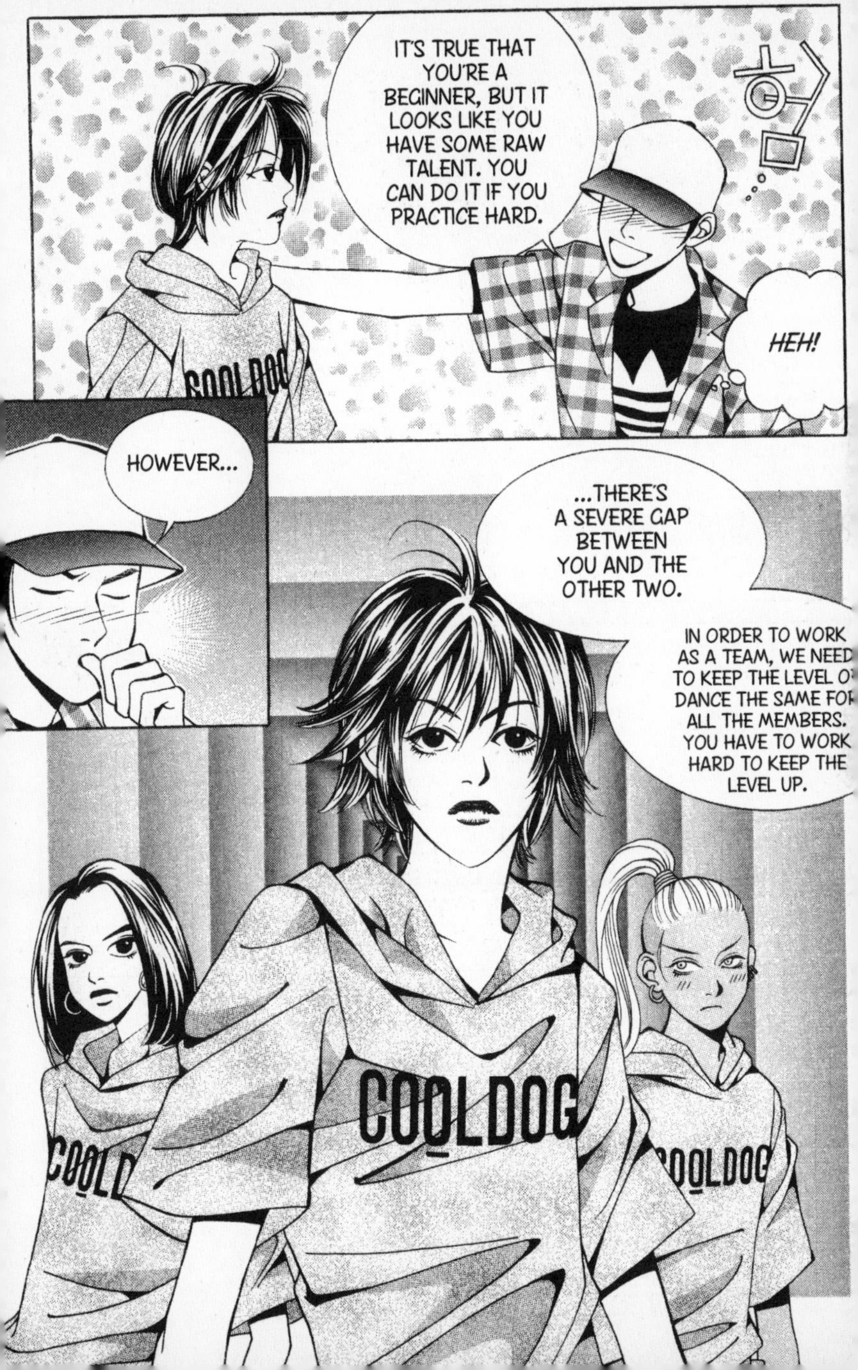
IT'S TRUE THAT YOU'RE A BEGINNER, BUT IT LOOKS LIKE YOU HAVE SOME RAW TALENT. YOU CAN DO IT IF YOU PRACTICE HARD.
HEH!
HOWEVER...
...THERE'S A SEVERE GAP BETWEEN YOU AND THE OTHER TWO.
IN ORDER TO WORK AS A TEAM, WE NEED TO KEEP THE LEVEL OF DANCE THE SAME FOR ALL THE MEMBERS. YOU HAVE TO WORK HARD TO KEEP THE LEVEL UP.
COOLDOG
COOLDOG
COOLDOG
COOLDOG

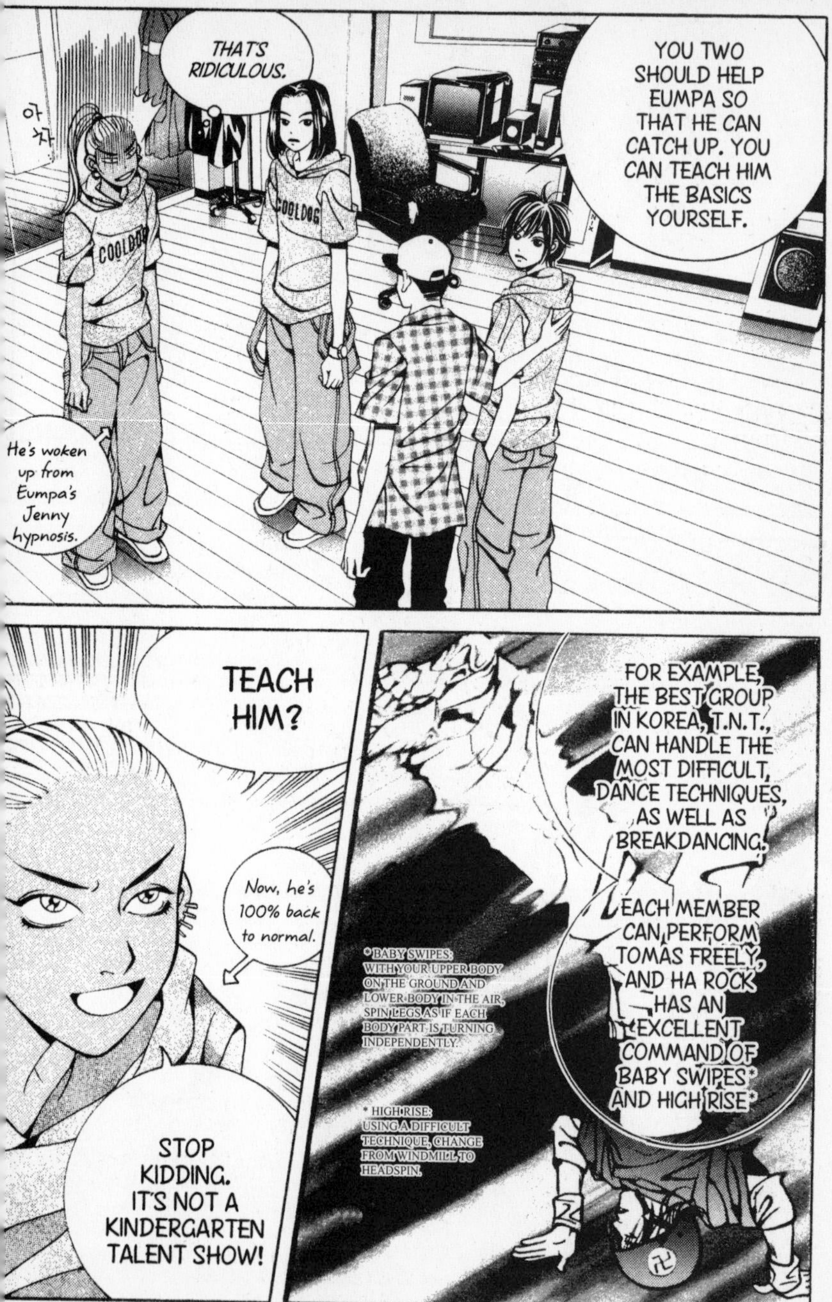

아차
THAT'S RIDICULOUS.
YOU TWO SHOULD HELP EUMPA SO THAT HE CAN CATCH UP. YOU CAN TEACH HIM THE BASICS YOURSELF.
He's woken up from Eumpa's Jenny hypnosis.
TEACH HIM?
Now, he's 100% back to normal.
STOP KIDDING. IT'S NOT A KINDERGARTEN TALENT SHOW!
FOR EXAMPLE, THE BEST GROUP IN KOREA, T.N.T., CAN HANDLE THE MOST DIFFICULT DANCE TECHNIQUES, AS WELL AS BREAKDANCING.
EACH MEMBER CAN PERFORM TOMAS FREELY, AND HA ROCK HAS AN EXCELLENT COMMAND OF BABY SWIPES* AND HIGH RISE*
* BABY SWIPES: WITH YOUR UPPER BODY ON THE GROUND AND LOWER BODY IN THE AIR, SPIN LEGS AS IF EACH BODY PART IS TURNING INDEPENDENTLY.
* HIGH RISE: USING A DIFFICULT TECHNIQUE, CHANGE FROM WINDMILL TO HEADSPIN.

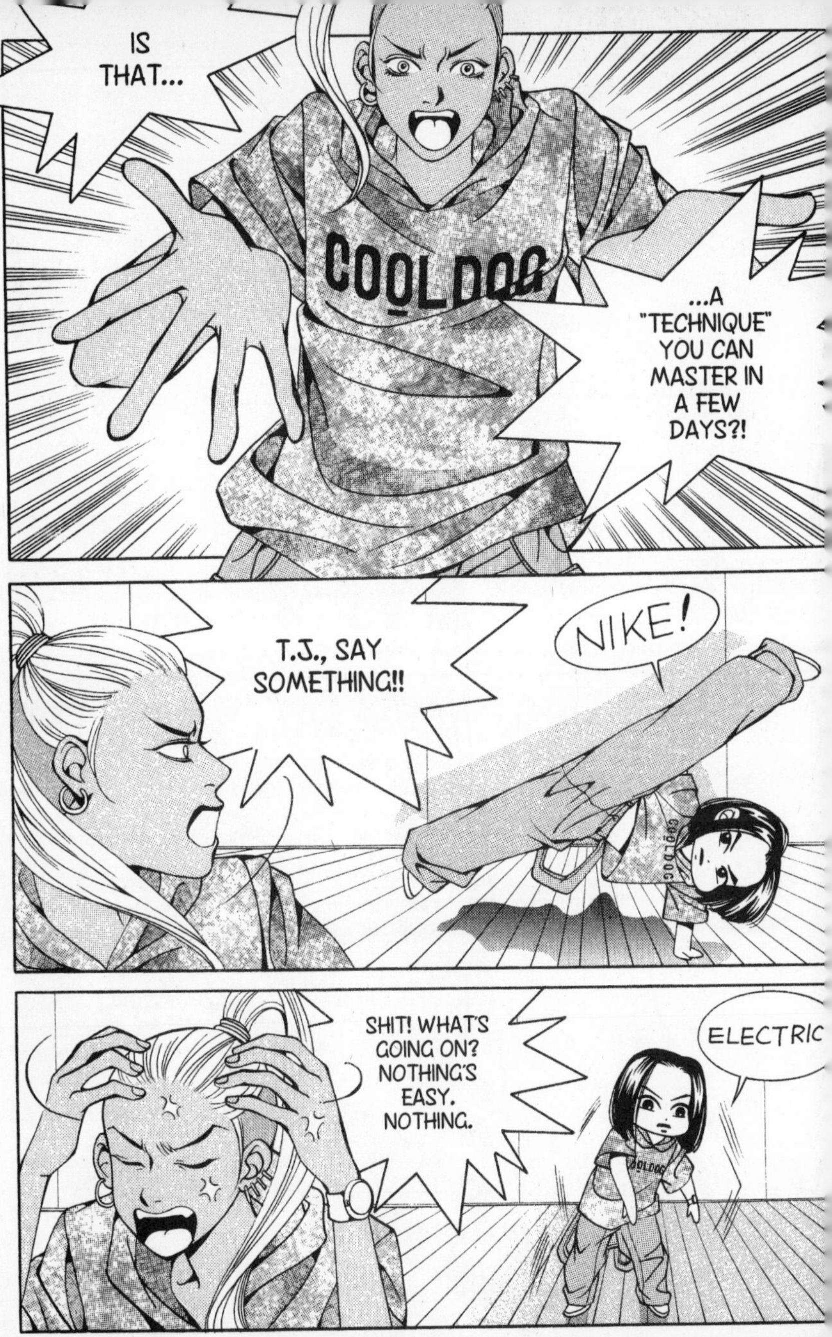
IS THAT...
...A "TECHNIQUE" YOU CAN MASTER IN A FEW DAYS?!
T.J., SAY SOMETHING!!
NIKE!
SHIT! WHAT'S GOING ON? NOTHING'S EASY. NOTHING.
ELECTRIC

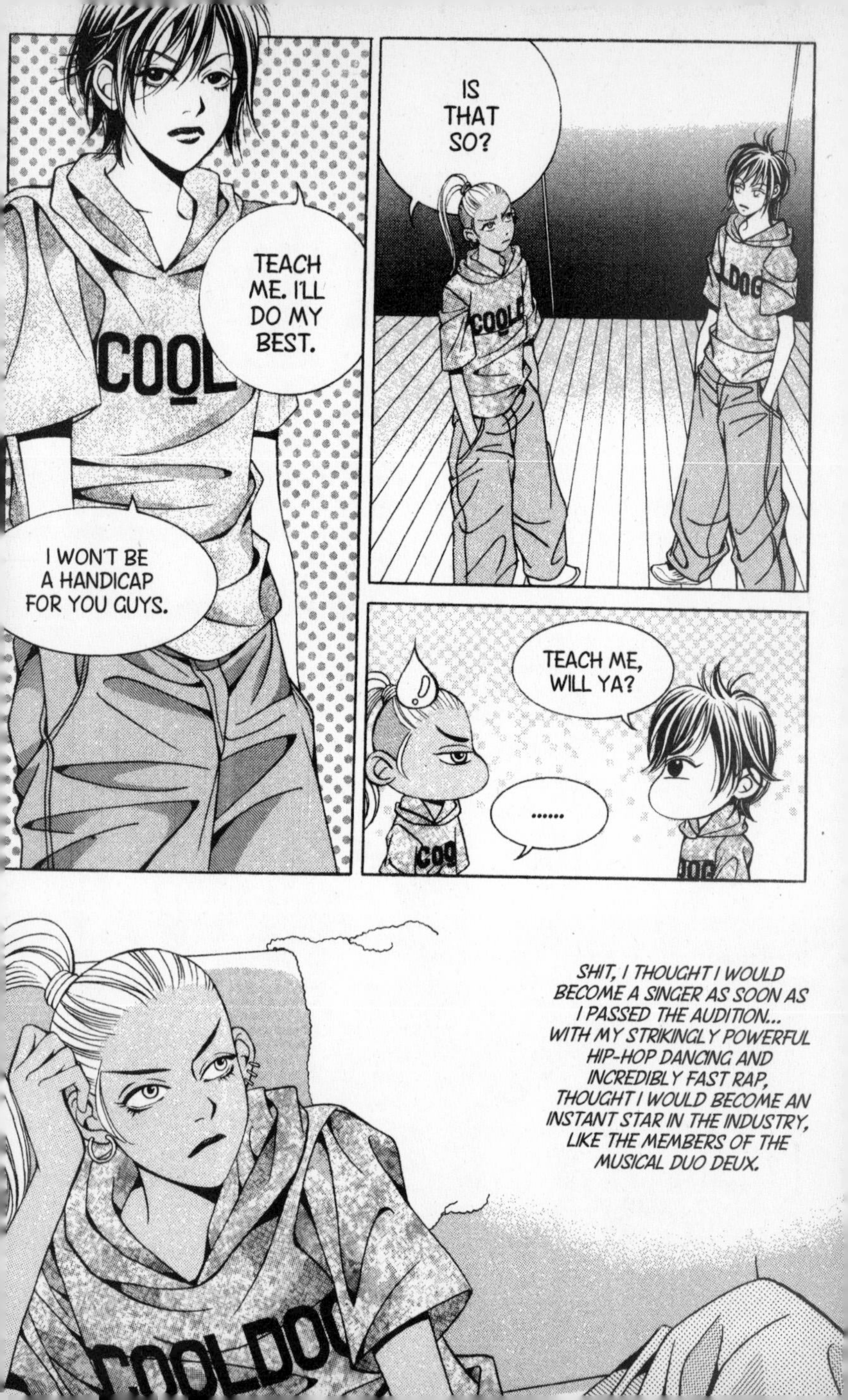
TEACH ME. I'LL DO MY BEST.
I WON'T BE A HANDICAP FOR YOU GUYS.
IS THAT SO?
TEACH ME, WILL YA?
......
SHIT, I THOUGHT I WOULD BECOME A SINGER AS SOON AS I PASSED THE AUDITION... WITH MY STRIKINGLY POWERFUL HIP-HOP DANCING AND INCREDIBLY FAST RAP, THOUGHT I WOULD BECOME AN INSTANT STAR IN THE INDUSTRY, LIKE THE MEMBERS OF THE MUSICAL DUO DEUX.

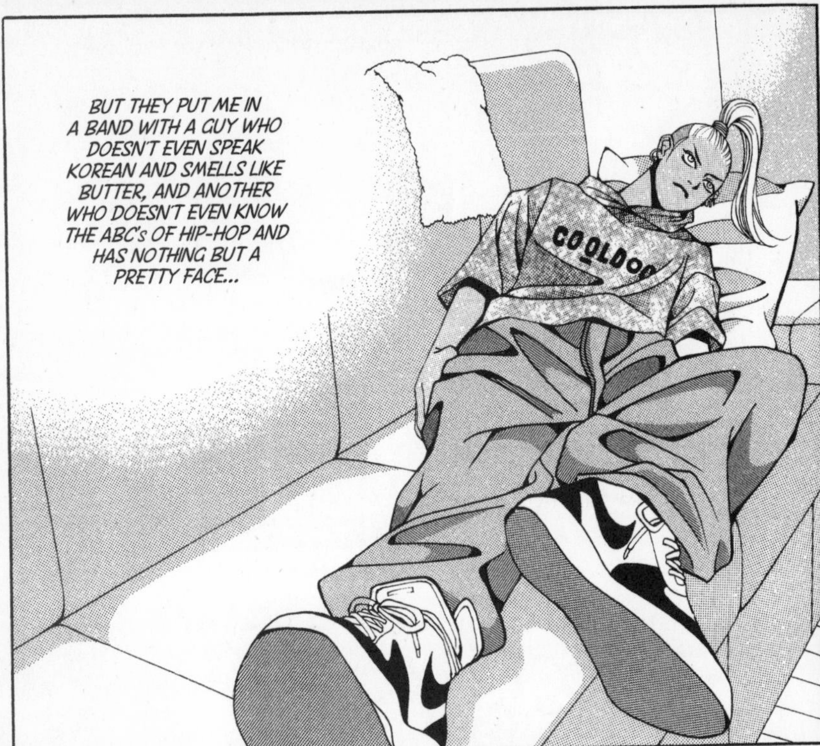
BUT THEY PUT ME IN A BAND WITH A GUY WHO DOESN'T EVEN SPEAK KOREAN AND SMELLS LIKE BUTTER, AND ANOTHER WHO DOESN'T EVEN KNOW THE ABC's OF HIP-HOP AND HAS NOTHING BUT A PRETTY FACE...

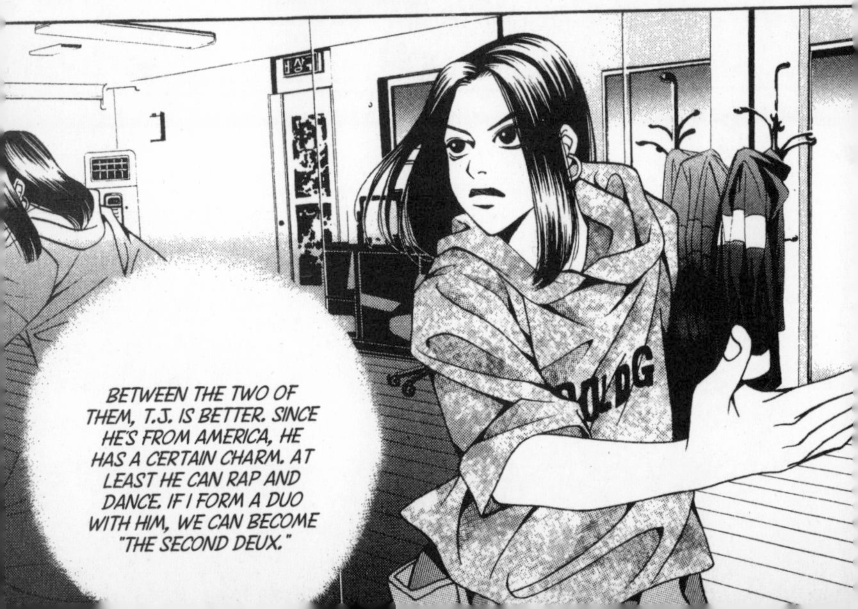
BETWEEN THE TWO OF THEM, T.J. IS BETTER. SINCE HE'S FROM AMERICA, HE HAS A CERTAIN CHARM. AT LEAST HE CAN RAP AND DANCE. IF I FORM A DUO WITH HIM, WE CAN BECOME "THE SECOND DEUX."

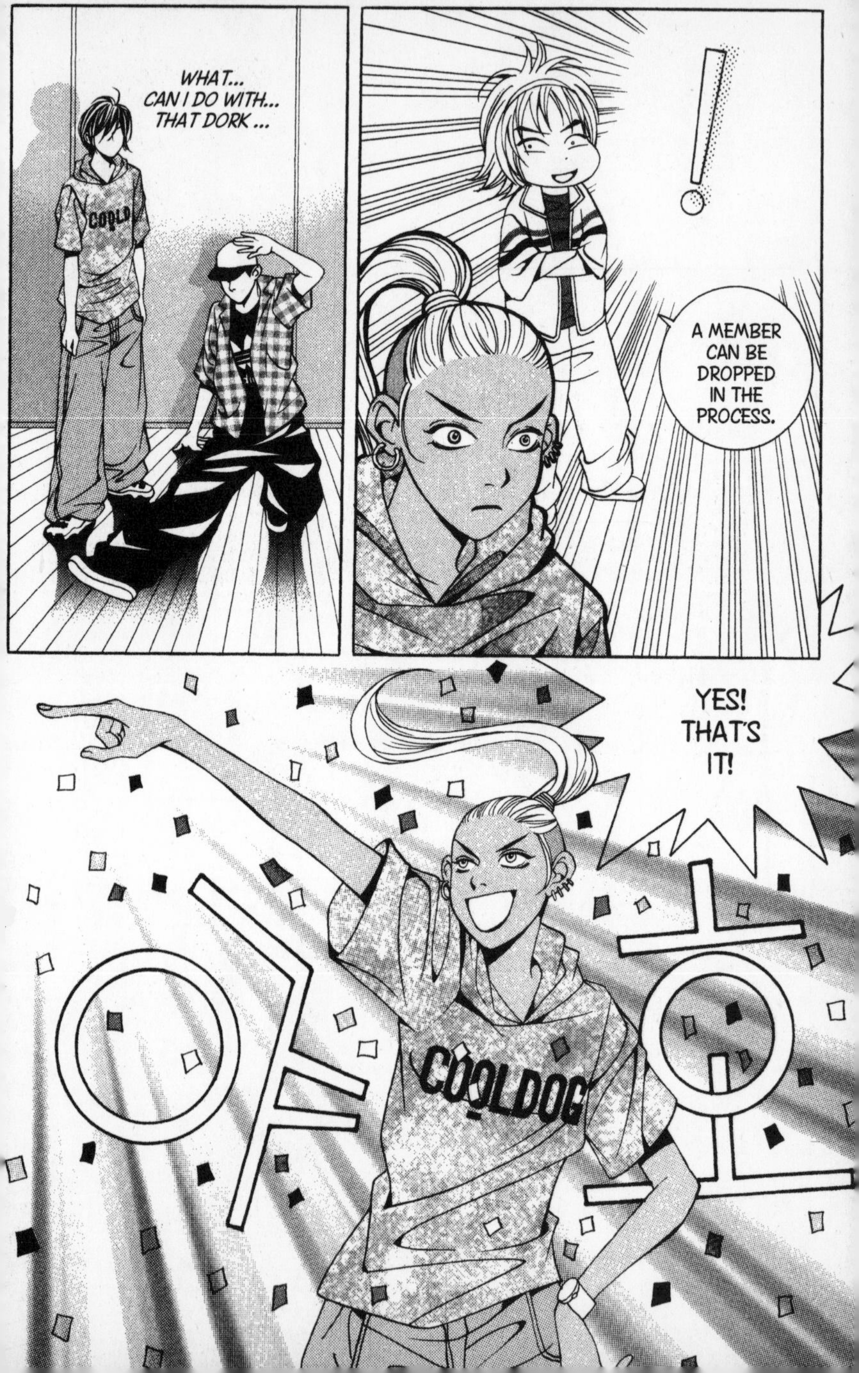
WHAT... CAN I DO WITH... THAT DORK...
A MEMBER CAN BE DROPPED IN THE PROCESS.
YES! THAT'S IT!

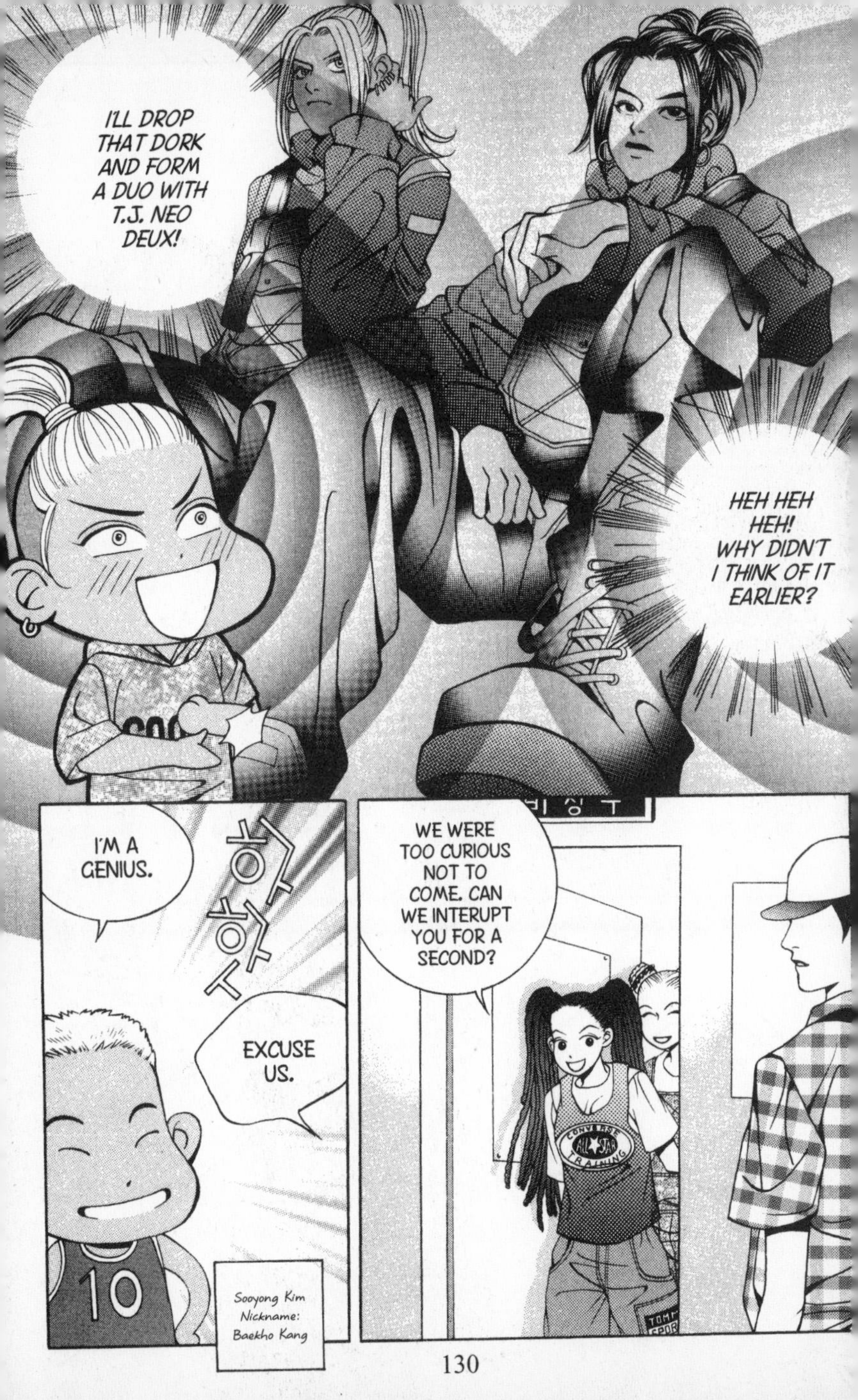
I'LL DROP THAT DORK AND FORM A DUO WITH T.J. NEO DEUX!
HEH HEH HEH! WHY DIDN'T I THINK OF IT EARLIER?
I'M A GENIUS.
EXCUSE US.
Sooyong Kim Nickname: Baekho Kang
WE WERE TOO CURIOUS NOT TO COME. CAN WE INTERUPT YOU FOR A SECOND?

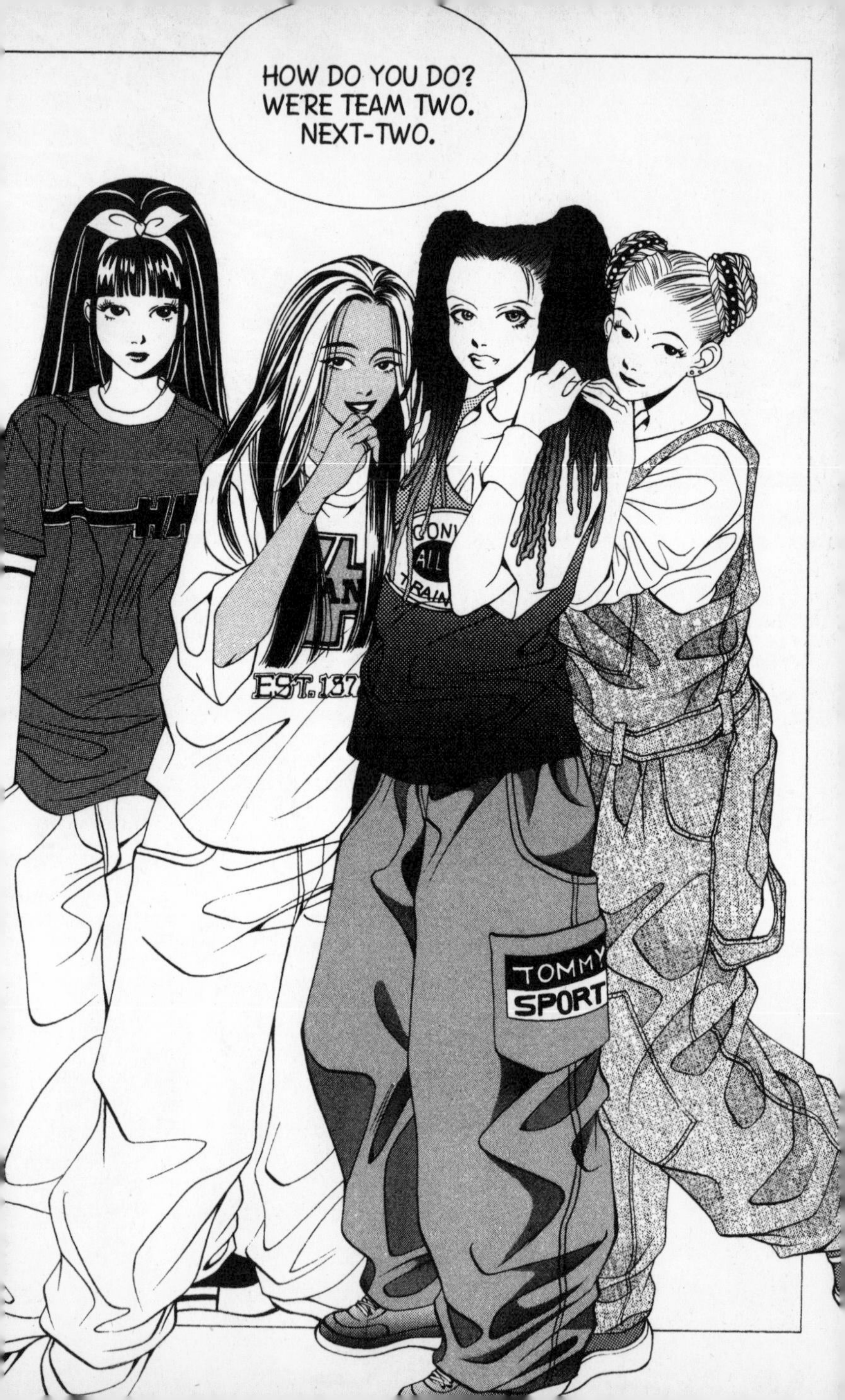
HOW DO YOU DO? WE'RE TEAM TWO. NEXT-TWO.
TOMMY SPORT

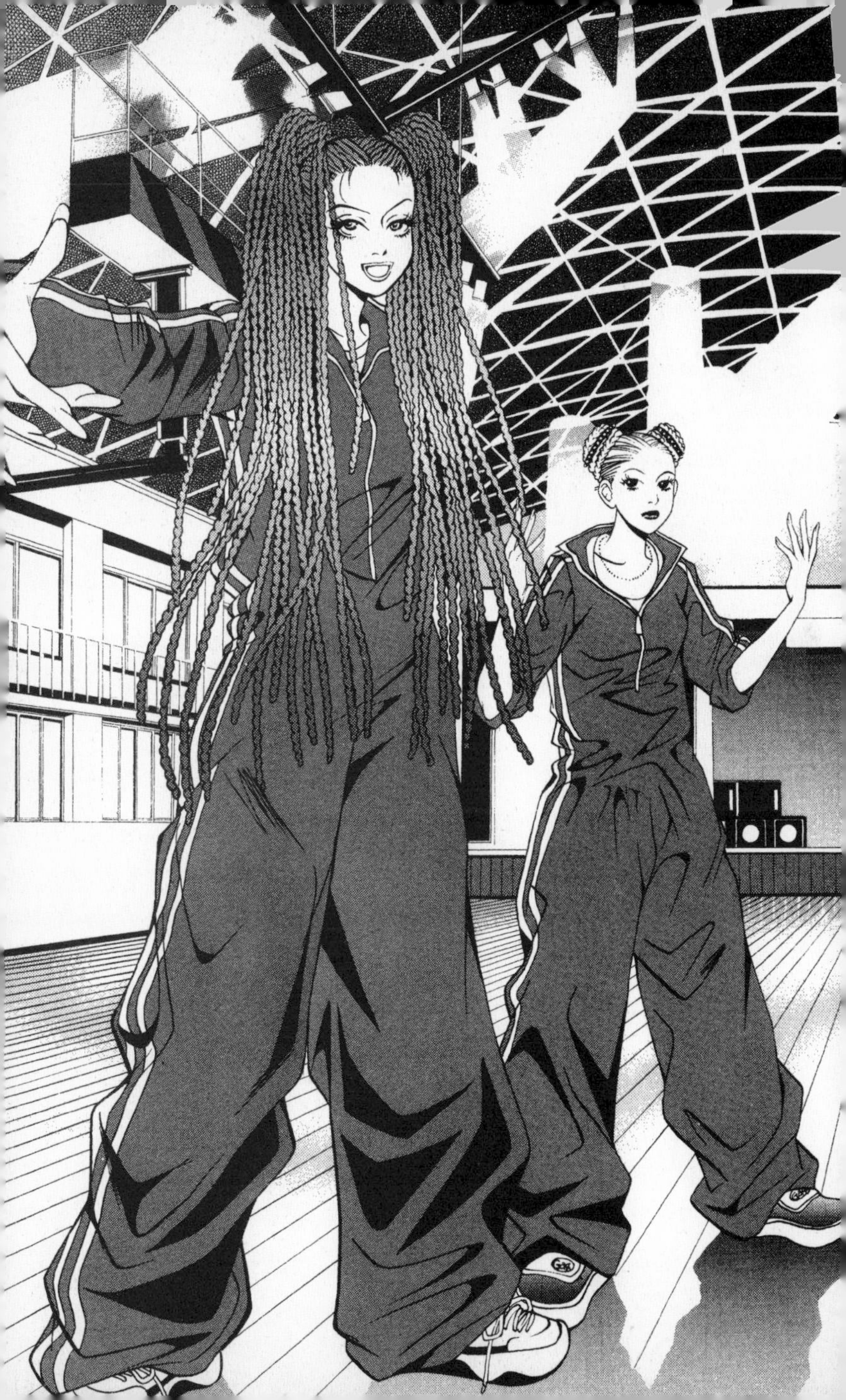

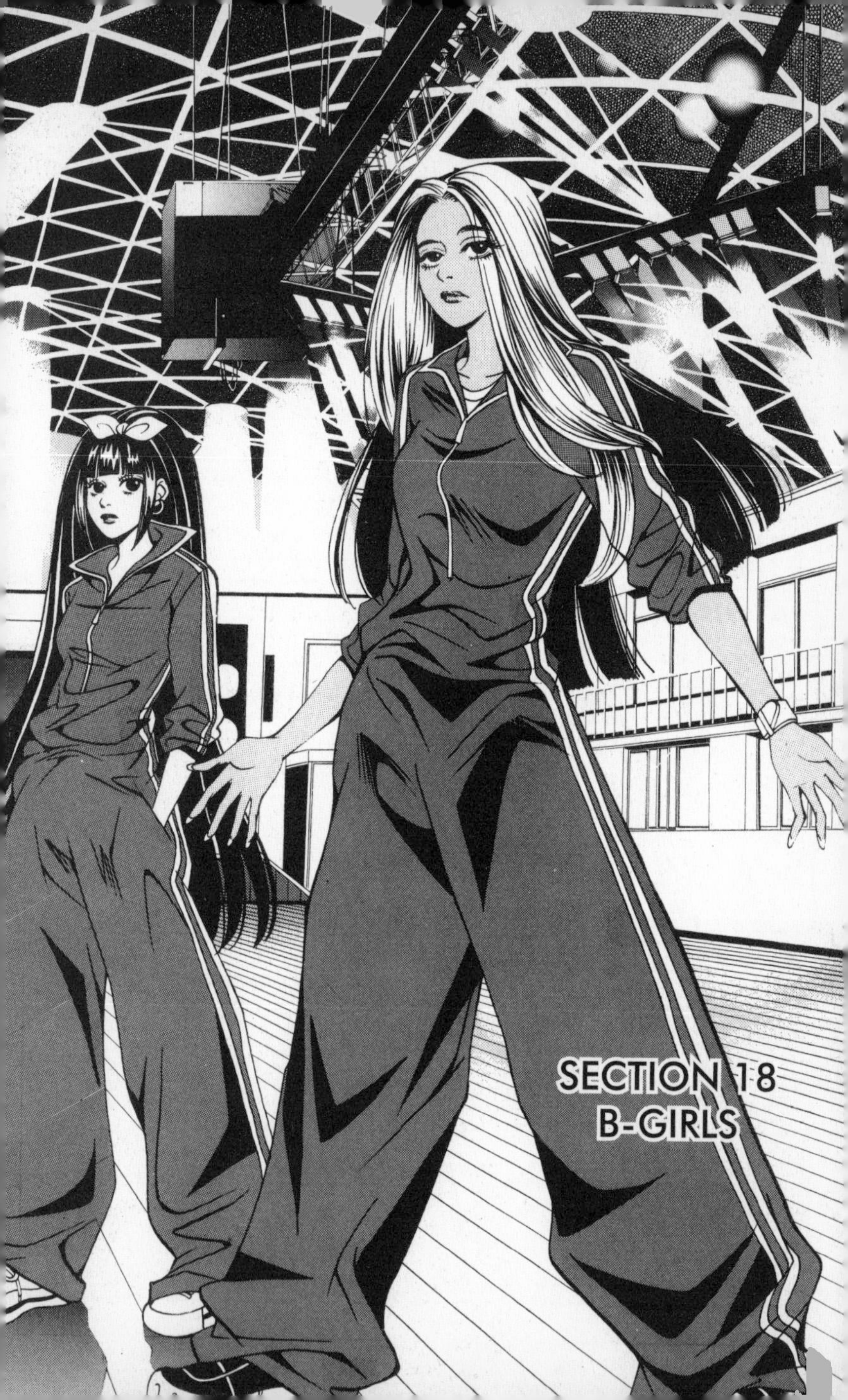
SECTION 18
B-GIRLS

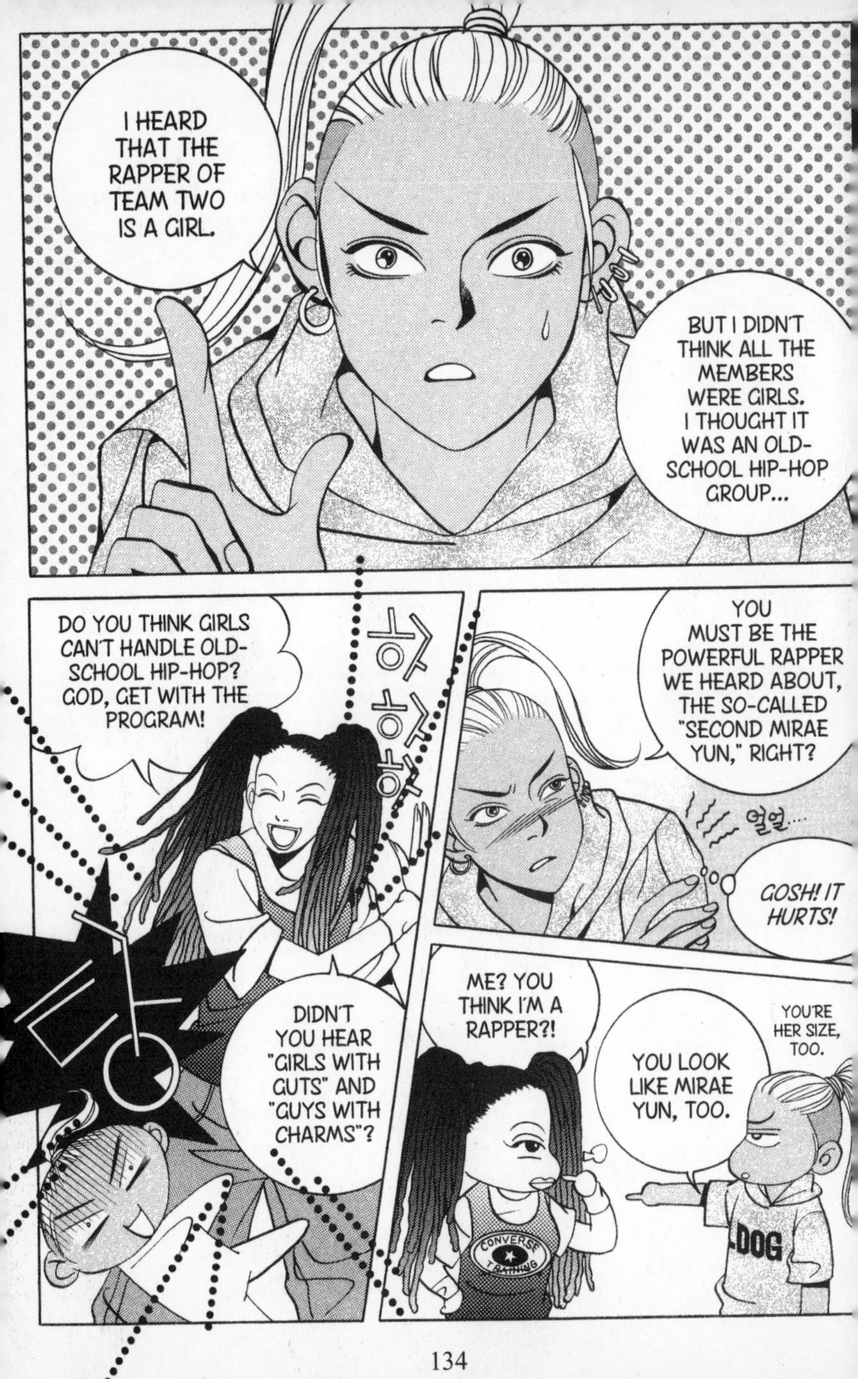
I HEARD THAT THE RAPPER OF TEAM TWO IS A GIRL.
BUT I DIDN'T THINK ALL THE MEMBERS WERE GIRLS. I THOUGHT IT WAS AN OLD-SCHOOL HIP-HOP GROUP...
DO YOU THINK GIRLS CAN'T HANDLE OLD-SCHOOL HIP-HOP? GOD, GET WITH THE PROGRAM!
YOU MUST BE THE POWERFUL RAPPER WE HEARD ABOUT, THE SO-CALLED "SECOND MIRAE YUN," RIGHT?
얼얼...
GOSH! IT HURTS!
DIDN'T YOU HEAR "GIRLS WITH GUTS" AND "GUYS WITH CHARMS"?
ME? YOU THINK I'M A RAPPER?!
YOU LOOK LIKE MIRAE YUN, TOO.
YOU'RE HER SIZE, TOO.
CONVERSE TRAINING
DOG

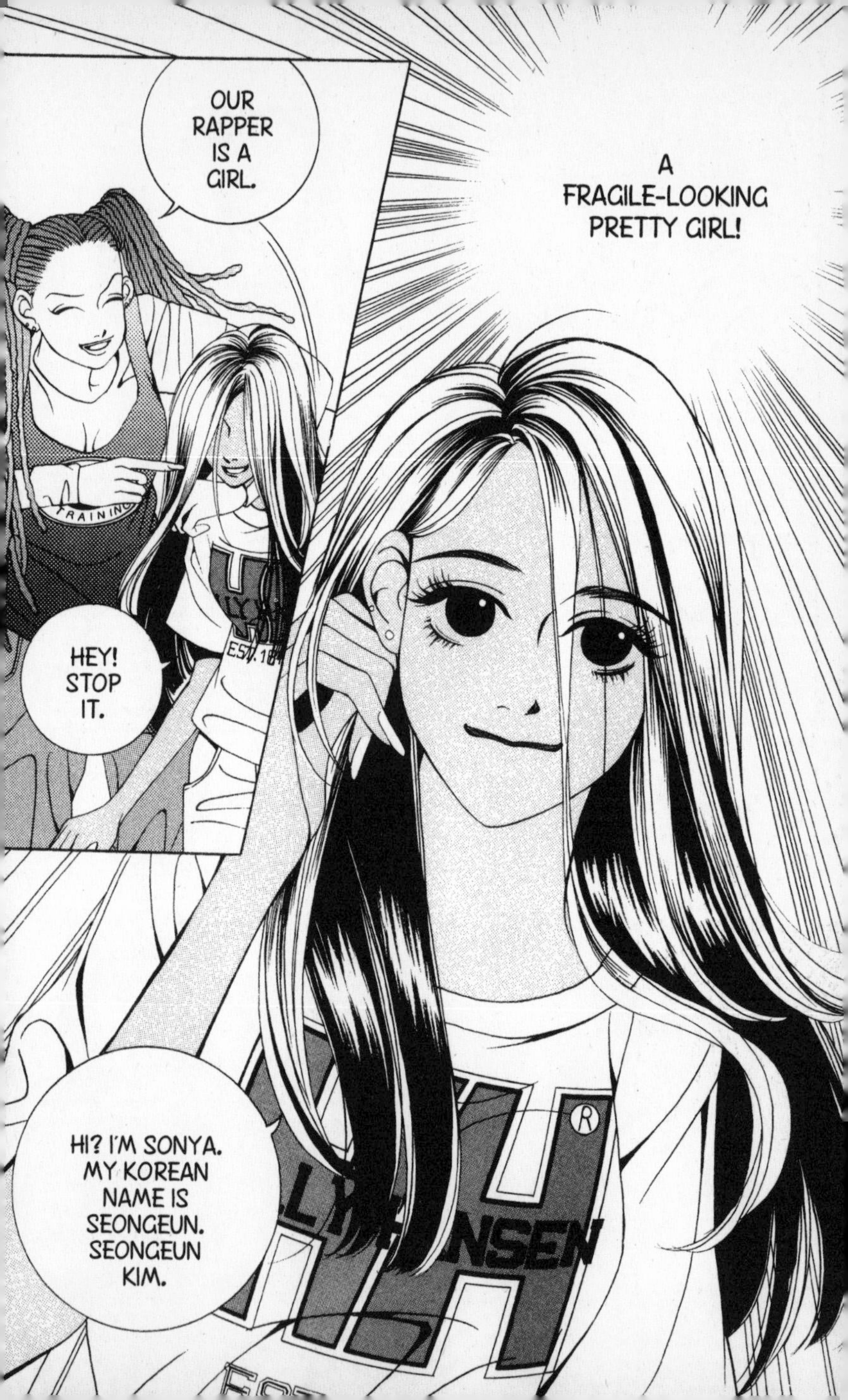
OUR RAPPER IS A GIRL.
HEY! STOP IT.
A FRAGILE-LOOKING PRETTY GIRL!
HI? I'M SONYA. MY KOREAN NAME IS SEONGEUN. SEONGEUN KIM.

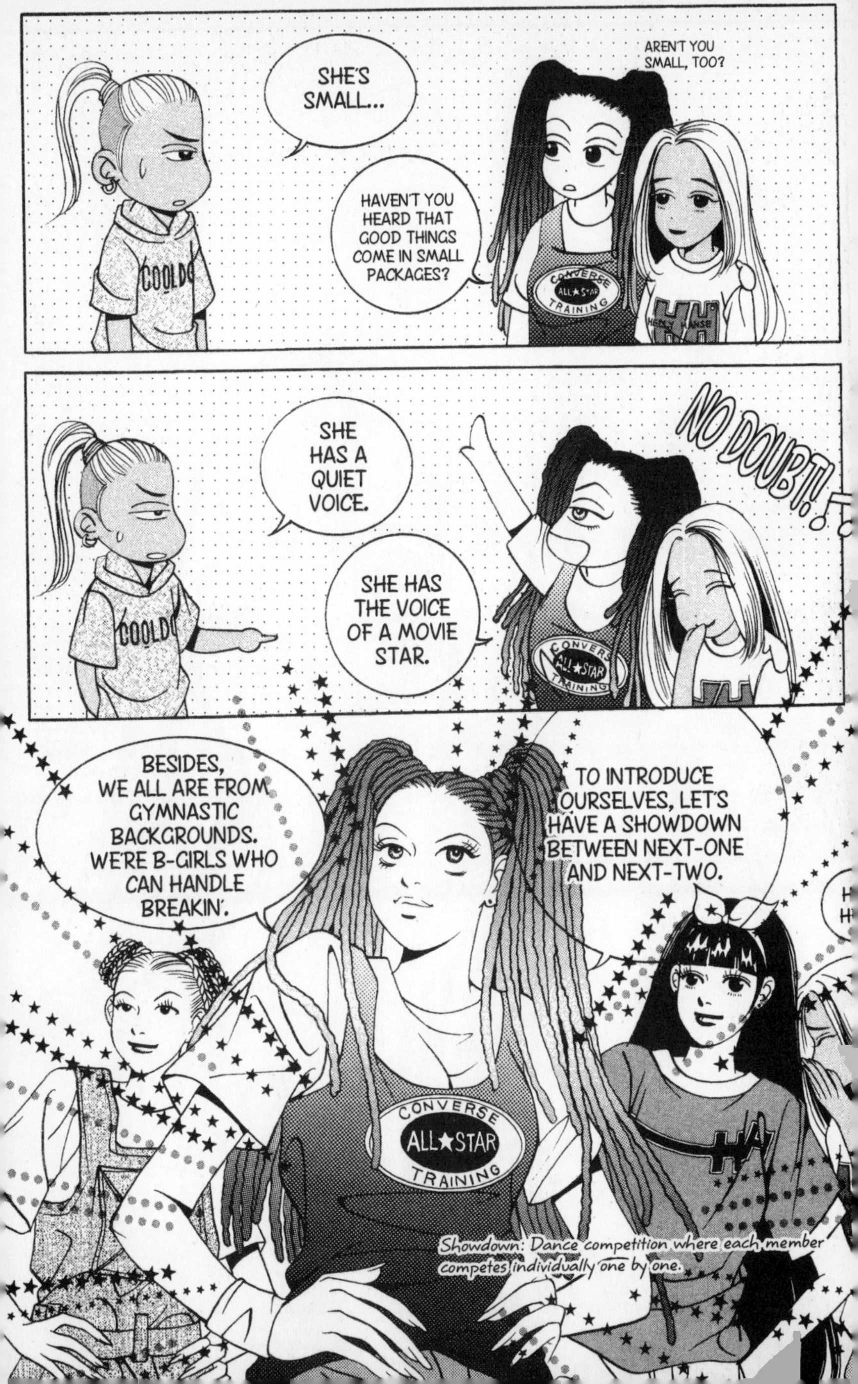
SHE'S SMALL...
HAVEN'T YOU HEARD THAT GOOD THINGS COME IN SMALL PACKAGES?
AREN'T YOU SMALL, TOO?
SHE HAS A QUIET VOICE.
SHE HAS THE VOICE OF A MOVIE STAR.
NO DOUBT!!
BESIDES, WE ALL ARE FROM GYMNASTIC BACKGROUNDS. WE'RE B-GIRLS WHO CAN HANDLE BREAKIN'.
TO INTRODUCE OURSELVES, LET'S HAVE A SHOWDOWN BETWEEN NEXT-ONE AND NEXT-TWO.
Showdown: Dance competition where each member competes individually one by one.

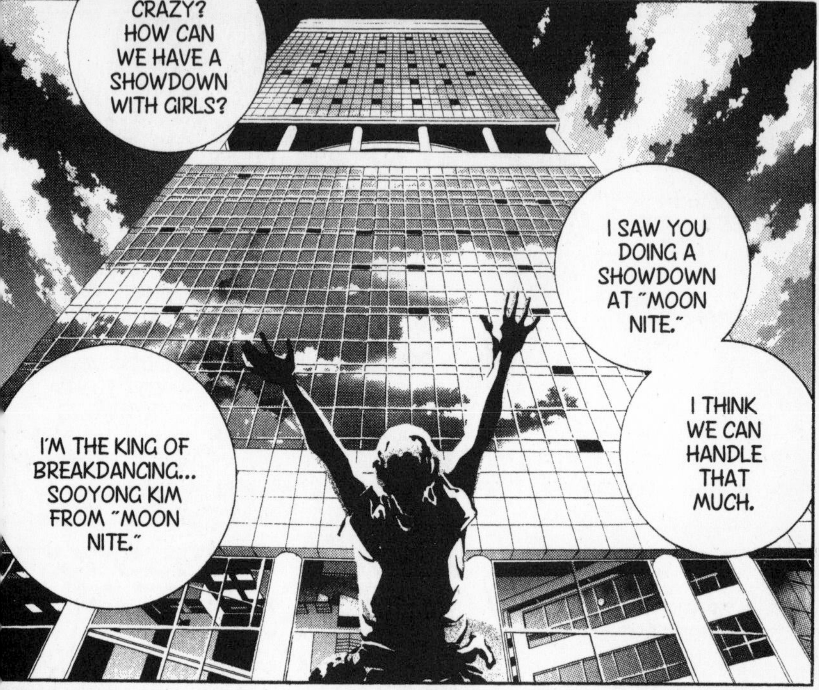
ARE YOU CRAZY? HOW CAN WE HAVE A SHOWDOWN WITH GIRLS?
I SAW YOU DOING A SHOWDOWN AT "MOON NITE."
I THINK WE CAN HANDLE THAT MUCH.
I'M THE KING OF BREAKDANCING... SOOYONG KIM FROM "MOON NITE."

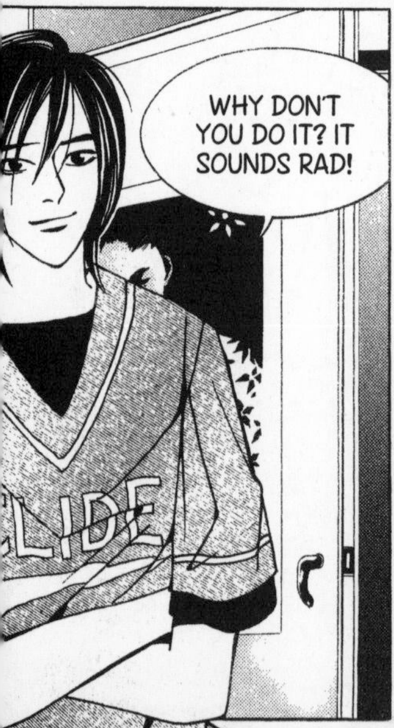
WHY DON'T YOU DO IT? IT SOUNDS RAD!
CLIDE

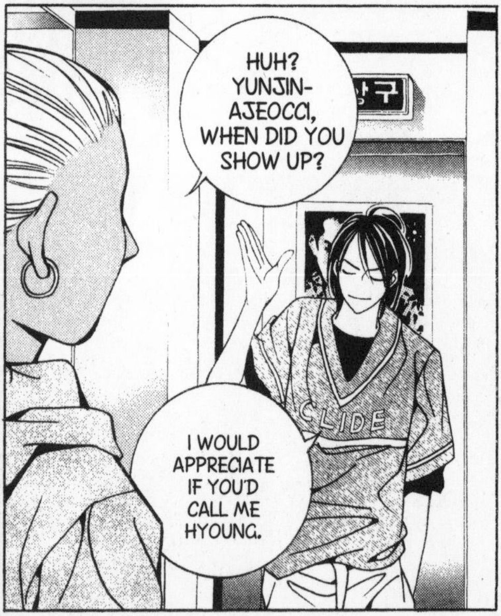
HUH? YUNJIN-AJEOCCI, WHEN DID YOU SHOW UP?
I WOULD APPRECIATE IF YOU'D CALL ME HYOUNG.
CLIDE

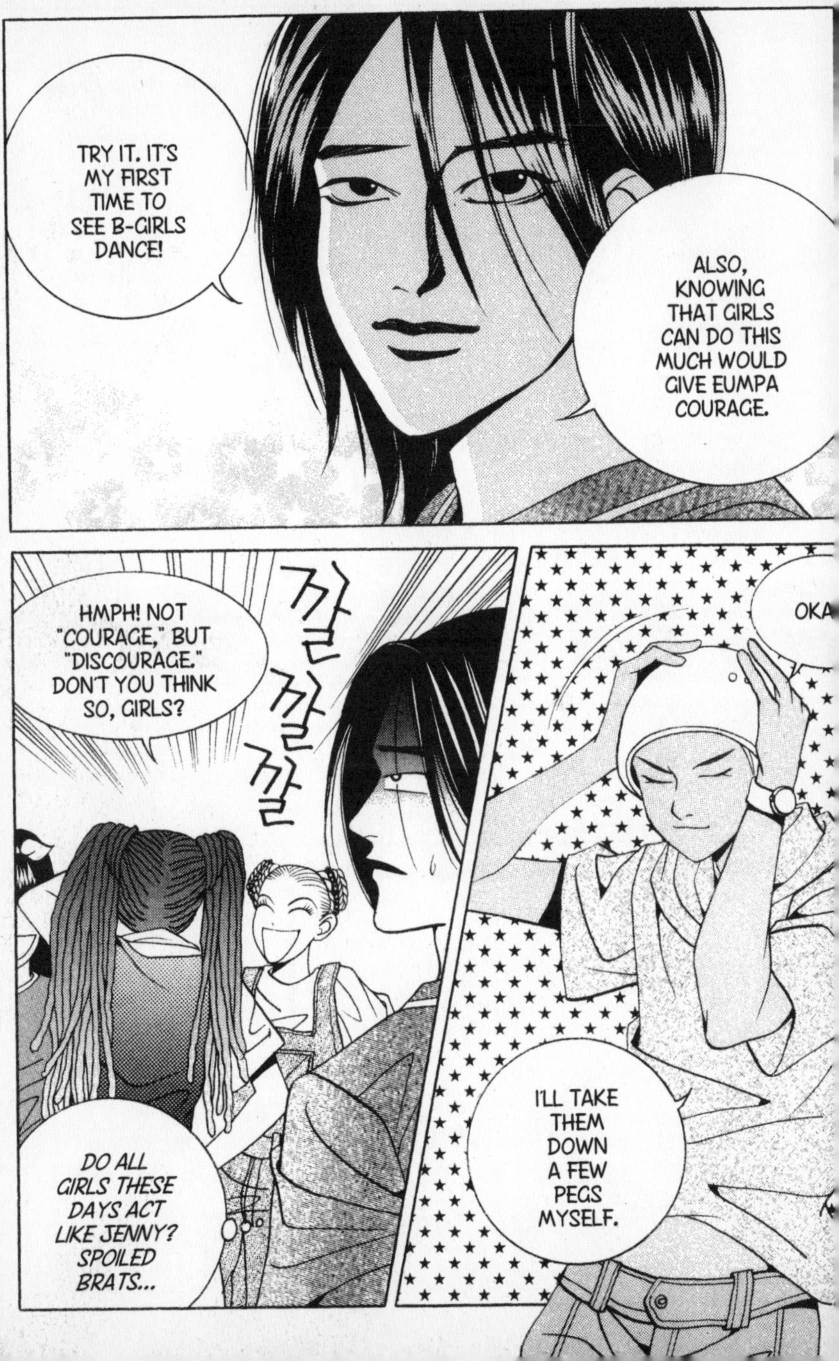
TRY IT. IT'S MY FIRST TIME TO SEE B-GIRLS DANCE!
ALSO, KNOWING THAT GIRLS CAN DO THIS MUCH WOULD GIVE EUMPA COURAGE.
HMPH! NOT "COURAGE," BUT "DISCOURAGE." DON'T YOU THINK SO, GIRLS?
깔깔깔
DO ALL GIRLS THESE DAYS ACT LIKE JENNY? SPOILED BRATS...
OKA
I'LL TAKE THEM DOWN A FEW PEGS MYSELF.

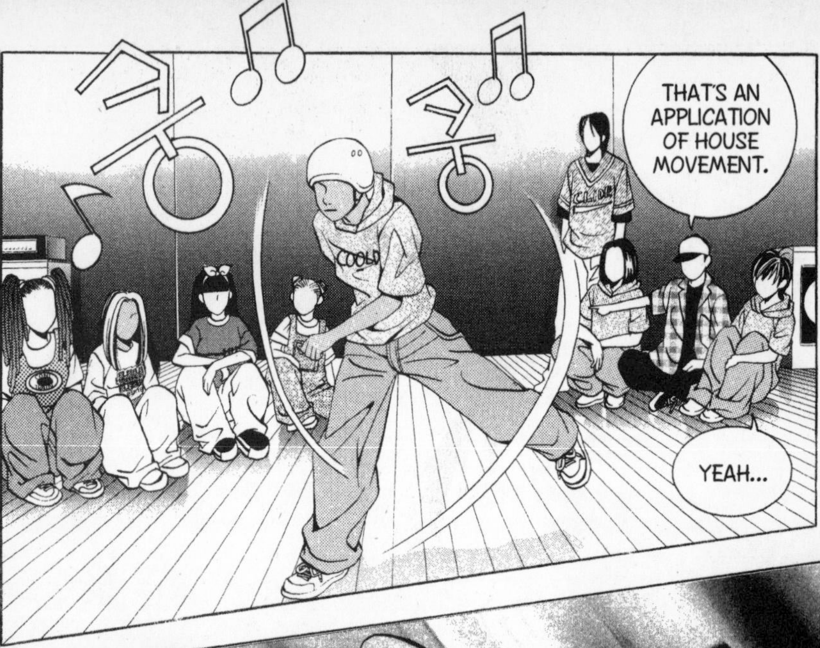
THAT'S AN APPLICATION OF HOUSE MOVEMENT.
YEAH...

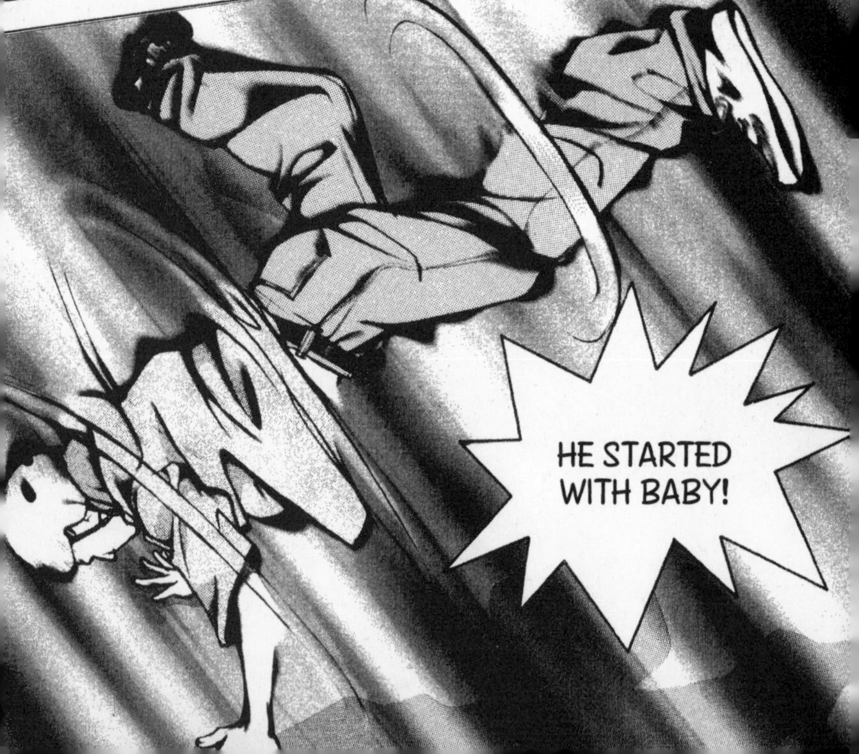
HE STARTED WITH BABY!

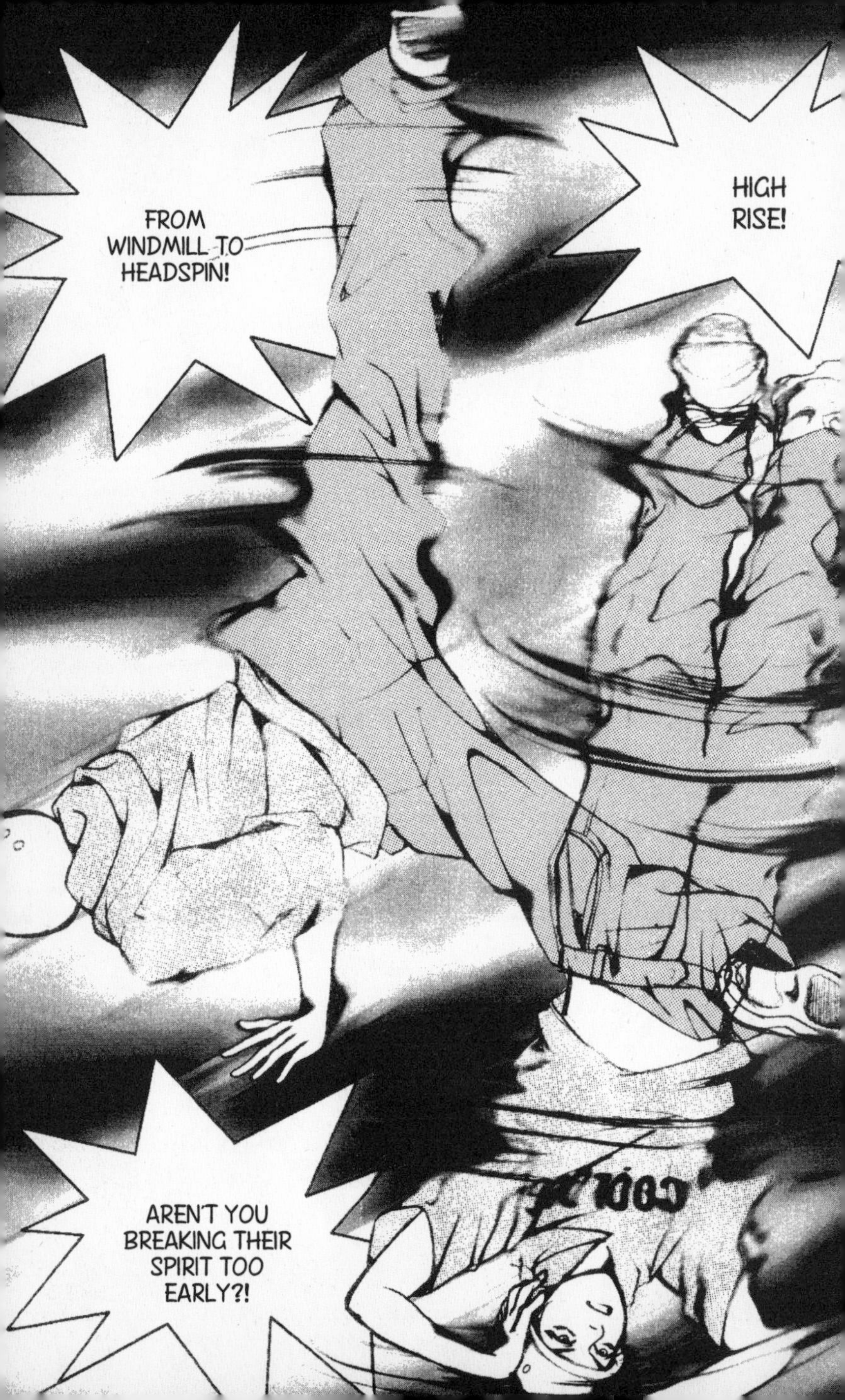
HIGH RISE!
FROM WINDMILL TO HEADSPIN!
AREN'T YOU BREAKING THEIR SPIRIT TOO EARLY?!

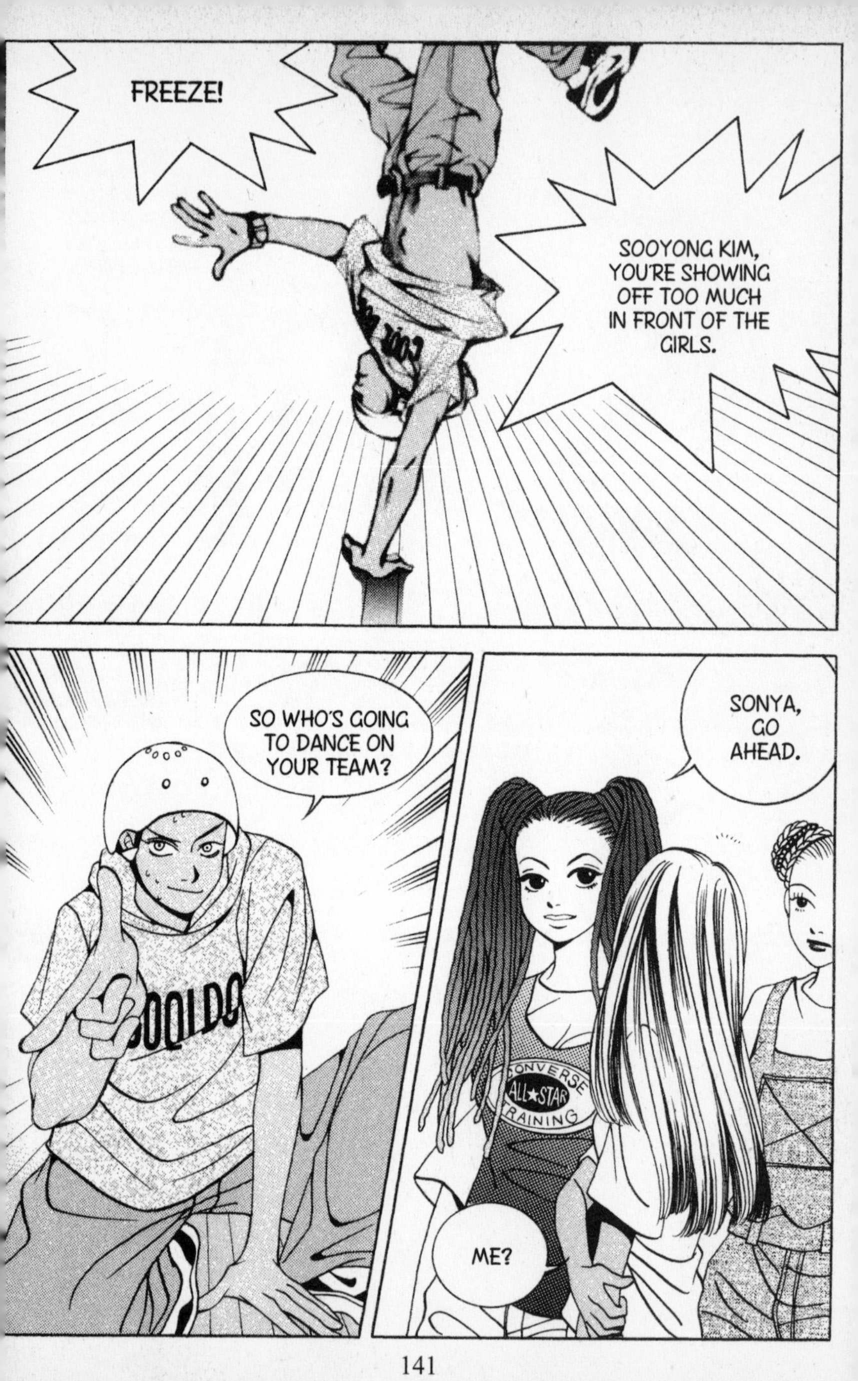
FREEZE!
SOOYONG KIM, YOU'RE SHOWING OFF TOO MUCH IN FRONT OF THE GIRLS.
SO WHO'S GOING TO DANCE ON YOUR TEAM?
SONYA, GO AHEAD.
ME?

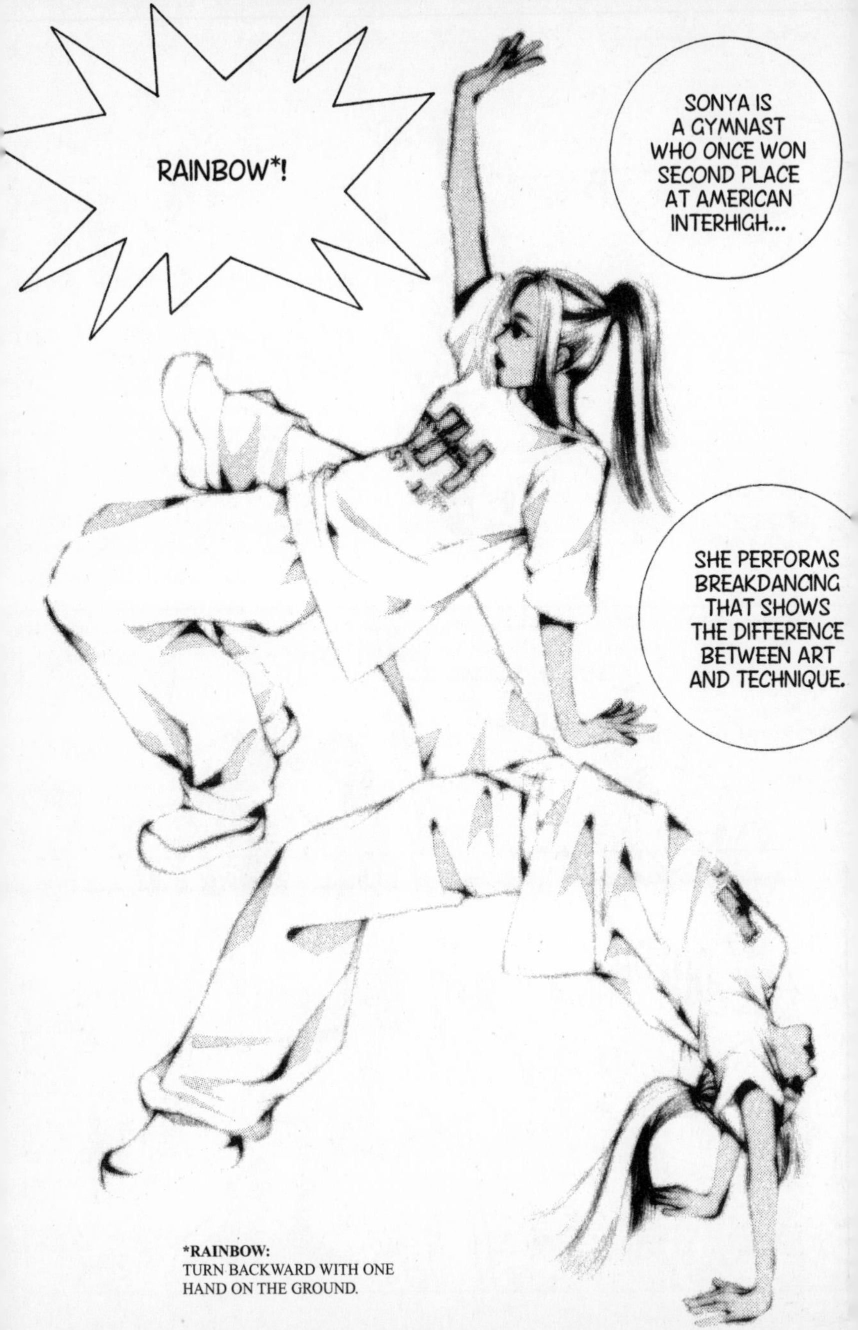
SONYA IS A GYMNAST WHO ONCE WON SECOND PLACE AT AMERICAN INTERHIGH...
RAINBOW*!
SHE PERFORMS BREAKDANCING THAT SHOWS THE DIFFERENCE BETWEEN ART AND TECHNIQUE.

***RAINBOW:**
TURN BACKWARD WITH ONE HAND ON THE GROUND.

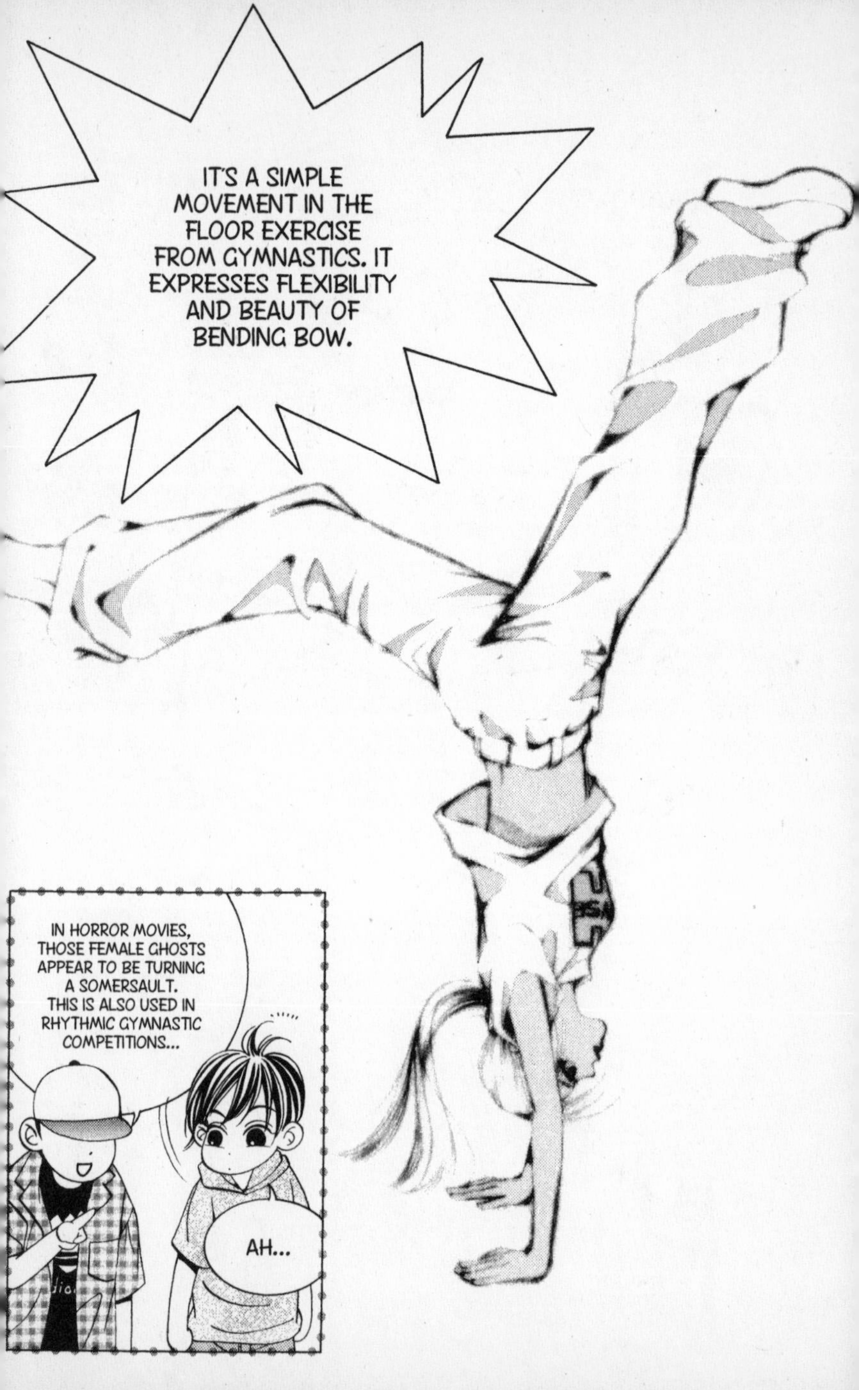
IT'S A SIMPLE MOVEMENT IN THE FLOOR EXERCISE FROM GYMNASTICS. IT EXPRESSES FLEXIBILITY AND BEAUTY OF BENDING BOW.
IN HORROR MOVIES, THOSE FEMALE GHOSTS APPEAR TO BE TURNING A SOMERSAULT. THIS IS ALSO USED IN RHYTHMIC GYMNASTIC COMPETITIONS...
AH...

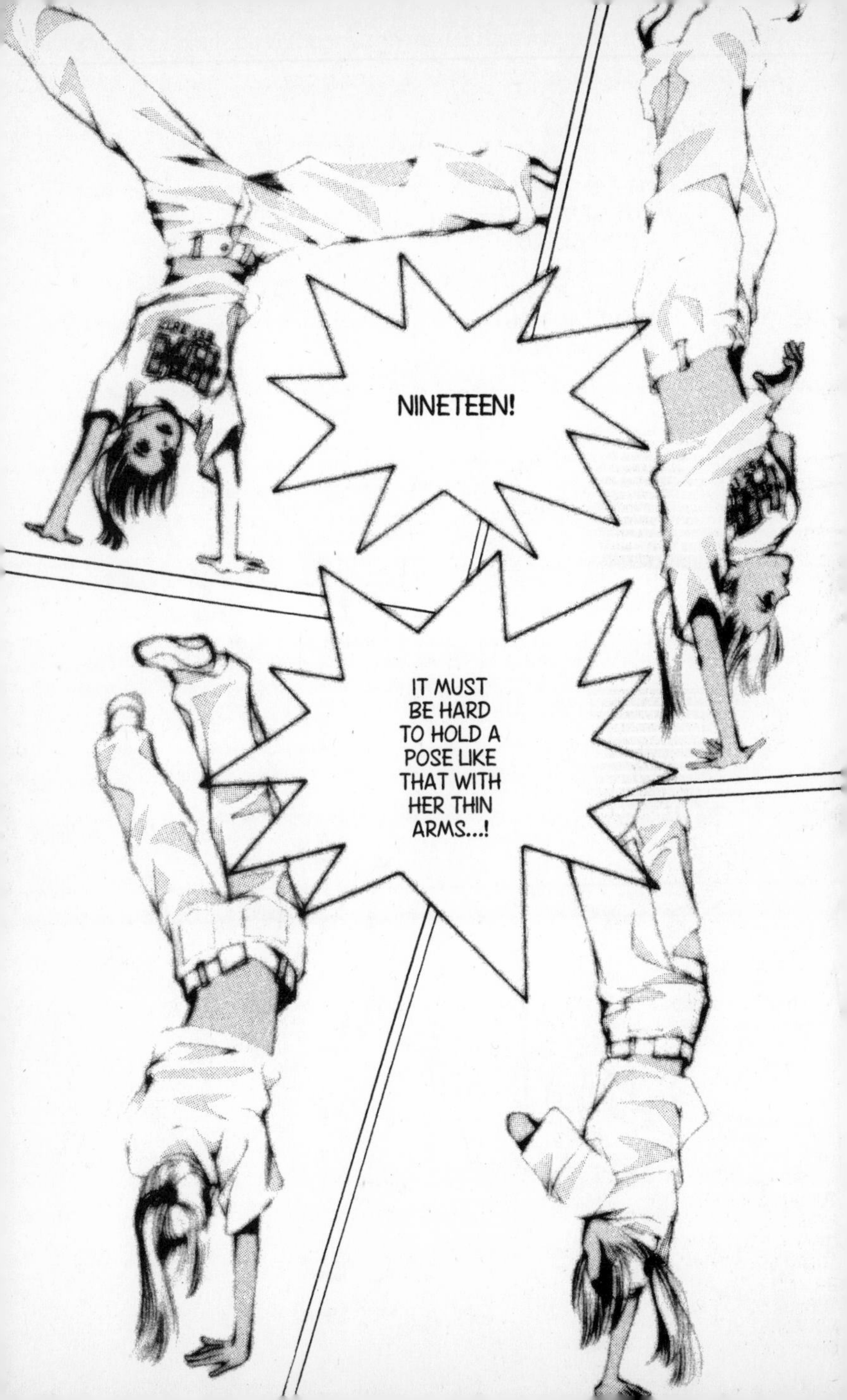
NINETEEN!
IT MUST BE HARD TO HOLD A POSE LIKE THAT WITH HER THIN ARMS...!

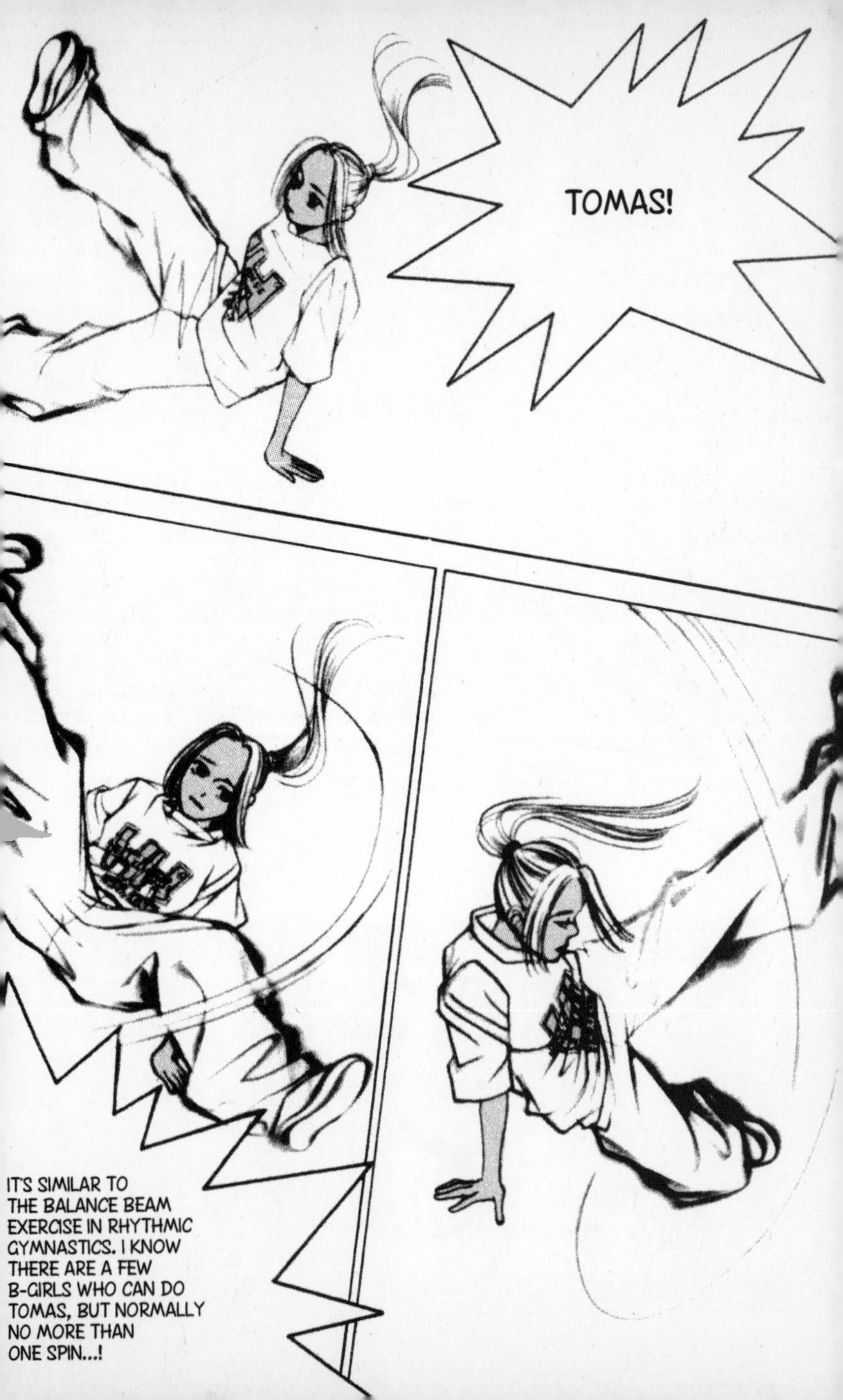
TOMAS!
IT'S SIMILAR TO THE BALANCE BEAM EXERCISE IN RHYTHMIC GYMNASTICS. I KNOW THERE ARE A FEW B-GIRLS WHO CAN DO TOMAS, BUT NORMALLY NO MORE THAN ONE SPIN...!

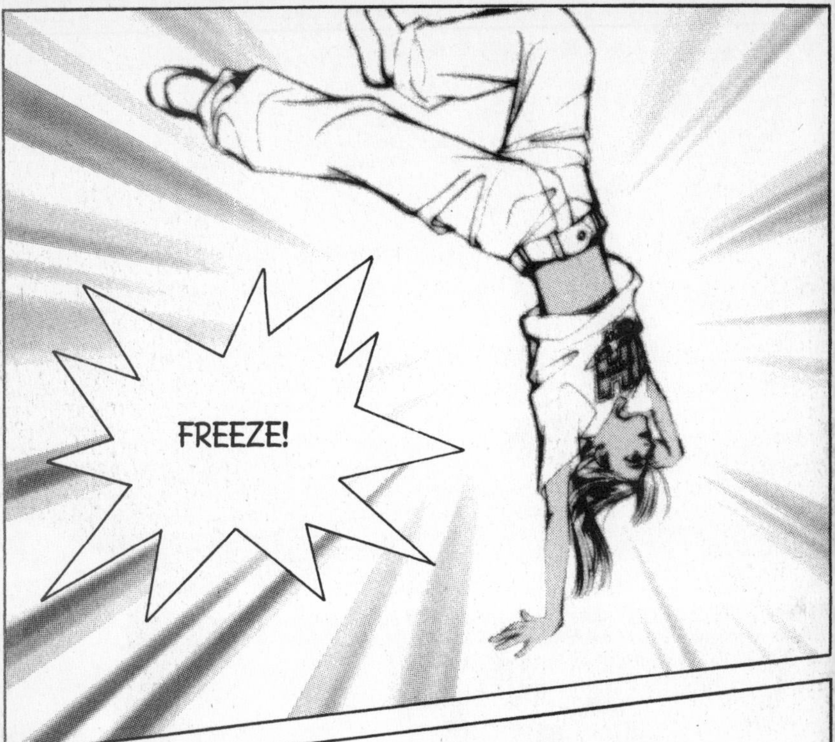
FREEZE!

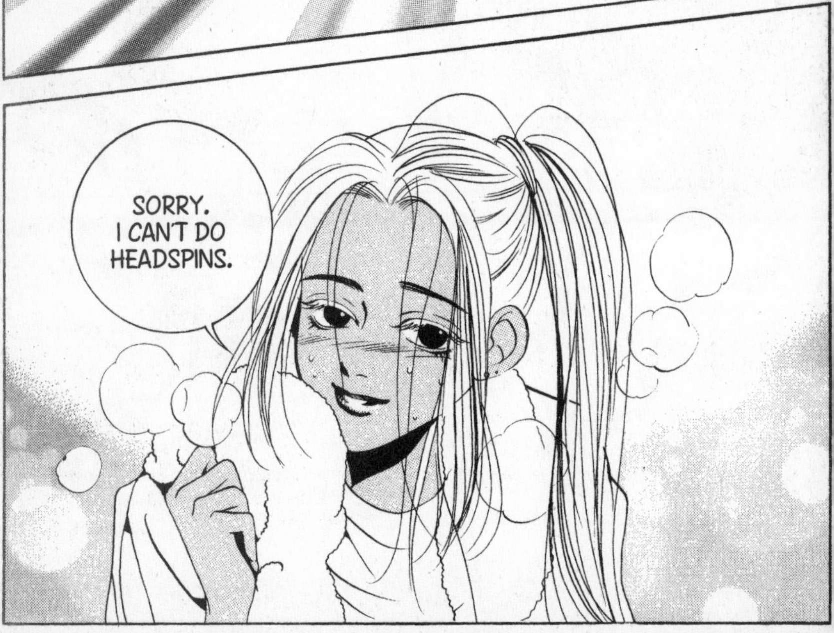
SORRY.
I CAN'T DO
HEADSPINS.

Showdown between Next-One and Next-Two
The dance of Team Two was striking enough to inspire
not only dance-deaf Eumpa, but also arrogant, self-involved Sooyong.
As ex-gymnasts, Team Two demonstrated both artistic and technical prowess.
Gymnastics shows the marvelous beauty of the human body.
Breakin' originally took many movements from gymnastics.
In a way, the beautiful breakdance performance of Team Two
was something of a culture shock to Team One.

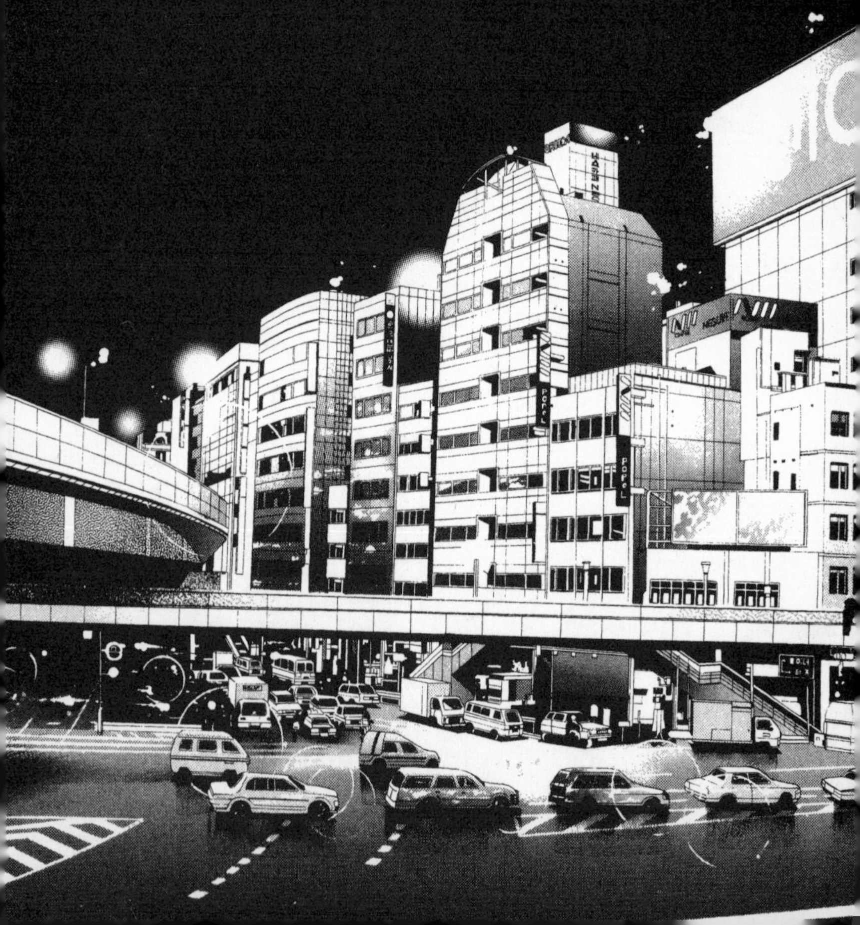

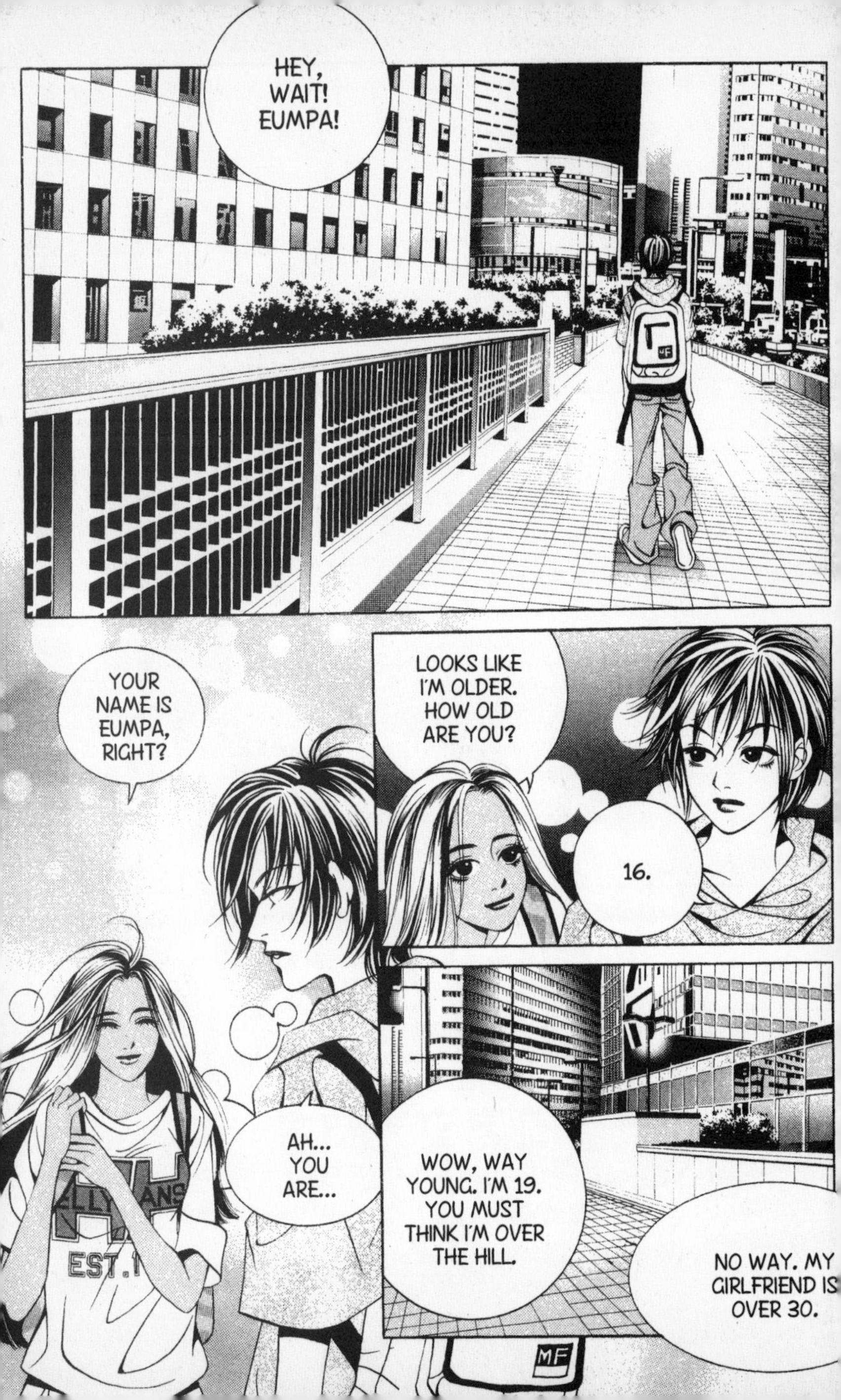
HEY, WAIT! EUMPA!
YOUR NAME IS EUMPA, RIGHT?
AH... YOU ARE...
LOOKS LIKE I'M OLDER. HOW OLD ARE YOU?
16.
WOW, WAY YOUNG. I'M 19. YOU MUST THINK I'M OVER THE HILL.
NO WAY. MY GIRLFRIEND IS OVER 30.

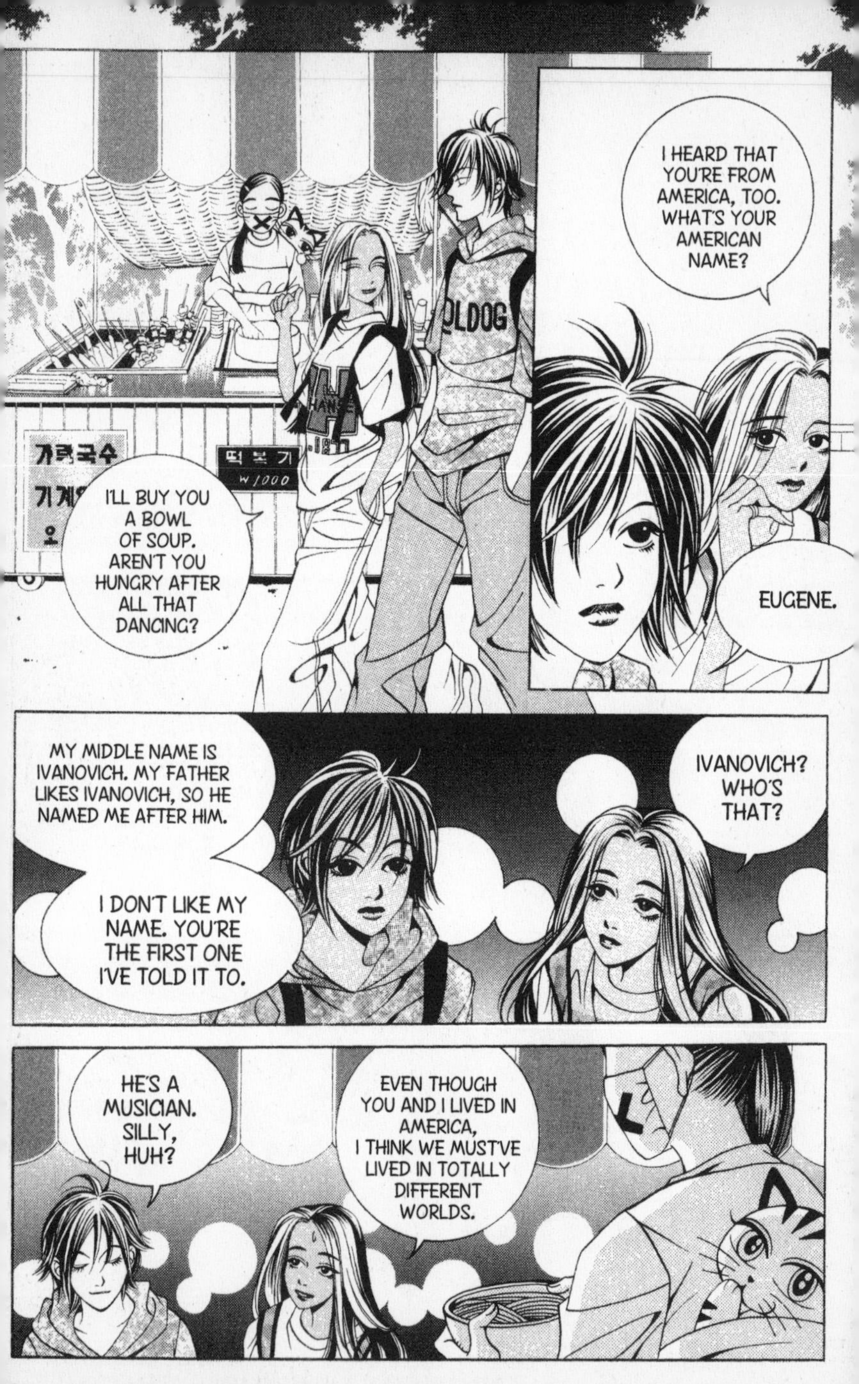
가락국수
I'LL BUY YOU A BOWL OF SOUP. AREN'T YOU HUNGRY AFTER ALL THAT DANCING?
I HEARD THAT YOU'RE FROM AMERICA, TOO. WHAT'S YOUR AMERICAN NAME?
EUGENE.
MY MIDDLE NAME IS IVANOVICH. MY FATHER LIKES IVANOVICH, SO HE NAMED ME AFTER HIM.
IVANOVICH? WHO'S THAT?
I DON'T LIKE MY NAME. YOU'RE THE FIRST ONE I'VE TOLD IT TO.
HE'S A MUSICIAN. SILLY, HUH?
EVEN THOUGH YOU AND I LIVED IN AMERICA, I THINK WE MUST'VE LIVED IN TOTALLY DIFFERENT WORLDS.

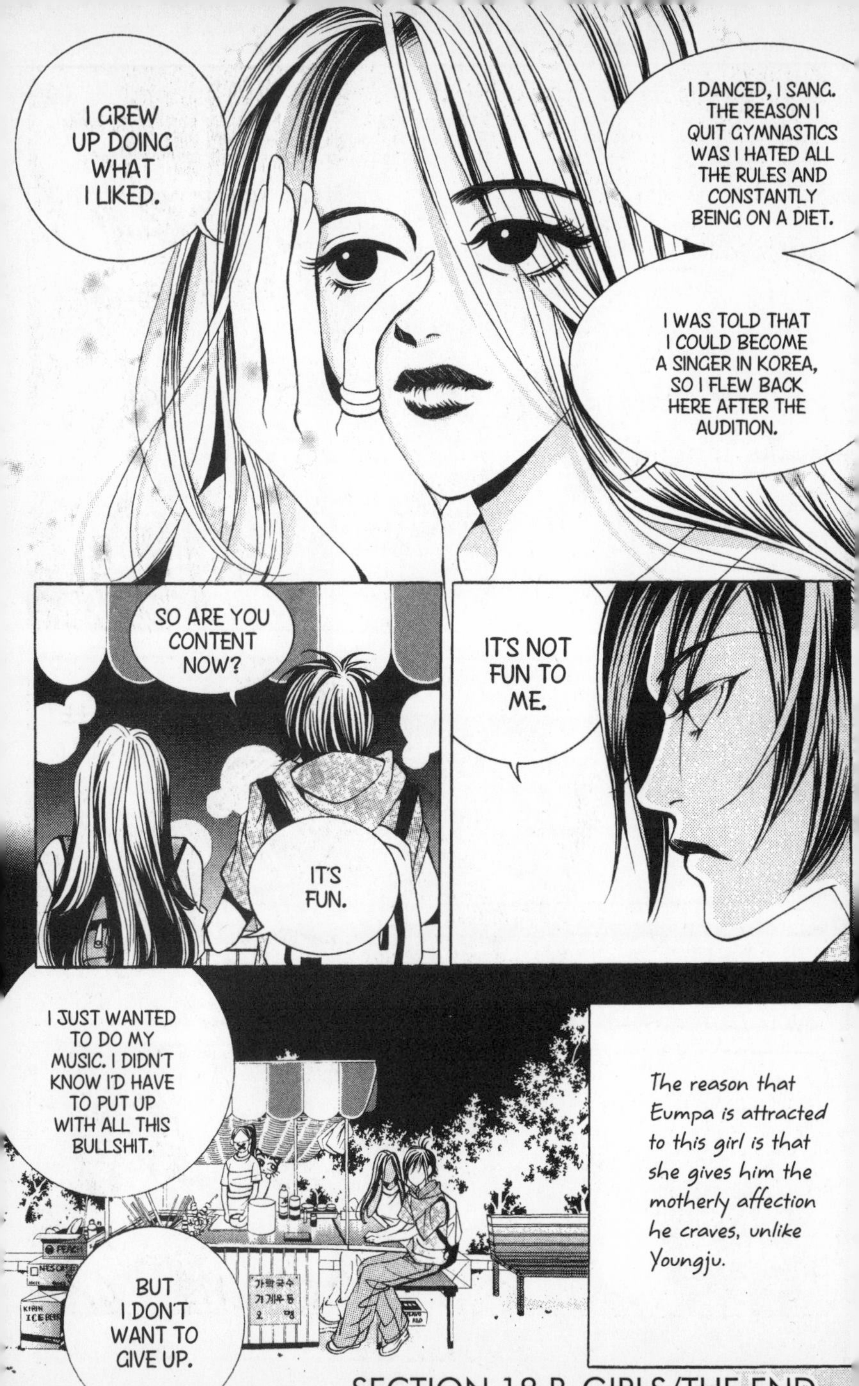
I GREW UP DOING WHAT I LIKED.
I DANCED, I SANG. THE REASON I QUIT GYMNASTICS WAS I HATED ALL THE RULES AND CONSTANTLY BEING ON A DIET.
I WAS TOLD THAT I COULD BECOME A SINGER IN KOREA, SO I FLEW BACK HERE AFTER THE AUDITION.
SO ARE YOU CONTENT NOW?
IT'S FUN.
IT'S NOT FUN TO ME.
I JUST WANTED TO DO MY MUSIC. I DIDN'T KNOW I'D HAVE TO PUT UP WITH ALL THIS BULLSHIT.
BUT I DON'T WANT TO GIVE UP.
The reason that Eumpa is attracted to this girl is that she gives him the motherly affection he craves, unlike Youngju.

SECTION 18 B-GIRLS/THE END

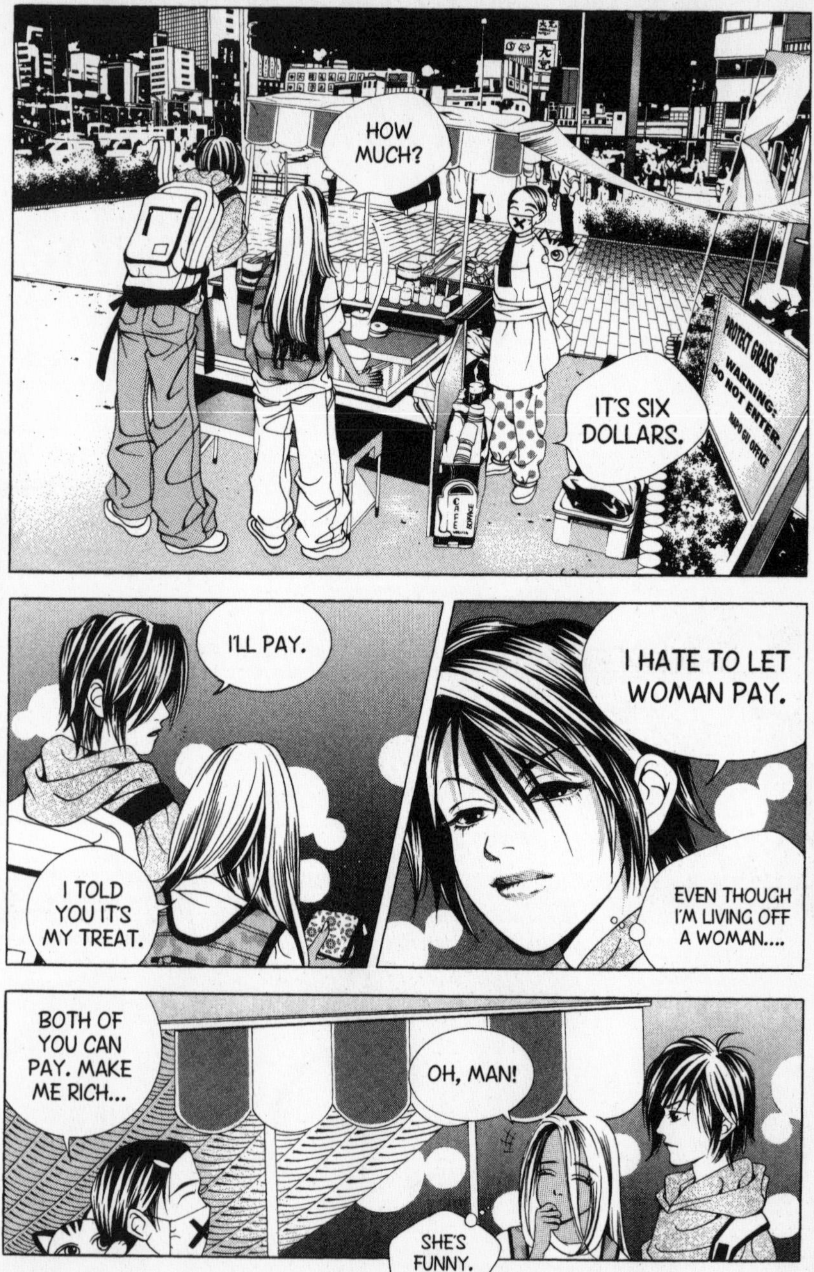
HOW MUCH?
IT'S SIX DOLLARS.
PROTECT GRASS
WARNING: DO NOT ENTER.
MAPO GU OFFICE
I'LL PAY.
I TOLD YOU IT'S MY TREAT.
I HATE TO LET WOMAN PAY.
EVEN THOUGH I'M LIVING OFF A WOMAN....
BOTH OF YOU CAN PAY. MAKE ME RICH...
OH, MAN!
SHE'S FUNNY.

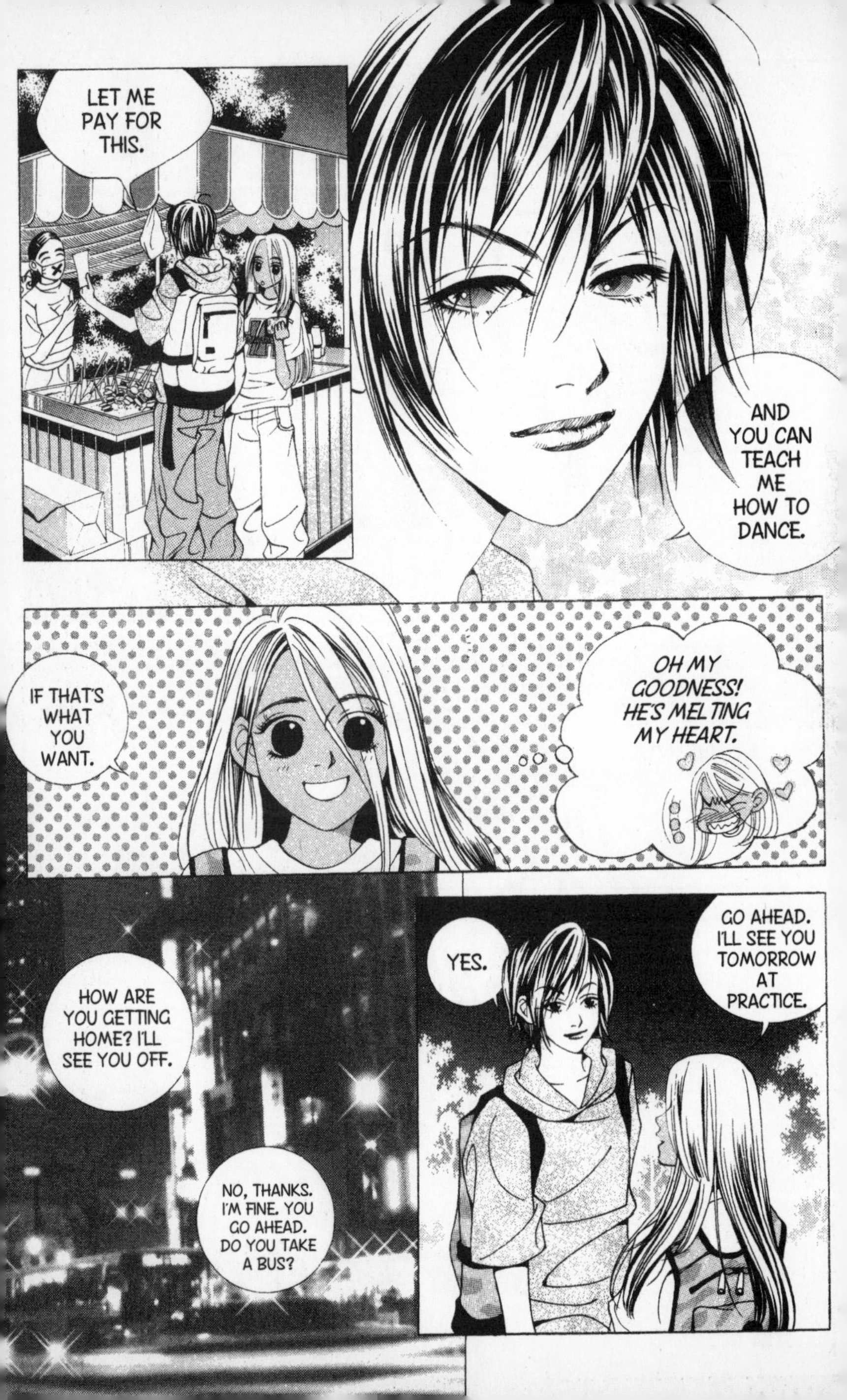
LET ME PAY FOR THIS.
AND YOU CAN TEACH ME HOW TO DANCE.
IF THAT'S WHAT YOU WANT.
OH MY GOODNESS! HE'S MELTING MY HEART.
HOW ARE YOU GETTING HOME? I'LL SEE YOU OFF.
NO, THANKS. I'M FINE. YOU GO AHEAD. DO YOU TAKE A BUS?
YES.
GO AHEAD. I'LL SEE YOU TOMORROW AT PRACTICE.

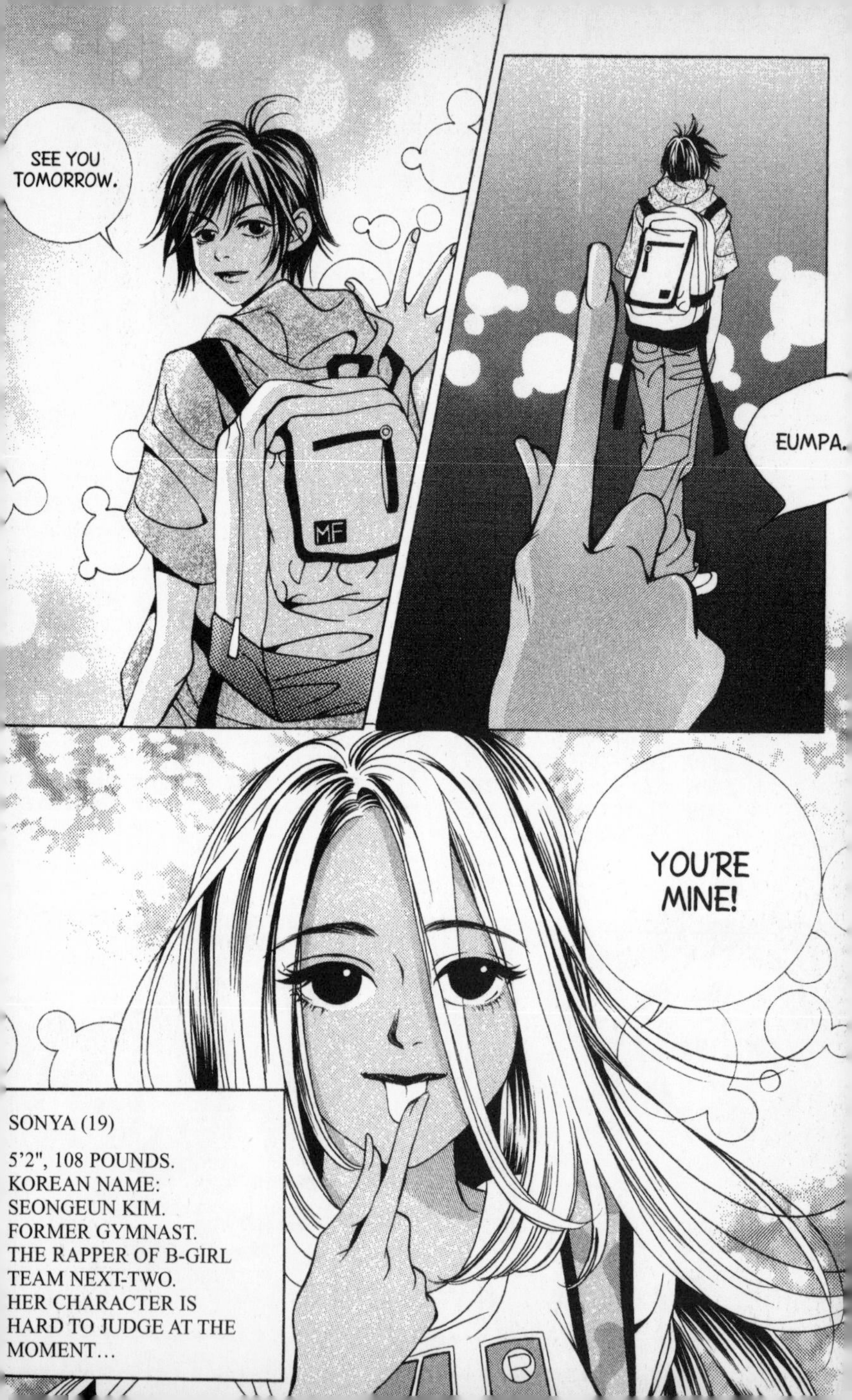
SEE YOU TOMORROW.
EUMPA.
YOU'RE MINE!
SONYA (19)
5'2", 108 POUNDS. KOREAN NAME: SEONGEUN KIM. FORMER GYMNAST. THE RAPPER OF B-GIRL TEAM NEXT-TWO. HER CHARACTER IS HARD TO JUDGE AT THE MOMENT…

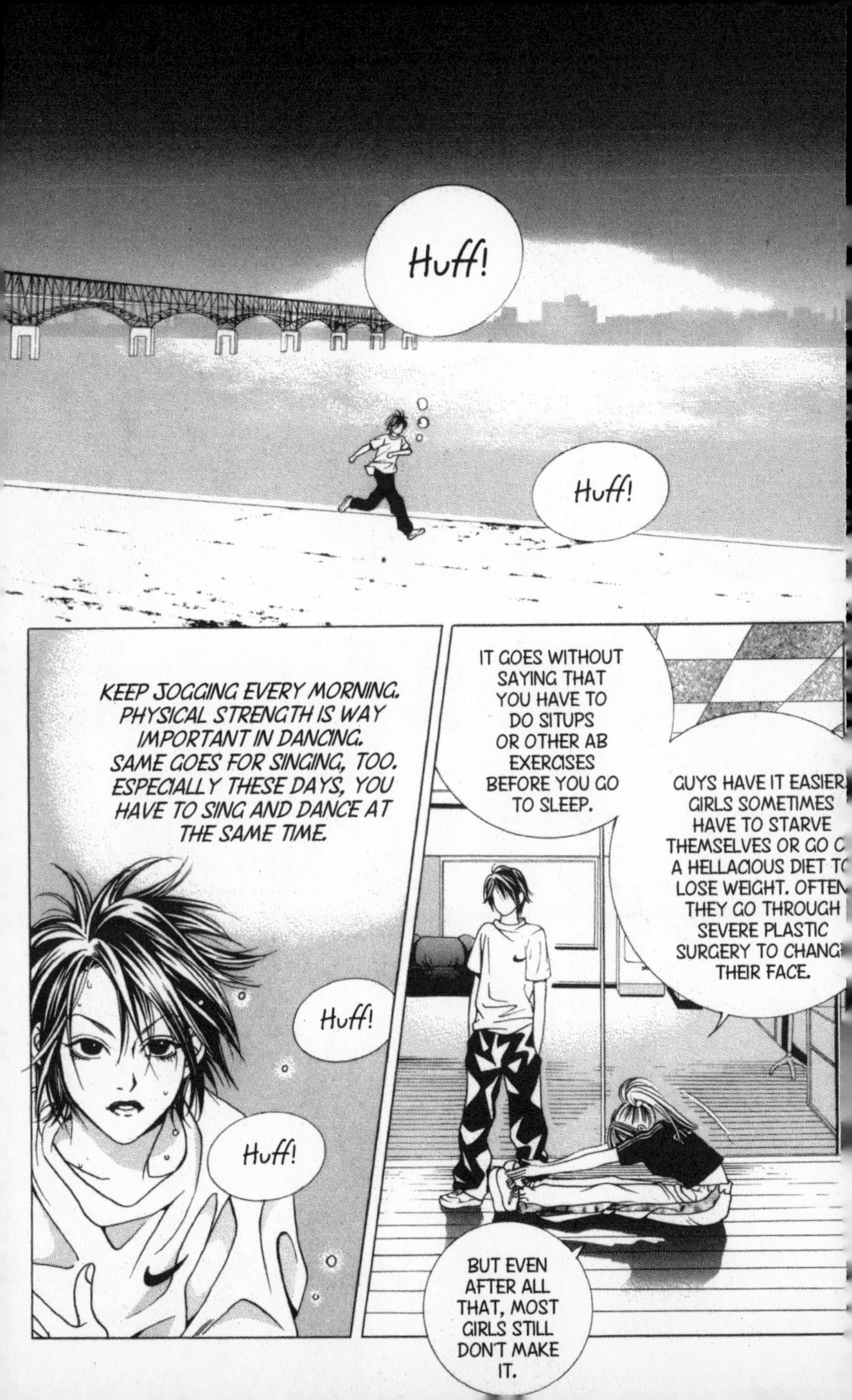
Huff!
Huff!
KEEP JOGGING EVERY MORNING. PHYSICAL STRENGTH IS WAY IMPORTANT IN DANCING. SAME GOES FOR SINGING, TOO. ESPECIALLY THESE DAYS, YOU HAVE TO SING AND DANCE AT THE SAME TIME.
Huff!
Huff!
IT GOES WITHOUT SAYING THAT YOU HAVE TO DO SITUPS OR OTHER AB EXERCISES BEFORE YOU GO TO SLEEP.
GUYS HAVE IT EASIER GIRLS SOMETIMES HAVE TO STARVE THEMSELVES OR GO C A HELLACIOUS DIET T LOSE WEIGHT. OFTEN THEY GO THROUGH SEVERE PLASTIC SURGERY TO CHANG THEIR FACE.
BUT EVEN AFTER ALL THAT, MOST GIRLS STILL DON'T MAKE IT.

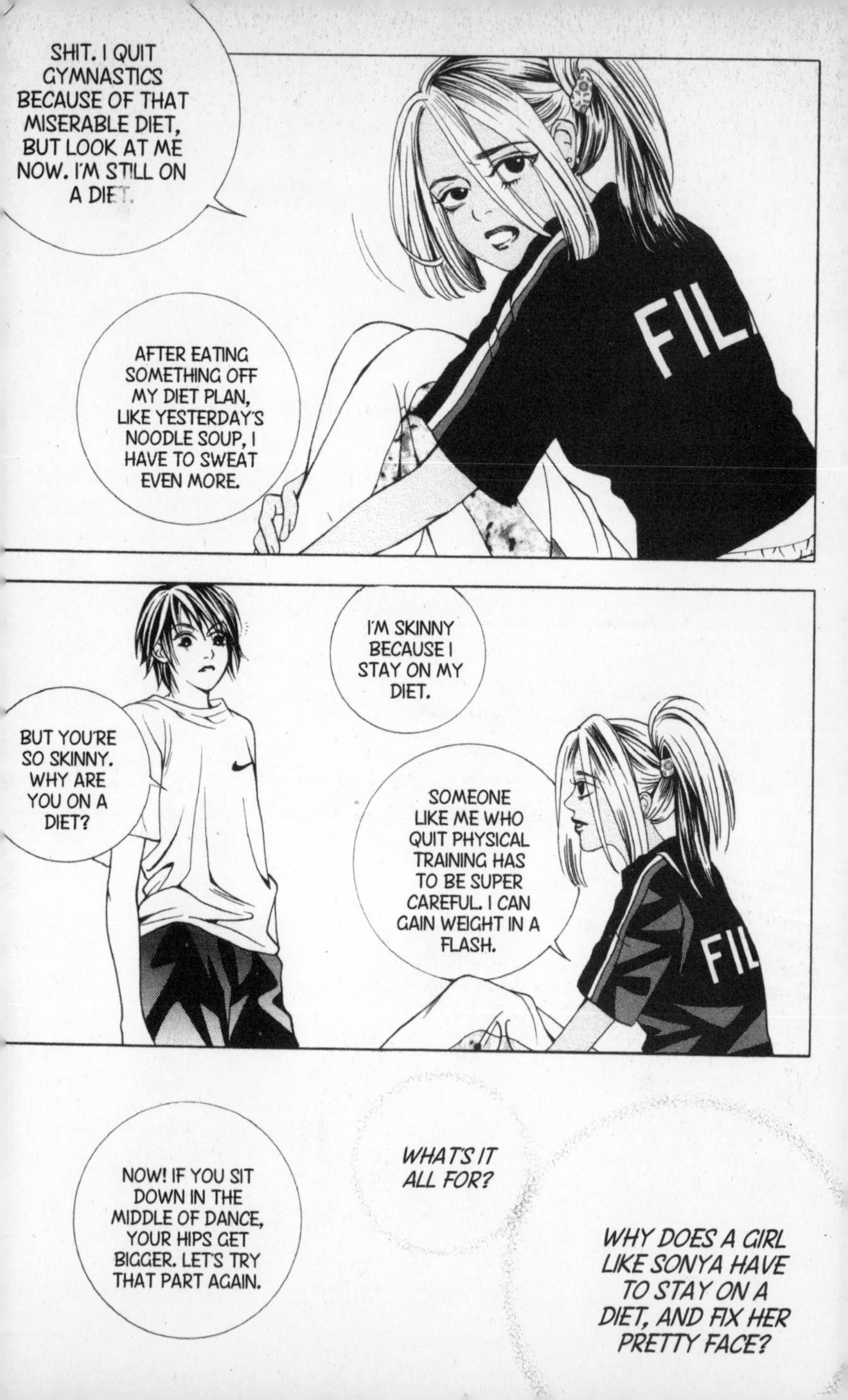
SHIT. I QUIT GYMNASTICS BECAUSE OF THAT MISERABLE DIET, BUT LOOK AT ME NOW. I'M STILL ON A DIET.
AFTER EATING SOMETHING OFF MY DIET PLAN, LIKE YESTERDAY'S NOODLE SOUP, I HAVE TO SWEAT EVEN MORE.
FIL
BUT YOU'RE SO SKINNY. WHY ARE YOU ON A DIET?
I'M SKINNY BECAUSE I STAY ON MY DIET.
SOMEONE LIKE ME WHO QUIT PHYSICAL TRAINING HAS TO BE SUPER CAREFUL. I CAN GAIN WEIGHT IN A FLASH.
FIL
NOW! IF YOU SIT DOWN IN THE MIDDLE OF DANCE, YOUR HIPS GET BIGGER. LET'S TRY THAT PART AGAIN.
WHAT'S IT ALL FOR?
WHY DOES A GIRL LIKE SONYA HAVE TO STAY ON A DIET, AND FIX HER PRETTY FACE?

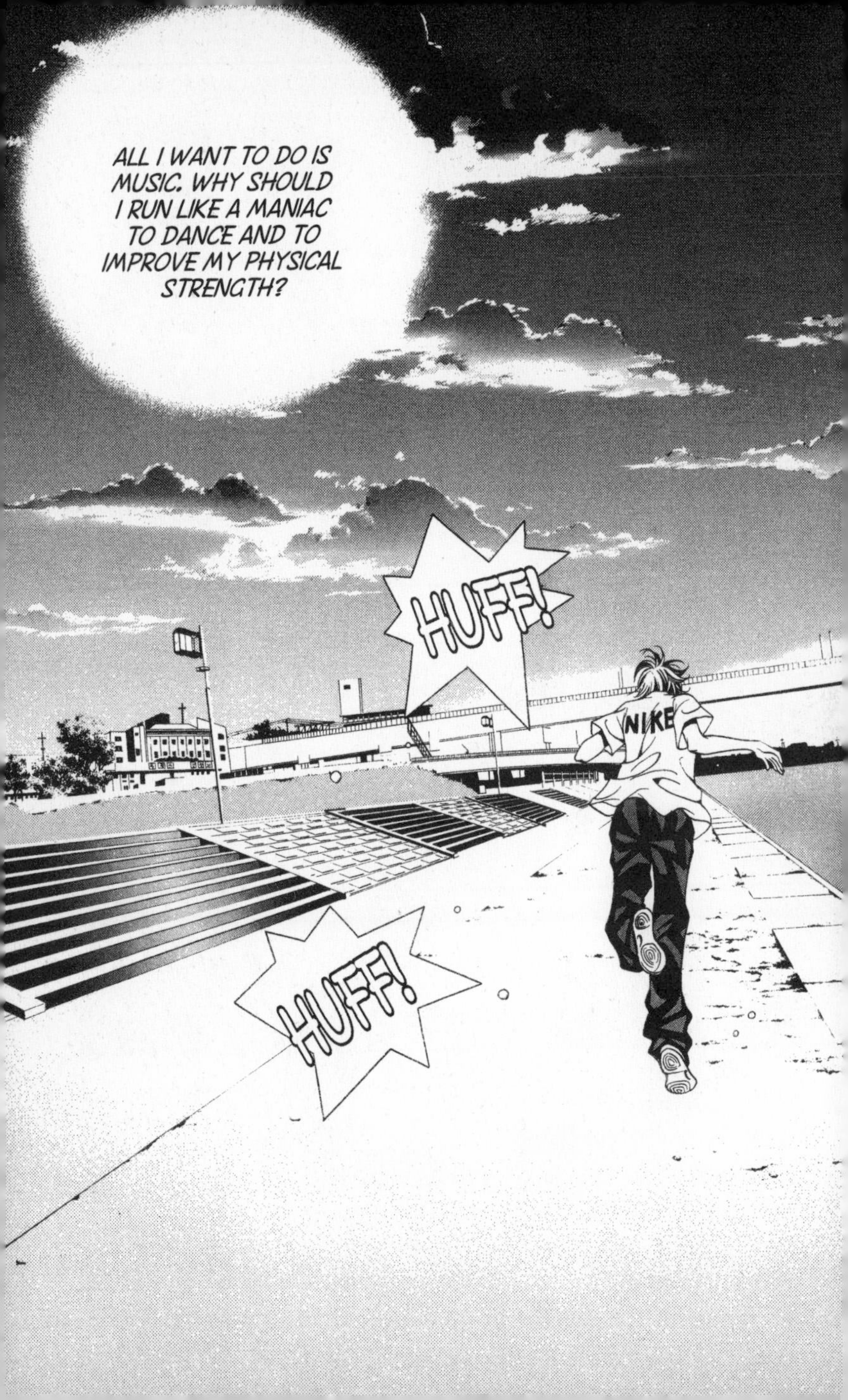
ALL I WANT TO DO IS MUSIC. WHY SHOULD I RUN LIKE A MANIAC TO DANCE AND TO IMPROVE MY PHYSICAL STRENGTH?
HUFF!
NIKE
HUFF!

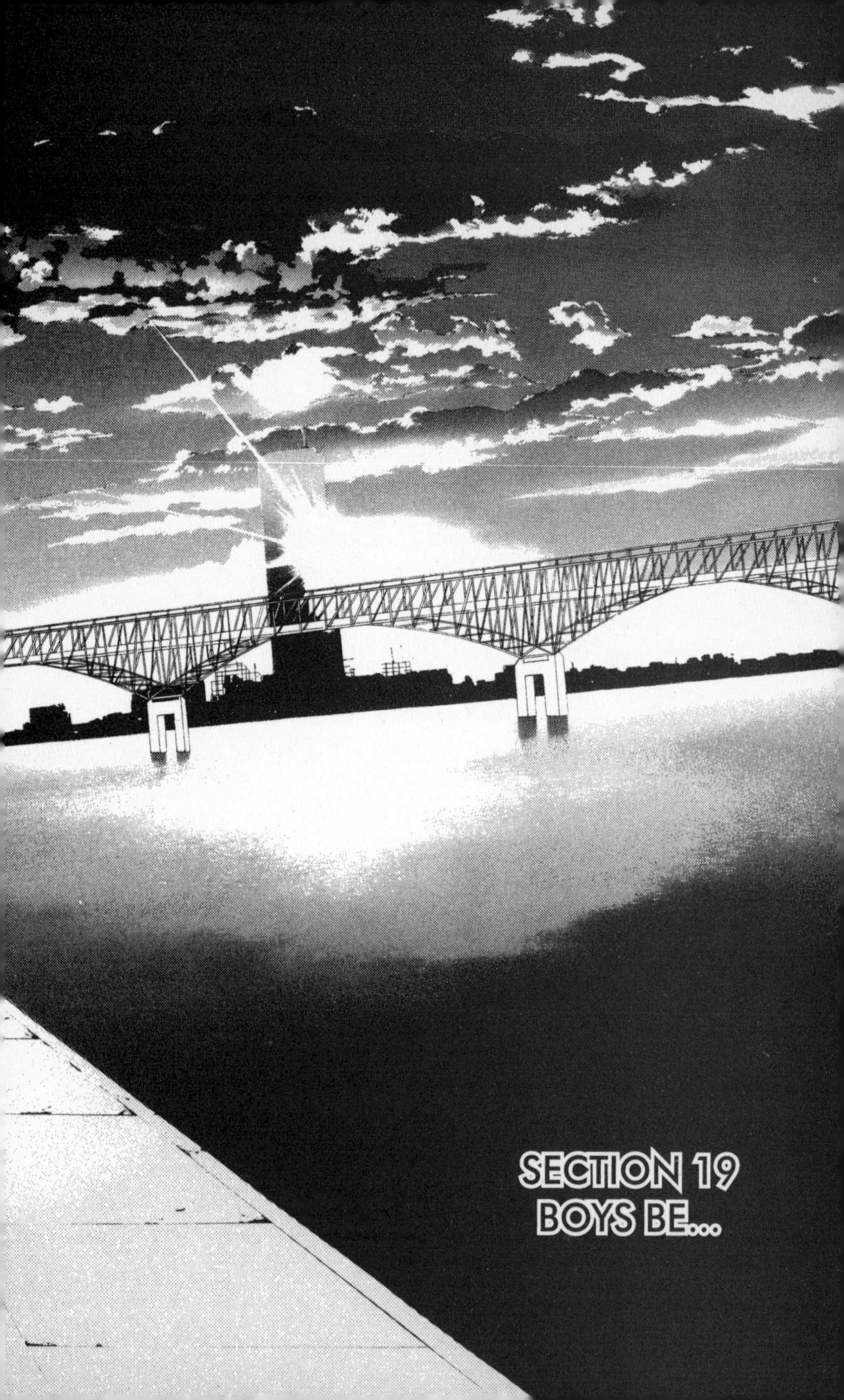
SECTION 19
BOYS BE...

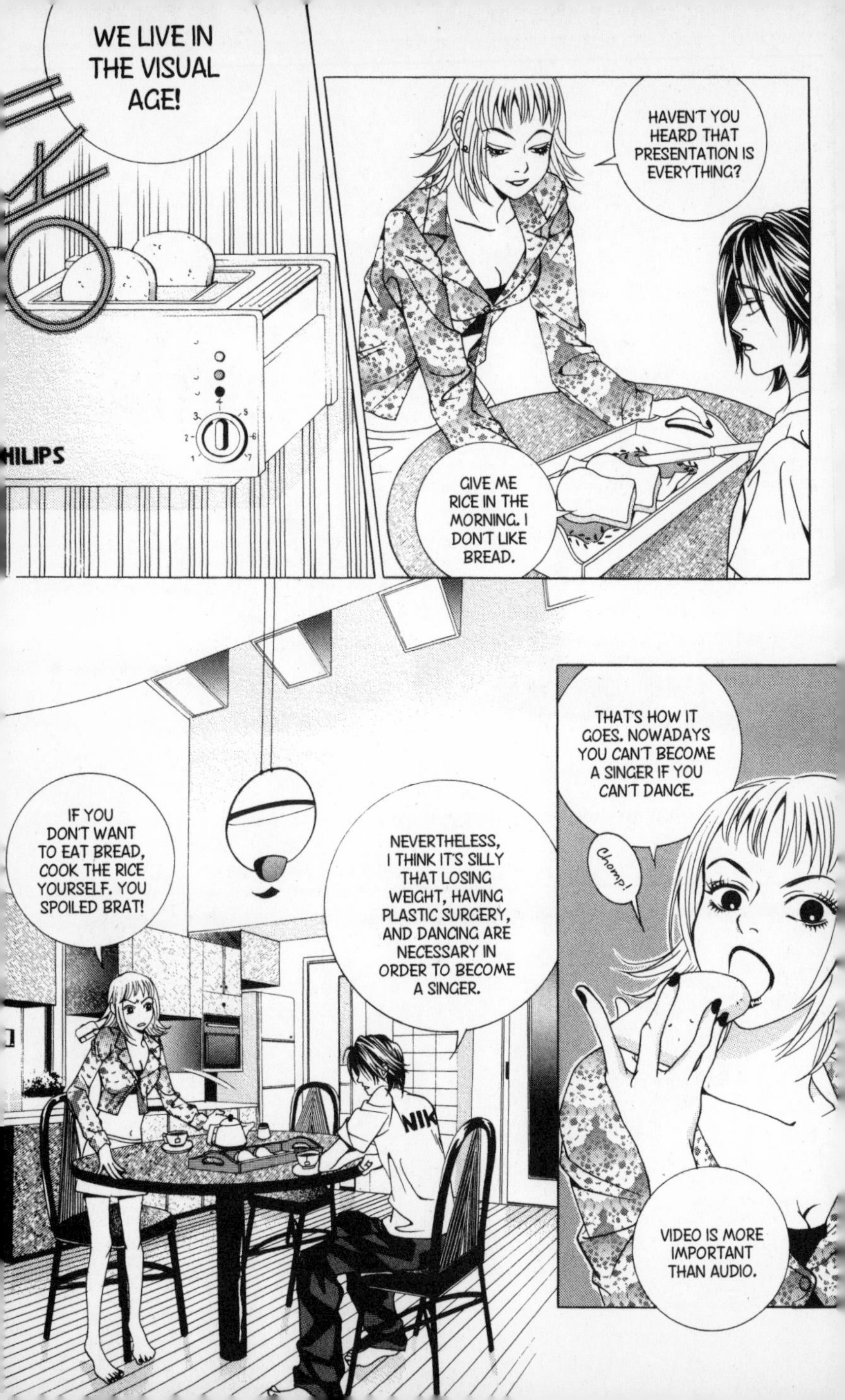
WE LIVE IN THE VISUAL AGE!
PHILIPS
HAVEN'T YOU HEARD THAT PRESENTATION IS EVERYTHING?
GIVE ME RICE IN THE MORNING. I DON'T LIKE BREAD.
IF YOU DON'T WANT TO EAT BREAD, COOK THE RICE YOURSELF. YOU SPOILED BRAT!
NEVERTHELESS, I THINK IT'S SILLY THAT LOSING WEIGHT, HAVING PLASTIC SURGERY, AND DANCING ARE NECESSARY IN ORDER TO BECOME A SINGER.
NIK
THAT'S HOW IT GOES. NOWADAYS YOU CAN'T BECOME A SINGER IF YOU CAN'T DANCE.
Chomp!
VIDEO IS MORE IMPORTANT THAN AUDIO.

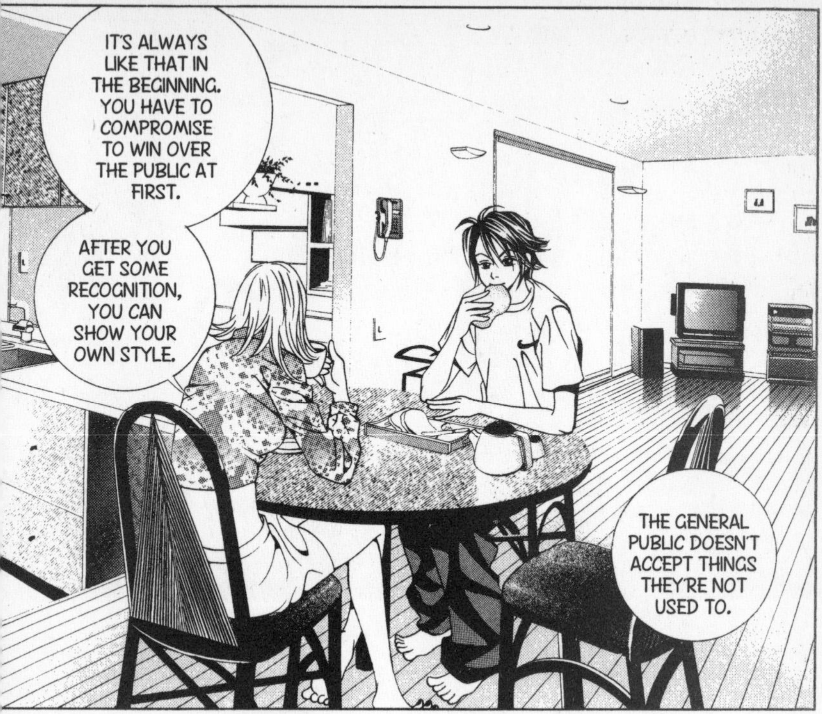
IT'S ALWAYS LIKE THAT IN THE BEGINNING. YOU HAVE TO COMPROMISE TO WIN OVER THE PUBLIC AT FIRST.
AFTER YOU GET SOME RECOGNITION, YOU CAN SHOW YOUR OWN STYLE.
THE GENERAL PUBLIC DOESN'T ACCEPT THINGS THEY'RE NOT USED TO.

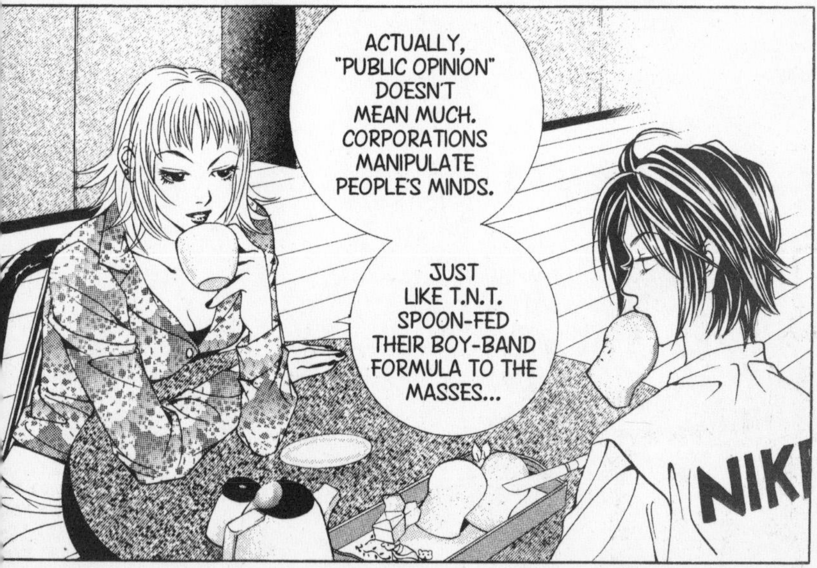
ACTUALLY, "PUBLIC OPINION" DOESN'T MEAN MUCH. CORPORATIONS MANIPULATE PEOPLE'S MINDS.
JUST LIKE T.N.T. SPOON-FED THEIR BOY-BAND FORMULA TO THE MASSES...
NIKE

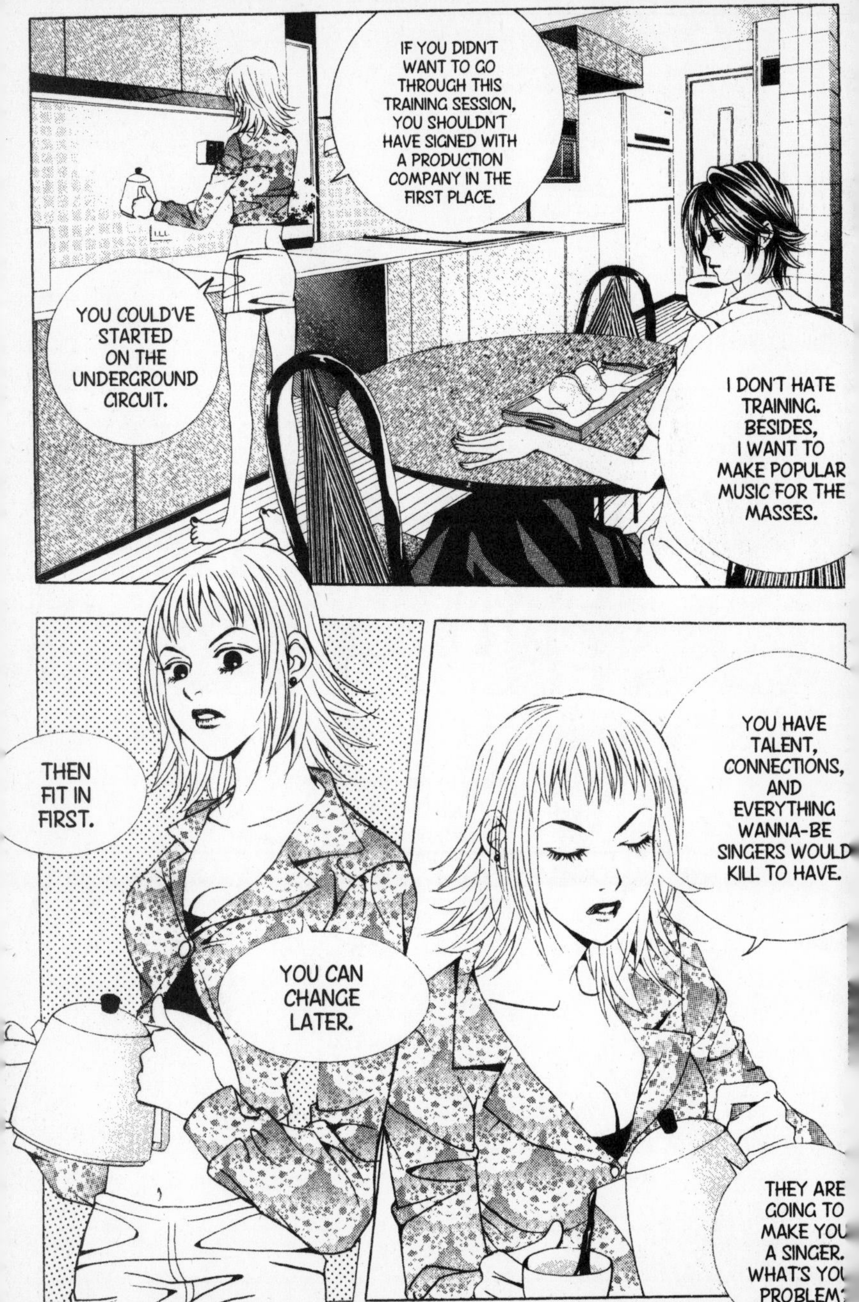
IF YOU DIDN'T WANT TO GO THROUGH THIS TRAINING SESSION, YOU SHOULDN'T HAVE SIGNED WITH A PRODUCTION COMPANY IN THE FIRST PLACE.
YOU COULD'VE STARTED ON THE UNDERGROUND CIRCUIT.
I DON'T HATE TRAINING. BESIDES, I WANT TO MAKE POPULAR MUSIC FOR THE MASSES.
YOU HAVE TALENT, CONNECTIONS, AND EVERYTHING WANNA-BE SINGERS WOULD KILL TO HAVE.
THEY ARE GOING TO MAKE YOU A SINGER. WHAT'S YOU PROBLEM?
THEN FIT IN FIRST.
YOU CAN CHANGE LATER.

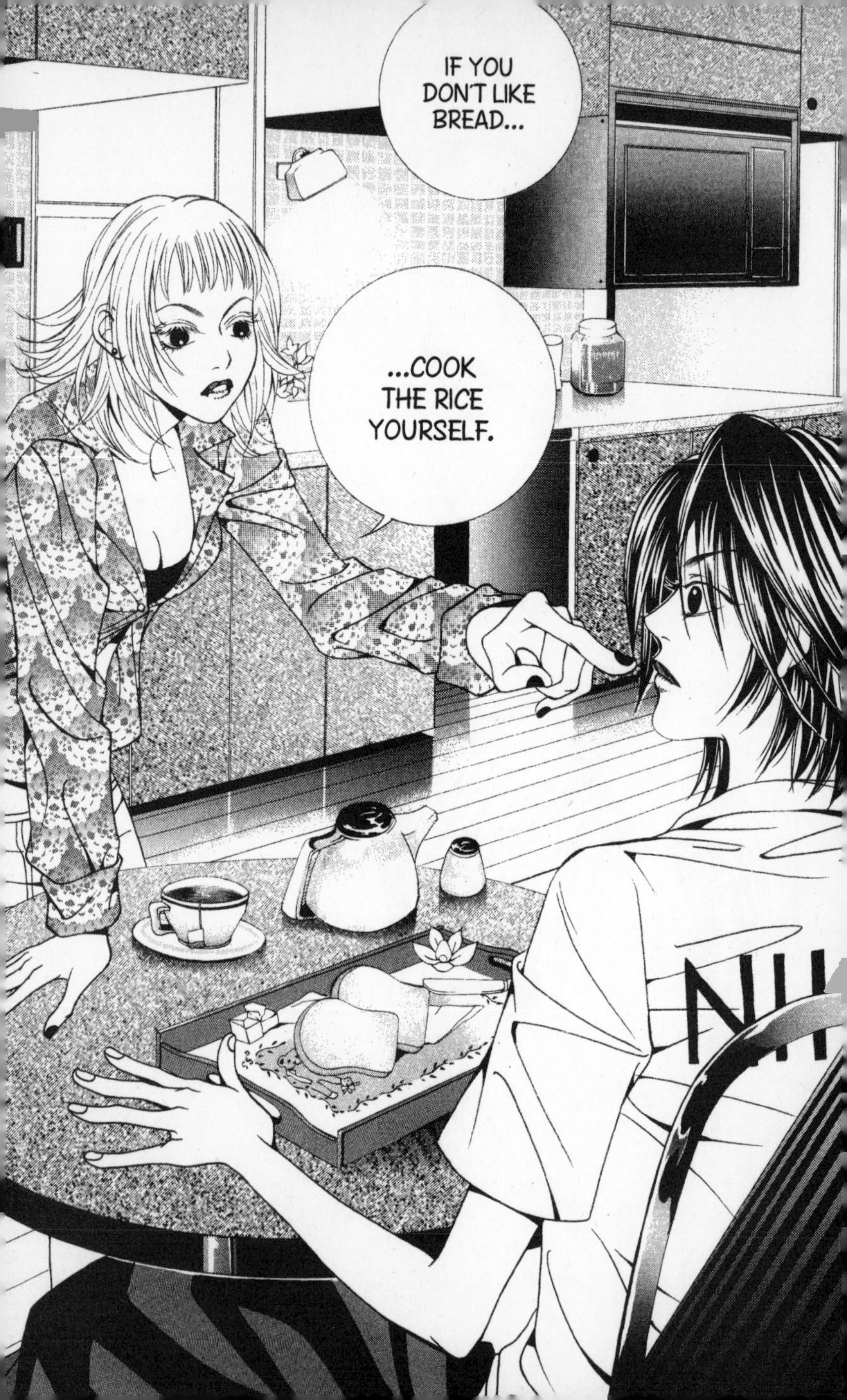
IF YOU DON'T LIKE BREAD...
...COOK THE RICE YOURSELF.
NH

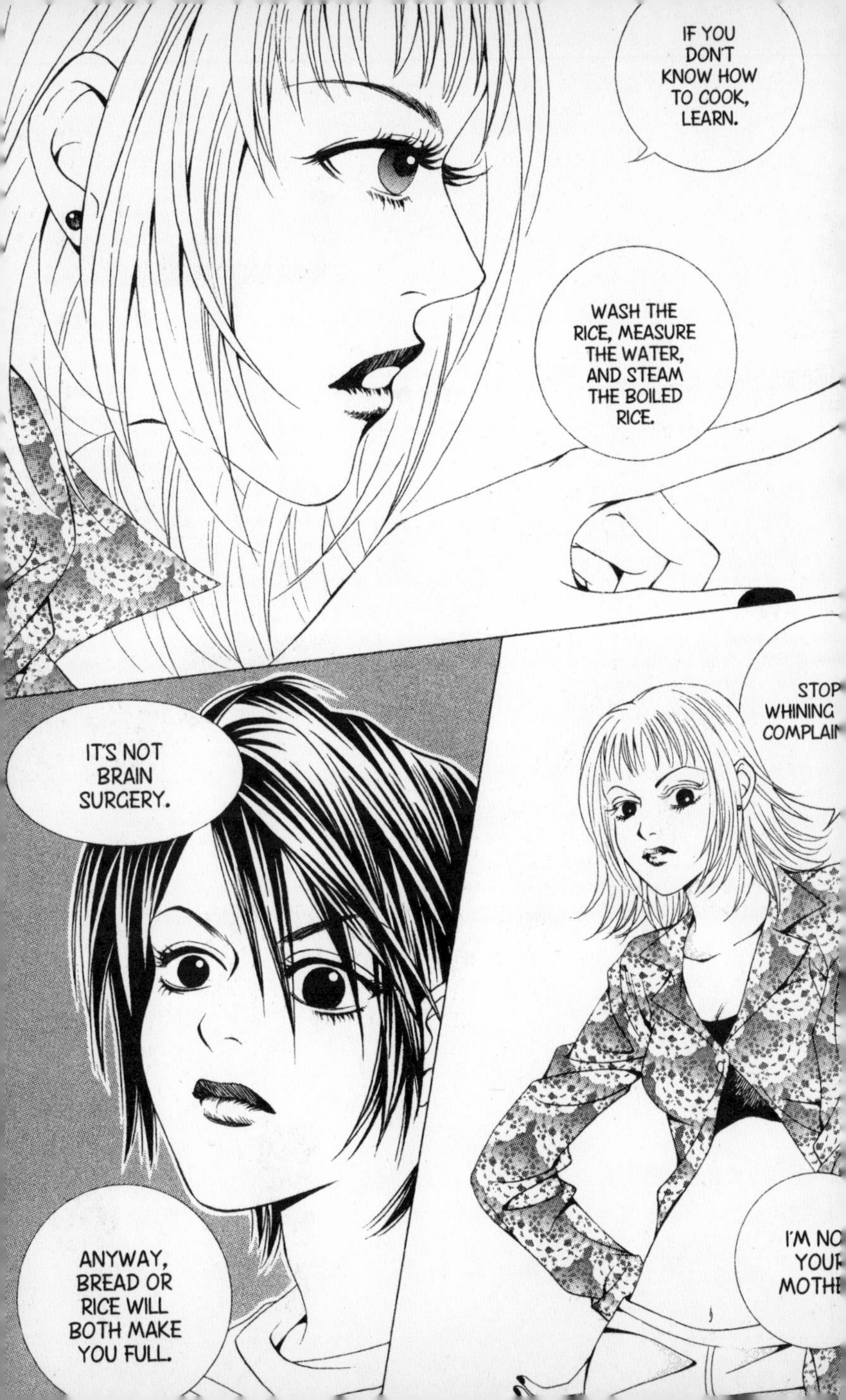
IF YOU DON'T KNOW HOW TO COOK, LEARN.
WASH THE RICE, MEASURE THE WATER, AND STEAM THE BOILED RICE.
STOP WHINING COMPLAI
I'M NO YOUR MOTHE
IT'S NOT BRAIN SURGERY.
ANYWAY, BREAD OR RICE WILL BOTH MAKE YOU FULL.

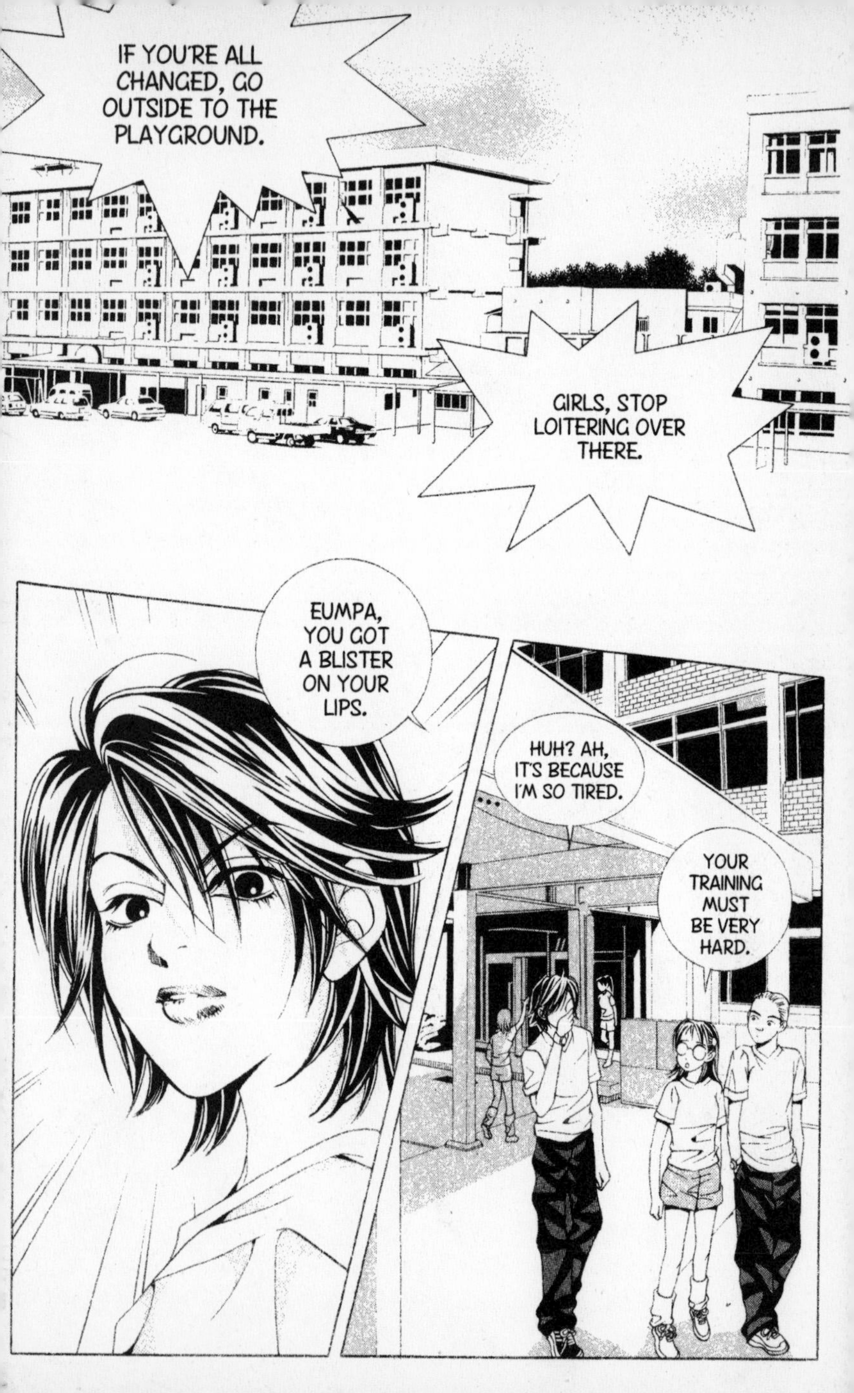
IF YOU'RE ALL CHANGED, GO OUTSIDE TO THE PLAYGROUND.
GIRLS, STOP LOITERING OVER THERE.
EUMPA, YOU GOT A BLISTER ON YOUR LIPS.
HUH? AH, IT'S BECAUSE I'M SO TIRED.
YOUR TRAINING MUST BE VERY HARD.

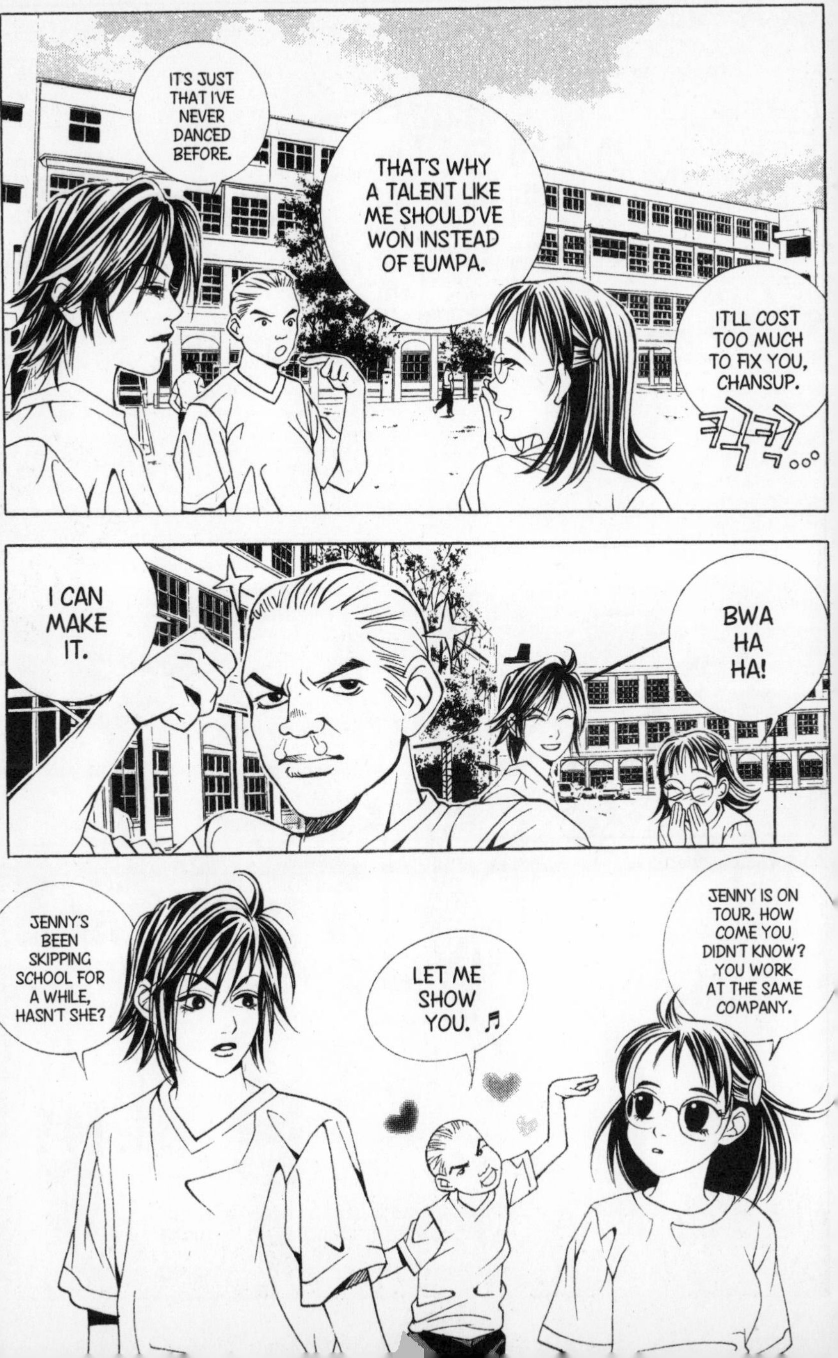
IT'S JUST THAT I'VE NEVER DANCED BEFORE.
THAT'S WHY A TALENT LIKE ME SHOULD'VE WON INSTEAD OF EUMPA.
IT'LL COST TOO MUCH TO FIX YOU, CHANSUP.
I CAN MAKE IT.
BWA HA HA!
JENNY'S BEEN SKIPPING SCHOOL FOR A WHILE, HASN'T SHE?
LET ME SHOW YOU. ♫
JENNY IS ON TOUR. HOW COME YOU DIDN'T KNOW? YOU WORK AT THE SAME COMPANY.

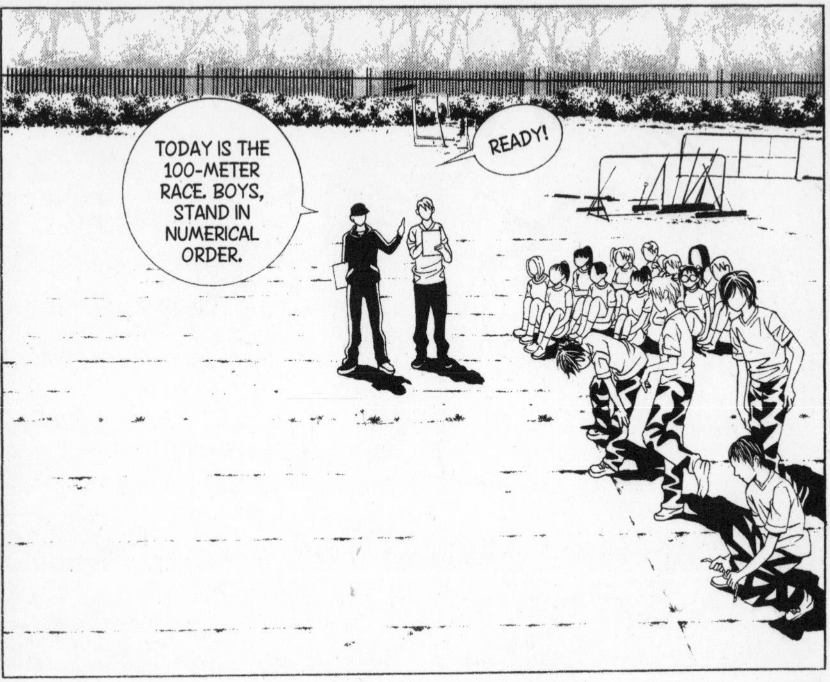
TODAY IS THE 100-METER RACE. BOYS, STAND IN NUMERICAL ORDER.
READY!

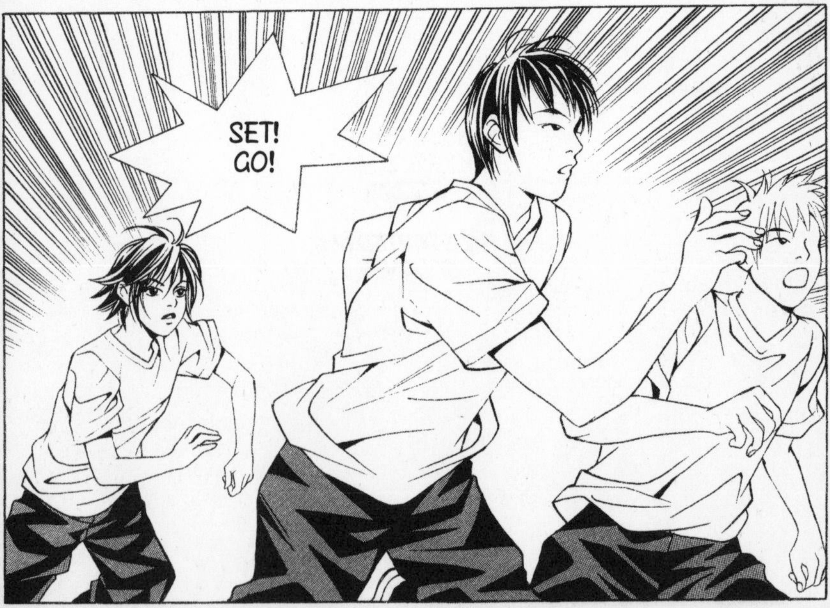
SET! GO!

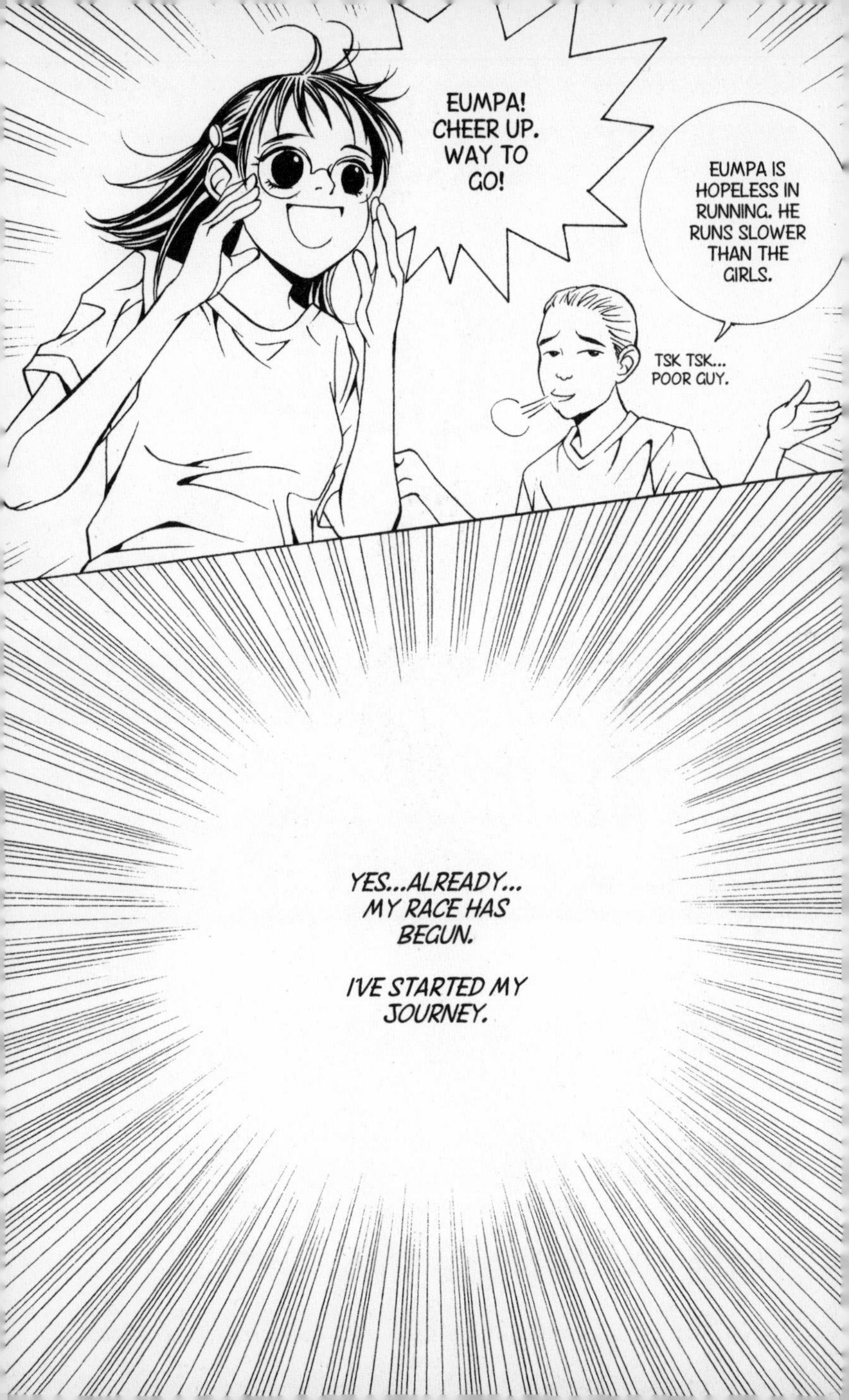
EUMPA IS HOPELESS IN RUNNING. HE RUNS SLOWER THAN THE GIRLS.
TSK TSK... POOR GUY.
EUMPA! CHEER UP. WAY TO GO!
YES...ALREADY... MY RACE HAS BEGUN.
I'VE STARTED MY JOURNEY.

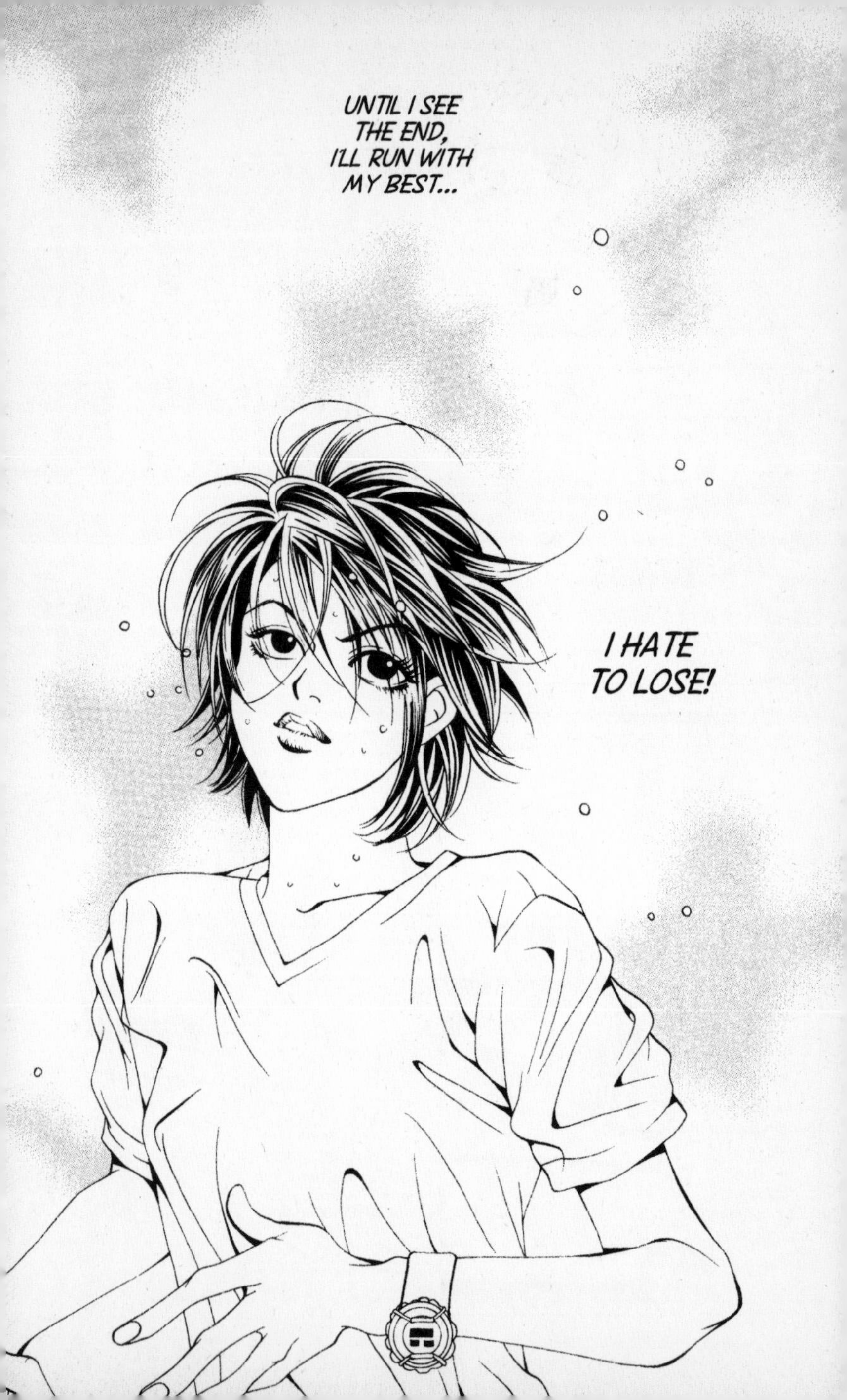
UNTIL I SEE THE END, I'LL RUN WITH MY BEST...
I HATE TO LOSE!

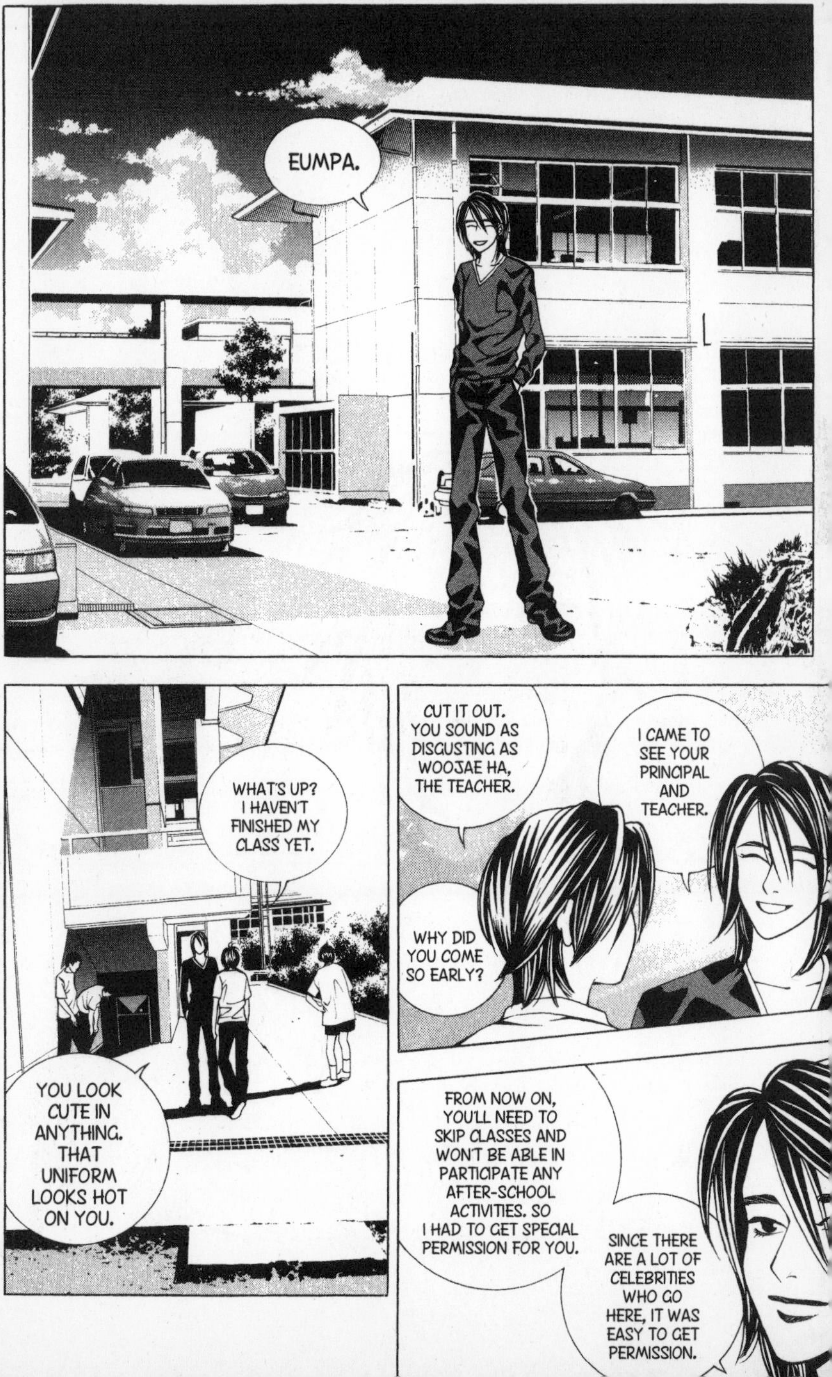
EUMPA.
WHAT'S UP? I HAVEN'T FINISHED MY CLASS YET.
YOU LOOK CUTE IN ANYTHING. THAT UNIFORM LOOKS HOT ON YOU.
CUT IT OUT. YOU SOUND AS DISGUSTING AS WOOJAE HA, THE TEACHER.
WHY DID YOU COME SO EARLY?
I CAME TO SEE YOUR PRINCIPAL AND TEACHER.
FROM NOW ON, YOU'LL NEED TO SKIP CLASSES AND WON'T BE ABLE IN PARTICIPATE ANY AFTER-SCHOOL ACTIVITIES. SO I HAD TO GET SPECIAL PERMISSION FOR YOU.
SINCE THERE ARE A LOT OF CELEBRITIES WHO GO HERE, IT WAS EASY TO GET PERMISSION.

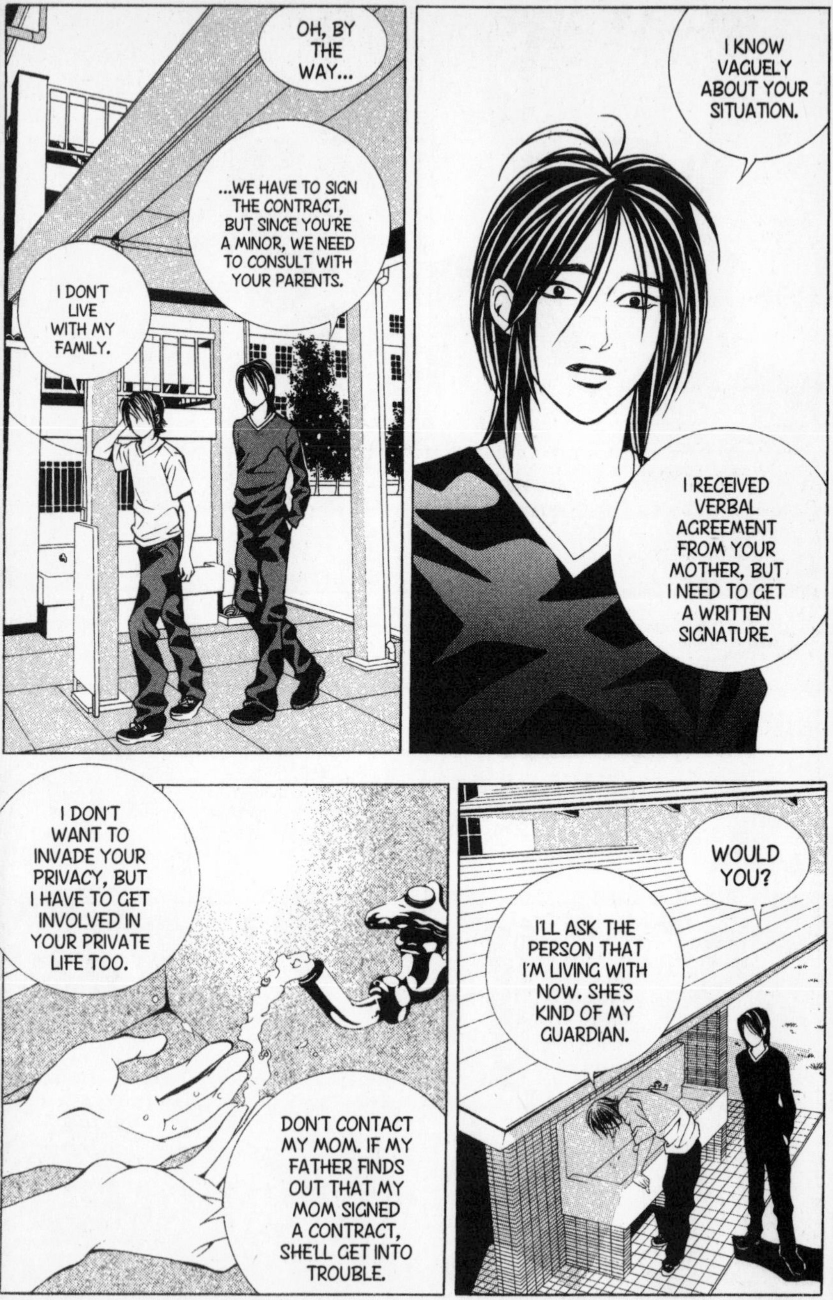
OH, BY THE WAY...
...WE HAVE TO SIGN THE CONTRACT, BUT SINCE YOU'RE A MINOR, WE NEED TO CONSULT WITH YOUR PARENTS.
I DON'T LIVE WITH MY FAMILY.
I KNOW VAGUELY ABOUT YOUR SITUATION.
I RECEIVED VERBAL AGREEMENT FROM YOUR MOTHER, BUT I NEED TO GET A WRITTEN SIGNATURE.
I DON'T WANT TO INVADE YOUR PRIVACY, BUT I HAVE TO GET INVOLVED IN YOUR PRIVATE LIFE TOO.
DON'T CONTACT MY MOM. IF MY FATHER FINDS OUT THAT MY MOM SIGNED A CONTRACT, SHE'LL GET INTO TROUBLE.
I'LL ASK THE PERSON THAT I'M LIVING WITH NOW. SHE'S KIND OF MY GUARDIAN.
WOULD YOU?

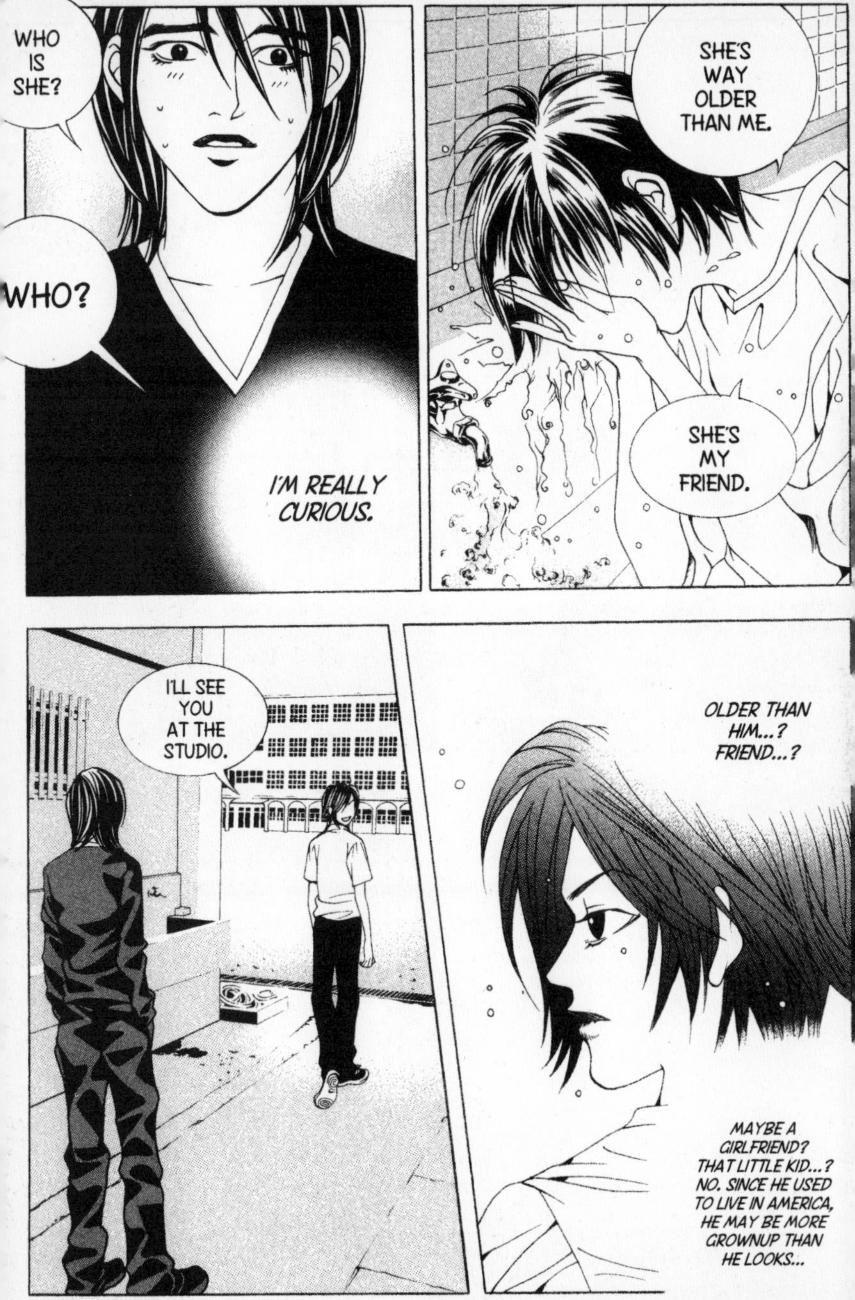
WHO IS SHE?
WHO?
I'M REALLY CURIOUS.
SHE'S WAY OLDER THAN ME.
SHE'S MY FRIEND.
I'LL SEE YOU AT THE STUDIO.
OLDER THAN HIM...? FRIEND...?
MAYBE A GIRLFRIEND? THAT LITTLE KID...? NO. SINCE HE USED TO LIVE IN AMERICA, HE MAY BE MORE GROWNUP THAN HE LOOKS...

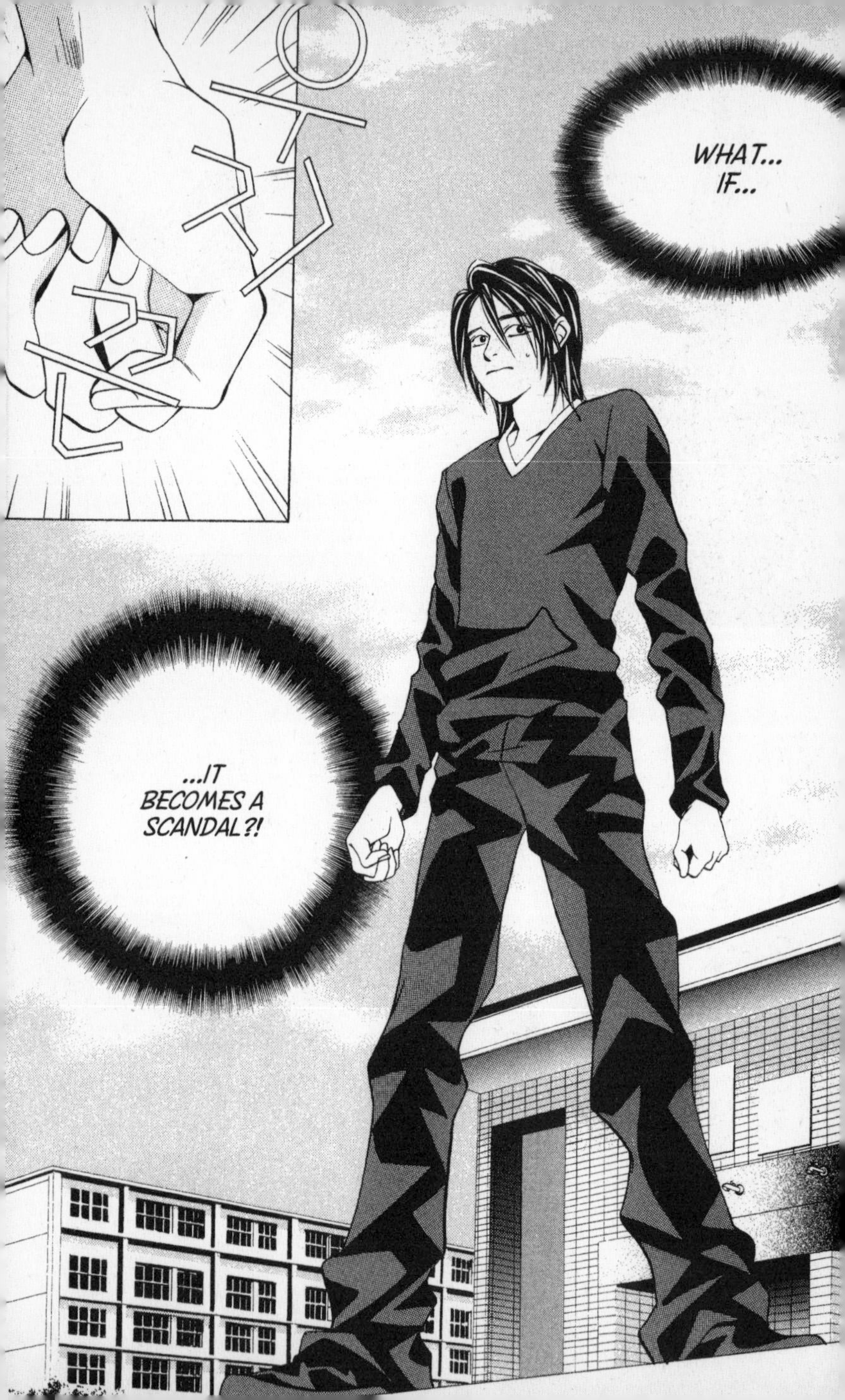
WHAT... IF...
...IT BECOMES A SCANDAL?!

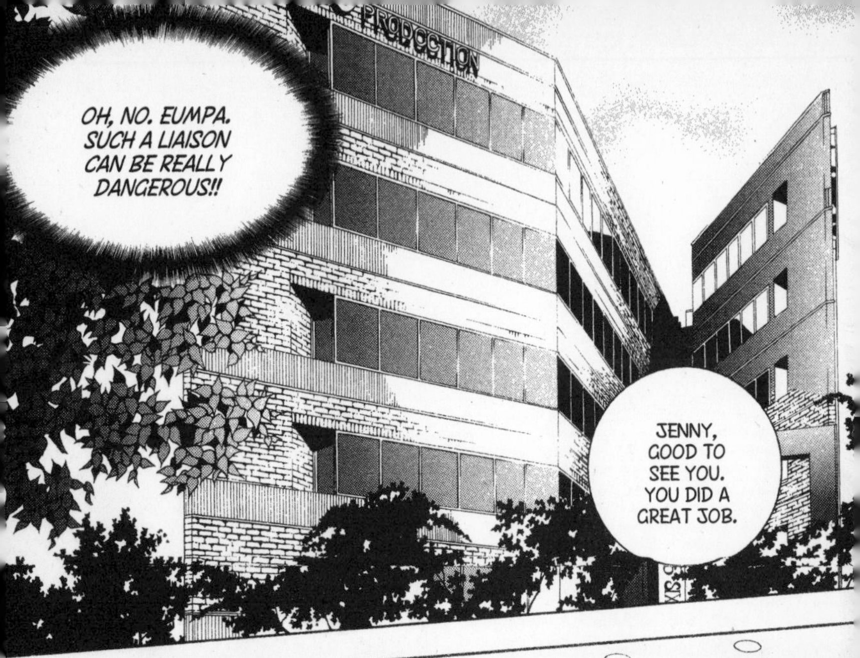
PRODUCTION
OH, NO. EUMPA. SUCH A LIAISON CAN BE REALLY DANGEROUS!!
JENNY, GOOD TO SEE YOU. YOU DID A GREAT JOB.

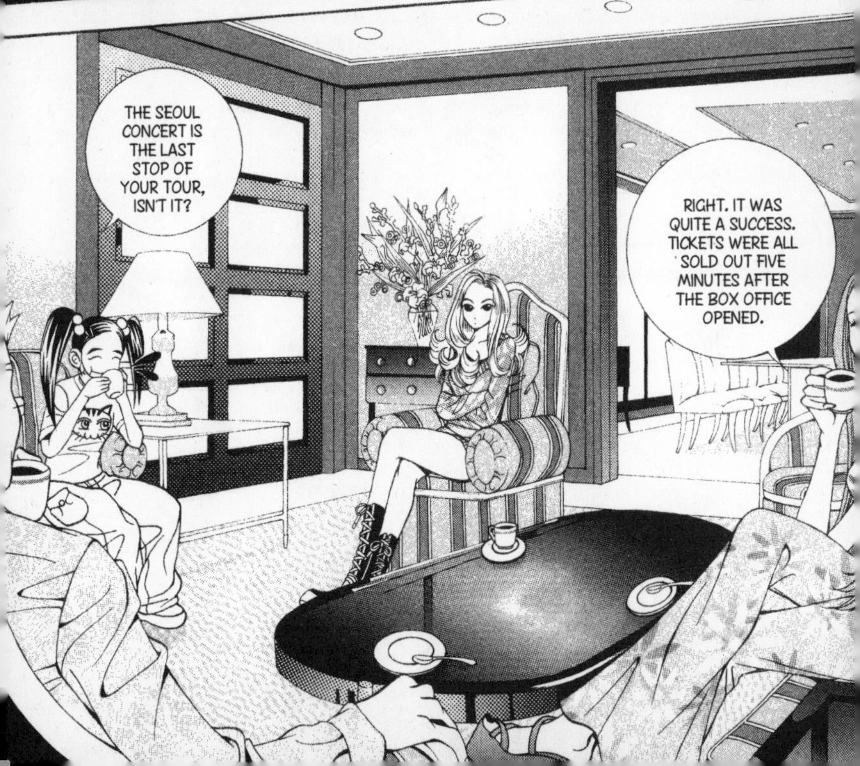
THE SEOUL CONCERT IS THE LAST STOP OF YOUR TOUR, ISN'T IT?
RIGHT. IT WAS QUITE A SUCCESS. TICKETS WERE ALL SOLD OUT FIVE MINUTES AFTER THE BOX OFFICE OPENED.

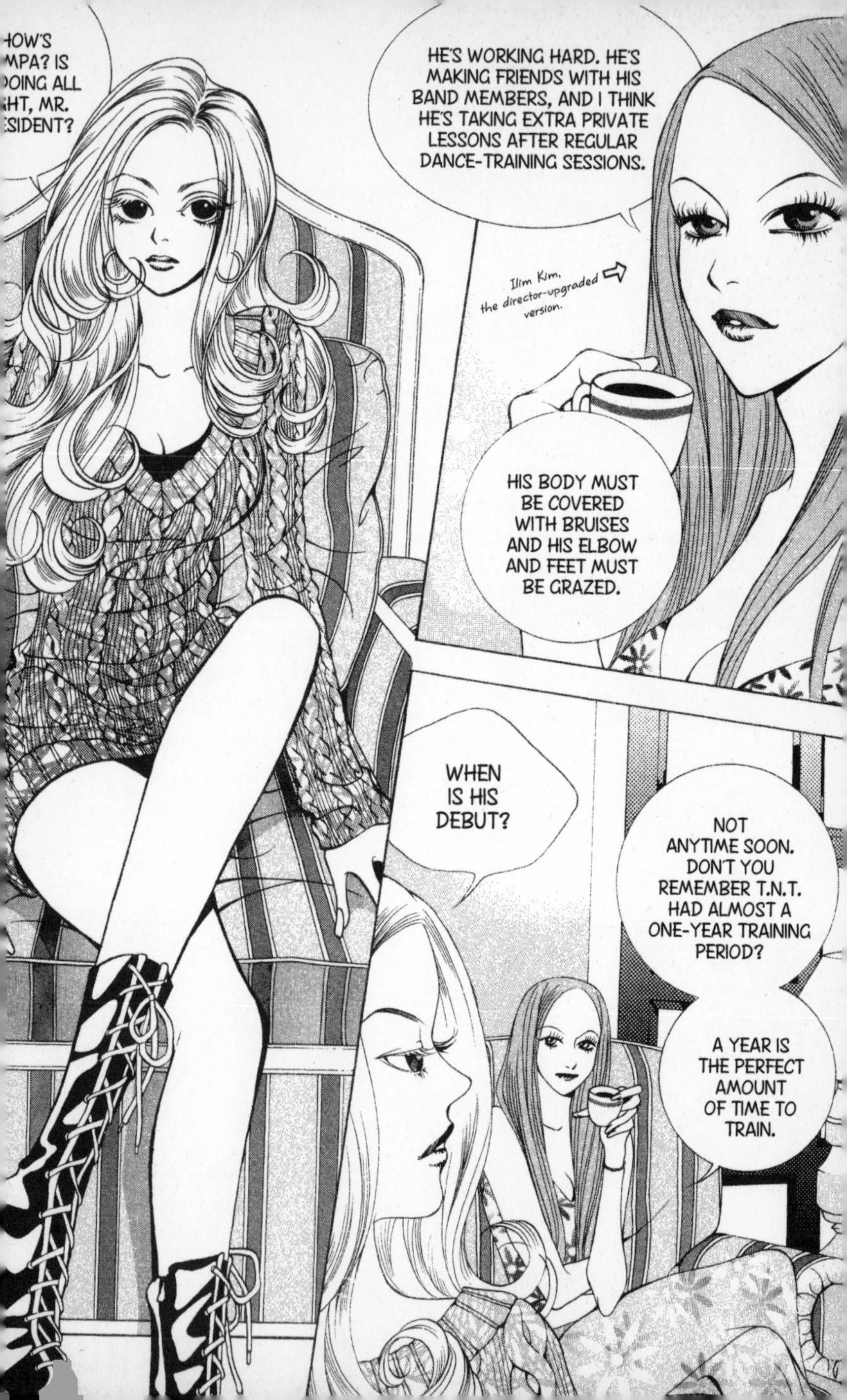
HOW'S MPA? IS DOING ALL HT, MR. ESIDENT?
HE'S WORKING HARD. HE'S MAKING FRIENDS WITH HIS BAND MEMBERS, AND I THINK HE'S TAKING EXTRA PRIVATE LESSONS AFTER REGULAR DANCE-TRAINING SESSIONS.
Ilim Kim, the director-upgraded version.
HIS BODY MUST BE COVERED WITH BRUISES AND HIS ELBOW AND FEET MUST BE GRAZED.
WHEN IS HIS DEBUT?
NOT ANYTIME SOON. DON'T YOU REMEMBER T.N.T. HAD ALMOST A ONE-YEAR TRAINING PERIOD?
A YEAR IS THE PERFECT AMOUNT OF TIME TO TRAIN.

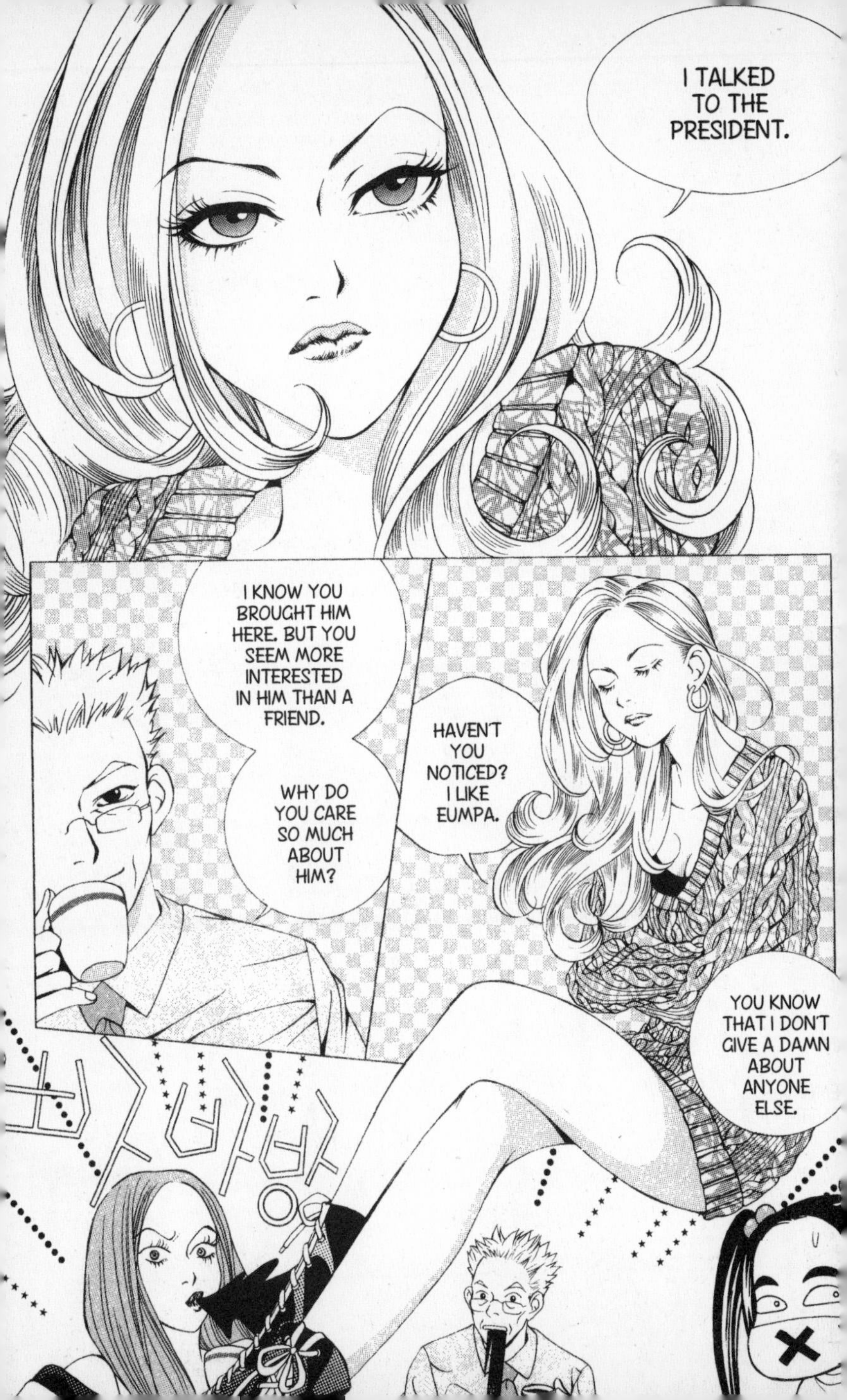
I TALKED TO THE PRESIDENT.
I KNOW YOU BROUGHT HIM HERE. BUT YOU SEEM MORE INTERESTED IN HIM THAN A FRIEND.
WHY DO YOU CARE SO MUCH ABOUT HIM?
HAVEN'T YOU NOTICED? I LIKE EUMPA.
YOU KNOW THAT I DON'T GIVE A DAMN ABOUT ANYONE ELSE.

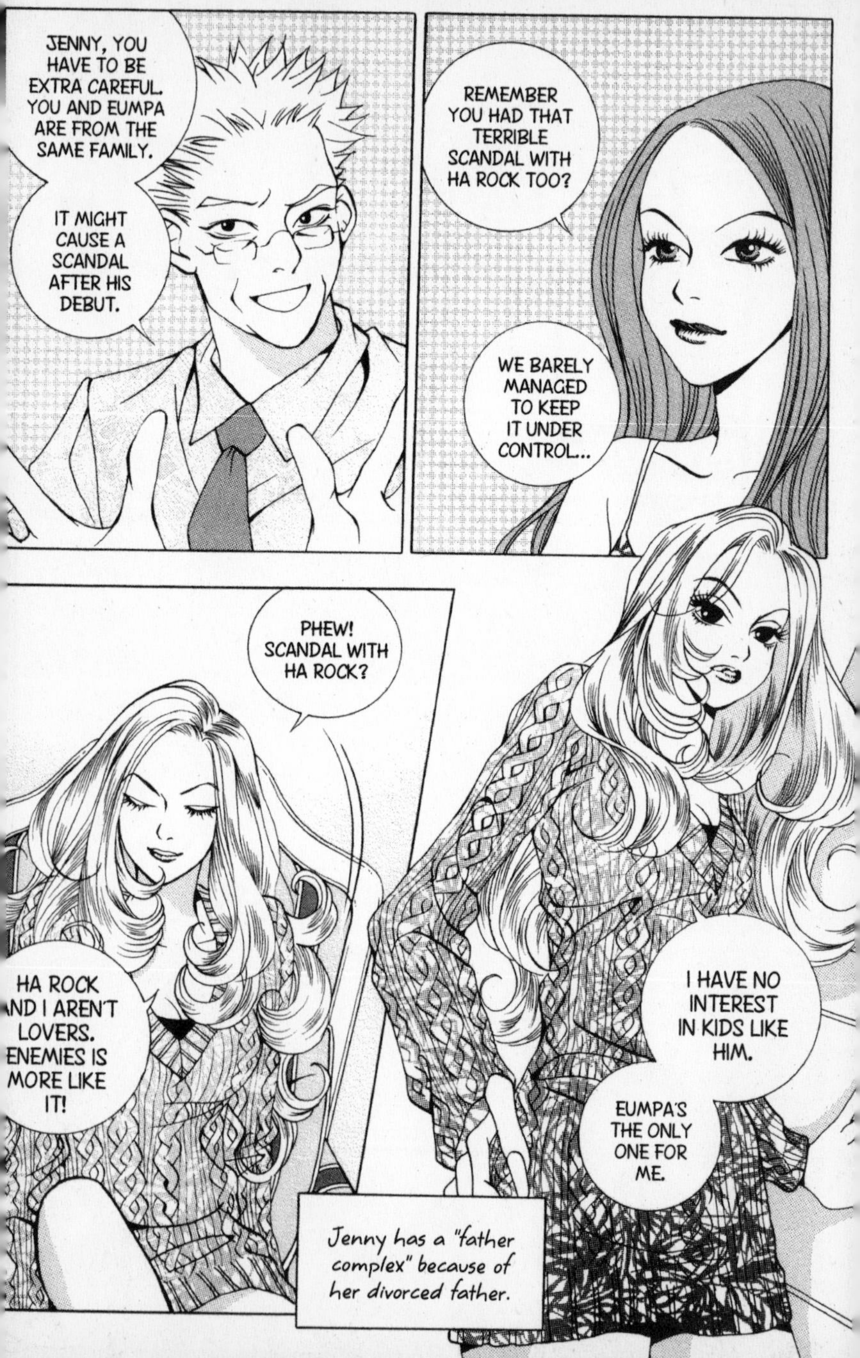
JENNY, YOU HAVE TO BE EXTRA CAREFUL. YOU AND EUMPA ARE FROM THE SAME FAMILY.
IT MIGHT CAUSE A SCANDAL AFTER HIS DEBUT.
REMEMBER YOU HAD THAT TERRIBLE SCANDAL WITH HA ROCK TOO?
WE BARELY MANAGED TO KEEP IT UNDER CONTROL...
PHEW! SCANDAL WITH HA ROCK?
HA ROCK ND I AREN'T LOVERS. ENEMIES IS MORE LIKE IT!
I HAVE NO INTEREST IN KIDS LIKE HIM.
EUMPA'S THE ONLY ONE FOR ME.
Jenny has a "father complex" because of her divorced father.

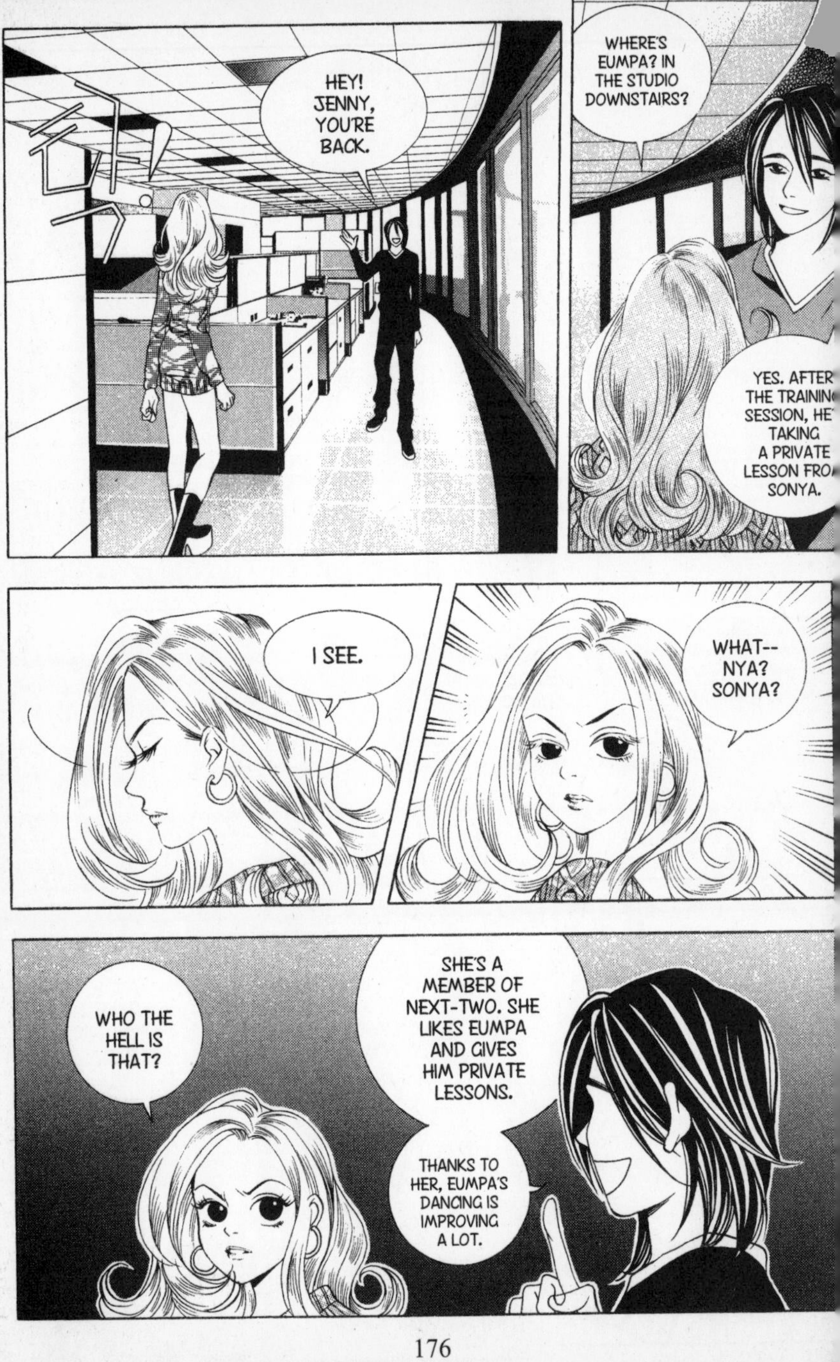
HEY! JENNY, YOU'RE BACK.
WHERE'S EUMPA? IN THE STUDIO DOWNSTAIRS?
YES. AFTER THE TRAININ SESSION, HE TAKING A PRIVATE LESSON FRO SONYA.
I SEE.
WHAT-- NYA? SONYA?
WHO THE HELL IS THAT?
SHE'S A MEMBER OF NEXT-TWO. SHE LIKES EUMPA AND GIVES HIM PRIVATE LESSONS.
THANKS TO HER, EUMPA'S DANCING IS IMPROVING A LOT.

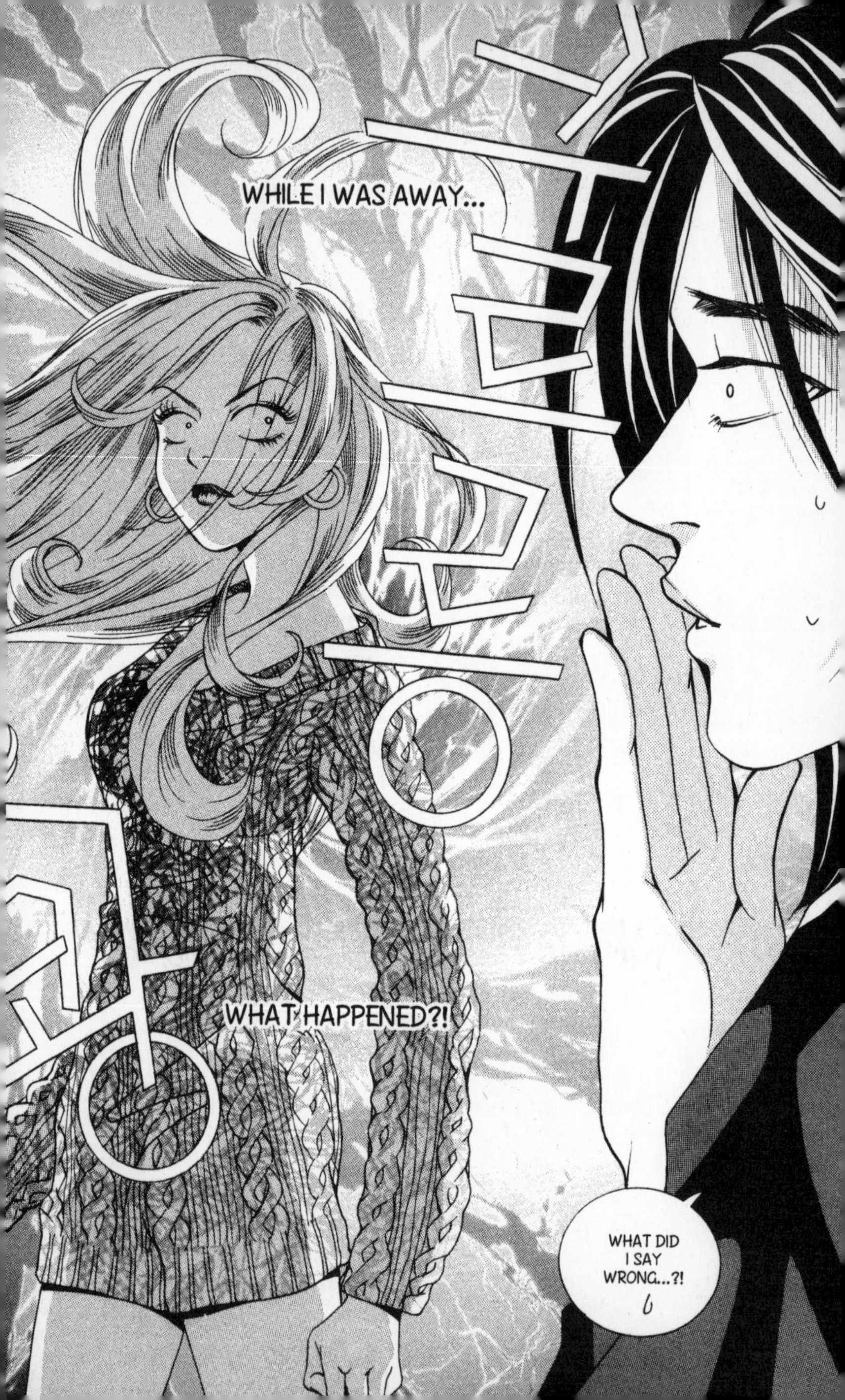
WHILE I WAS AWAY...
WHAT HAPPENED?!
WHAT DID I SAY WRONG...?!

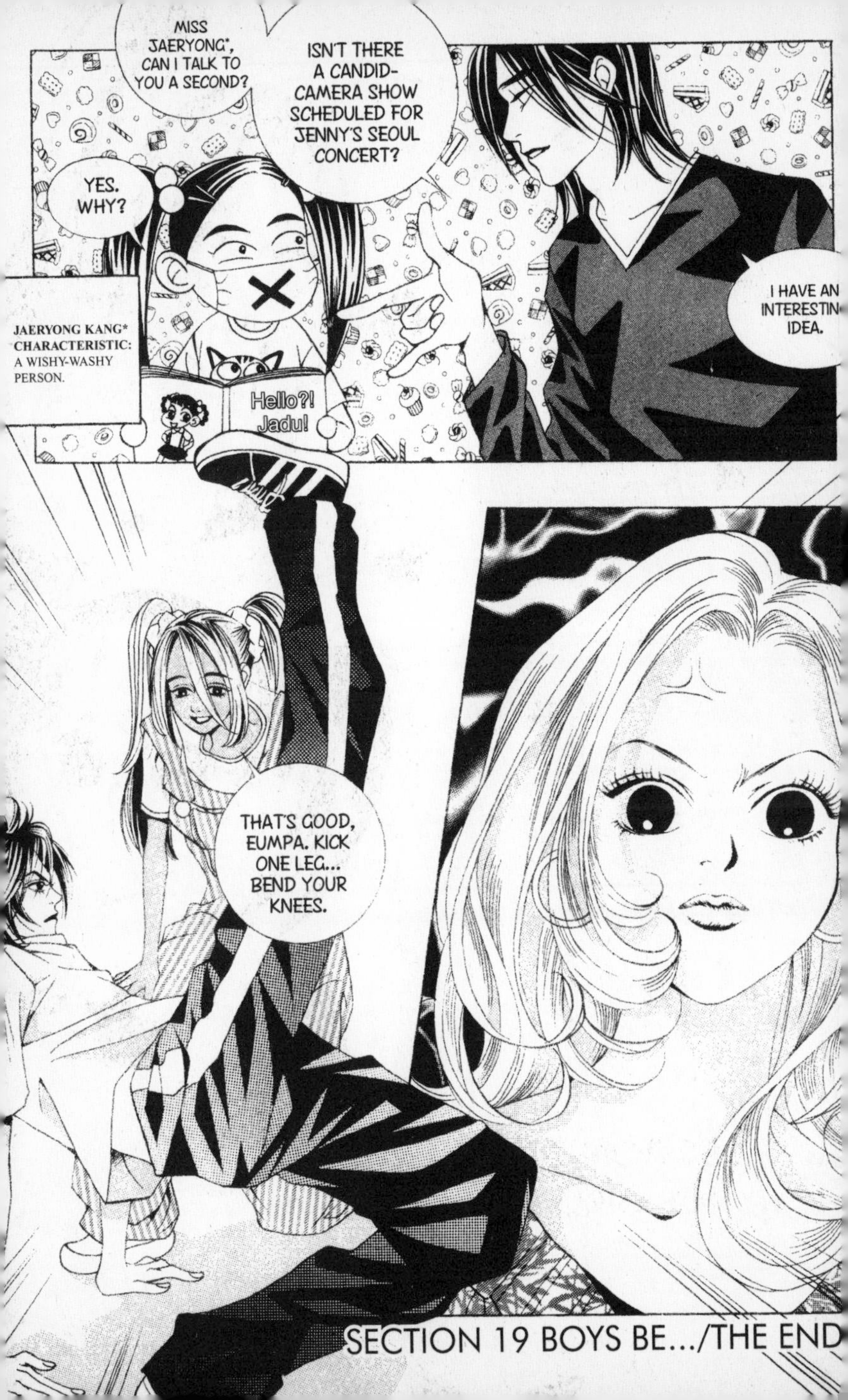
MISS JAERYONG*, CAN I TALK TO YOU A SECOND?
YES. WHY?
ISN'T THERE A CANDID-CAMERA SHOW SCHEDULED FOR JENNY'S SEOUL CONCERT?
JAERYONG KANG* CHARACTERISTIC: A WISHY-WASHY PERSON.
Hello?! Jadu!
I HAVE AN INTERESTIN IDEA.
THAT'S GOOD, EUMPA. KICK ONE LEG... BEND YOUR KNEES.
SECTION 19 BOYS BE.../THE END

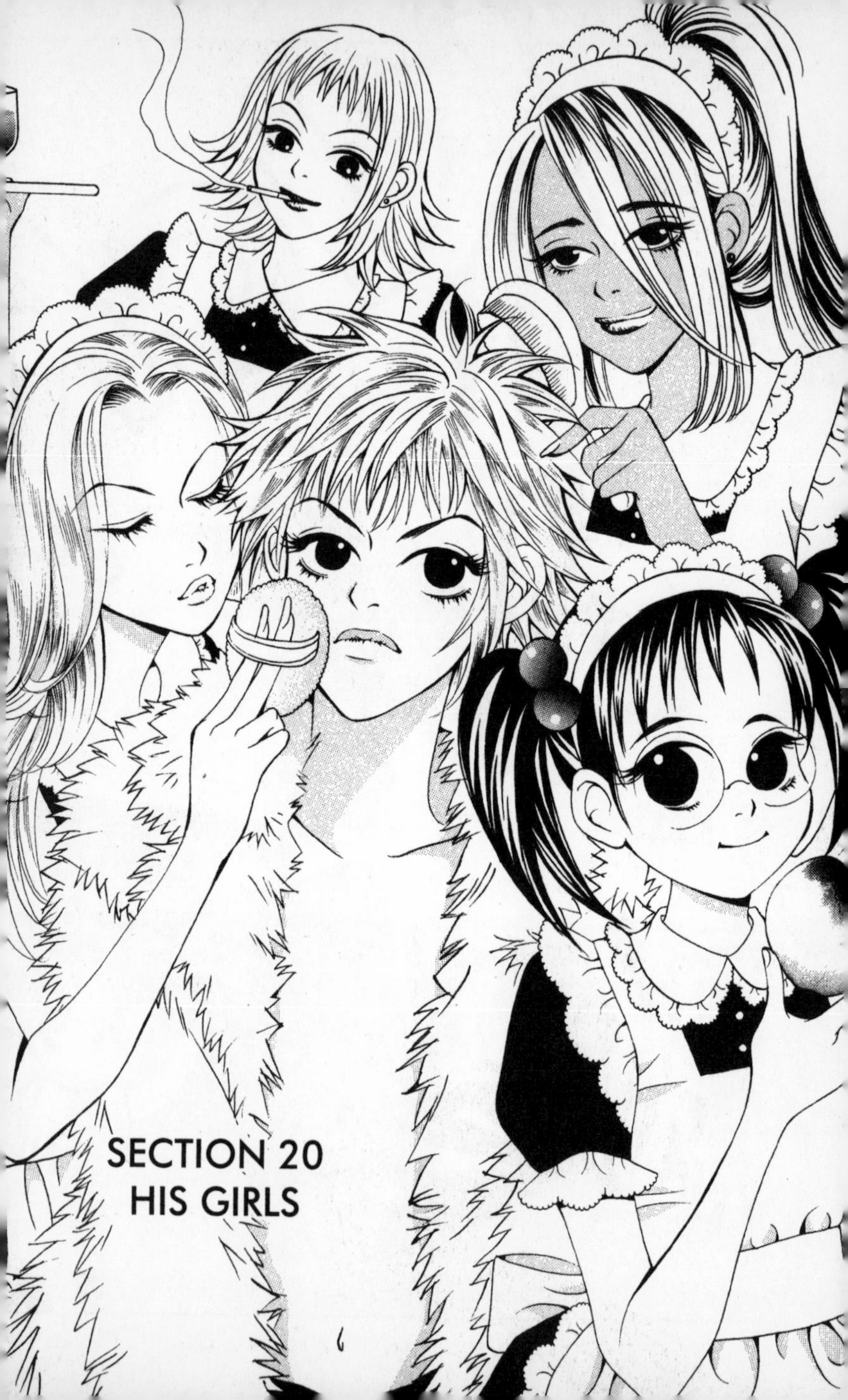
SECTION 20
HIS GIRLS

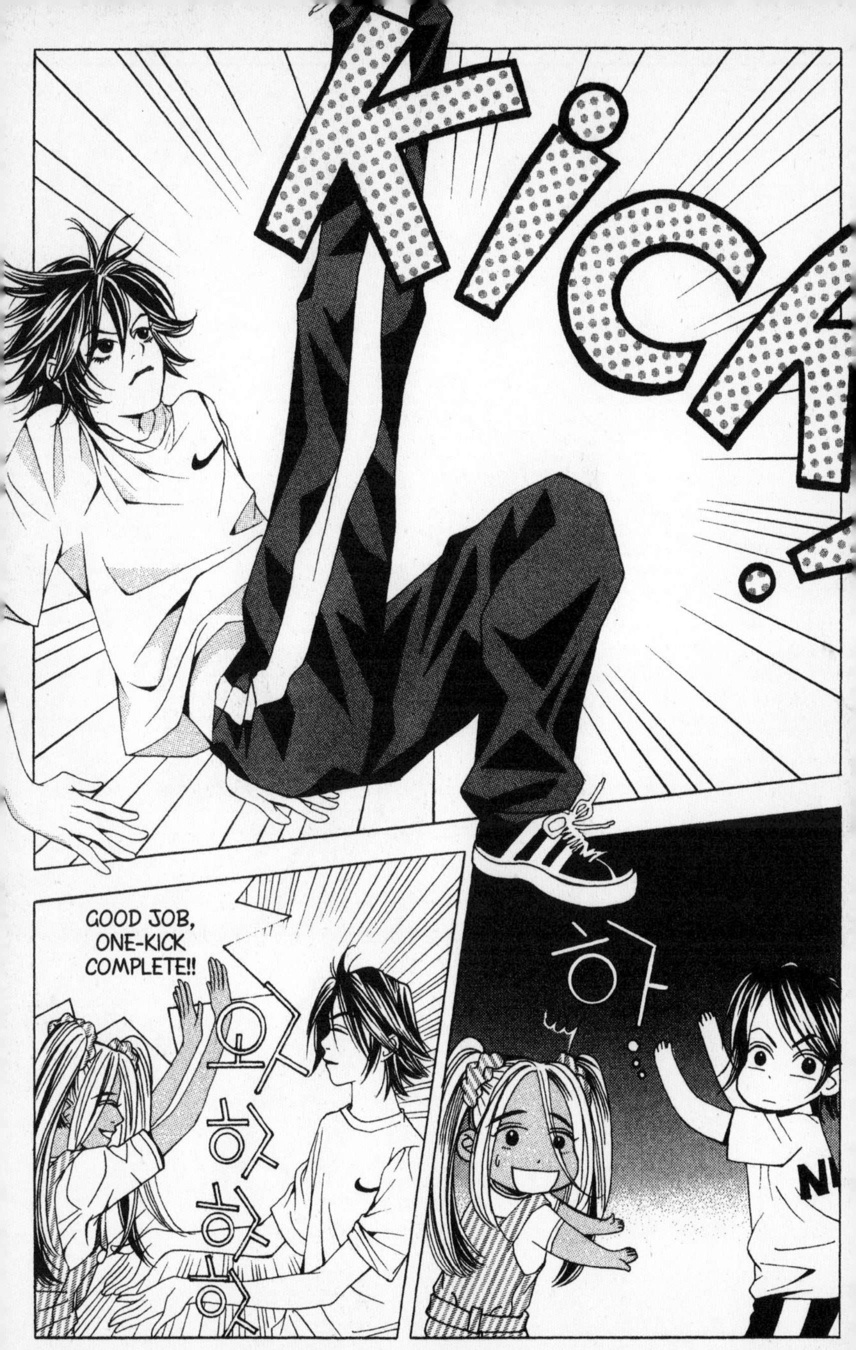
KICK!
GOOD JOB, ONE-KICK COMPLETE!!

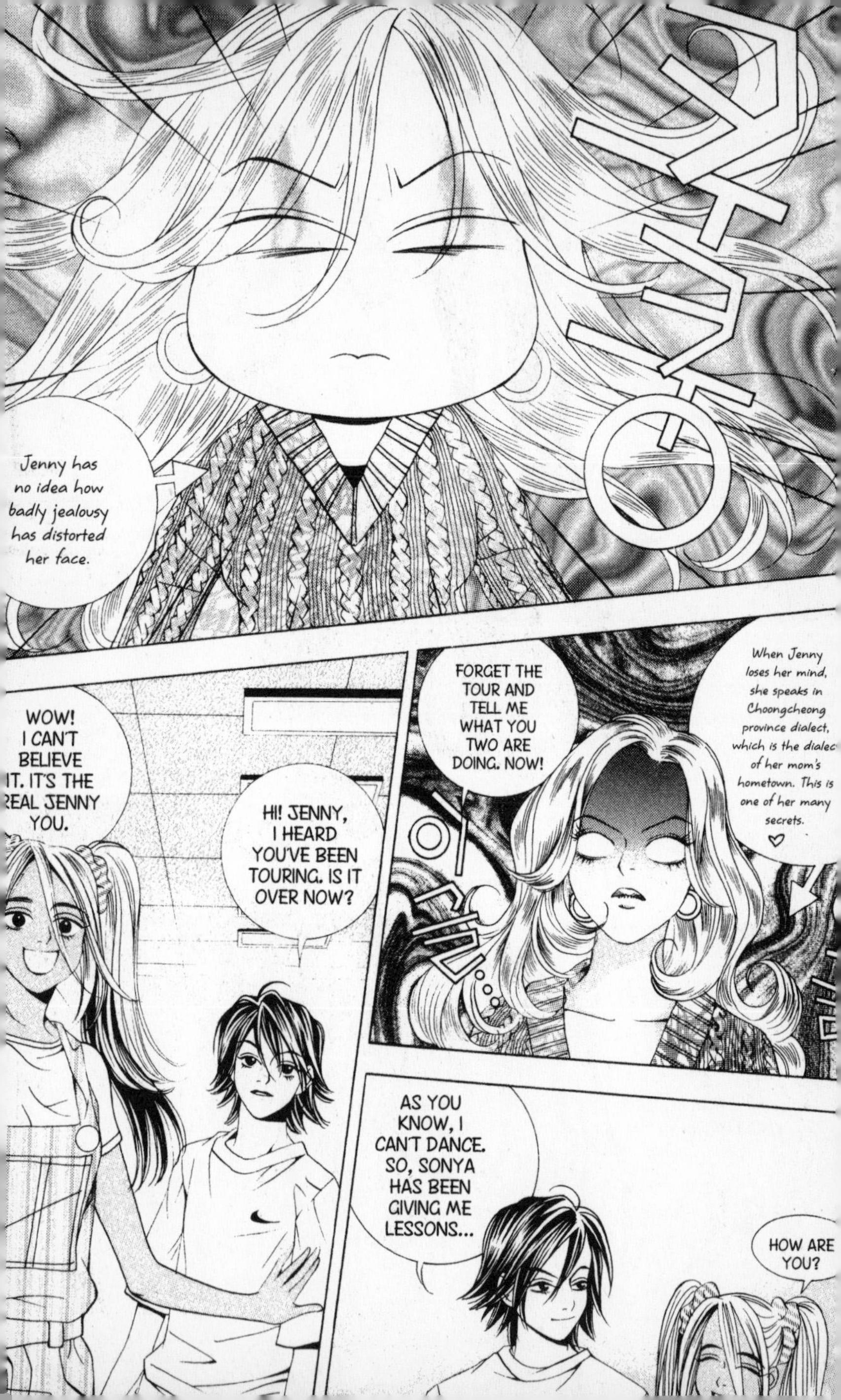
Jenny has no idea how badly jealousy has distorted her face.
WOW! I CAN'T BELIEVE T. IT'S THE EAL JENNY YOU.
HI! JENNY, I HEARD YOU'VE BEEN TOURING. IS IT OVER NOW?
FORGET THE TOUR AND TELL ME WHAT YOU TWO ARE DOING. NOW!
When Jenny loses her mind, she speaks in Choongcheong province dialect, which is the dialec of her mom's hometown. This is one of her many secrets. ♡
AS YOU KNOW, I CAN'T DANCE. SO, SONYA HAS BEEN GIVING ME LESSONS...
HOW ARE YOU?

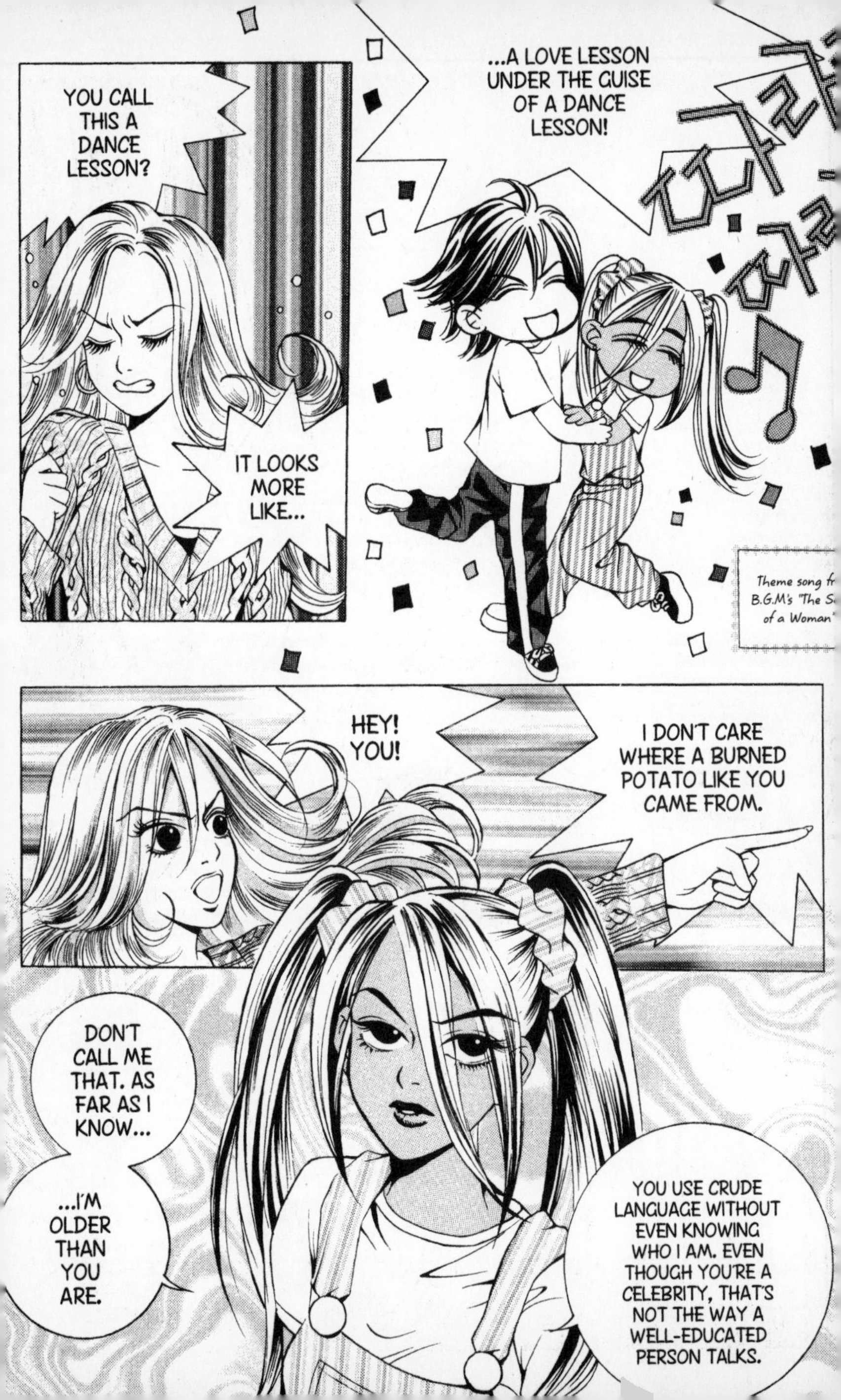
YOU CALL THIS A DANCE LESSON?
IT LOOKS MORE LIKE...
...A LOVE LESSON UNDER THE GUISE OF A DANCE LESSON!
Theme song fr B.G.M's "The S of a Woman"
HEY! YOU!
I DON'T CARE WHERE A BURNED POTATO LIKE YOU CAME FROM.
DON'T CALL ME THAT. AS FAR AS I KNOW...
...I'M OLDER THAN YOU ARE.
YOU USE CRUDE LANGUAGE WITHOUT EVEN KNOWING WHO I AM. EVEN THOUGH YOU'RE A CELEBRITY, THAT'S NOT THE WAY A WELL-EDUCATED PERSON TALKS.

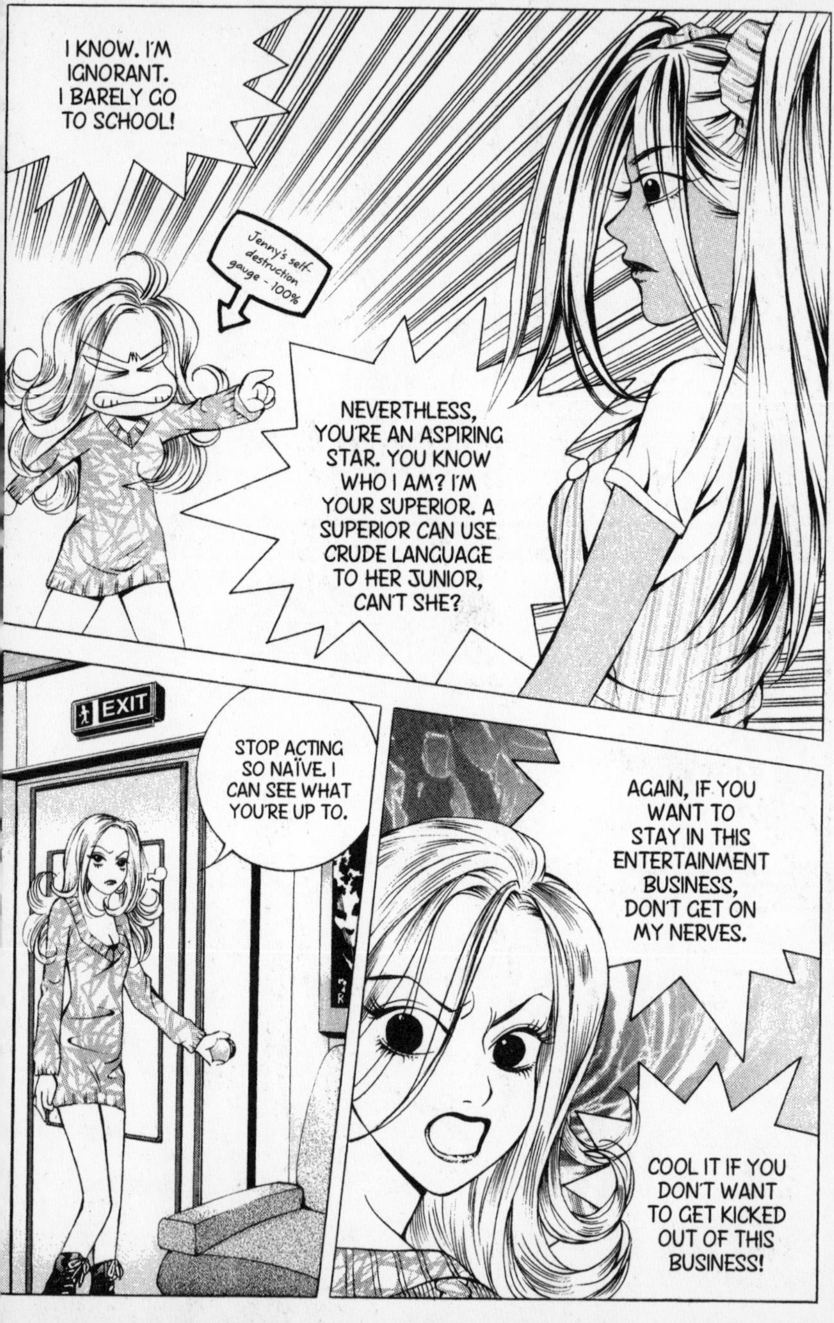
I KNOW. I'M IGNORANT. I BARELY GO TO SCHOOL!
Jenny's self-destruction gauge - 100%
NEVERTHLESS, YOU'RE AN ASPIRING STAR. YOU KNOW WHO I AM? I'M YOUR SUPERIOR. A SUPERIOR CAN USE CRUDE LANGUAGE TO HER JUNIOR, CAN'T SHE?
EXIT
STOP ACTING SO NAÏVE. I CAN SEE WHAT YOU'RE UP TO.
AGAIN, IF YOU WANT TO STAY IN THIS ENTERTAINMENT BUSINESS, DON'T GET ON MY NERVES.
COOL IT IF YOU DON'T WANT TO GET KICKED OUT OF THIS BUSINESS!

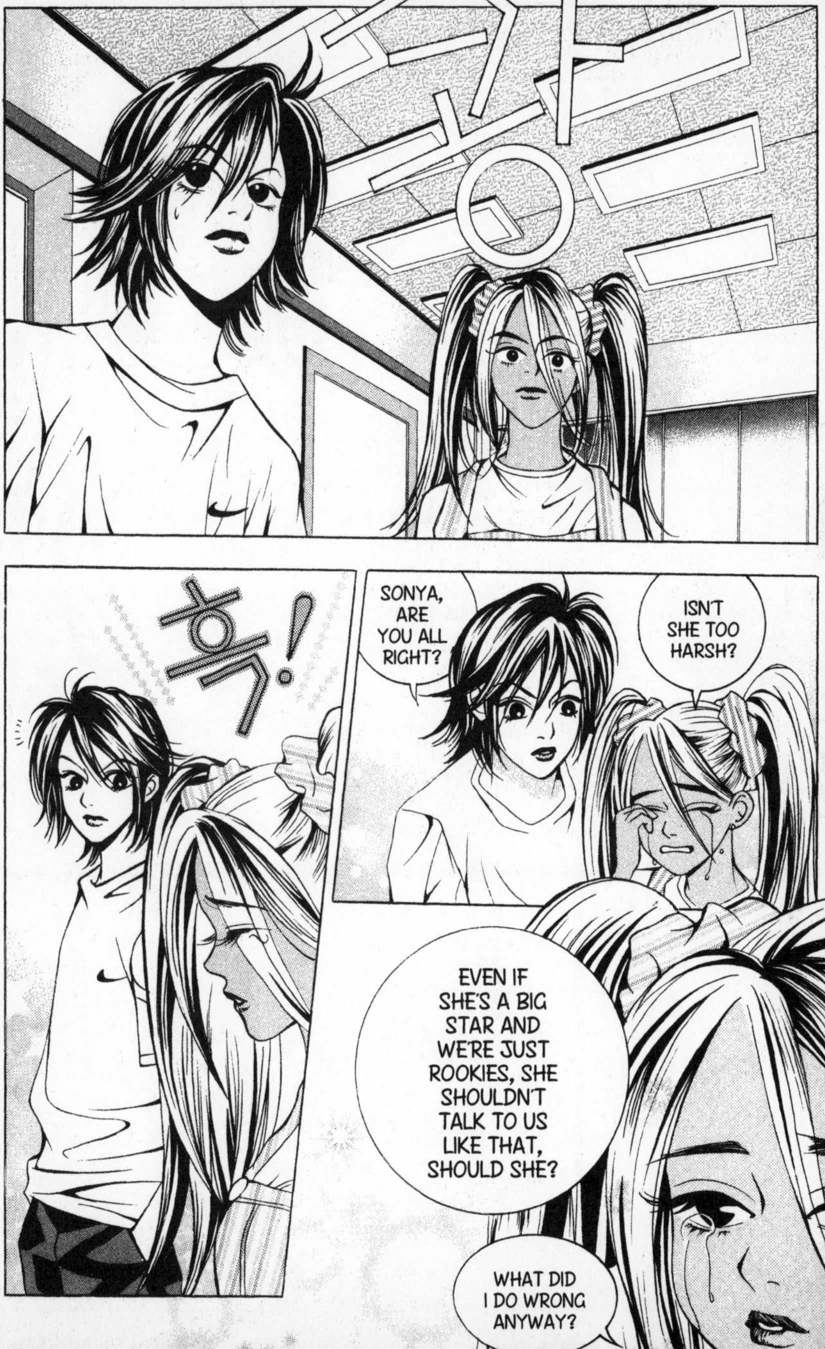
SONYA, ARE YOU ALL RIGHT?
ISN'T SHE TOO HARSH?
EVEN IF SHE'S A BIG STAR AND WE'RE JUST ROOKIES, SHE SHOULDN'T TALK TO US LIKE THAT, SHOULD SHE?
WHAT DID I DO WRONG ANYWAY?

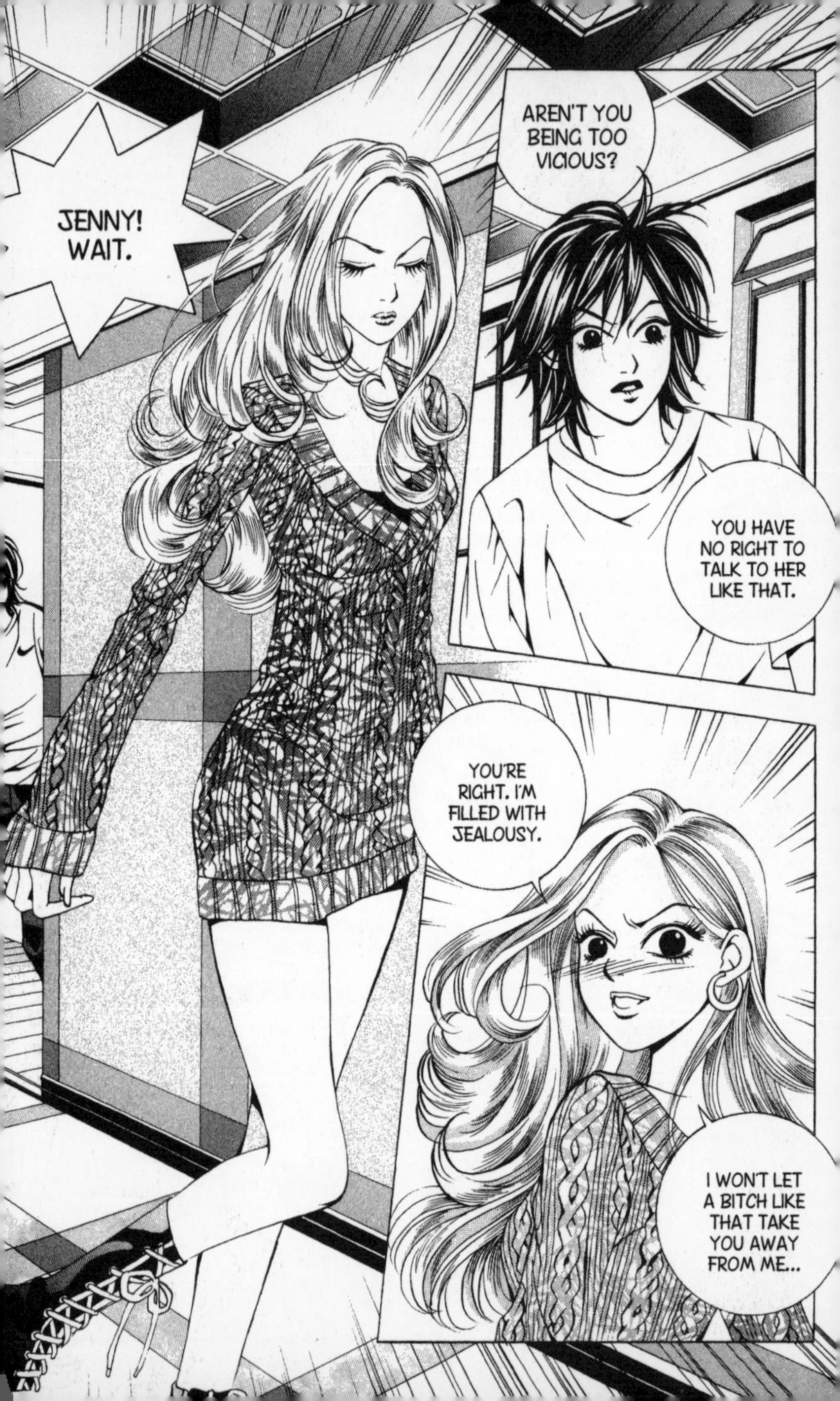
JENNY! WAIT.
AREN'T YOU BEING TOO VICIOUS?
YOU HAVE NO RIGHT TO TALK TO HER LIKE THAT.
YOU'RE RIGHT. I'M FILLED WITH JEALOUSY.
I WON'T LET A BITCH LIKE THAT TAKE YOU AWAY FROM ME...

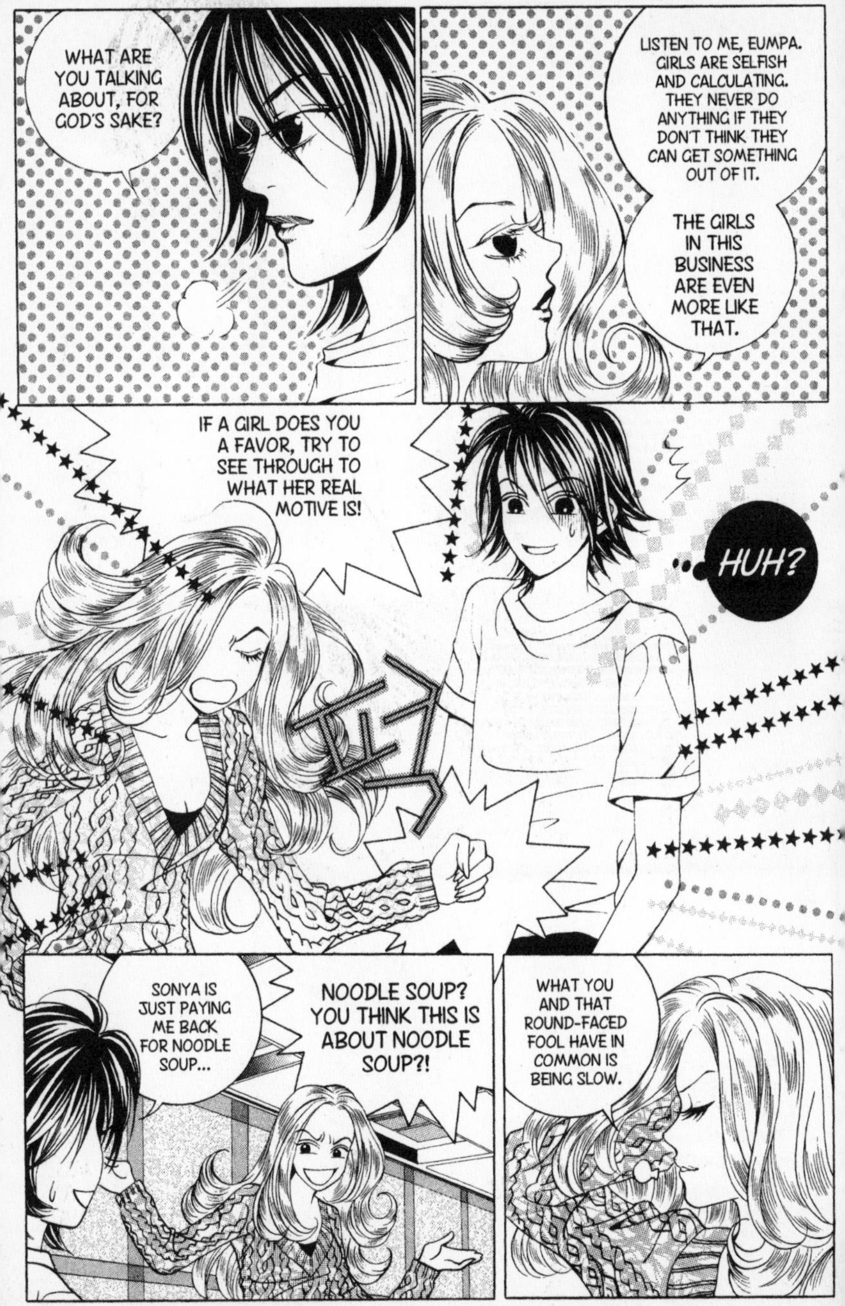
WHAT ARE YOU TALKING ABOUT, FOR GOD'S SAKE?
LISTEN TO ME, EUMPA. GIRLS ARE SELFISH AND CALCULATING. THEY NEVER DO ANYTHING IF THEY DON'T THINK THEY CAN GET SOMETHING OUT OF IT.
THE GIRLS IN THIS BUSINESS ARE EVEN MORE LIKE THAT.
IF A GIRL DOES YOU A FAVOR, TRY TO SEE THROUGH TO WHAT HER REAL MOTIVE IS!
...HUH?
SONYA IS JUST PAYING ME BACK FOR NOODLE SOUP...
NOODLE SOUP? YOU THINK THIS IS ABOUT NOODLE SOUP?!
WHAT YOU AND THAT ROUND-FACED FOOL HAVE IN COMMON IS BEING SLOW.

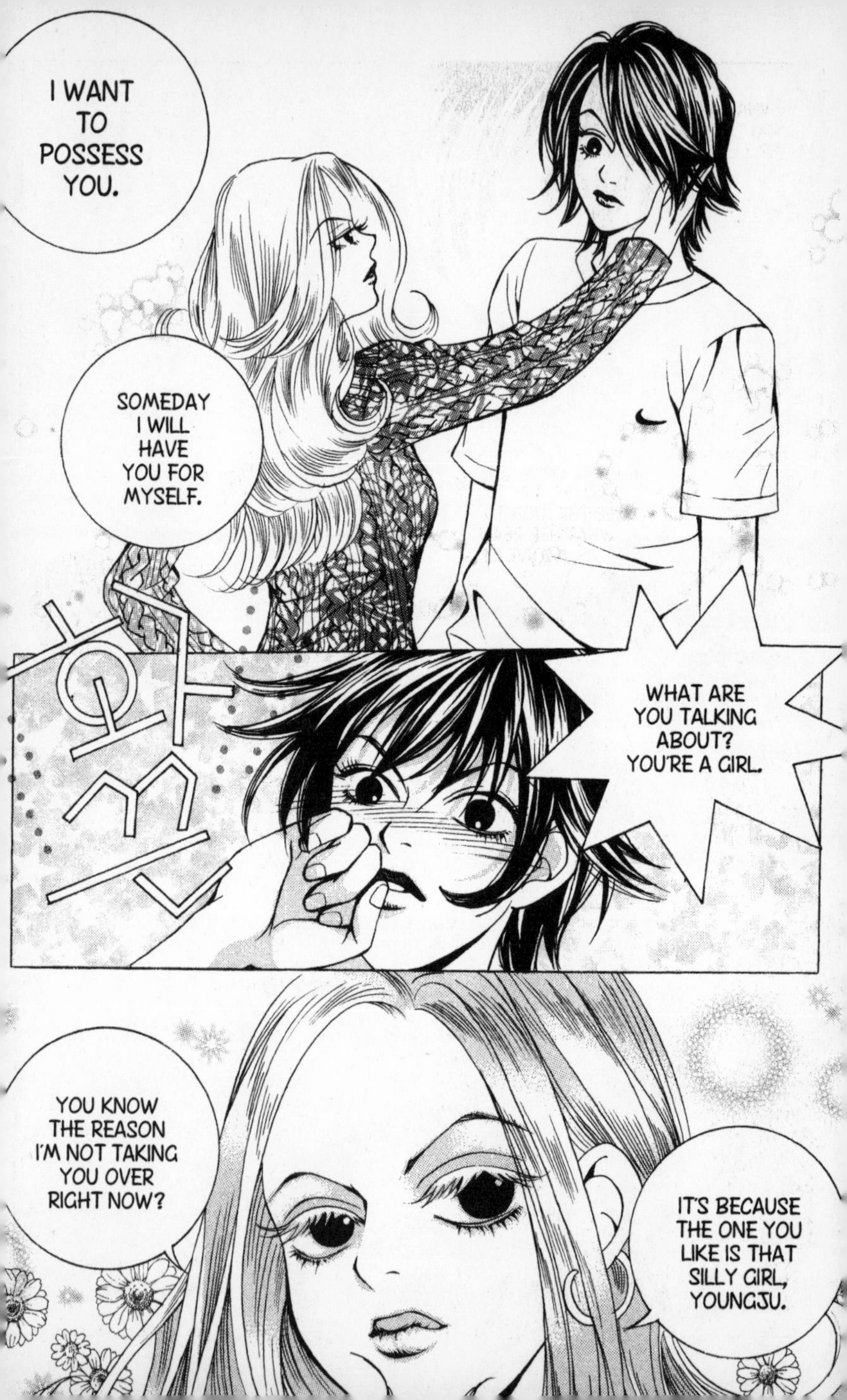
I WANT TO POSSESS YOU.
SOMEDAY I WILL HAVE YOU FOR MYSELF.
WHAT ARE YOU TALKING ABOUT? YOU'RE A GIRL.
YOU KNOW THE REASON I'M NOT TAKING YOU OVER RIGHT NOW?
IT'S BECAUSE THE ONE YOU LIKE IS THAT SILLY GIRL, YOUNGJU.

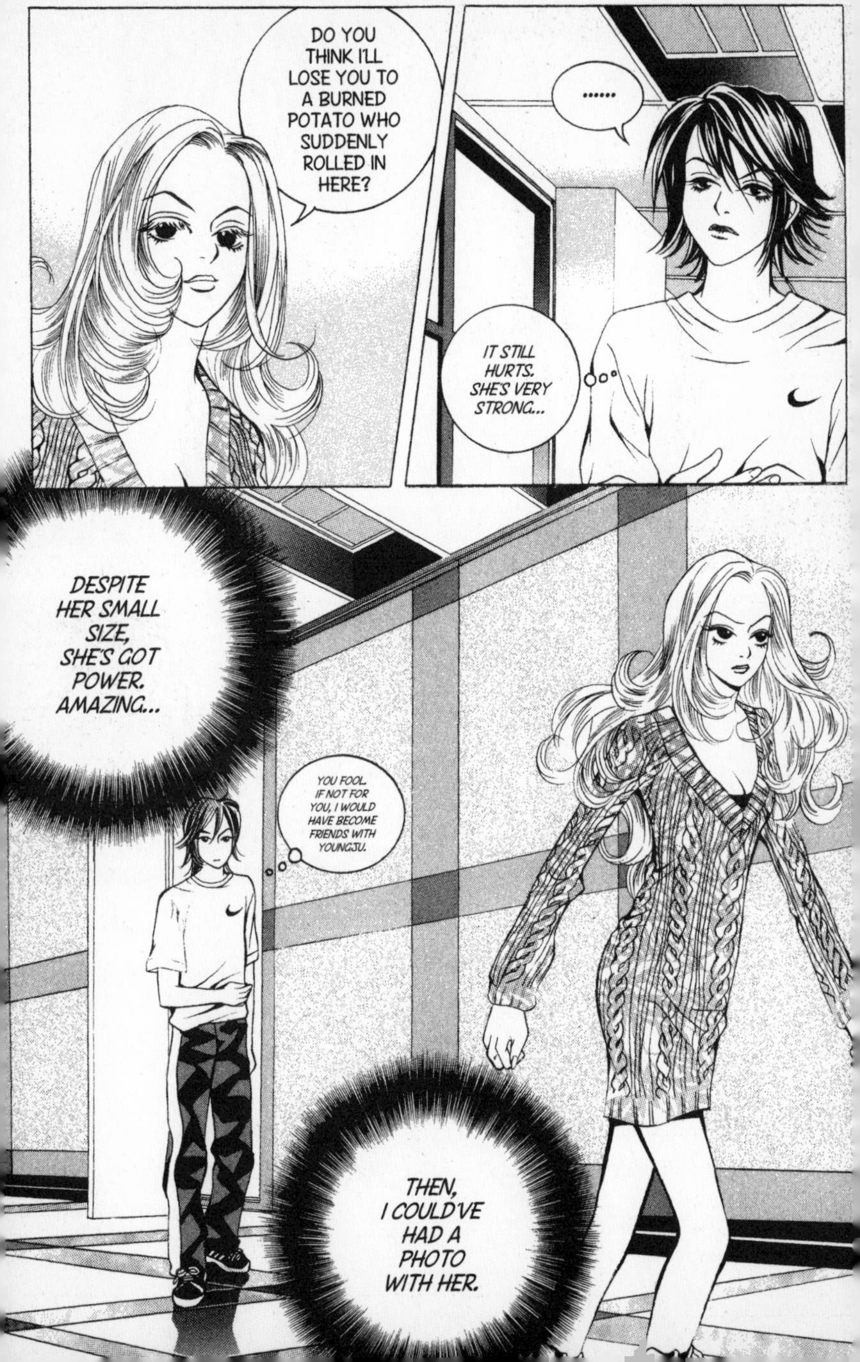
DO YOU THINK I'LL LOSE YOU TO A BURNED POTATO WHO SUDDENLY ROLLED IN HERE?
......
IT STILL HURTS. SHE'S VERY STRONG...
DESPITE HER SMALL SIZE, SHE'S GOT POWER. AMAZING...
YOU FOOL. IF NOT FOR YOU, I WOULD HAVE BECOME FRIENDS WITH YOUNGJU.
THEN, I COULD'VE HAD A PHOTO WITH HER.

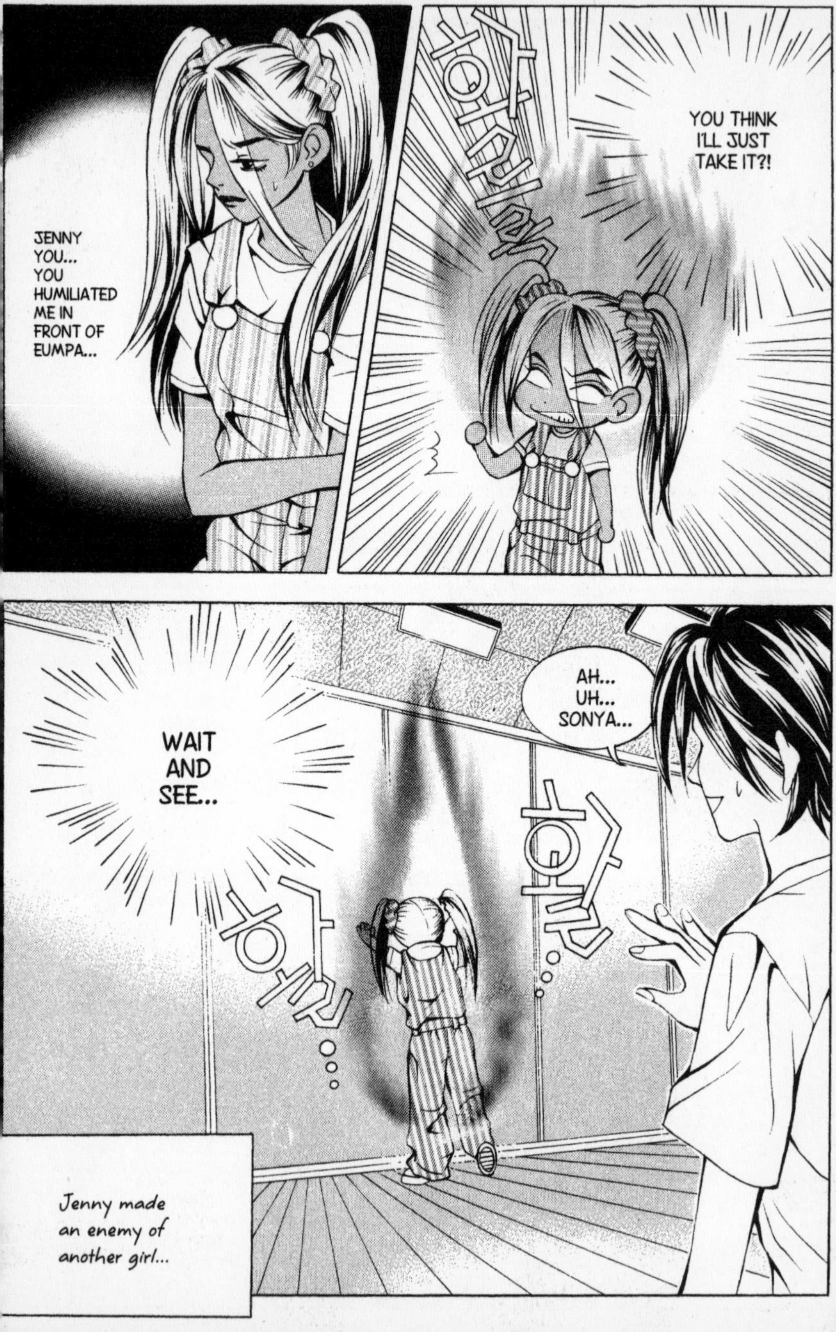
JENNY YOU... YOU HUMILIATED ME IN FRONT OF EUMPA...
YOU THINK I'LL JUST TAKE IT?!
WAIT AND SEE...
AH... UH... SONYA...
Jenny made an enemy of another girl...

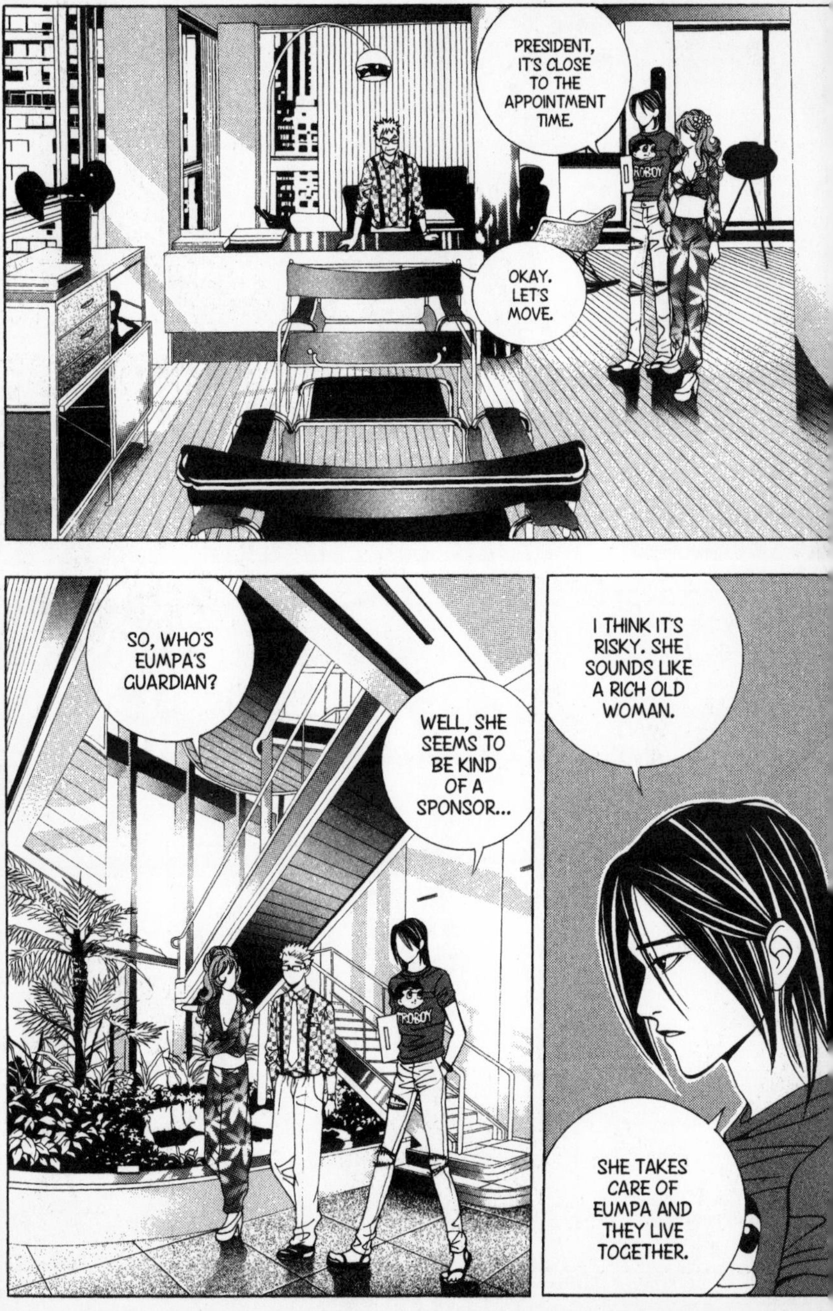
PRESIDENT, IT'S CLOSE TO THE APPOINTMENT TIME.
OKAY. LET'S MOVE.
SO, WHO'S EUMPA'S GUARDIAN?
WELL, SHE SEEMS TO BE KIND OF A SPONSOR...
I THINK IT'S RISKY. SHE SOUNDS LIKE A RICH OLD WOMAN.
SHE TAKES CARE OF EUMPA AND THEY LIVE TOGETHER.

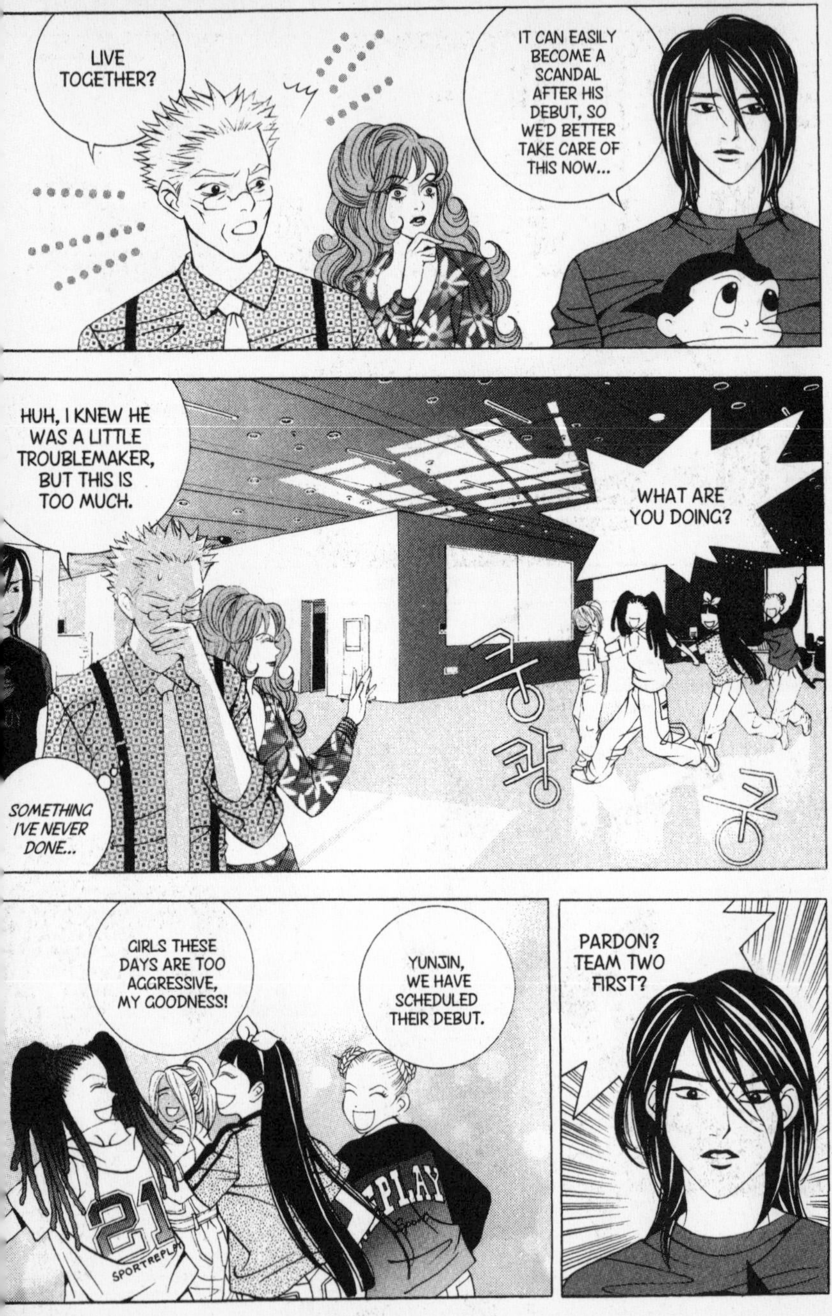
LIVE TOGETHER?
IT CAN EASILY BECOME A SCANDAL AFTER HIS DEBUT, SO WE'D BETTER TAKE CARE OF THIS NOW...
HUH, I KNEW HE WAS A LITTLE TROUBLEMAKER, BUT THIS IS TOO MUCH.
SOMETHING I'VE NEVER DONE...
WHAT ARE YOU DOING?
GIRLS THESE DAYS ARE TOO AGGRESSIVE, MY GOODNESS!
YUNJIN, WE HAVE SCHEDULED THEIR DEBUT.
PARDON? TEAM TWO FIRST?

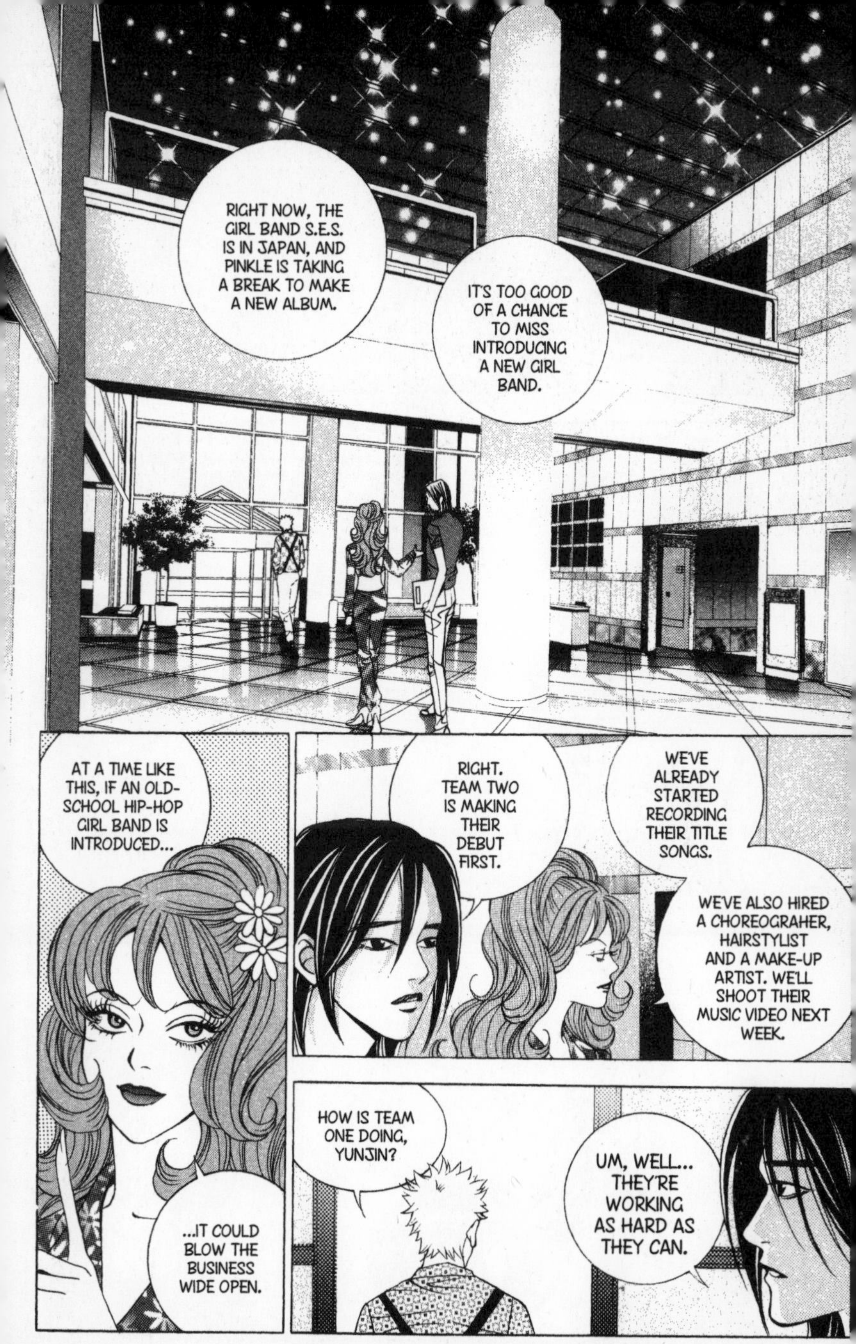
RIGHT NOW, THE GIRL BAND S.E.S. IS IN JAPAN, AND PINKLE IS TAKING A BREAK TO MAKE A NEW ALBUM.
IT'S TOO GOOD OF A CHANCE TO MISS INTRODUCING A NEW GIRL BAND.
AT A TIME LIKE THIS, IF AN OLD-SCHOOL HIP-HOP GIRL BAND IS INTRODUCED...
...IT COULD BLOW THE BUSINESS WIDE OPEN.
RIGHT. TEAM TWO IS MAKING THEIR DEBUT FIRST.
WE'VE ALREADY STARTED RECORDING THEIR TITLE SONGS.
WE'VE ALSO HIRED A CHOREOGRAHER, HAIRSTYLIST AND A MAKE-UP ARTIST. WE'LL SHOOT THEIR MUSIC VIDEO NEXT WEEK.
HOW IS TEAM ONE DOING, YUNJIN?
UM, WELL... THEY'RE WORKING AS HARD AS THEY CAN.

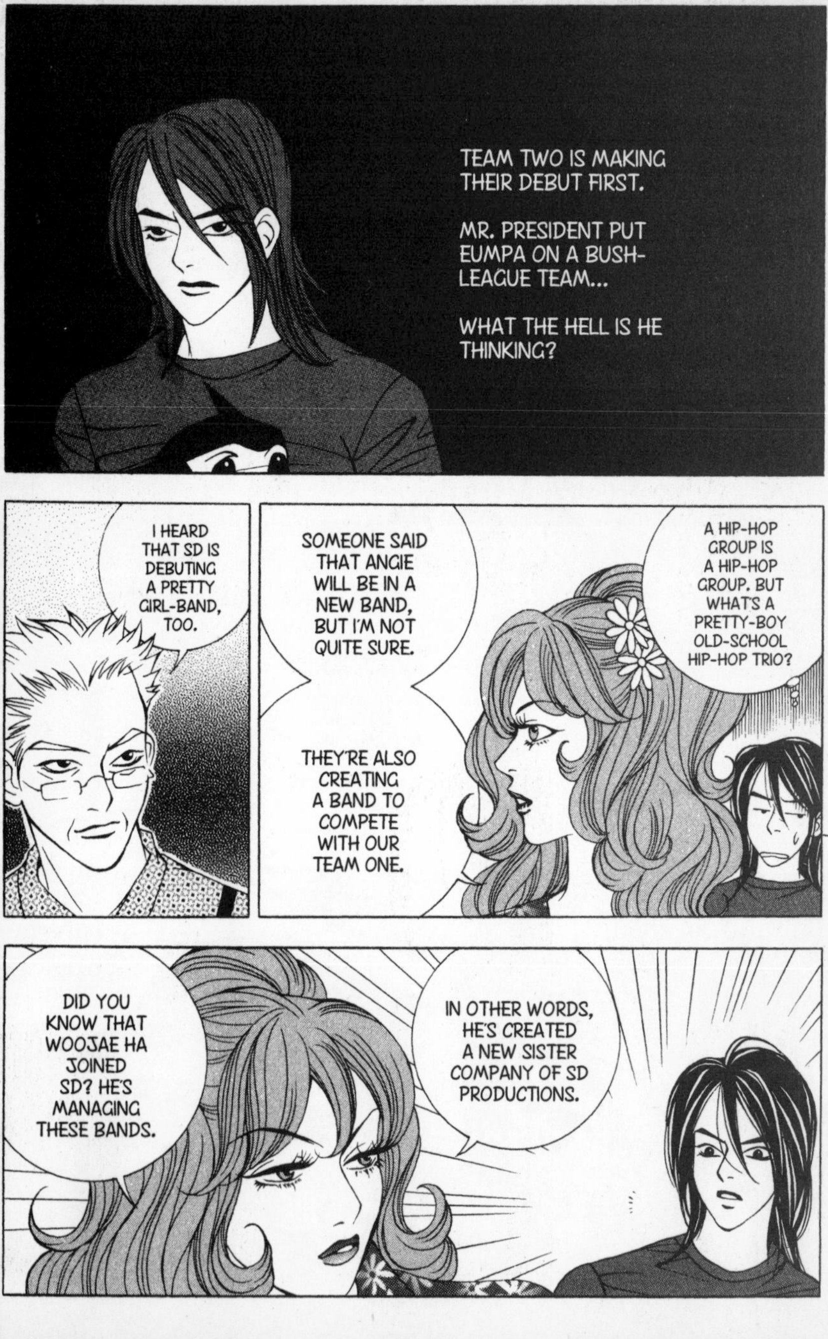
TEAM TWO IS MAKING THEIR DEBUT FIRST.
MR. PRESIDENT PUT EUMPA ON A BUSH-LEAGUE TEAM...
WHAT THE HELL IS HE THINKING?
I HEARD THAT SD IS DEBUTING A PRETTY GIRL-BAND, TOO.
SOMEONE SAID THAT ANGIE WILL BE IN A NEW BAND, BUT I'M NOT QUITE SURE.
THEY'RE ALSO CREATING A BAND TO COMPETE WITH OUR TEAM ONE.
A HIP-HOP GROUP IS A HIP-HOP GROUP. BUT WHAT'S A PRETTY-BOY OLD-SCHOOL HIP-HOP TRIO?
DID YOU KNOW THAT WOOJAE HA JOINED SD? HE'S MANAGING THESE BANDS.
IN OTHER WORDS, HE'S CREATED A NEW SISTER COMPANY OF SD PRODUCTIONS.

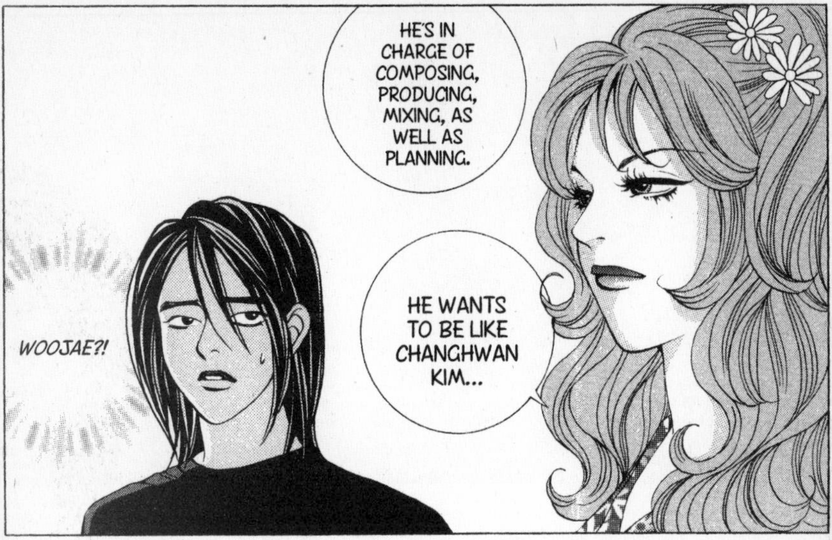
HE'S IN CHARGE OF COMPOSING, PRODUCING, MIXING, AS WELL AS PLANNING.
HE WANTS TO BE LIKE CHANGHWAN KIM...
WOOJAE?!

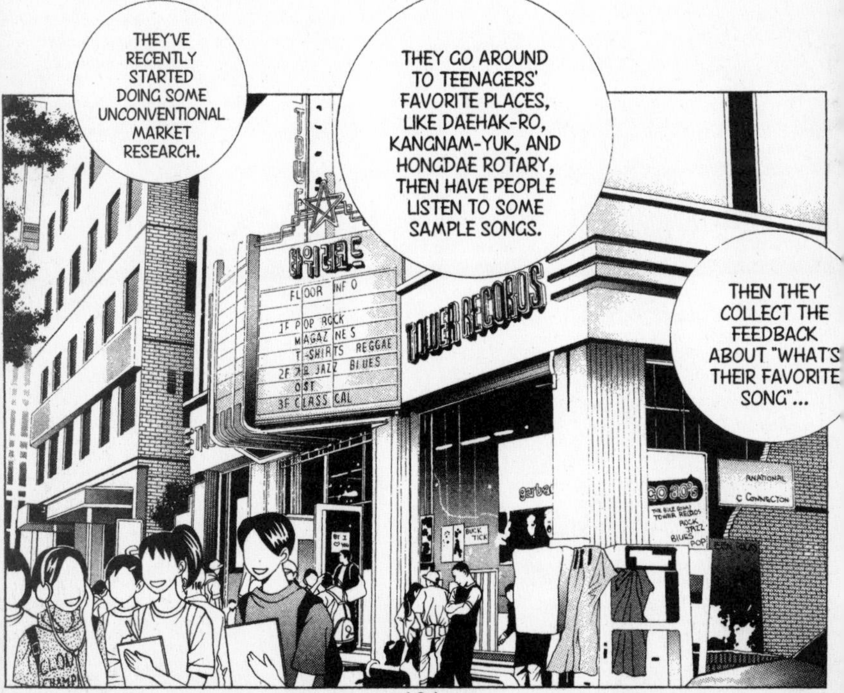
THEY'VE RECENTLY STARTED DOING SOME UNCONVENTIONAL MARKET RESEARCH.
THEY GO AROUND TO TEENAGERS' FAVORITE PLACES, LIKE DAEHAK-RO, KANGNAM-YUK, AND HONGDAE ROTARY, THEN HAVE PEOPLE LISTEN TO SOME SAMPLE SONGS.
TOWER RECORDS
THEN THEY COLLECT THE FEEDBACK ABOUT "WHAT'S THEIR FAVORITE SONG"...

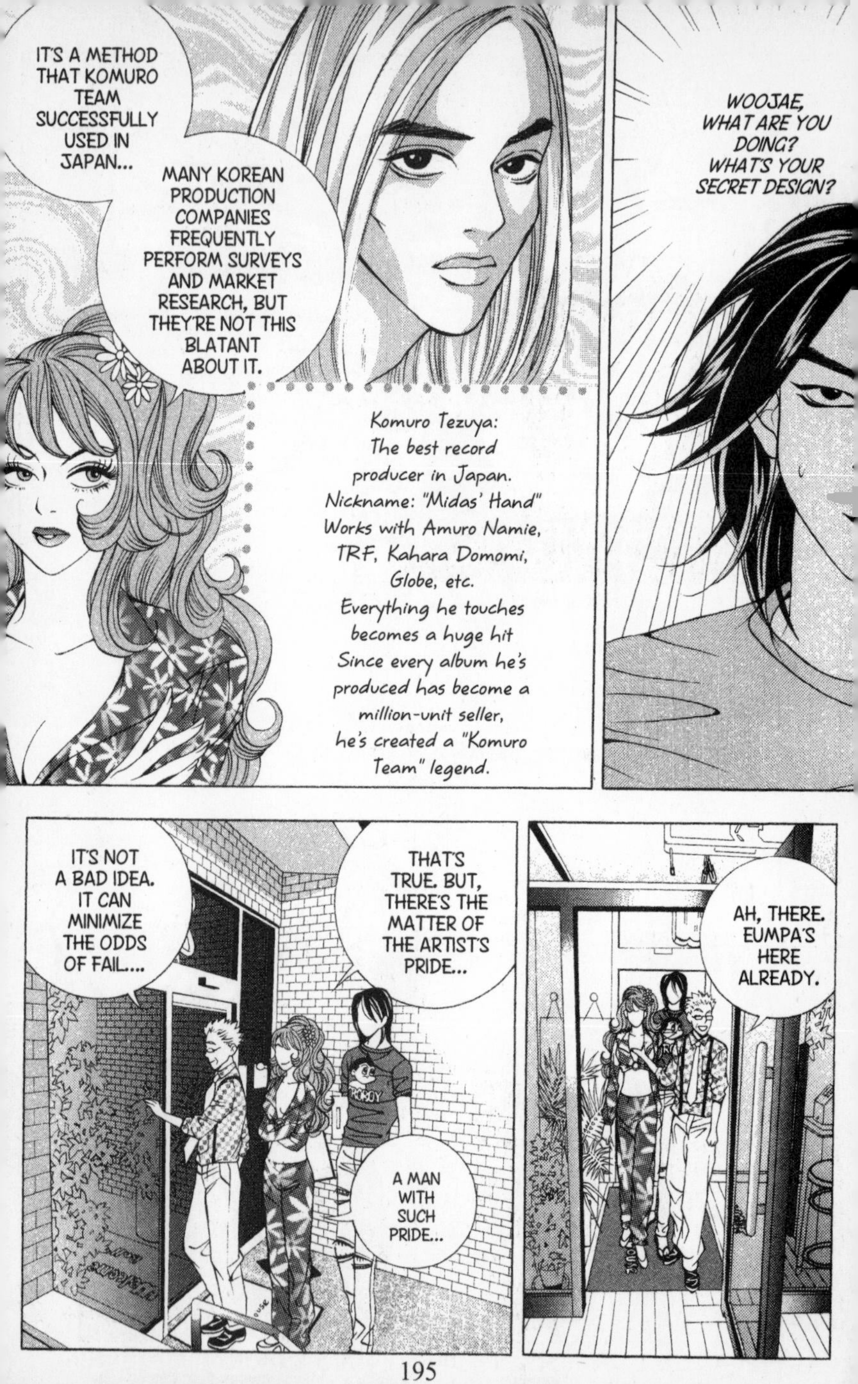
IT'S A METHOD THAT KOMURO TEAM SUCCESSFULLY USED IN JAPAN...
MANY KOREAN PRODUCTION COMPANIES FREQUENTLY PERFORM SURVEYS AND MARKET RESEARCH, BUT THEY'RE NOT THIS BLATANT ABOUT IT.
Komuro Tezuya: The best record producer in Japan. Nickname: "Midas' Hand" Works with Amuro Namie, TRF, Kahara Domomi, Globe, etc. Everything he touches becomes a huge hit Since every album he's produced has become a million-unit seller, he's created a "Komuro Team" legend.
WOOJAE, WHAT ARE YOU DOING? WHAT'S YOUR SECRET DESIGN?
IT'S NOT A BAD IDEA. IT CAN MINIMIZE THE ODDS OF FAIL....
THAT'S TRUE. BUT, THERE'S THE MATTER OF THE ARTIST'S PRIDE...
A MAN WITH SUCH PRIDE...
AH, THERE. EUMPA'S HERE ALREADY.

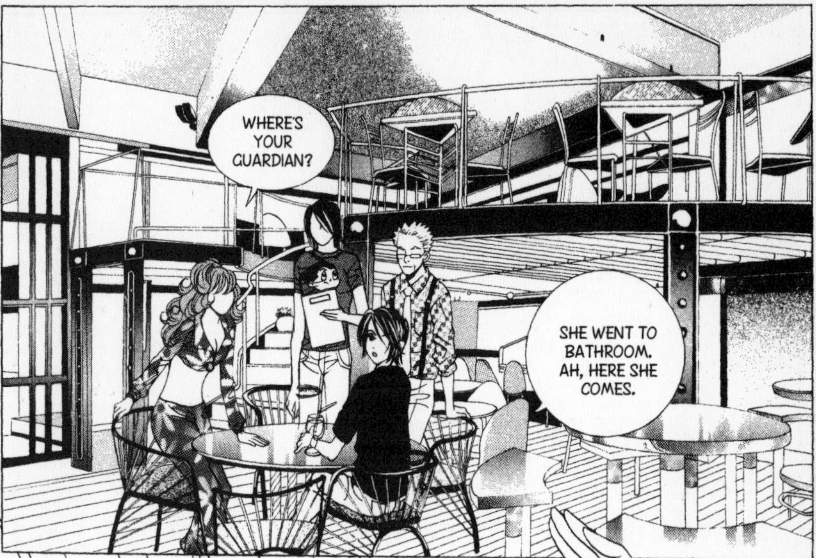
WHERE'S YOUR GUARDIAN?
SHE WENT TO BATHROOM. AH, HERE SHE COMES.

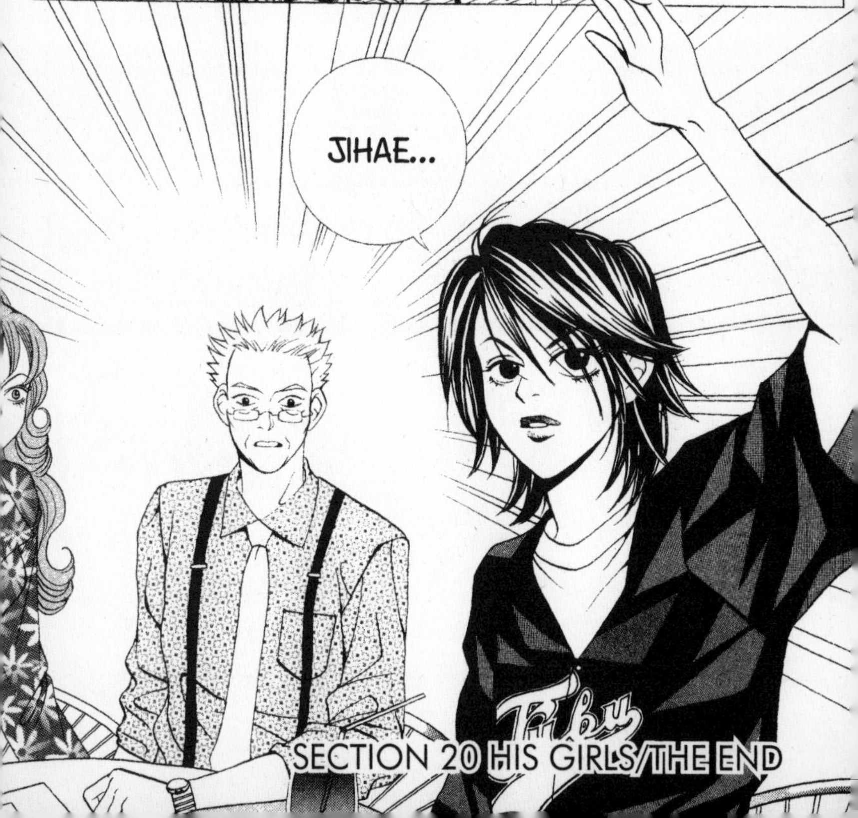
JIHAE...

SECTION 20 HIS GIRLS/THE END

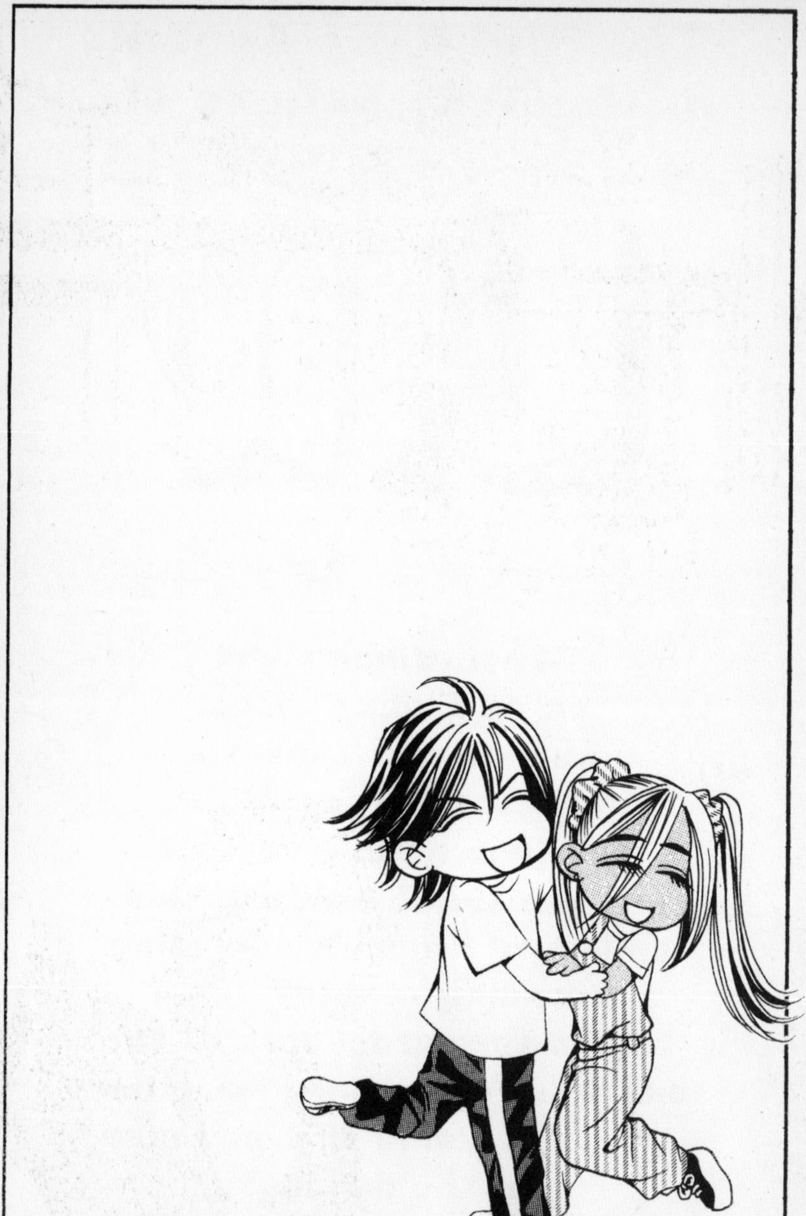

ONE VOLUME 3 – THE END

The Hits Keep Coming in the Next Volume of...

When Jihae signs on as Eumpa's legal guardian, it causes a huge controversy. What's the true nature of their relationship? And will this endanger Eumpa's exploding recording career? It's a behind-the-scenes look at the sometimes glamorous, sometimes stressful world of a pop star in the making!

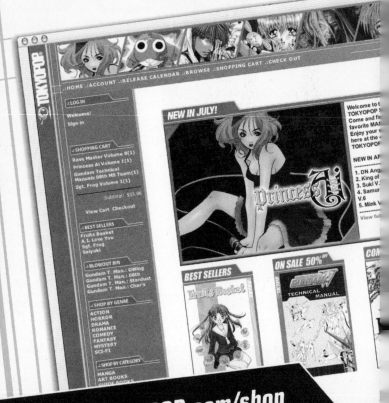

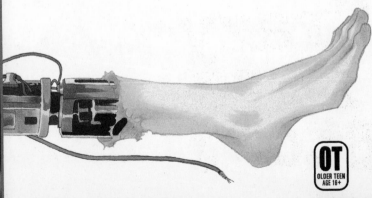

LOVE (TRIANGLES)
CAN DRIVE A GIRL TO THE EDGE.
TOKYOPOP®
Crazy Love Story™
T
TEEN AGE 13+
©2004 Lee Vin, DAIWON C.I. INC. ©2004 TOKYOPOP Inc. All Rights Reserved.
www.TOKYOPOP.com

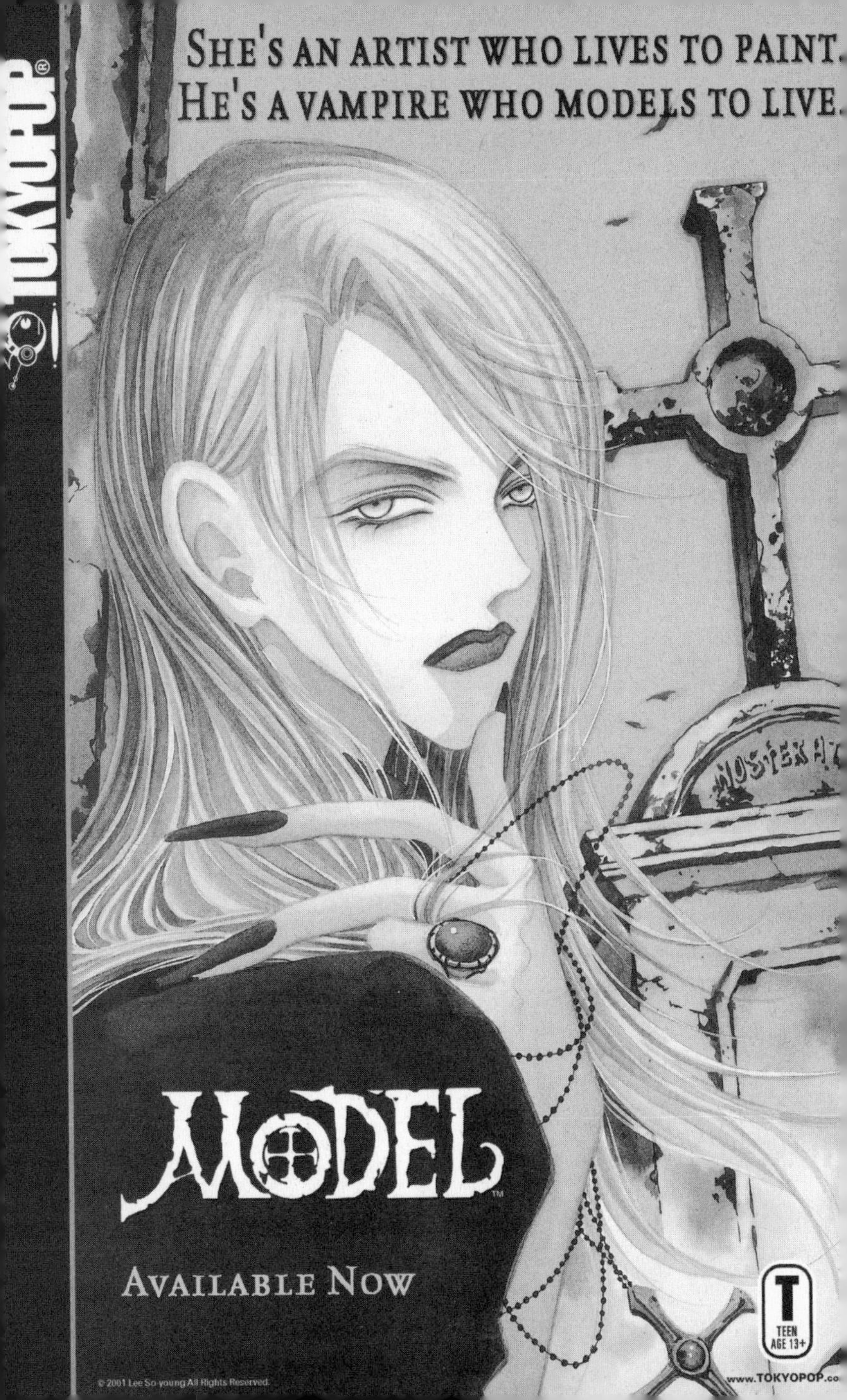
TOKYOPOP®
SHE'S AN ARTIST WHO LIVES TO PAINT.
HE'S A VAMPIRE WHO MODELS TO LIVE.
MODEL™
AVAILABLE NOW
T TEEN AGE 13+
© 2001 Lee So-young All Rights Reserved.
www.TOKYOPOP.co

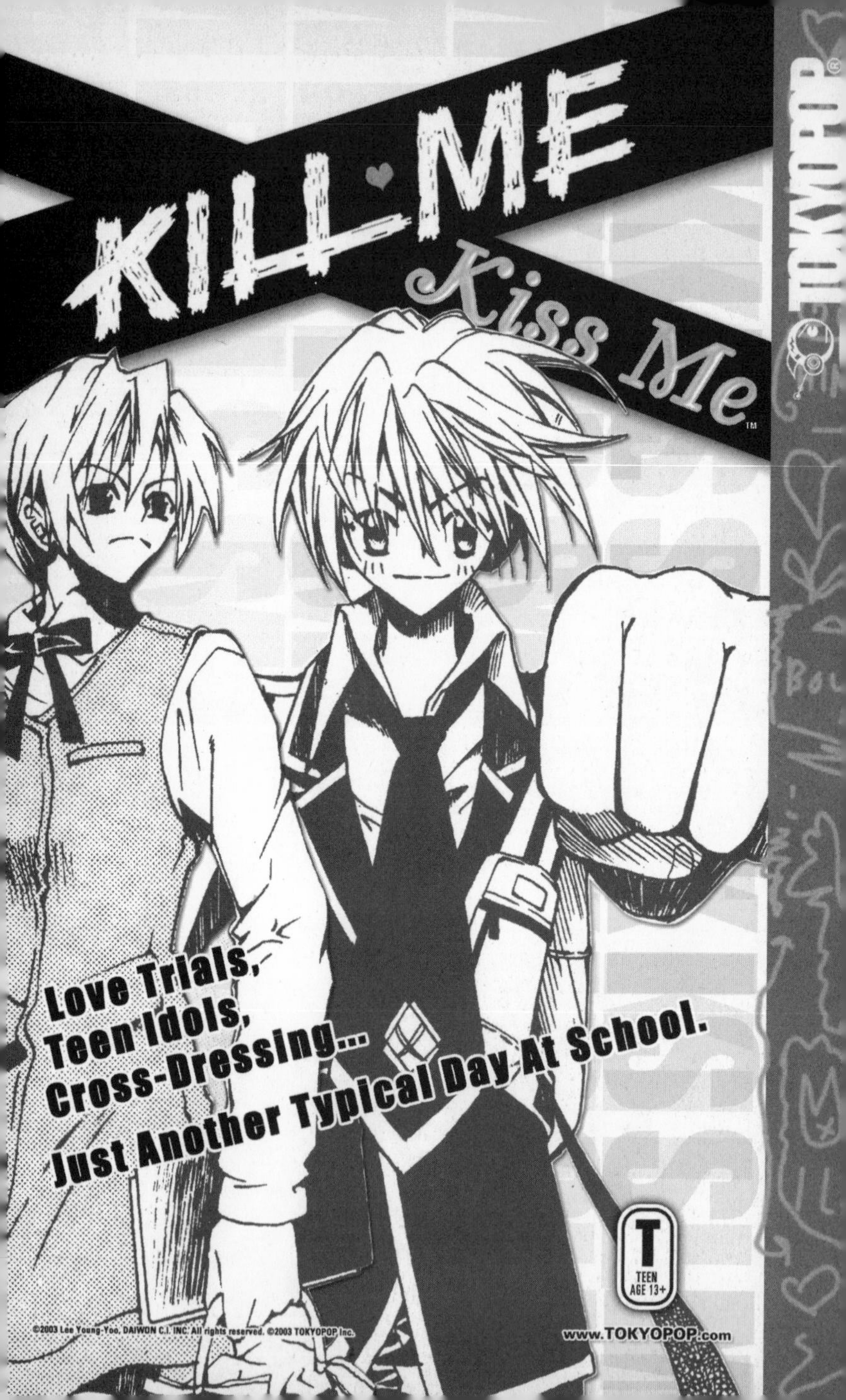
KILL ME
Kiss Me™
TOKYOPOP®
Love Trials,
Teen Idols,
Cross-Dressing...
Just Another Typical Day At School.
T
TEEN
AGE 13+
©2003 Lee Young-Yoo, DAIWON C.I. INC. All rights reserved. ©2003 TOKYOPOP Inc.
www.TOKYOPOP.com

TOKYOPOP
When darkness is in your genes,
only love can steal it away.
D•N•ANGEL
T
TEEN
AGE 13+
www.TOKYOPOP.com
©2004 Yukiru SUGISAKI. ©2004 TOKYOPOP Inc. All rights reserved.

ALSO AVAILABLE FROM  TOKYOPOP®

MANGA

.HACK//LEGEND OF THE TWILIGHT
@LARGE
ABENOBASHI: MAGICAL SHOPPING ARCADE
A.I. LOVE YOU
AI YORI AOSHI
ANGELIC LAYER
ARM OF KANNON
BABY BIRTH
BATTLE ROYALE
BATTLE VIXENS
BRAIN POWERED
BRIGADOON
B'TX
CANDIDATE FOR GODDESS, THE
CARDCAPTOR SAKURA
CARDCAPTOR SAKURA - MASTER OF THE CLOW
CHOBITS
CHRONICLES OF THE CURSED SWORD
CLAMP SCHOOL DETECTIVES
CLOVER
COMIC PARTY
CONFIDENTIAL CONFESSIONS
CORRECTOR YUI
COWBOY BEBOP
COWBOY BEBOP: SHOOTING STAR
CRAZY LOVE STORY
CRESCENT MOON
CROSS
CULDCEPT
CYBORG 009
D•N•ANGEL
DEMON DIARY
DEMON ORORON, THE
DEUS VITAE
DIABOLO
DIGIMON
DIGIMON TAMERS
DIGIMON ZERO TWO
DOLL
DRAGON HUNTER
DRAGON KNIGHTS
DRAGON VOICE
DREAM SAGA
DUKLYON: CLAMP SCHOOL DEFENDERS
EERIE QUEERIE!
ERICA SAKURAZAWA: COLLECTED WORKS
ET CETERA
ETERNITY
EVIL'S RETURN
FAERIES' LANDING
FAKE
FLCL
FLOWER OF THE DEEP SLEEP
FORBIDDEN DANCE
FRUITS BASKET
G GUNDAM

GATEKEEPERS
GETBACKERS
GIRL GOT GAME
GIRLS' EDUCATIONAL CHARTER
GRAVITATION
GTO
GUNDAM BLUE DESTINY
GUNDAM SEED ASTRAY
GUNDAM WING
GUNDAM WING: BATTLEFIELD OF PACIFISTS
GUNDAM WING: ENDLESS WALTZ
GUNDAM WING: THE LAST OUTPOST (G-UNIT)
GUYS' GUIDE TO GIRLS
HANDS OFF!
HAPPY MANIA
HARLEM BEAT
I.N.V.U.
IMMORTAL RAIN
INITIAL D
INSTANT TEEN: JUST ADD NUTS
ISLAND
JING: KING OF BANDITS
JING: KING OF BANDITS - TWILIGHT TALES
JULINE
KARE KANO
KILL ME, KISS ME
KINDAICHI CASE FILES, THE
KING OF HELL
KODOCHA: SANA'S STAGE
LAMENT OF THE LAMB
LEGAL DRUG
LEGEND OF CHUN HYANG, THE
LES BIJOUX
LOVE HINA
LUPIN III
LUPIN III: WORLD'S MOST WANTED
MAGIC KNIGHT RAYEARTH I
MAGIC KNIGHT RAYEARTH II
MAHOROMATIC: AUTOMATIC MAIDEN
MAN OF MANY FACES
MARMALADE BOY
MARS
MARS: HORSE WITH NO NAME
MINK
MIRACLE GIRLS
MIYUKI-CHAN IN WONDERLAND
MODEL
MY LOVE
NECK AND NECK
ONE
ONE I LOVE, THE
PARADISE KISS
PARASYTE
PASSION FRUIT
PEACH GIRL
PEACH GIRL: CHANGE OF HEART
PET SHOP OF HORRORS
PITA-TEN

05.11.04T

ALSO AVAILABLE FROM TOKYOPOP®

TOKYOPOP®

Ai Yazawa's

Paradise Kiss™

Our Fabulous New Look for Your Fashion Favorite

Paradise Kiss
Vol. 1
Ai Yazawa
Paradise Kiss
Ai Yazawa
Vol. 2
Paradise Kiss
Yazawa
Vol. 3
Paradise Kiss
Ai Yazawa
Vol. 4
Paradise Kiss
5

From
Japan's #1
Shojo Creator

OT
OLDER TEEN
AGE 16+

www.TOKYOPOP.com